The Idea of Poetry
in France

The Idea of Poetry
in France

FROM HOUDAR DE LA MOTTE

TO BAUDELAIRE

BY

MARGARET GILMAN

HARVARD UNIVERSITY PRESS

Cambridge, Massachusetts

1958

172280
011046

C C

© Copyright 1958 by the President
and Fellows of Harvard College

Distributed in Great Britain by
Oxford University Press
London

The publication of this book was aided
by a grant from the Ford Foundation.

Printed in the United States of America

Library of Congress Catalog Card Number 58-12968

Sainte-Beuve, writing in 1866, observed that ideas about poetry had changed almost completely in his time. Formerly, he says, the great poet was the one who had composed the most finished and beautiful work, the most clear and pleasant to read. But now the great poet is the one who gives the greatest latitude to his reader to imagine and to dream, the one who suggests the most. Sainte-Beuve's remarks characterize admirably the movement of ideas about poetry from the beginning of the eighteenth century to the time at which he was writing. It is a period during which the conception of poetry changed from that of embellished statement to "suggestive magic," to use Baudelaire's phrase. The story of that change is the subject of this book.

It is, of course, only a chapter of the long story of poetry and poetic theory in France, a chapter which begins at a time when poetry, after a gradual decline from its great flowering during the Renaissance, had reached so low an ebb that its complete disappearance could be, and was predicted. Towards the middle of the eighteenth century the tide slowly turned, and poetry began to come into its own again. But the process was a long and slow one, and the triumphant boast of the romantic poets that they had carried out a poetic revolution as spectacular as the great political revolution of the preceding century was not a little exaggerated. Romantic poetry by no means succeeded in freeing itself completely from the shackles of the eighteenth century, and the emancipation was fully achieved only towards the middle of the nineteenth century. Baudelaire is justly considered the starting point of modern poetry, but it is equally true that he represents the culmination of the long upward struggle of poetry which lasted more than a century.

This progress of poetry itself was accompanied by a vast

amount of discussion and theorizing about poetry. Nearly all the questions which are still at issue today were considered and debated: the essence of poetry; the function of the poet; the nature of poetic experience and poetic creation; the relative importance of inspiration, imagination, and craftsmanship; the language and imagery of poetry; clarity and obscurity; the relation of poetry to prose. At the heart of these discussions, though not always explicitly stated, are two fundamental questions which are particularly relevant to the conception of poetry as suggestion. The first is that of the relation between art and reality. To this the classical doctrines of imitation had long given comparatively easy answers. With Diderot the whole question was opened again. Later it slipped into the background, and the romantic debates on fidelity to nature versus the autonomy of art brought no real solution. Only with Baudelaire did the question again become a focal one. The second great question is that of the relation between matter and form in poetry. One is conscious of a perpetual dialogue between the conceptions of poetry as form and poetry as spirit, and the divorce of the two was a major obstacle to a poetic renascence. Only with the gradual realization that in poetry matter and form are one and indivisible did a true renewal of poetry become possible. The separation of the two, undue stress on one or the other, are disastrously reflected in the poetry of certain periods. The balance is a delicate and precarious one, and the cycle repeats itself, happy union being followed by divorce, then by slow reconciliation. The period I am treating here is one of such reconciliation, and one which seems to me particularly significant in relation to many present-day discussions of poetry.

While this study is focused on poetic theory rather than on poetry itself, I have tried throughout to relate the two, and thus to avoid the aridity of a discussion of theories alone. Theory is never a completely adequate explanation of poetry; as Victor Hugo said, "La poésie ne tient dans aucun art poétique, pas plus que la mer dans aucun vase, cruche ou amphore." It must be remembered too that poetry and theory do not always go hand in hand. Good theory does not suffice to produce good poetry; a bad cook can spoil the best of recipes. On the other hand it is difficult to make a good dish from a bad recipe, although the instincts of a number of poets have guided them to a poetic creation far superior to their expressed doctrines. But I believe that by and large there is a fairly close connection between a poet's practice and his theory. As Baudelaire said, the poetry should come first, then the theory; a critic turned poet would be a monstrosity. "On the contrary, all great poets naturally, inevitably, become critics." So my interest has lain first of all in what the poets themselves thought and wrote about poetry. Then I have examined the countless treatises on poetry, the ideas of critics and reviewers, and the more informal opinions set down in letters and records of conversations. I have tried to give particular attention to the precise meaning given to certain key terms, such as imagination and enthusiasm, image and symbol, and to the way in which these meanings changed.

I have in general organized this study around the problems and questions I have mentioned, rather than around individual writers, in order to keep the main lines of development, the focal points of discussion, more clear. To treat the work of each critic individually would have resulted in a lengthy and repetitious catalogue, many of the names being undeserving of individual treatment. Moreover the poetic doctrines of a number — though not all — of the writers have already been treated either in special studies or in general works on the author. I have however devoted a chapter each to the two figures who seem to me most significant: Diderot, the first in the eighteenth century to have a clear vision of what poetry should be; and Baudelaire, who by his doctrine as well as by his poetry is the culminating point of this development.

Since my discussion is centered on the fundamental and

persistent problems of poetry, I have dealt only briefly with a number of fairly technical questions, such as versification and the genres of poetry. The fact that at certain periods poets and theorists were much concerned with such questions is indeed of importance. But a detailed study of them would often have led me far from my real subject. Moreover the period is marked by the gradual emergence of lyric poetry as the chief of all poetic genres; in 1872 Banville wrote that the ode "has absorbed all the genres of poetry, just as it has become all modern poetry." Since the whole trend is towards the modern tendency to define poetry almost exclusively in terms of the lyric genre, I have kept that in the foreground, and omitted any detailed discussion of the special problems of epic and dramatic poetry.

It will be apparent to anyone familiar with the history of poetic theory in Europe that France lagged far behind both England and Germany in arriving at a new idea of poetry. It is significant that in *Can You Forgive Her?*, published in 1864, Trollope should have put into the mouth of one of his less cultivated, as well as less attractive characters, George Vavasor, in the middle of a somewhat banal speech, the sentence, "Poetry is precious chiefly because it suggests more than it declares." What seemed to Sainte-Beuve an innovation had long since become a commonplace in England.

The consequence of this historical situation is that an impressive array of possible foreign sources for the ideas that developed in France can be lined up. The problem of how far French writers drew on these is a very thorny one indeed. As will be seen, many of these ideas were adumbrated early in French theory, even though they developed slowly and met with much resistance. It is undeniable that the contacts with English and German writers in the late eighteenth and early nineteenth centuries encouraged and fortified them. But I believe that too many critics have tended to give to foreign influences, especially German ones, too exclusive an importance, forgetting the many signposts in earlier French theory pointing in this direction. In any case, any valid judgment on this question would have to be based on a series of studies, running into many volumes, on the sources of the critical ideas of each French author of any importance; what he read or might have read; whether an influence might well have been second or third hand, rather than direct; whether, in the case of foreign influences, the French writer knew the foreign language; whether there had been translations, and at what date.

Given this situation, I have made no attempt to treat this complex interplay of influences in any detail. Sometimes an influence is obvious, sometimes an author has been obliging enough to mention his sources, and I have cited a number of such instances. Occasionally a decisive change has seemed inexplicable without some reference to sources outside the French literary tradition, such as the English conception of imagination or the illuminist and occultist doctrines, and here I have sketched the background briefly. Otherwise I have contented myself with noting a number of parallels which might lead to a detailed study of influences.

Even with these restrictions, the amount of material available for such a study as this is enormous, and to try to present all of it would have been as tedious for the writer as for the reader. The wood would merely be obscured by a large number of identical trees. So I have focused my attention on the major figures and presented a sufficient number of examples drawn from the minor ones to give the reader some idea of what the average poets and critics, as well as the great ones, were thinking. In the text I have in general translated French prose passages of any length into English, although I have not hesitated, when the French text was particularly significant in its wording, or seemed to lose its flavor in translation, to give it in the original. The translations are in all cases my own; I have however found some helpful hints in previous translations, when they existed. In the French texts I have consistently modernized the spelling, and in some cases the punctuation and capitalization.

The text is attended by a large retinue of notes, whose presence perhaps needs some justification. First of all, the sources I have used are legion, and I have wished to spare my readers the exasperation I have so often felt in trying to track down a quotation or allusion for which the reference was either incomplete or missing. Secondly, I have given additional references to both primary and secondary sources, for the benefit of those who may wish to pursue the subject further. The bibliography of the subject is voluminous, and I have referred only to those books and articles which I have found most useful and significant. Lastly, I have relegated to the notes references to the scholarly controversies which have raged around some of the problems treated in the text, and which are of interest to the specialist rather than to the general reader. In any case the notes are, to use John Livingston Lowes' happy phrase, "securely kenneled in the rear," where the reader so inclined may leave them undisturbed.

No theories of poetry, and even less a book about those theories, can have any validity dissociated from poetry itself. My hope is that the reader and lover of poetry who has felt, as Baudelaire did, the urge to "transformer sa volupté en connaissance," to know what other readers, what the poets themselves thought about the nature and function of poetry and the mysteries of the poetic process, may find some satisfaction in these pages.

The debts I have incurred to colleagues and students and other friends during the years I have been working on this book are far too many to enumerate here. But a few deserve special mention. Professor Henri Peyre has encouraged me in the project from the start, and given me many valuable suggestions. Professor Jean Seznec has read part of the manuscript, and has helped me in many ways, not least perhaps by continually prodding me to get the book finished. Professor Norman L. Torrey has also read part of the manuscript, and has given me unfailing support and encouragement.

I am most grateful to the John Simon Guggenheim Memorial Foundation for the fellowship which made the completion of my research possible.

M. G.

Bryn Mawr, Pennsylvania
April 10, 1958

PUBLISHER'S NOTE

Professor Gilman died in May 1958, before this book had gone to press. The publishers are grateful to her friends Norman L. Torrey and W. M. Frohock for reading the proofs and to Mrs. W. M. Frohock for compiling the index.

CONTENTS

I

THE NADIR OF POETRY

In 1754 Abbé Trublet wrote in his essay, "De la poésie et des poètes": "As reason is perfected, judgment will more and more be preferred to imagination, and, consequently, poets will be less and less appreciated. The first writers, it is said, were poets. I can well believe it; they could hardly be anything else. The last writers will be philosophers." [1] The statement epitomizes the low estate that poetry had reached during the first half of the eighteenth century. This was the culmination of a gradual decline from the lofty conception of poetry attained in the sixteenth century, and can hardly be understood without a rapid survey of that decline and fall.

The numerous *arts poétiques* of the Middle Ages had been largely concerned with versification, the genres of poetry, the moral lessons to be derived from it, with the aid of the allegorical method if necessary. Little distinction other than a purely formal one was made between prose and poetry, and only here and there were there hints as to the nature of poetry and the function of the poet. In the sixteenth century an intense interest in these problems was manifested; poets and critics alike were eager to have their say, and towards the middle of the century treatises and prefaces came thick and fast.[2] These theoretical works are closely related to the poetry of the period, a poetry remarkable not only for its supreme achievements but also for the high poetic level maintained both by the minor poets and by the great poets in their lesser moments. In spite of a frequent sameness of subject matter and method, an often all too faithful imitation of the ancients, the reading of large doses of this poetry rarely offends the reader's poetic susceptibilities, and gives him a steady, if not always intense pleasure. Most of the theories come from the poets them-

selves, or from writers in close touch with them, and in spite
of their heavy debt to classical and Italian sources the theories
have something of the new life, the springtime freshness of the
poetry.

At the center of this poetic doctrine is the proclamation of
the high calling of the poet. Fired by the divine madness without which no lasting poetic achievement can be hoped for, he
must seek the silence and solitude dear to the Muses, that the
divine spark may not be lost. Poetry is first and foremost a
divine gift. Yet inspiration is not sufficient in itself, and must
always be seconded by art and labor. What has been written in
the white heat of inspiration must be laid aside, then corrected
and revised. Poets, says Du Bellay, must like bears lick their
offspring into form and shape.[3] Ronsard, too, for all his stress
on inspiration, on the fact that nothing can be good or perfect
unless it be heaven-sent, insists that the poet, like a good gar-
dener, must correct and prune his verses. Nature and art must
go hand in hand.

Closely allied to this is the doctrine of imitation, with all its
gamut of meanings. For Du Bellay, preoccupied with the *illustration* of his native language, imitation is above all imitation of the ancients; the poet must follow the example of the
Romans, who wrote their great works in imitation of the
Greeks, devouring, digesting, and absorbing them, but not
slavishly copying them. Other writers were more fully aware
of the latent dangers of the doctrine. Peletier du Mans warns
the poet that greatness is not achieved merely by following
in the footsteps of others, and advises him rather to observe in
nature what he has studied in books, to contemplate living
images.[4] For Ronsard the key word is *invention*, the work of
"an imagination which conceives the ideas and forms of all
imaginable things." [5]

Some problems that have harassed poets in other ages were
little discussed at this time. Truth and fiction, utility and pleasure dwell together in peace, all being essential elements of

poetry. The poetic obscurity which had flourished earlier in the century is roundly berated by Peletier, who maintains that the chief virtue of poetry is clarity, which must not be obscured by an excess of poetic ornament. But the essence of this doctrine of poetry lies in its conception of the high nature of poetry, the loftiness of the poet's calling, which must of necessity set him apart from other men.

It is enlightening to consider this doctrine in relation to the poetry of the period. Obviously no theory of poetry will furnish an adequate explanation of the workings of a great poetic genius; one would be hard put to it to explain Villon by the *arts poétiques* of the late Middle Ages. Yet I do believe that the general level of poetry at any given period has a close relationship to the beliefs generally held about poetry at the time. Poets write with some sort of conception, whether it be clear or confused, of what they are trying to do, whether it be to yield themselves wholly to the rushing torrent of inspiration, or to make a given number of verses according to certain fixed rules. In the sixteenth century the doctrine of poetry, keeping the balance between inspiration and technique, nature and art, saved poetry both from the hard bright conventionality of the eighteenth century, the cold implacable perfection of the minor Parnassians, and from the overgrown luxuriance of much romantic poetry, the chaotic confusion of certain modern poets. The sixteenth-century poets left untouched many themes and moods which have since been discovered, they were often much too ready to repeat a theme or a pattern with only minor variations, to pluck the laurels of their great masters. But their poetry, while often not reaching the highest levels, rarely descends to the lower ones, and for this the conception of poetry by which they were guided is in no small measure responsible.

The gradual decline of poetry from this high estate to the

depths it reached in the early eighteenth century has often been traced.[6] This decline was due not so much to causes inherent in the poetry itself as to a general movement of ideas which swept poetry, to its great damage, along with it. The strong social pressure, the worldly spirit brought poetry down from Parnassus to the salons. The regimentation of the language, its tendency to abstraction, logic, and clarity, the development of rules, all combined to harness Pegasus and make him into a docile coach horse. In vain did Régnier, in his ninth *Satire*, contrast Malherbe and his followers, driven by "nul aiguillon divin," with the poets of the Pléiade, "ces divins esprits, hautains et relevés,/ Qui des eaux d'Hélicon ont les sens abreuvés." The abundant production of odes and elegies during the early seventeenth century is marked by frequent preciosity, a wealth of versified maxims, often allied indeed with a wit and charm, a concise and suggestive quality, which have won for it in recent years a revival of popularity somewhat akin to that achieved by the English metaphysical poets. Théophile, Saint-Amant, Racan, Malherbe, and Maynard can still please, and sometimes move us. As the century moves on, poetry more and more takes refuge in tragedy, where, within the framework of the rigid dramatic pattern, some of the greatest of French lyric poetry is to be found.

In the theories of poetry, we find the lofty earlier conception of the poet swept away by Malherbe's pronouncement that a good poet is of no more use to the state than a good skittles player. In Malherbe's hands poetic doctrine becomes the rigid regimentation of syntax, vocabulary, and versification. For him poetry is essentially the same as prose, the only difference being that poetry is subject to a few more rules.[7] Malherbe is but the embodiment of the spirit of the time, and even without him poetry would sooner or later have been engulfed in the current. More and more reason becomes supreme: reason, whose function is to eliminate the particular and the individual, to generalize, to clarify. Here is the very antithesis of poetry. It is true that the need of genius and of imagination is not denied, but they are more and more cabined and confined. Poetry continues to be considered an imitation of nature, but the conception of nature is narrowed to the average, the typical. Utility comes to the fore; the aim of poetry is moral instruction as well as pleasure. The rules teach a double imitation; the imitation of an idealized nature, with its corollaries of *vraisemblance* and *bienséances*, and an enlightened imitation of the ancients. Everywhere the local and the temporal give place to the universal and the general. Clarity is the supreme poetic virtue. This doctrine is set forth in countless treatises in the course of the century.

In Boileau's *Art poétique* we have the final codification of the classic doctrine. The legislator of Parnassus starts off, to be sure, with an acknowledgement of the need for native genius:

> C'est en vain qu'au Parnasse un téméraire auteur
> Pense de l'art des vers atteindre la hauteur:
> S'il ne sent point du ciel l'influence secrète,
> Si son astre en naissant ne l'a formé poète,
> Dans son génie étroit il est toujours captif;
> Pour lui Phébus est sourd, et Pégase est rétif.

But after this initial sop to Pegasus the *Art poétique* is largely devoted to putting poetry safely under the control of reason:

> Aimez donc la raison: que toujours vos écrits
> Empruntent d'elle seule et leur lustre et leur prix.

Villon and Ronsard had clouded the clarity of poetry, but at last Malherbe came and "réduisit la muse aux règles du devoir." This was the supreme achievement in Boileau's eyes; but it sounded the knell of poetry. Clarity is placed among the chief virtues of poetry, and the poet is advised, "Vingt fois sur le métier remettez votre ouvrage." He has a moral function:

> Qu'en savantes leçons votre muse fertile
> Partout joigne au plaisant le solide et l'utile.

And he must not withdraw from society and devote himself wholly to poetry: "Il faut savoir encore et converser et vivre." Boileau does not indeed deny that emotion and passion have a role in poetry; "Il faut que le cœur parle seul dans l'élégie." And to the writer of tragedy he says:

> Que dans tous vos discours la passion émue
> Aille chercher le cœur, l'échauffe, et le remue,

and concludes: "Pour me tirer des pleurs, il faut que vous pleuriez." Such lines are however rare, and later writers, less wise than their master, tended to forget or ignore them. The effect of the *Art poétique* was to bring the poet down from the heights, to subject him like other men to the laws of reason, clarity, and usage, and to establish the Muse in her salon. It was the point of departure for the movement which, by sealing up the springs of spontaneity, was to make a barren desert of poetry. With the early years of the eighteenth century we reach the depths of the valley which lies between the two great peaks of French poetry; the ascent to the second was to be a laborious and difficult one.

Poetry itself fell low indeed.[8] In 1735 Voltaire wrote to Cideville: "Verse is no longer fashionable in Paris. Everyone is beginning to play the geometrician and the physicist. Sentiment, imagination, the graces are banished. . . . I don't regret that philosophy is cultivated, but I don't want it to become a tyrant." [9] Of quantity there is indeed no lack; odes, idylls, epigrams, fables, satires, didactic poems, all came off the poetic assembly line with appalling regularity. One has but to leaf through the numerous anthologies that appeared in the course of the century, such as the *Trésor du Parnasse*, the *Etrennes du Parnasse*, the *Portefeuille d'un homme de goût*, to realize that the epithet used in the subtitle of one of them, *Elite de poésies fugitives*, is all too apt. At their best the poems are characterized by technical virtuosity and by elegance and wit. The poets are most successful in epigram and satire, though even here there is too often a superficiality that soon palls. One feels the lack of emotion, of imagination, of concrete detail, of any personal touch. The poets seem to believe, like Imlac, that the business of a poet "is to examine, not the individual, but the species; to remark general properties and large appearances; he does not number the streaks of the tulip, or describe the different shades in the verdure of the forest." [10]

Even when the point of departure seems to have been a personal experience, this is transformed into abstraction, and the abstraction often further transformed into allegory. Here is a concrete example, from the poet hailed by his contemporaries as the great lyric poet of their time, Jean-Baptiste Rousseau.[11] His *cantate*, *Le Triomphe de l'amour*, has as its theme the victory of love over poetry, the poet who leaves his poetic solitude and liberty to submit himself gladly to the bondage of love. At the beginning the poet apostrophizes the Muses and boasts of the joy and glory of the poet:

> Il partage avec les héros
> La gloire qui les environne,
> Et le puissant Dieu de Délos
> D'un même laurier les couronne.

Presently the tranquil scene is interrupted by the appearance of a whole mythological cortège, Graces, Nymphs, and their ilk, all paying homage to the god of love. The blind god wins a swift and easy victory over the poet, who promptly bids farewell to the Muses. Whatever personal experience may have lain behind the poem has been lost. The poet yields, not to a woman, but to an abstraction personified. The form is equally artificial; the poem is built up of exclamations, rhetorical questions, periphrases:

> Nymphes, quel est ce dieu qui reçoit votre hommage?
> Pourquoi cet arc et ce bandeau?
> Quel charme en le voyant, quel prodige nouveau
> De mes sens interdits me dérobe l'usage!

The merit of the poem lies in its metrical construction, which by skilful variation of form of stanza and length of line lifts it above the dreary monotony of most of its fellows. Rousseau, too, is not devoid of a sense of music, and if one can forget the banality of content many of his verses are pleasant to the ear:

> Filles du Dieu de l'Univers,
> Muses, que je me plais dans vos douces retraites!
> Que ces rivages frais, que ces bois toujours verts
> Sont propres à charmer les âmes inquiètes!

But the technical skill, the pleasing music cannot obscure the artificiality of content, the paraphernalia of rhetoric.

If one can give only such faint praise to the chief lyric poet of his time, it is harder still to find a kind word for most of his contemporaries. The poetry that has best stood the test of time is the *poésie de circonstance*, the light verse, such as that of Chaulieu and above all of Voltaire, in which the poet, often with gentle mockery, sometimes with a wistfulness rare in French poetry, gives to passing events and ephemeral feelings a delicate and harmonious form.[12] Voltaire regrets the flight of time, the passing of the age for love, with a resignation and grace which are a restful contrast to the torrents of rhetoric, the frantic appeals to Nature with which the romantic poets were to treat the same theme:

> Si vous voulez que j'aime encore,
> Rendez-moi l'âge des amours.
> Au crépuscule de mes jours
> Rejoignez s'il se peut l'aurore.
>
> .   .   .   .
>
> Que le matin touche à la nuit!
> Je n'eus qu'une heure, elle est finie.
> Nous passons. La race qui suit
> Déjà par une autre est suivie.

But in general the poetic level of the period is incredibly low. The poets write prosaic lines on poetical subjects, such as Fontenelle's *Vers sur un clair de lune*, which begins:

Quand l'amour nous fait éprouver
Son premier trouble, avec ses premiers charmes,
Contre soi-même encor c'est lui prêter des armes
Que d'être seul et de rêver.
La dominante idée à chaque instant présente,
N'en devient que plus dominante.

Or else prosaic subjects are treated in a style which only the bare bones of versification distinguish from prose. Here the supreme example is Houdar de la Motte. A small sample of his verse will suffice, the first stanza of *Le Mérite personnel*, an ode addressed to Jean-Baptiste Rousseau:

On ne se choisit point son père;
Par un reproche populaire
Le sage n'est point abattu.
Oui: quoi que le vulgaire en pense,
Rousseau, la plus vile naissance
Donne du lustre à la vertu.

Even his own century, however, had its reservations on La Motte as a poet. Chaulieu wrote of him:

C'est dans un dictionnaire
De rimes que prend Houdart
Ce bel essor, cet écart,
Qui, froids enfants d'un libraire,
Sentent trop la peine et l'art.

Voltaire called La Motte "le patriarche des vers durs," and Cardinal de Bernis pilloried him in his ode, *Les Poètes lyriques*:

Plus philosophe que poète
Il touche une lyre muette;
La raison lui parle, il écrit;
On trouve dans ses strophes sensées
Moins d'images que de pensées
Et moins de talent que d'esprit.

An anonymous epigram of the period applies not only to La Motte but to all too many other poets of the time:

Certain rimeur, qui jamais ne repose,
Me dit hier arrogamment
Qu'il ne sait point écrire en prose;
Lisez ses vers; vous verrez comme il ment.

In short the poetry of the first half of the eighteenth century, with rare exceptions, at its best has faint echoes of the poetry of the preceding century; at its worst it echoes nothing but prose, from which it differs only in form. Thus poetry becomes fixed in a formalism never to be equaled except perhaps by the minor Parnassian poets. One can but conclude with Master Holofernes: "Here are only numbers ratified; but, for the elegancy, facility, and golden cadence of poesy, *caret*."

When one turns from the poetry of the period to its poetic doctrine, the agreement between the two is all too evident. Few of the treatises are the work of poets who have based their theory on the practice of poetry. Fontenelle indeed apologizes for having written his eclogues before composing the "Discours sur la nature de l'églogue" which precedes them. Most of the theories are produced by critics and professors, who set up a code of laws for both the judgment and the production of poetry. The title of Père Du Cerceau's work, published in 1742, puts the matter in a nutshell; *Réflexions sur la poésie française, où l'on fait voir en quoi consiste la beauté des vers, et où l'on donne des règles sûres pour réussir à les bien faire.*

In this welter of discussion it is possible to discern three different tendencies. The first two represent in many respects a prolongation of the "Querelle des Anciens et des Modernes." [13] The extreme "modern" position led to a restriction and deflation of poetry which so undermined its nature that its very right to existence was questioned. Against this attack there was a defense based on traditional grounds, an attempt to maintain the seventeenth-century conception of poetry and thus save it from annihilation. Finally, though rarely, a new note is heard, a clearer distinction between poetry and prose, a more courageous defense of the role of enthusiasm, imagination, imagery, and harmony in poetry. These three tendencies correspond to three different ideas of the function of literature: to instruct, to please, and to move. Often these are not considered mutually exclusive; pleasure, particularly, is often combined with one of the other two. The belief that literature must be useful leads to a subordination of poetry to reason and truth, accompanied by a certain distrust. The emphasis on pleasure is tied up with the question of taste, the "organ of pleasure," a taste educated and trained to take pleasure only in poetry which conforms to traditional rules. Only when theorists begin to present the idea that poetry should appeal to feeling as well as to taste does the emancipation begin.

Most of the critics can be attached to one of these groups, but only in rare cases do we find entire consistency. The most vehement enemies of the autonomy of poetry often echo the traditional view, and many of the traditionalists make concessions to their opponents, while others show unexpected vision and penetration on certain points. And there is no critic, however "advanced," who does not pay at least lip service to the classical doctrine.

With the first group the movement begun in the seventeenth century marches on to its logical conclusion. The equilibrium of the classical period is destroyed, the elements of its synthesis disintegrated. Reason, after succeeding in controlling inspiration, now attempts to replace it.[14] The demise of poetry seems imminent. But the theorists were in no wise content to let it die a natural and peaceful death. Its deathbed is surrounded by all manner of doctors, some shaking their heads in despair, others proposing various remedies, some drastic, some moderate. Rarely has so much been written about poetry as at this time when it seems close to dissolution. Countless treatises classify, divide, and subdivide its genres, define its rules with pedantic precision. One begins to feel with Tristram Shandy that "their heads, Sir, are stuck so full of rules and compasses, and have that eternal propensity to apply them upon all occasions, that a work of genius had better go to the Devil at once, than stand to be pricked and tortured to death by 'em."

In the seventeenth century poetry had already begun to lose its independence; it had been brought down from Parnassus, tamed and groomed to make its appearance in the salons. Nevertheless it had still been considered as belonging to a different order than prose, as having its own laws, however much these were in need of amendment. Though the spirit might no longer blow where it listed, its existence was not denied. But the eighteenth-century extremists were not to be satisfied with putting poetry into leading-strings; it must be annexed, and finally absorbed into the empire of reason. Even Voltaire says at one point: "I esteem poetry only in so far as it is the ornament of reason." [15] But it should not be forgotten that this is in a letter of good advice to a young man about not wasting his time, finding a useful occupation, and so on; Voltaire has better things to say about poetry elsewhere.

The real leaders in the undermining of poetry were Fontenelle and Houdar de la Motte. In their wake come a host of critics and pedants, such as Abbé Terrasson, Abbé Trublet, and Abbé de Pons.[16] With them we find a series of efforts to bring poetry into line with the ideas of the century. Poetic enthusiasm is attacked in the name of reason; the "frivolity" of poetry in the name of morality; its "fictions" in the name of imitation and verisimilitude; versification and rhyme in the name of the "natural." And it is demonstrated that by the laws of progress poetry itself will inevitably disappear. Gradually a conception of poetry is established which is a denial of its very essence.

However, poetry had its defenders, often indeed rather timid ones, whose chief effort was to maintain the *status quo* of the seventeenth century. Enthusiasm is controlled rather than condemned; the moral value of poetry is upheld; poetry is distinguished from prose by its imagery as well as by its technique; and the "difficulté vaincue" is considered a merit rather than a reproach. Nearly all these critics, explicitly or implicitly, base their doctrine on Boileau's, putting him above

Aristotle and Horace, and venturing to disagree with him here and there only with great diffidence.[17] In some cases, just as the attacks on poetry were associated with the new philosophic ideas, so the defense of tradition in poetry was allied with the defense of traditional religion. One of the most die-hard treatises of the period puts it plainly: "Let us reject all new opinions in matters of literature, as in those of religion." [18] But more often the appeal is simply to literary tradition, and above all to the doctrine of imitation. In *Les Beaux-arts réduits à un même principe*, Batteux, inquiring into the essence of poetry, rejects in turn fiction, versification, and enthusiasm, in favor of imitation. Poetry is simply "l'imitation de la belle nature exprimée par le discours mesuré." [19]

A host of more or less well-known writers joined in this defense of the great tradition. Louis Racine followed somewhat timidly in his father's footsteps.[20] The greatest among them was of course Voltaire. Although he occasionally exaggerates the role of reason, his taste saves him from a narrow and geometrical conception of poetry. His thinking on poetry is often most penetrating, and some of the most perceptive observations of the century come from his pen. But he, with a goodly number of disciples, was particularly concerned with the defense of tradition, and above all of verse.

The majority of treatises on poetry toe the classical line fairly strictly. Abbé Mallet, who was later to contribute a number of the articles on poetry in the first edition of the *Encyclopédie*, begins his *Principes pour la lecture des poètes* by asserting his fidelity to Malherbe's doctrine. But some of those whose main line of thought is traditional show some originality and initiative. Batteux, once he is off his hobbyhorse of reducing all the arts to the principle of imitation, writes some admirable pages on the language and harmony of poetry. And Vauvenargues, who says that he owed most of his ideas on poetry to Voltaire, illuminates his theories with a real poetic sensitivity. Earlier Jean-Baptiste Rousseau sets forth in some

of his letters a much bolder poetic doctrine than his poems
would lead one to suspect.

The critics who venture to give to emotion an important
place in poetry are few, but important. The first is Fénelon,
who in *Télémaque* set the great example of the prose poem,
and in the *Lettre à l'Académie* and the *Dialogues sur
l'éloquence* stressed the importance of naturalness, simplicity,
and passion in poetry.[21] The work, however, which has long
been considered the most significant of its time, and which
elicited the highest praise from Voltaire, is Du Bos' *Réflexions
critiques sur la poésie et sur la peinture*, first published in 1719.
Du Bos proclaims an "esthétique du sentiment"; for him "the
true way to know the value of a poem will always be to con-
sult the impression that it makes on us." [22] André Monglond
does not hesitate to say that Du Bos, in spite of his perpetua-
tion of the classical emphasis on rules and order, is the founder
of romantic aesthetics.[23] This statement seems to me slightly
exaggerated, but there is no doubt that Du Bos is the first to
carry over the sensualist philosophy into the literary domain.
While he maintains the doctrine of imitation in his constant
stress on *ut pictura poesis*, he conceives the great aim of that
imitation as an appeal to the heart, an awakening of the emotions. His weakness lies in a certain deficiency in his own
sensitivity to poetry; one has the impression that he is dis-
coursing about poetry rather than experiencing it.

The feeling for poetry which is missing in Du Bos can be
found in a work which, perhaps because of its extremely un-
prepossessing title, has received little attention from students
of eighteenth-century poetics: the *Examen philosophique de
la poésie en général* of Rémond de Saint-Mard, first published
in 1729, and five years later expanded into a larger volume.[24]
In the "Lettres sur la décadence du goût" appended to the later
volume the author proclaims himself a partisan of the ancients,
attributing the decline in taste which he deplores to the scorn
in which they are held. He castigates the sacrifice of feeling

to reason, the pride taken in precision, and cites as the two authors most responsible for this lamentable state of affairs Fontenelle and La Motte. But Rémond de Saint-Mard is no mere traditionalist; he is an enthusiast about poetry, "le plus bel art du monde." He is, to the best of my knowledge, the only writer of his time in France to assert unhesitatingly that poetry comes first, then rules. In his preface to the *Réflexions* he asks how it happened that Aristotle and Horace, to whom we should indeed be grateful for having set down the rules of poetry, did not go further and tell us just what these rules are based on, verify them by the impression poetry makes on the reader. Not only would this give greater authority to the rules, but it would also give us the satisfaction of knowing the real basis of the rules, "c'est-à-dire leur rapport avec notre manière de sentir." [25] This insistence that rules must be judged by poetry, not poetry by rules, gives to the *Réflexions* a freshness, a personal quality, all too rare in such treatises.[26]

In all these treatises and commentaries certain focal points of discussion recur constantly: enthusiasm, feeling, imagination, imagery, poetic language and technique. What conception did the poets and critics have of each of these? What did they believe the role of each in poetry to be?

The history of the idea of enthusiasm and of the word itself reflects faithfully the poetic movement of the century.[27] The first edition of the *Dictionnaire de l'Académie* (1694) defines it as "an extraordinary movement of the spirit, by which a poet, an orator, or a man who works with genius rises in some way above himself." This definition is maintained in the 1718 and 1740 editions of the *Dictionnaire*, which however add "an extraordinary activity of the spirit, caused by an inspiration which is or seems to be divine." [28] But enthusiasm became more and more suspect in the early years of the century, and the leader in the attack on it was La Motte. Much of what he says had indeed been said in the seventeenth century. It is La

Motte's initial definition of enthusiasm that does most to be-
little it: "it is an ardor of the imagination which one arouses
in oneself, and to which one abandons oneself, a source of
beauties and of defects, depending on whether it is blind or
enlightened." The very nature of enthusiasm is changed. It
is no longer a divine and mysterious gift of the gods, but a
state produced deliberately and artificially by the poet. La
Motte can say triumphantly: "Voilà tout le mystère, une
imagination échauffée." [29] To be sure, he has not really eliminated the mystery; he never explains just how the poet is to set
about arousing this fervor of imagination in himself. But on
the surface at least reason is satisfied, divine intervention is
excluded. La Motte's own enthusiasm was certainly no divine
madness, but, as Fontenelle said in his *éloge*, "a determination
to make verses, which he carried out, because he was very intelligent." [30]

La Motte's subjugation of poetry to reason is echoed by his
faithful disciples, such as Trublet and Terrasson. And many
writers who make fewer concessions to reason adopt La
Motte's definition of enthusiasm, repeating his very words.
Even for Du Bos enthusiasm has no element of mystery; he
defines it as a "qualité du sang jointe avec l'heureuse disposition
des organes," and concludes "voilà en quoi consiste cette
fureur divine." After describing the poet carried away by the
enthusiasm of composition and by the ideas aroused in his
"imagination échauffée," he warns poets not to be satisfied
with what they have produced in a state of delirium rather
than of true enthusiasm, and stresses the need for a "travail de
limer et de polir," however wearisome it may be.[31] Here it is
interesting to note that Du Bos, unlike most of his contemporaries, puts the work of intelligence after that of enthusiasm,
instead of restraining enthusiasm while it is at work. Batteux
describes the moments of enthusiasm when the soul, glowing
as if with a divine fire, illuminates all nature, but later says that
it is the poets themselves who excite their own imaginations,

and uses the phrase "une imagination échauffée par l'art." [32] Although the distrust of enthusiasm is usually based on rationalistic grounds, it was also the target of certain ardent defenders of religion, who considered it nothing but a pagan heritage.

It is in connection with one genre, the ode, that enthusiasm is allowed the greatest freedom. Even La Motte makes some concessions here, allowing more liberty to lyric poets than to others. Batteux likewise grants special privileges to the writer of odes; he is allowed bold, strong terms, extraordinary images, asides and digressions, all the "beau désordre," so much more pleasing than reality, which results from enthusiasm.[33] The most elevated conception of enthusiasm and its role in the ode is found in a fragment of Jean-Baptiste Rousseau: "Thus this disorder which characterizes the ode, far from being guided by reason, should guide, transport, do violence to reason by another and higher reason of which the poet is but the instrument. This is what leads Plato to say that the poet is sacred, the enthusiasm essential for him being a kind of divinity which, so to speak, takes the place of his own soul as long as the fervor of composition lasts." [34] Although Vauvenargues uses Rousseau's own odes as example of what the ode should not be, putting them in the same category as La Motte's, his theory is very close to Rousseau's: "My idea of the ode is that it is a kind of madness, a rapture of the imagination; but this rapture and this madness, if they are real and not feigned, should fill odes with feeling; for never is the imagination truly stirred without the soul being moved: now nothing is colder than very fine verses in which one finds only harmony and images, without fire and without imagination." [35] Likewise Rémond de Saint-Mard sees the lyric poet driven half mad by his passions, and asserts that nothing is so admirable as this state of enthusiasm. For Rémond enthusiasm is not limited to poetry; even prose writers such as Pascal, Montaigne, and Malebranche have their "petit enthousiasme," their "ivresse sage." But in general it is only in the ode that free rein is given to

> . . . . . . cet aveugle délire,
> Qui du poète échauffant les transports,
> Dicte ses vers, et forme ses accords.[36]

For the majority of writers enthusiasm remains the effect of an artificial stimulation of the imagination, shorn of mystery. But mystery was not to be eliminated so easily, and found refuge in another conception, less discussed at this time than later in the century, that of genius. For Louis Racine genius is a divine power, a secret inspiration, an illumination of the soul. With some writers the distinction between enthusiasm and genius is far from clear, as when Du Bos says that genius is the enthusiasm by which poets are possessed. On the other hand, genius is even more frequently paired with talent, as in Girard's *Synonymes français* (1737): "Both are natural gifts . . . but *genius* seems to be more inward, and to be somewhat akin to the spirit of invention; *talent* seems to be more outward, and to be more akin to brilliant execution." [37] For Du Bos genius most often seems to be the same as talent: "we call by the name of genius the aptitude with which a man has been endowed by nature for doing certain things well and easily." But genius must be cultivated; it is "a plant, which, so to speak, grows of itself; but the quality, like the quantity of its fruits depends on the cultivation it receives. The most fortunate genius can be perfected only by long study." [38] So genius, like enthusiasm, must be controlled and guided by reason. Vauvenargues, however, has a broader conception of genius, in which he finds a combination of many qualities. In his *Dialogues* he asks: "What is a great poet if not a great genius, a man who dominates other men by his imagination, who is superior to them in acuteness of feeling, who has an intuitive and luminous knowledge of the passions, the vices, and the spirit of men; who paints nature faithfully because he knows it perfectly and has more vivid ideas of everything than others; a soul capable of lofty flights." [39]

Another poetic faculty which received little attention is sentiment. Enthusiasm is distrusted, but emotion is almost ignored. This explains in part the difficulty in defining enthusiasm, which by later writers was to be so closely allied with emotion; the man of deep and strong feelings is the one whose imagination is easily stirred to a state of enthusiasm. Fénelon indeed constantly insists that, although poetry is imitation, imitation in itself is not enough, and he calls to witness his beloved classical authors: "The ancients were not satisfied with simply painting from nature; to truth they added passion. . . . The beautiful which is only beautiful, that is to say brilliant, is only half beautiful; it must express passions in order to inspire them; it must take possession of the heart in order to guide it towards the legitimate goal of a poem." [40] And it is in his realization of the importance of emotion that Du Bos is so far ahead of his time, putting the appeal to feeling as one of the primary aims of poetry: "le sublime de la poésie et de la peinture est de toucher et de plaire, comme celui de l'éloquence est de persuader." *Toucher* first; poetry "songe à nous émouvoir préférablement à toute chose." [41] For Du Bos sentiment is a sixth sense, the touchstone of all true poetry.

Only a few other writers allow sentiment its place. For Batteux lyric poetry is "toute consacrée aux sentiments." The poet must arouse his heart, and then immediately take up his lyre.[42] And Batteux insists that everything that is meant to be sung must be filled with sentiment, and hence free and natural.[43] Vauvenargues too considered that the greatest and commonest weakness of poets was their inability to preserve "la naïveté du sentiment." This is his main criticism of Fontenelle; "his subtle and profound mind deceived him only in questions of sentiment." [44] The one aim of poetry, for Rémond de Saint-Mard; is to "remuer un cœur qui veut continuellement être agité." [45] But with these exceptions sentiment is little considered before the middle of the century.

Even though enthusiasm was harnessed, emotion ignored, poetry was still suspect on other grounds. Its usefulness is denied, its sole function is to please. The next step is to accuse it of frivolity and of extravagance, and, as the famous passage in the *Lettres persanes* shows, it is above all the lyric poets who were attacked on these grounds. "Here are the poets . . . that is, those authors whose business it is to shackle common sense, and to load down reason with trimmings just as women used to be buried beneath their ornaments and jewels. . . . Here are the lyric poets, whom I despise as much as I esteem the others, and who made of their art a harmonious extravaganza." [46] Poetry is unfit for the serious-minded; the Abbé de Pons states categorically, "L'art des vers est un art frivole." [47] There is a widespread feeling that poetry lacks the seriousness which belongs to a philosophic age, and again and again Plato's exclusion of poets from the republic is cited.

But champions to defend the great tradition of the utility of poetry were not lacking. Fénelon wrote in 1718: "Just as we should despise bad poets, we should admire the great poet who makes of poetry not a means of gaining empty glory but a means of moving men to wisdom, virtue, and religion." [48] Du Bos maintains that the portrayal of virtuous actions stirs the soul, and Louis Racine assures his readers that poetry need not necessarily be dangerous to morality, and that its aim should be to make men better. A strong defense of poetry on both philosophic and moral grounds is made by Abbé Massieu, who rebukes those who despise and condemn poetry either because it corrupts the mind or because it corrupts the heart.[49]

The wisest words on the morality of poetry come from Voltaire, writing to his friend Cideville: "No moral lesson, I beg of you. . . . Those moral lessons which are inherent in the picture itself and enter into the heart of the story, are the only ones which can please, because they at the same time paint, and everything in poetry should be painting." [50] Here

Voltaire is far ahead of his times in his realization that the moral must be implicit in the work of art, and not attached to it. But for Voltaire poetry should not be an end in itself: "In this century, woe be to the versifier who is only a versifier." Verses which do not teach new and moving truths do not deserve to be read.[51]

The charge of frivolity is indeed based more often on philosophical grounds than on moral ones; the danger is not so much that poetry will corrupt morals as that it will distort truth. At this point the spirit of the age comes into conflict with the faculty which during the next hundred years was to become for the poet the "reine des facultés," imagination. And in its distrust of imagination philosophic truth finds a strong ally in the aesthetic field in the classical doctrine of imitation.

Imagination is by no means the focus of discussion in the early part of the century that enthusiasm is. First of all it had no such established and traditional position. Enthusiasm had to be dethroned and exiled; imagination was but a timid pretender. Moreover the concept of imagination had never been very closely associated with literature in France.[52] Ronsard, it is true, had assigned to it the work of *invention*: "Invention is only the natural bent of an imagination which conceives ideas and forms of all imaginable things, heavenly as well as earthly, animate and inanimate, in order later to represent, describe, and imitate them." [53] But Ronsard immediately restricts the role of the imagination, warning against the fanciful or melancholy inventions which arise from a disordered mind.

In the seventeenth century imagination plays practically no part in discussions of literature and poetry; it is not so much as mentioned by Boileau. What attention is paid to it comes from the philosophers, who regard it with varying degrees of suspicion. It is an image-making faculty, with a dangerous tendency to distort and falsify the images produced. This distrust of imagination is found in the *Discours de la méthode* when Descartes says: "Neither our imagination nor our senses can assure us of anything whatever, if our understanding does not intervene." [54] Later in the *Discours*, in a passage where he uses the word *fantaisie* instead of *imagination*, Descartes suggests the distinction between memory and imagination, the modifying power of the imagination which was to become so important.[55] In his later works Descartes's distrust of imagination is somewhat lessened; he distinguishes between a passive dream-imagination, with the senses in control, and a waking and conscious imagination controlled by thought. Only the latter is to be trusted. Much the same attitude is found in Malebranche. When imagination, "the mind's power to form images of objects," is in control, it is a dangerous faculty and a form of madness.[56] The most vehement condemnation of imagination is Pascal's famous phrase, "C'est cette partie décevante dans l'homme, cette maîtresse d'erreur et de fausseté." [57] Condemned by reason, it was also to be restrained in the name of taste and morality. La Bruyère warns his readers against the danger of too much imagination in conversation and in writing, which "often produces only vain and childish ideas, which improve neither taste nor morals." [58]

Thus the conception of imagination inherited by the eighteenth century was that of an image-making faculty, inherent in human nature, but dangerous as a potential enemy of reason and judgment. The 1694 *Dictionnaire de l'Académie* defines it as "la faculté de l'âme qui imagine" (*imaginer* is defined as "former quelque chose dans son idée, dans son esprit"), and adds, "Encore, fantaisie erronée et bizarre." The definition is maintained, with only minor changes, in the 1718 and 1740 editions of the *Dictionnaire*. It is then hardly surprising that the role of imagination in poetry received scant attention during the first half of the century. The faculty was first of all suspect on philosophic and moral grounds. It is named constantly, as we have seen, in the most common definition of enthusiasm, "une imagination échauffée," but it is rarely discussed in any detail, and always subjected to the rule of reason, as when Fénelon says that if a poet is to equal the ancients he must display judgment superior to the liveliest and most fertile imagination.[59] Budding poets are warned by Mallet that the safest rule is not to be carried away by the flights of the imagination, but to weigh all one's thoughts in the scales of reason, the only source of the durable beauties of poetry.[60] In *Le Pour et le Contre* Prévost quotes a fable sent him by a correspondent, which says that imagination,

> . . . . de l'hypogriffe empruntant le secours,
> Sans sujet et sans art se perdait dans les nues.[61]

The distrust of imagination was due not only to its bad reputation with the philosophers, but to a conflict on aesthetic grounds, sometimes explicit, more often implicit, between imagination and the doctrine of imitation. The more narrowly imitation is conceived, the less scope there is for imagination. Fénelon insists that the only way to rival the ancients is to follow even more closely than they had, their ideas on the imitation of "la belle nature." On this point Du Bos keeps close to tradition, insisting that verisimilitude cannot be too closely observed in both painting and poetry, that "la vraisemblance est l'âme de la poésie." However he does say that the man of genius sees nature with different eyes, and in his imitation brings out differences between objects which are imperceptible to ordinary men.[62] Batteux, whose entire poetic doctrine is grounded on imitation, insists that the function of genius is not to imagine what does not exist, but to discover what does exist. However, imitation should not be of nature in the raw, but of "la nature telle qu'elle peut être." [63] Here again is the idea of "la belle nature," which, as Louis Racine points out, leads to the conception of a beauty independent of time, of language, and of passing fashion.[64] This is the fixed and invariable beauty of Crousaz's and Père André's treatises,[65] to which was to be opposed later a beauty composed of two elements, one eternal and unchangeable, the other relative and variable. The change in the conception of beauty goes hand in hand with the increasing importance of imagination.

With the aesthetic prejudice added to the philosophical one, imagination stood little chance. For Gaillard "a poet who is a prey to the vagaries of his imagination produces only monsters." [66] Batteux gives imagination a limited role: "Imagination is an aptitude for conceiving objects in the form of material images. It gives form and color to everything it represents, whether the object be material or not." [67] The "poètes légers" do indeed welcome imagination lightheartedly; Chaulieu addresses an ode to his goddess, imagination, "Reine aimable des mensonges." [68] But the only author before the middle of the century to give much thought to the question is Vauvenargues, who both defines imagination and recognizes its importance; "I call imagination the gift of conceiving things in a figurative manner, and of representing thoughts by images." [69] He maintains that, although imagination is not all that the poet needs, great poetry is impossible without imagination.

On the whole the writers of the early eighteenth century viewed imagination, when they considered it at all, with much the same distrust they felt towards enthusiasm. At worst it was a danger to reason, truth, and verisimilitude; at best it was the purveyor of the images which are the ornament of poetry and help to distinguish it from prose. When Voltaire wrote that "an Epic poem ought to be grounded upon judgment, and embellished by imagination," [70] he was putting imagination in the place to which most of his contemporaries would have assigned it.

Whereas enthusiasm, however much decried, was never without defenders, imagination was for a long time less fortunate. Only about the middle of the century does it move into the forefront of poetic discussion. The change is due largely to the impact of English thought on French writers. For English writers and philosophers had long been interested in the problem of the imagination, mainly in its physiological and psychological aspects, but occasionally in its relation to poetry. And it is, I think, impossible to understand the new importance attached to the imagination in France towards 1750 without a brief backward glance at its antecedents in England.

The distrust of the imagination is not indeed entirely lacking in England. In *The Rambler* Doctor Johnson calls it "a licentious and vagrant faculty, unsusceptible of limitations, and impatient of restraint." But such philosophers as Hobbes, Locke, Berkeley, and Hume had adopted a more objective attitude towards imagination, and were concerned with defining it more precisely, relating it to the other human faculties, and establishing distinctions between imagination and memory. Their point of departure is stated at the beginning of the *Leviathan*: "There is no conception in a man's mind, which hath not at first, totally, or by parts, been begotten upon the organs of sense." Coming to imagination, Hobbes states: "After the object is removed, or the eye shut, we still retain an image of the thing seen, though more obscure than when we see it. And this is what the Latins call *Imagination*, from the image made in seeing; and apply the same, though improperly, to all the other senses. But the Greeks call it *Fancy*; which signifies *apparence*, and is as proper to one sense as to another. IMAGINATION therefore is nothing but decaying sense . . . when we would express the *decay*, and signify that the sense is fading, old and past, it is called *Memory*. So that *Imagination* and *Memory* are but one thing." In this passage Hobbes raises several of the questions which were to be most discussed later: the basic nature of imagination (the retention of images), its validity for senses other than sight, and the relation of imagination to memory. Then Hobbes distinguishes between two types of imagination: *"Simple Imagination*; as when one imagineth a man, or horse, which he hath seen before. The other is *Compounded*, as when from the sight of a man at one time, and of a horse at another, we conceive in our mind a Centaur." [71] This distinction was to recur constantly, the "simple" imagination being considered as either identical with, or closely allied to memory, and the "compounded" leading to the idea of the "creative" imagination.

Like Dryden and other earlier writers, Locke uses the term *wit* rather than imagination. Memory is "the storehouse of our ideas," while wit consists in "the assemblage of ideas, and putting those together with quickness and variety, wherein can be found any resemblance or congruity, thereby to make up pleasant pictures and agreeable visions in the fancy. Unlike judgment, which separates ideas, wit compounds and enlarges." [72] This last distinction was to be taken up by Diderot. The power of the imagination to change and modify images is also stressed by both Berkeley and Hume.[73] So the French writers found in many of the English philosophers they read with such interest lengthy discussions of the imagination and the problems it presents, and found it viewed, not with alarm, but with scientific curiosity. It is true that the philosophers were little concerned with the role of imagination in literature. But this is to be found in other writers, first of all in Bacon, who furnished the divisions of human learning set forth in the *Discours préliminaire* of the *Encyclopédie*: "The parts of human learning have reference to the three parts of man's understanding, which is the seat of learning: history to his memory, poesy to his imagination, and philosophy to his reason." [74] Imagination has its part in English literary theory in the seventeenth century, but the treatment of it which was to have the greatest influence in France was Addison's series of essays "On the Pleasures of the Imagination," which appeared in the *Spectator* in 1712, and are frequently referred to by French writers. Addison discusses at length the importance of imagination in the arts. He makes no distinction between imagination and fancy, and limits images to the visual field. But he stresses the "compounding" imagination: "We cannot indeed have a single image in the fancy that did not make its first appearance through the sight; but we have the power of retaining, altering and compounding those images which we have once received." [75] Imagination is essential for the writer: "A noble writer should be born with this faculty in its full strength and vigor, so as to be able to receive lively ideas from outward objects, to retain them long, and to range them together, upon occasion, in such figures and representations as are most likely to hit the fancy of the reader." [76] Imagination produces the poetic figures which Addison praises: "Allegories, when well chosen, are like so many tracks of light in a discourse that make everything about them clear and beautiful. A noble metaphor, when it is placed to an advantage, casts a kind of glory round it, and darts a lustre through the whole sentence." [77] Addison's actual conception of imagination is a somewhat looser one than that of the philosophers; his great contribution is his stress on imagination as a primary faculty of the writer. The English conception of the free imagination which, in Dryden's happy phrase, "like a nimble Spaniel, beats over and ranges through the fields of memory, till it springs the quarry it hunted after," [78] contrasts strikingly with the French idea of an imagination which cannot be trusted and must always be kept on a leash.

The great champion of the imagination in France was to be Diderot. But the first important treatment of the subject comes just before the middle of the century, in Condillac's *Essai sur l'origine des connaissances humaines* (1746).[79] In his preface the author acknowledges his debt to the English empiricists, especially Bacon and Locke, and maintains with Locke that we have no ideas which do not come to us from our senses. He first defines imagination in the passive sense, then in a later chapter, "Des vices et des avantages de l'imagination," points

out that this power of arousing images also gives us the power
of combining and uniting the most disparate ideas, so that
there is nothing which cannot take on a new form in our
imagination. Nothing would seem so contrary to truth as this
activity, yet if imagination is rightly controlled it can be one
of the principal instruments of knowledge. In a footnote he
distinguishes the two types of imagination, that which merely
awakens images in the absence of objects, and that which
makes new combinations.[80] After a warning on the dangers
of imagination, including that of novel-reading for "les jeunes
personnes du sexe," which brings Emma Bovary to mind,
Condillac turns to the brighter side in the chapter, "Où
l'imagination puise les agréments qu'elle donne à la vérité."
Imagination is "a bee which gathers its treasures from the most
beautiful flowers in a garden-bed." It is not really opposed to
truth; its function is rather to embellish truth, which otherwise would often be bare and cold; "L'imagination est à la
vérité ce qu'est la parure à une belle personne." [81]

Condillac reintegrates imagination in its proper place
among human faculties, emphasizes its passive and active
aspects, and reconciles it with truth. He adds nothing to what
his English predecessors had said, and is often less precise,
as well as more timid. And at no point does he suggest the
role of imagination in literature. Nevertheless the section on
imagination in the *Essai* marks the beginning of its rehabilitation in France. Its literary importance comes to the fore only
in Voltaire's *Encyclopédie* article "Imagination," published
in 1765, but written some seven years earlier. I am treating it
here rather than later both because it synthesizes the English
conceptions just discussed, and because of its importance in
the development of Diderot's conception of the imagination.

For Voltaire imagination is first of all "le pouvoir que
chaque être sensible éprouve en soi de se représenter dans son
esprit les choses sensibles," a power which depends on memory. Then Voltaire refers to the essays on imagination of "le

célèbre Adisson," but disagrees with Addison as to the sense of sight being the only one involved in imagination. Sight indeed furnishes the most important images, but the blind man has memories of sound and of touch. Next comes the distinction between the "passive" imagination, which merely retains impressions, and the "active," which arranges and combines them. It is interesting to note that Voltaire sees in dreams more than memory, a kind of involuntary active imagination, uncontrolled by reason. The true active imagination joins reflexion and combination to memory; it brings together distant objects, separates those which are joined, arranges and changes them. Thus imagination seems to create, but Voltaire insists that creation is impossible, "for man cannot make images, he can only modify them." Imagination is the source of poetic enthusiasm, where emotion and image meet.

Looking forward to the idea of the creative imagination, it is worth while to pause for a moment over the controversy on the use of the word *créer* as applied to the imagination. The English writers had used it freely, though often modifying it, as when Addison says that imagination "has something in it like creation. It bestows a kind of existence." [82] But in France there was much resistance to the use of the term. Voltaire indeed addresses some verses to Helvétius in 1740 in which he says "Le vrai poète est créateur." [83] But this is poetic licence, for in his prose writings he is strongly opposed to the use of the term. Batteux, with his emphasis on imitation, refuses, as might be expected, to call the work of the imagination creative: "The human mind cannot create, properly speaking; all its productions bear the imprint of a model. Even the monsters conceived by a lawless imagination in its ravings can only be composed of parts taken from nature." [84] Vauvenargues too insists that man cannot create, but only modify. And Condillac is categoric: "We do not create ideas properly speaking, we only combine, by a process of composition and decomposition, those which we received from the senses." [85]

This argument on the use of *créer* was to continue through the century. There is general agreement as to what the imagination does; the only point is whether the word *créer* can rightly be applied to this activity, as a convenient glorification of the poetic imagination. The objection is partly linguistic, a desire to reserve to the word its primary meaning of a creation *ex nihilo*, God's creation of the world. But the objection is also on philosophical grounds, on the basis that there is no mystery involved, that imagination works only on impressions received by the senses. The quarrel is primarily over words, but the gradual triumph of *créer* was to be a significant concomitant of the increasing importance of imagination, culminating in the nineteenth century in the complete acceptance of the "creative" imagination.

In modern poetic theory the creation of poetic images has been closely allied with imagination, and considered one of its most important functions. But in eighteenth-century French theory images, though accepted as a product of imagination, are most discussed as a mark of poetic style, one of the characteristics that differentiate the language of poetry from that of prose. How great that difference was, or should be, was a moot point. The tendency was to minimize the distinction, and there is a good deal of truth in Thomas Gray's statement, made later in the century: "The language of the age is never the language of poetry, except among the French, whose verse, where the thought or image does not support it, differs in nothing from prose." [86] Most of the French theorists would agree. Louis Racine says: "In a language as discreet as ours, the difference between poetry and prose should not be as great as in other languages." [87] For Fénelon poetry differs from eloquence only in that it paints with enthusiasm, and with bolder strokes.[88] And one of Mallet's precepts is: "Poetry requires a simple, precise, and easy language; at a first reading one should be able, with moderate attention, without difficulty

and without effort, to find a clear and well-developed meaning." [89] The road to hermetic poetry was to be a long one.
This lack of any great distinction between the language of
poetry and that of prose was one of the major obstacles to the
renascence of poetry. As will be seen again when we come to
the quarrel between the partisans of prose poetry and of verse,
poetry is constantly allied with eloquence. The same laws
govern both; the same rhetorical conventions are common to
both. The difference is not of kind, but of degree.

But insofar as there is a difference between the two
languages, the use of images is one of the distinguishing
characteristics of poetry. There is some difficulty here in that
the precise meaning of *image* is not always clear. When the
word is used in connection with the imagination, it most often
has the simple meaning of a picture, or sense image, present
to the imagination in the absence of the object. At other times
it is a word picture, a description. The 1694 *Dictionnaire de
l'Académie* gives the two meanings of a representation in the
fine arts and an image perceived by the imagination; the 1718
edition adds: "En parlant d'un ouvrage de prose ou de vers
orné de descriptions on dit qu'*il est plein d'images*." And in
1730 Gibert's *Rhétorique* has: "On appelle *Image* en rhétorique, une manière de s'exprimer, qui pourrait fournir à un
peintre la matière d'un tableau." [90] But at the same time *image*
is beginning to take on its modern sense of metaphor, simile,
and the like, although writers on rhetoric, in particular, keep
to the terms of *figure* or *trope*. Gibert, however, refers to
simile and metaphor as "images sensibles," and many writers,
La Motte among them, use *figure* and *image* indifferently.
Gradually the latter term comes to replace the former in ordinary usage. With these changes taking place it is not always
certain whether *image* means merely a concrete description,
or a figure of speech, though in most cases the meaning is
clarified by the context.

One thing is unmistakably clear: the image, in either sense, is an "embellishment," something added to the poem, which can be taken away or changed at will. Among the most important developments in poetic doctrine during the next hundred years was to be the movement of the image from a peripheral place to a central one, from ornament to symbol. The eighteenth-century critics, particularly the champions of reason in poetry, consider the image merely as one characteristic of the language of poetry. Fontenelle, though he subordinates images to thoughts, asserting that a poetical work which had fewer images than thoughts would be so much the more worthy of praise,[91] still puts images above verse form as a source of poetic pleasure. He rejects the traditional "images fabuleuses," preferring the "image réelle" ("la diligente abeille"), but above all the "image spirituelle" ("le Remords incorruptible"). The closer an image is to abstract thought, the more acceptable Fontenelle finds it. For La Motte images constituted one of the two distinctions between poetry and prose, the other being "un arrangement mesuré des paroles." By images he means "such bold figures as eloquence would not dare to use." [92] So in general images are accepted as a mark of poetry. But Abbé Trublet will have none of them: "It is said that in verse the images have more value than the thoughts. So much the worse for verse; for this is an excellent proof of its inferiority to prose." [93]

The exponents of the classical tradition stress the importance of images in both senses. Voltaire admires a poem because he finds in it what he likes, "beaucoup d'images, *ut pictura poesis*." [94] The author of the *Connaissance des beautés*, long attributed to Voltaire, sees in the poetic image a product of the imagination: "Metaphor is the mark of a genius who represents images vividly to himself. He makes a keen and swift comparison between the things which move him and the images presented by nature. This is the result of a lively and felicitous imagination." [95] But figures must be used with moderation and not multiplied unduly, and above all must not prevent clarity: "As soon as tropes and figures make a discourse obscure, as soon as *Allegory* comes close to Enigma, . . . Eloquence thus adorned has only false beauties." [96] On allegory opinion is divided. Voltaire has words of warning: "An allegory must not be strained, everything in it must appear natural, nothing must seem extraneous." [97] Abbé Massieu, on the other hand, praises allegory, for "everyone knows that there are two ways of teaching truth to men; one cryptical and mysterious, the other open and simple." [98]

The classical work on images, which was to be reprinted again and again in the eighteenth and nineteenth centuries and to be pilfered, with or without acknowledgement, by writer after writer, is Du Marsais' *Des tropes* (1730). Du Marsais lists the different uses of the trope: to support the principal idea by accessory ideas; to give added energy; to adorn and ennoble discourse; to disguise harsh or disagreeable ideas. He warns against certain wrong uses of metaphor; metaphors should not be drawn from base subjects, and they should not be forced. For the latter Du Marsais gives as an example Théophile's "je baignerai mes mains dans les ondes de tes cheveux"; what he would have thought of Baudelaire's *La Chevelure* is all too easy to imagine. Moreover metaphors must be suited to the style, and they can be "softened" by such expressions as "pour ainsi dire" and the like. Finally mixed metaphors must be avoided. Du Marsais concludes by making the distinction between literal meaning (strict or figurative) and spiritual meaning (moral, allegorical, and anagogic). [99]

Batteux sees in images the expression of strong feeling by things rather than words. The poet does not say *"mon mal est cruel*, mais, *c'est un tigre impitoyable*. De là naissent les métaphores, les allégories, les comparaisons." [100] The image is a "tour poétique," but it is suitable also to prose; "C'est la parure et non le corps de la poésie." [101] Here Batteux, mindful of his basic principle that the essence of poetry is imitation, is opposing those who find that essence in "fiction." He is undoubtedly thinking of the long discussion of images in Du Bos, and his insistence on *ut pictura poesis*. Du Bos advises the poet to give up the use of "emblematic figures": "on produit tant qu'on veut de ces symboles par le secours de deux ou trois livres qui sont des sources intarissables de pareils colifichets."[102] Images must not be the chimeras of a capricious imagination, mysterious allegories and enigmas more obscure than those of the sphinx. The imagination must find images which will move the reader, not puzzle him. Du Bos' famous "poésie du style" "consiste à prêter des sentiments intéressants à tout ce qu'on fait parler, comme à exprimer par des figures et à représenter sous des images capables de nous émouvoir, ce qui ne nous toucherait pas, s'il était dit simplement en style prosaïque." For Du Bos this "poésie du style" constitutes the greatest difference between poetry and prose: "Many metaphors which would be considered too daring in the most lofty oratorical style are accepted in poetry. . . . It is in order to invent images which shall paint truly what the poet means, to find expressions to give them form, that the poet needs a divine fire — not in order to make rhymes."[103] Du Bos' emphasis on images and on the conformity between images and ideas is one of the most important and original aspects of his work. But it is in a passage of Rémond de Saint-Mard that we find the most striking anticipation of later conceptions: "Les images ne servent pas seulement à peindre et à nous rendre attentifs, par la chaleur qu'elles portent avec elles; elles ont encore des rapports secrets, une analogie sourde, des convenances délicates avec les principales affections du cœur; et c'est en vertu de ces convenances qu'on est quelquefois si vivement touché." And again: "Nos passions sont des espèces de cordes toujours tendues et toujours prêtes à recevoir l'unisson de quelque image."[104] It is often dangerous to interpret earlier theory in the light of modern connotations, but even so *rapports secrets, analogies sourdes, convenances délicates* strike a note that has not been heard before in France.

In Condillac's *Origine des connaissances humaines* the section on language is of particular interest for the future conception of the poetic image. The chapter on the origins of poetry begins with familiar ideas; style was at the beginning poetic, since it depicted ideas by images and used a regular and measured language. When Condillac comes to written language he acknowledges his great debt to an English source, which he refers to as Warburton's "Essai sur l'écriture hiéroglyphe." Warburton's thesis was that at the beginning hieroglyphs had been "picture" writing, gradually developed into "character" writing. At first the hieroglyph was intended to communicate, not to conceal; it had its origin in necessity, and only later was it employed for secrecy and mystery. Language followed a parallel development. Finally figurative expressions, originating in necessity, later becoming "dark sayings," came to be used for ornament. But their common foundation was "a picture or image, presented to the imagination through the eyes or ears." "*Wit* consists in using *strong metaphoric Images* in uncommon and adequate allusions; just as ancient *Egyptian Wisdom* did in *Hieroglyphic Symbols* fancifully adopted by analogy." [105] Again images are related to imagination; Warburton quotes Shakespeare, "as imagination bodies forth/ The form of things unknown."

In his chapter, "De l'origine de la fable, de la parabole et de l'énigme, avec quelques détails sur l'usage des figures et des métaphores," Condillac follows this outline of the development of hieroglyphs and of language, and ends with a quotation from Warburton: "En un mot, le style prophétique semble être un hiéroglyphe parlant." [106] This notion of the hieroglyph was to play an important part in later conceptions of the image, from Diderot's "tissu d'hiéroglyphes" to Baudelaire's "tout est hiéroglyphique." Indeed the history of the image during the next hundred years can be envisaged as a return from the image as embellishment to the image as dark saying. Condillac himself, faithful to the doctrine of progress, was far from seeing any great virtue in the use of images. He notes that as writing became more simple style became more simple. "It is thus that figures and metaphors, first invented from necessity, then chosen as instruments of mystery, became the ornaments of speech, when employed with discrimination; thus the abuse made of them was the first step in the decadence of language." [107] Condillac, though he put into circulation ideas that were to be allied to poetry, had nothing of the poet in him; his interest is psychological in the case of imagination, linguistic in the case of images. Only later writers, above all Diderot, were to perceive the significance of these ideas in relation to literature.

In nearly all discussions of poetic style the image has the lion's share. Another point comes up often: the use of inversion. Voltaire, writing to Frederick the Great, distinguishes the "idée poétique," which is "une image brillante substituée à l'idée naturelle de la chose dont on veut parler," from the "tour poétique," which is "une inversion que la prose n'admet pas." [108] For Louis Racine too inversion is one of the two chief marks of poetic style, the other being a more frequent and bold use of images. Père Du Cerceau goes so far as to say that the essence of poetry is not in versification, not in vocabulary, not in imagery, but in the construction and turn of the sentence, the use of inversion and transposition.[109] It is Du Cerceau whom Batteux is refuting when he says that inversion cannot be the essence of poetry: "L'inversion n'est qu'un sel du style poétique." [110]

In all this discussion little is said of what was to be so much stressed in the next century, the music of poetry. Nothing could be more remote from most eighteenth-century theory than "De la musique avant toute chose." La Motte says that "the sounds of a language are a matter of indifference. . . . They please or shock us only by the meaning we attach to them." [111] Yet some at least of the poets did not neglect the musical aspect of poetry. Jean-Baptiste Rousseau writes: "It is the ear which carries verses to the soul . . . consequently it should be the first to be satisfied . . . then it is for the intelligence to decide whether the ear was right . . . so the poet who would please both must unite accuracy of harmony with accuracy of thought. . . . One can succeed in this only by a precise and scrupulous balance between ideas and words." [112] The last sentence suggests a realization, rare at this time in France, of the relationship between sound and sense.

In the preface to his poems Chaulieu claims that the ear is the only judge of poetry, and that he has sacrificed everything to number and harmony. Voltaire too was well aware of the musical values of poetry: "Poetry is a kind of music; one must hear it to judge it." [113] Likewise Vauvenargues maintains that imagination, enthusiasm, a talent for description are not enough to make a poet; he must be born with a sense of harmony, a gift for language and for the art of verse. And Du Bos puts beside his "poésie du style," the art of painting images and pleasing the imagination, the "mécanique de la poésie," the art of making harmonious verses and pleasing the ear. He adds: "I shall be told that their interests are often opposed; I agree, and would only point out that to reconcile them one must be born a poet." [114] Here again is a recognition of the relation of sound and sense. In many of these discussions one finds what is so often lacking in eighteenth-century theory, the use of precise examples. Thus Abbé d'Olivet analyzes in great detail the line of Boileau which Diderot was to use later as an example of the poetic hieroglyph:

Soupire, étend les bras, ferme l'œil et s'endort.[115]

The general question of music and harmony is often overshadowed by a quarrel which was to be prolonged through the century, between the opponents and the partisans of verse and rhyme. The former are clearly divided into two categories. There are those to whom poetry is suspect, who see in the difference between poetry and prose only a difference between verse and prose, and then, finding in verse an obstacle to natural expression, go on to deny to poetry any reason to exist. But there are also those who attack verse in order to preserve poetry, by freeing it from the intolerable shackles which bind it. For both groups verse was an unnecessary obstacle; but its elimination meant for one the deathblow of poetry, for the other its salvation. But the defenders of verse and rhyme, led by Voltaire, attacked both groups impartially.

Among the first to question the value of verse was La Motte. He states that the charm of poetry is due to "la surprise agréable qui naît de la difficulté vaincue." [116] But he goes on, with imperturbable logic, to say that since rhyme and measure are obstacles, and the poet's aim is to *appear* not to be cramped by them, it would be as well not to be cramped in reality, and to speak equally well with less difficulty. La Motte put his theory into practice by writing "La Libre Eloquence, ode en prose," in which he exclaims: "Rime, aussi bizarre qu'impérieuse, mesure tyrannique, mes pensées seront-elles toujours vos esclaves?" [117] The ode, it must be admitted, is hardly calculated to convince the reader of the merits of the theory on which it is based. Gradually, however, the conviction spreads that prose is superior to verse. Soubeiran de Scopon writes: "La belle prose est préférable aux plus beaux vers parce qu'elle fatigue moins dans les longs ouvrages et que la prose plaît toujours." [118] The conception of poetry as a "difficulté vaincue" is added to that of poetry as a primitive language, which for the believers in progress is by definition inferior to prose. On both counts its disappearance seems inevitable.

Fontenelle, however, while declaring that prose is always the natural language, and poetry only an artificial one, admits that poetry pleases the ear by a kind of music, though a somewhat imperfect one. This pleasure is due in large measure to an agreeable surprise on the part of the reader that the poet, cramped by rules, is able to express himself as well as he does.

For Fontenelle poetry is essentially a "difficulté vaincue," [119] a term which was to be reiterated throughout the eighteenth century. He grants it a certain charm, but would allow its existence only on condition that it give less room to ornament and more to thought. At best it is a humble handmaid of philosophy.

But there were also those who, believing in poetry, also believed that the only hope for it was to dissociate it from verse. Fénelon, whose *Télémaque* was so often cited as a model of prose poetry, claimed that "poetry differs from eloquence only in that it paints with enthusiasm and with bolder strokes." Poetry is not versification: "On the contrary, many people make verses without poetry, and many others are filled with poetry without making verses; so away with versification." [120] One of the focal points of the discussion was Madame Dacier's translation of the *Iliad*, the preface to which contains a strong plea for the translation of poetry into prose. Later De Longue follows the same line. Maintaining that rhyme, instead of arousing and supporting genius, stupefies and chills it, he proposes a new style, a chain of "vers libres" freed from the fetters of rhyme, and truly poetic because it will be sustained by noble expressions and vivid images.[121] Rhyme had no more determined opponent than Abbé Prévost. He attacks it repeatedly in *Le Pour et le Contre;* in 1735 in answer to a letter from a reader, he says that rhyme is not a perfection in poetry, and should even be considered as a flaw.[122] In the next year he returns to the charge apropos of President Bouhier's translation of Petronius, the preface of which defended rhyme against its detractors.[123] Prévost gives lengthy quotations from Bouhier, endeavoring to refute him on every point, and concluding with the statement that the constraint of rhyme is the only reason for the weaknesses in Racine.[124]

This discussion of poetic prose goes on interminably, and its story has often been told.[125] The question often comes up in connection with prose translations of poetry. Can the "poetry" be preserved? And if it can, is not this the strongest of arguments for the validity of prose poetry? Furthermore, the success of *Télémaque* and of Montesquieu's *Temple de Gnide* inspired a host of imitators. But these attempts to dispose of verse were far from passing unchallenged. For the sake of clarity, I have grouped the enemies and the defenders of verse, but what we actually have, chronologically speaking, is a continual battle between the two camps, attack and riposte following each other in swift succession. The most ardent defenders of verse were naturally found among the staunch upholders of the classical tradition, for whom verse, if not the whole of poetry, was an essential and inseparable part of it. The "difficulté vaincue," far from being a hindrance to poetry, was considered a major source of poetic beauty. According to Jean-Baptiste Rousseau, "it is from these very difficulties that spring all the wealth and beauty of a language that has no other advantage over prose than that of harmony and exact proportion of sounds." [126]

One of the most celebrated contributions to the defense of verse was La Faye's "Ode en faveur des vers" (1731), in which the author says of the poet:

> De la contrainte rigoureuse
> Où l'esprit semble resserré,
> Il reçoit cette force heureuse
> Qui l'élève au plus haut degré:
> Telle, dans les canaux pressée,
> Avec plus de force élancée,
> L'onde s'élève dans les airs;
> Et la règle qui semble austère,
> N'est qu'un art certain de plaire,
> Inséparable des beaux vers.[127]

Further on in the ode there are terms which suggest those used by Gautier in *L'Art*:

> Tous ceux que son burin aimable
> N'a pas gravés d'un trait durable
> Sont peu lus, ou sont effacés.
> . . . . . Médite, polis, remanie.

It must be admitted that, as poetry, La Faye's ode is hardly a better argument for verse poetry than La Motte's had been for prose poetry.

The most ardent and constant defender of verse was Voltaire. Although he was painfully aware of the difficulty of writing poetry in French, to the point of saying that of all civilized nations France was the least poetical, he found in this very fact an argument for differentiating poetry from prose in every possible way. "We are slaves to rhymes in France. . . . Our poetry, being fettered by too strict rules . . . would have nothing but loftiness of style to distinguish it from prose, if it were not for rhyme." [128] He insists on the potential value of the "difficulté vaincue"; replying to La Motte he says: "Quiconque se borne à vaincre une difficulté pour le mérite seul de la vaincre est un fou; mais celui qui tire du fond de ces obstacles mêmes des beautés qui plaisent à tout le monde est un homme très sage et presque unique." [129] The idea is close to Valéry's: "Est poète celui auquel la difficulté inhérente à son art donne des idées, — et ne l'est pas celui auquel elle les retire." [130] Voltaire's attack on La Motte is reiterated in *La Pucelle*:

> Que chaque troupe en ce moment compose
> Un hymne en vers, non pas une ode en prose.
> Houdard a tort; il faut dans ces hauts lieux
> Parler toujours le langage des dieux.[131]

No less than La Motte, Fénelon was the target for Voltaire's shafts. In 1740 he remarks that *Télémaque* gives the impression of a Greek poem translated into prose,[132] and later, more bluntly: "Fénelon wrote his *Télémaque* in prose because he was incapable of writing it in verse." [133] Echoing Voltaire, Marmontel says in his preface to the *Henriade* (1746) that *Télémaque* comes first among novels, but cannot be put in even the lowest class of poems: "It lacks number, rhythm, measure, rhyme, inversions, in a word everything which constitutes this most difficult art of poetry, an art which has no more to do with prose than music has with our ordinary tone of voice." [134] Voltaire never ceases to insist both that "the art of being eloquent in verse is the most difficult and the rarest of all the arts," and that without verse poetry cannot exist. As he puts it more than once: "we are slaves who wish to dance in our chains." [135] Yet he would not have the chains unreasonably heavy, especially as far as the rules of rhymes are concerned. Rhyme is for the ear, not for the eye: "We should not multiply obstacles unnecessarily, for thus we lose beauties. We must have severe laws, not abject slavery." [136]

Voltaire is supported by Louis Racine, by Du Cerceau defending rhyme in answer to Abbé Pons, by Abbé d'Olivet supporting Bouhier, and by many others. At the middle of the century the defenders of verse were still holding the fort valiantly. At the same time it is curious to note how both parties agree on the close relation between poetry and eloquence. Fénelon emphasizes it, as we have seen, and from the other camp Vauvenargues says: "As for poetry, I do not believe that it is very different from eloquence. A great poet [Voltaire] calls it harmonious eloquence; I do myself the honor of thinking as he does." [137] The premises are the same; the conclusions are different.

Of all the discussions relating to poetry, this one seems to a reader who has plowed through the interminable pages on the subject the most sterile. It constantly runs into a dead end. The difficulty lies in the lack of an adequate conception of poetry; the whole discussion degenerates into an artificial opposition of poetry as a language embellished by more daring imagery and permitted more syntactical freedom than prose, and poetry as rhymed and measured verse. The distinction between prose and verse either is or is not accepted as the basic distinction between prose and poetry.

Certainly the discussion is not without basis; no one can read the poetry of the eighteenth century without feeling that something should be done about it. The attempt to save poetry by freeing it from verse, however questionable, has at least a realistic foundation. The attempt to maintain verse, on the other hand, is largely a theoretical and idealistic one; with all the talk of the beauties which result from the "difficulté vaincue," hardly ever is any adequate explanation of the nature of those beauties given, beyond the general statement that measured and rhymed verse is pleasing to the ear. The argument, implicit in Du Bos's and Batteux's discussion of poetic harmony, that measure and rhyme can reinforce and intensify the meaning of the poem, is not picked up in the quarrel, which was as arid and artificial as it was repetitious. It was to have prolonged and regrettable consequences by its encouragement of the separation of matter and form in poetry.

Looking back over the first half of the century, we see a picture less simple than has sometimes been suggested. It is indeed for the most part as arid a stretch in poetic theory as it is in poetry. The attempts to subjugate enthusiasm to reason and imagination to imitation, to see in poetic images only an embellishment to be used in moderation, to assimilate poetry and eloquence: all this, carried to its logical conclusions, dried up the springs of poetry. It is somewhat surprising that just at the time when poetry, as well as poetic theory, reached its lowest ebb the *Dictionnaire de l'Académie* (possibly through Fénelon's influence?) amplified its definition of poetry. The 1694 edition had given: "the art of representing or recounting in verse human actions and passions by means of ingenious fictions. . . . Is also used sometimes for the art of making verses or versification." In the 1718 edition two significant additions are made to the original definition: "Is used also for the fire of poetry. *These are verses, but there is no poetry in them* . . . . Is used also for a way of writing full of figures and fictions. In this sense, one says that *There is poetry in a work, either in prose or in verse*, meaning that there is a poetic style full of this kind of images." A faint breath of enthusiasm has stirred even the dictionary.

But at this time the partisans of reason were bearing down hard on poetry, and much of the defense of it, based on tradition rather than on experience, was timid and inadequate, and all too ready to compromise. From Du Bos on, statements, often isolated, sometimes made without full awareness of their implications, open the way for a larger understanding of poetry. Even in this age of poetry conceived as embellished statement, its suggestive aspect is occasionally touched upon. Batteux finds three kinds of harmony in poetry: pure harmony of sound, harmony of sound and words with thought, and a third kind, "a certain art which, besides the choice of sound and words in relation to their meaning, so arranges them that all the syllables of a line, taken together, produce by their sound, their number, their quantity, another kind of expression, which adds to the natural meaning of the words." This is a harmony which belongs to poetry alone.[138] Here Batteux, who usually keeps close to classical tradition, suggests an idea which was to be developed by Diderot in the *Lettre sur les sourds et muets*. Later, in a long passage on the "ton élevé," Batteux justifies the differences between prose style and poetic style, the use of inversion, of epithets, of figures. Poetry gives bodily form to the spiritual, life to the inanimate, wraps itself in allegory, and "ne dit les choses qu'à demi." [139] This passage, more than any other before Diderot, foreshadows a poetry of suggestion. Yet this idea is implicit in Voltaire's terse words: "C'est l'essence de la poésie de dire plus et mieux que la prose." [140] But such suggestions were not to bear fruit for a long time.

One of the major obstacles to the recovery of poetry was the fact that poets and critics alike were almost completely cut off from the great lyric tradition of their own poetry, that of the late Middle Ages and the sixteenth century. Although this poetry was not so entirely forgotten as has sometimes been said — certain poems of Ronsard and his contemporaries appear in anthology after anthology — the critical works are almost unanimous in their condemnation, and paraphrase Boileau *ad nauseam*. A few examples will suffice. La Motte says that Ronsard's fame hardly survived him, and that he quickly relapsed into an oblivion from which any recovery is unlikely. Mallet is vehement: after Marot, who had begun to perfect French poetry, Ronsard "replongeait insensiblement nos Muses dans une barbarie pire que celle d'où elles commençaient à peine de sortir." [141] For Du Bos, Ronsard was very learned, but had little talent; his language was not French, and the poets who followed him were superior to him. [142] The most understanding treatment of the poetry of the past is found in Massieu's *Histoire de la poésie française* (completed only up to Marot). Massieu treats a number of mediaeval poets, and devotes some twenty pages to Villon, "le premier qui soit bien entré dans le génie de notre langue." [143] Most of this is biography and summary, with little real criticism. But the space devoted to Villon, the quotation of some of his greatest lines, such as "Je connais pauvres et riches. . . ." put Massieu far ahead of his contemporaries. Nearly all discussions of lyric poetry are dissociated from the greatest lyric poetry written in France before the eighteenth century. Theorists of tragedy propose Corneille and Racine as their great models, however imperfect their understanding of them; for theorists of lyric poetry the models in France are Malherbe and, above all, Jean-Baptiste Rousseau.

Equally striking is the lack of any feeling for poetry on the part of so many critics. Poetry is analyzed and judged, but rarely experienced and enjoyed. In a painfully revealing passage of his introduction Batteux tells his readers that after having finished the usual studies of poetry he thought himself well enough informed on this part of literature to go on to other subjects. However, "I realized then that in judging authors I had been guided by a kind of instinct rather than by reason: I sensed the risks I had run, and the errors into which I might well have fallen." [144] The study of earlier critics did not satisfy him, and he mocks at the idea of poetry he found in them. Only when he has reduced poetry to the single principle of imitation is he satisfied. Likewise for Mallet all that is necessary is the study of the rules: "In such limited arts as eloquence and poetry everything is clear, the rules are established, and as they are all founded in nature, in a short time one can acquire, with a modicum of attention, a sufficiently exact and extensive knowledge of them to form one's taste." [145] The study of poetry has become the business of the judgment which analyzes, not of the imagination which synthesizes. The theorists struggle to find a single quality which constitutes the "essence" of poetry, and in so doing strip it to a skeleton.

Poetic theory is thus dissociated from poetry. The rarity with which poetry is quoted in most treatises is painful; one sighs as one plods through page after page of solid prose. Poetry is treated as an abstract and general problem, as the number of treatises on "la poésie en général" attests, and the language of the critics is equally abstract. Images, grudgingly allowed in poetry itself, have an even smaller place in poetic theory. Here is no spaniel Imagination ranging through the fields of Memory, no poet licking his verse into shape as a mother bear licks her cub. What rare images there are quickly become banal, like that of poetry shackled in the chains of verse.

It must always be remembered that the theorists in general were thinking more of epic and of dramatic verse than of lyric, which is the focus of modern theory. When they do treat the ode and other lyric genres, they tend to allow them greater liberty, sometimes indeed a "désordre sacré," to give a freer rein to enthusiasm and imagination, a larger place to imagery and harmonious language. Even so, all too many of their pronouncements are arbitrary and rigid, and fated to lead to a poetical dead end. Yet it would be unjust to forget the critics, few as they were, who kept the idea of poetry alive and had their moments of insight into its true nature. They suggested ideas which were to be fully developed later, and above all by Diderot.

II

A NEW VISION OF POETRY: DIDEROT

DIDEROT's conception of poetry leads us out of the somewhat dreary stretch through which we have made our way.[1] While he is far from owing nothing to his predecessors, Diderot goes more deeply into the questions they had raised, and is perpetually bringing up new ones.[2] Most important of all, he brings a judgment and a conception of poetry not based on any arbitrary set of rules but derived from his own personal appreciation of literature.[3] He could have said of literature as he did of painting: "I have given the impression time to reach me and to enter into me. I have opened my soul to its effects, and let them penetrate me." [4]

Yet Diderot was no mere impressionistic critic; his taste was refined by study and experience. "Nature has endowed me with a taste for simplicity," he writes, "and I endeavor to perfect it by reading the Ancients." [5] He believed that "one rarely becomes a great writer, a great man of letters, a man of great taste, without having become closely acquainted with the Ancients." [6] He advises the young writer to translate the ancient poets and orators in order to form his taste, just as young artists copy from the antique.[7] For him Homer was the greatest of all poets, and he never tired of singing his praises and acknowledging his debt to him. "The language of poetry seems to be Homer's native language. May I be forgiven for the little grain of incense that I burn before the statue of a master to whom I owe all that I am worth, if I am worth anything." [8] And there are many passages on the beauties of Virgil, of Horace, and of Terence. Yet Diderot was no blind and narrow partisan of the Ancients. He admired Racine, with only occasional reservations. And perhaps no writer except Homer stirred him as did Richardson.[9]

Diderot was a philosopher as well as a lover of literature and a writer, and as such could not but proceed from the individual to the general, meditate as well as enjoy, and, in Baudelaire's phrase, "transformer [sa] volupté en connaissance." He turned out no neatly organized *art poétique*, yet he believed that rules there are, and that they are not to be despised: "Genius knows no rules; however in its successes it never deviates from them. . . . It is for the past century to provide examples; it is for our century to prescribe the rules." [10] Diderot's own ideas on poetry must be tracked down all through his works, not only in such obvious spots as the *Entretiens* and *De la poésie dramatique*, but in such scientific works as the *Lettre sur les sourds et muets* and the *Rêve de D'Alembert*, in the *Paradoxe sur le comédien* and especially in the *Salons*. The fact is in itself significant; Diderot constantly considers poetry in its relation to literature as a whole (again and again he uses the word *poète* where we should say "creative writer"), to the other arts, to philosophy and to science. With his central interest in *rapports*, his ideas on the nature and special faculties of the poet are linked with his physiological and psychological interests.[11]

It has been an easy game for critics to point out what they considered contradictions and paradoxes in Diderot's theories.[12] It is of course true that Diderot was more interested in asking the right questions than in finding consistent answers. As he himself said, he was more concerned with forming clouds than with dissipating them, with suspending judgment than with judging. Yet this does not mean that he arrived at no solid conclusions, and one may well apply to him his own words: "Our real opinion is not the one in which we have never wavered, but the one to which we have most constantly returned." [13] By paying careful attention to chronology one discovers that, with rare exceptions, what we have is not perpetual paradox but development and variation. This is particularly true of such important questions as the role of

sensibility and the conception of imitation. The former develops in connection with Diderot's physiological studies, the
latter especially in relation to his interest in the fine arts. It is
also important to realize that in some cases Diderot's vocabulary and language lag behind his thought. A superficial reading, particularly of certain passages on enthusiasm and on the
"modèle intérieur," can easily give the impression that Diderot
is following traditional conceptions, and only with a careful
reading of all he has to say on a subject does his real position
become clear.

For a long time Diderot was considered almost exclusively
as a precursor of the romantic belief in sentiment and emotion
as the source and essence of poetry.[14] Recent criticism has
shown the inadequacy and falseness of this view. Diderot
was indeed an "âme sensible"; "si Nature a pétri une âme
sensible, c'est la mienne." [15] The question of sensibility runs
through all his thinking about poetry.[16] In his earlier writings
its role is a central one: "Poets, actors, musicians, painters,
singers of the first rank, great dancers, tender lovers, truly
devout people, all this enthusiastic and passionate troop feels
strongly and thinks little." But before long Diderot begins to
be wary of unrestrained feeling: "Sensibility, when it is extreme, no longer has any discernment, it is moved by everything indiscriminately." [17] In the *Rêve de D'Alembert* this
distrust of sensibility is developed in connection with Diderot's
ideas on sensation and the nervous system. Here sensibility,
"l'extrême mobilité de certains filets du réseau," is dominant
in mediocre individuals. The term has a variety of shades of
meaning for Diderot, which go far to explain his varying
attitude.[18] Basically it is sensitivity, receptivity to sense impressions, and in this sense it is essential to the artist. But there
is also a "sensibilité du diaphragme," which overshadows the
"sensibilité de l'âme" of the earlier writings. A man who is

at the mercy of his diaphragm is so overwhelmed by what he sees and hears that he shudders, sighs, weeps, and loses all reason and judgment. The only hope of greatness for those thus afflicted is a constant self-control: "The great man, if he has unfortunately been endowed with this natural disposition, will make a constant effort to decrease and dominate it, to become master of his impulses." [19] Greatness can be achieved only by a victory over one's native sensibility.

In the *Paradoxe sur le comédien* Diderot reaches his extreme position. In seemingly direct contradiction to the passage from the *Second Entretien* quoted above he says: "Great poets, great actors, and perhaps all great imitators of nature, whoever they may be, who are endowed with a vivid imagination, great judgment, delicate tact, and very sure taste, are the least sensitive of men. . . . Sensibility is hardly the quality of a great genius." Indeed it is an entire lack of sensibility which makes great actors. Sensibility is defined in terms very close to those used in the *Rêve*: "Sensibility, according to the only definition which has hitherto been given to this term, is, it seems to me, that tendency which accompanies organic weakness, and is the result of a mobile diaphragm, a lively imagination, delicate nerves, which leads a man to sympathize, to shudder, to admire, to fear, to falter, to weep, to faint, to succour, to flee, to shout, to lose his senses, to exaggerate, to despise, to disdain, to have no precise idea of the good, the true, and the beautiful, to be unjust, to go mad." [20]

It should be noted that Diderot applies the paradox strictly only to the actor, and that when he extends it to the poet and the painter he tends to make the reservation already noted in the *Rêve* and suggest the possibility of controlled emotion. How conscious this is, I cannot say; I do not think that Diderot anywhere suggests a possible justification for carrying the paradox to its limit only in the case of the actor by the fact that the actor, more than any other artist, is bound by times and seasons, that he has his exits and his entrances and cannot wait on feeling or inspiration.[21] At all events the rigor of the paradox is definitely mitigated when it is applied to the poet. Towards the end of the *Paradoxe* there is a close parallel to the passage from the *Rêve* quoted above: "The sensitive man is too much at the mercy of his diaphragm to be . . . a profound observer and hence a sublime imitator of nature, unless he can forget himself and get outside himself, and with the aid of a powerful imagination be able to create for himself phantoms to serve as models, and by a retentive memory keep his attention fixed upon them; but then it is no longer he who acts, it is the spirit of another which possesses him." [22] Here the "unless" clause opens the way to a control of sensibility not only by judgment, but by imagination and memory. And another passage in the *Paradoxe* clarifies the relation between emotion and poetry by bringing out the idea of emotion recollected in tranquillity:

Is it at the moment when you have just lost your friend or your mistress that you will compose a poem on their deaths? No. Woe be to him who at that moment chooses to exercise his talent! It is when the great grief is past, when extreme sensibility is deadened, when the catastrophe is far behind, that the spirit is calm again, that one recalls one's vanished happiness, that one can estimate one's loss, that memory joins with imagination, the one to retrace, the other to magnify, the pleasure that is past; then one has control of oneself, then one can give tongue. You may say that you are weeping, but you do not weep when you are hot on the trail of a forceful epithet which evades you; you may say that you are weeping, but you do not weep when you are absorbed in making your verse harmonious: or if the tears do flow, the pen falls from your hands, you surrender to your feelings, and you stop writing.[23]

The poet must write, not without feeling, but after the tyranny of emotion is overpast. The emotion must be stored away in the "deep well of unconscious cerebration," where memory and imagination do their hidden work.

Thus Diderot never completely refuses to sensibility a share in poetic creation, though it is not in itself sufficient: "One must feel in order to be an orator, a scholar, a poet, a philosopher, but one is not a philosopher, a poet, an orator, a scholar, just because one feels." [24] In his final word on the subject, referring to the phrase Marmontel had applied to him, "l'homme de génie, le grand écrivain, et l'homme sensible," Diderot says: "of these three qualities, I accept only the last: it is enough for me; one can possess it and be without the other two, which one rarely possesses without it." [25] Although his position is less episodic than has often been assumed, and the rigor of the *Paradoxe* is always attenuated for the poet, there is a definite change. Unless one is satisfied with seeing in it merely an example of Diderot's own phrase, "la tête d'un Langrois est sur ses épaules comme un coq d'église en haut d'un clocher," [26] one feels the urge to look into the reasons for this change. First of all it is noticeable that with the increasingly important role the judgment takes on in Diderot's thought the role of feeling decreases. In the *Réfutation* he sets down his idea of the particular function of the judgment and its relation to the senses: "Here are the five witnesses; but where is the judge or rapporteur? There is a special organ, the brain, to which the five witnesses make their report." The brain judges all our sensations, and records everything that happens to us. This clarifies the distinction made in the *Paradoxe*: "C'est qu'être sensible est une chose, et sentir est une autre. L'une est une affaire d'âme, l'autre une affaire de jugement." *Etre sensible*, a nervous susceptibility, "la mobilité du diaphragm"; *sentir*, the communication of sensation to the central organ. The role of judgment is further clarified when Diderot says of man as contrasted with the animal: "Among his senses there is a harmony such that no one of them dominates the others enough to be able to lay down the law to his understanding; on the contrary it is his understanding, or the organ of his reason, which is the most powerful. It is a judge who is neither corrupted by nor subservient to any of the witnesses; it keeps its authority entire, and uses it to perfect itself; it combines all sorts of images and sensations, because it feels nothing

strongly." [27] So with Diderot's increasing interest in physiological and psychological problems and his effort to find
more and more precise definitions of certain faculties and their
relation to each other, sensibility is gradually reduced from an
"émotion de l'âme" to a "mobilité du diaphragme" which may
be a hindrance rather than a help to creative activity, and
therefore needs to be controlled by the "origine du faisceau,"
the judgment.

The problem of sensibility is a very general one, and far
from being limited to the poet or to the artist. The poet shares
the faculty with many who have no creative gift, who indeed
may be prevented from any great achievement by an excess
of sensibility. The poet must indeed have sensibility, but it
does not suffice to make him a poet. What else is needed?

In Diderot's earlier works the first quality of the poet seems
to be enthusiasm. In a famous passage in the *Lettre sur les
sourds et muets*, to which we shall return later, though the
word enthusiasm is not used, there is no doubt, I think, that
it is meant. "Then there enters into the language of the poet a
spirit which moves and quickens every syllable," a spirit which
stirs the emotions and the imagination, and at the same time
creates a language which is not prose but poetry.[28] It is a state
which Diderot himself had experienced, as more than one
passage of his correspondence shows: "Je leur semblais extraordinaire, inspiré, divin. . . . Nous avons passé une soirée
d'enthousiasme dont j'étais le foyer." [29]

The poet in search of enthusiasm must seek solitude and the
inspiration of nature. His experience is described by Diderot
in the *Second Entretien*:

Here is the sacred abode of enthusiasm. Has a man been endowed
with genius? He leaves the city and its inhabitants. Following the
dictates of his heart, he delights in mingling his tears with the crystal
waters of a fountain; in laying flowers on a grave; in treading with a
light step over the tender meadow grass; in passing through the fertile
countryside with slow steps; in contemplating men at their work; in

escaping into the heart of the forests. He delights in their secret awesomeness. He roams about. He seeks out a cave to inspire him. Who mingles his voice with that of the torrent which falls from the mountain? Who feels the sublimity of a solitary spot? Who listens to his heart in silence and solitude? It is he. Our poet dwells on the shore of a lake. He casts his eyes over the waters, and his genius expands. . . . Enthusiasm is born of some object in nature. If the spirit of the poet has perceived its striking and varied aspects, he is absorbed, agitated, tormented by it. Imagination is aroused; passion is stirred. In turn one is amazed, touched, indignant, angry. Without enthusiasm, either the true idea does not make its appearance, or, if one runs across it by chance, it eludes one. . . . At the moment of enthusiasm the poet feels; this is after he has meditated. This moment announces itself by a tremor which begins in his heart and then moves, in a swift and pleasurable fashion, to all the extremities of his body. Soon it is no longer a tremor; it is a strong and lasting fervor which inflames him, takes his breath away, devours him, slays him, but gives spirit and life to all he touches. If this fervor were to increase still more, crowds of phantoms would rise up before him. His passion would increase almost to madness. His only relief would be to pour out in a torrent the images which crowd, jostle, and harry each other.[30]

This passage brings together a number of different aspects of Diderot's conception of enthusiasm. Here are all the scenes dear to the "âme sensible" and later to the romantics: fountains, tombs, fields, forests with their secret terror, mountains, lakes, all wrapt in silence and in solitude. But there is more to it than a catalogue of romantic properties, a background against which the poet performs. Here nature supplies and induces enthusiasm; the spirit is stirred, the imagination aroused, the passions moved. Poetry, weakened and made effete by civilization, must go back to nature: "La poésie veut quelque chose d'énorme, de barbare et de sauvage." [31]

Yet it is amusing to note that in spite of all its romantic panoply the passage recalls at points the earlier eighteenth-century idea that the contemplation of nature is the source of enthusiasm. Here is the familiar phrase, "l'imagination s'échauffe." But Diderot, wiser than his predecessors, does not confuse cause and effect; quickened imagination is not itself enthusiasm, it is the result of enthusiasm. What then is enthusiasm? Diderot gives his most precise answer in the *En-cyclopédie* article "Eclectisme" (1755): "I will observe in passing that in poetry, in painting, in eloquence, in music, it is impossible to produce any sublime work without enthusiasm. Enthusiasm is a vehement impulse of the spirit by which we are transported into the midst of the objects we have to represent; then we see a whole scene take place in our imagination, as if it were outside us; and indeed it is, for as long as this illusion lasts all beings that are present to our senses are annihilated, and in their place our ideas take material form; it is only our ideas that we perceive; yet our hands touch bodies, our eyes see living beings, our ears hear voices." [32] Here, as in the end of the passage from the *Second Entretien*, with its detailed description of physical symptoms, enthusiasm is closely allied to hallucination. As with sensibility, and later with imagination, Diderot finds a psychosomatic relationship. Enthusiasm is a frenzy; "Il y a une *fureur* particulière qu'on appelle *fureur poétique*; c'est l'enthousiasme." [33] Yet it is a frenzy explicable in physiological terms, an agitation of the entire nervous system, rather than a divine inspiration.

In some passages, however, Diderot does use the language of the earlier conception: "An invocation is always a fruit of enthusiasm. The poet has meditated. His fertile spirit is eager to bring forth. His tumultuous thoughts struggle to emerge. . . . He sees the full extent of his subject. He calls to his aid some divinity to sustain him. He sees this divinity. She stretches out her hand to him. He advances." [34] One might well argue that this is a figure of speech, left over from tradition. Yet even at a time when Diderot was becoming suspicious of unrestrained enthusiasm he says: "Poetry presupposes a spiritual exaltation which is close to divine inspiration." [35] And in a passage where the word *inspiration* is used rather than *enthousiasme* a certain sense of mystery is unmistakable: "What then is inspiration? The art of lifting a corner of the veil and showing to men an unknown, or rather forgotten recess of the world they live in. The man who is inspired is sometimes uncertain whether what he presents is a reality or a chimera, whether it ever existed outside himself. He has then reached the last limit of the force of human nature, and the outermost extremity of the resources of art." [36] However material in its origins this enthusiasm that makes men dream dreams and see visions may be, Diderot cannot but pause in wonder before its workings.

Whatever the exact nature of enthusiasm, Diderot never ceases to repeat that without it there can be no true poetry: "L'enthousiasme est le germe de toutes les grandes choses, bonnes ou mauvaises." [37] One of his chief criticisms of Saint-Lambert, the poet of the *Saisons*, is that he "*prophesied*, to use Naigeon's expression, *before the descent of the Spirit. . . .* On seeing a beautiful country scene, he would say: O what a beautiful scene to describe! What he should have done was to be silent, to feel, to drink in the scene, and then to take up his lyre." [38] Here Diderot emphasizes again a point made in the *Second Entretien*, the necessity for a period of meditation, of contemplation, to prepare the way for enthusiasm.

There is indeed much the same increasing restraint on enthusiasm as on sensibility. As early as the "Eclectisme" article, Diderot says after his description of enthusiasm, "if this state is not madness, it is very close to it," and goes on, "for this reason great good sense is needed to balance enthusiasm." [39] Here again judgment must play its part; even the ode "requires qualities which are almost incompatible, great judgment in organization and a frenzied muse in execution." [40] Yet even in the *Paradoxe* enthusiasm, though restricted, is still essential for the artist: "Why should the actor be different from the poet, the painter, the orator, the musician? It is not in the frenzy of the 'premier jet' that characteristic traits present themselves, it is in quiet and passionless moments, in quite unexpected moments. One does not know where these traits come from; they are the work of inspiration. When, halfway between nature and their rough sketch, these geniuses gaze attentively first at one, then at the other; then the beauties due to inspiration, the chance strokes distributed in the works of geniuses, whose sudden appearance astonishes their authors, have a far more certain effect and success than those they tossed off capriciously. Deliberation must temper the frenzy of enthusiasm." [41] This is indeed a refined and tempered enthusiasm, but still enthusiasm there must be.

Closely related to the idea of enthusiasm is that of genius.[42] For the French critics of the seventeenth century genius had been a somewhat vague power, "un feu céleste." In the early eighteenth century, like enthusiasm, it gradually lost its extraordinary and mysterious quality, and was often simply equated with talent. But in the course of the century interest became focused on *le génie*, the individual permanently endowed with the gift of genius, previously regarded as separate and transient. In this change Diderot is in the forefront of the discussion. In his *Réfutation de l'ouvrage d'Helvétius intitulé L'Homme* he takes issue with Helvétius' thesis that genius is the result of chance and circumstance, and again hardly distinguishable from talent. For Diderot the genius is a unique type of individual, essentially different from other men; he forges ahead bearing his torch, while they lag behind, groping in the darkness. He has been endowed by Nature with a special gift.

Just what this gift is, Diderot finds it difficult to say. The man of genius possesses "some special, secret, indefinable quality, without which nothing very great or very good can be produced." This quality is neither imagination, nor judgment, nor wit; neither ardor, sensibility, nor taste. "Is it a certain structure of the head and the viscera, a certain organization of the humors? I will accept this, but only on condition that we agree that neither I nor anyone else has an exact notion of it, and that 'l'esprit observateur' be included in it." Genius is thus a physiological, possibly pathological state, closely akin to enthusiasm, and Diderot often discusses it in these terms. But it transcends the purely physiological. The "esprit observateur" is a higher instinct with which ordinary men are not endowed, a kind of "esprit prophétique" which is a permanent condition of genius. In other men enthusiasm can be controlled by judgment; in the man of genius the two are raised to a higher power, and are coexistent and inseparable, fused in a single great faculty.[43]

Diderot's conception of genius, as well as his attitude towards sensibility and enthusiasm, indicates clearly how far he is from being an unmitigated "preromantic." Sensibility and enthusiasm are indeed essential for the poet, but the excesses of both must be modified by judgment. This modification is closely connected with the development of Diderot's aesthetic ideas, and particularly with the notion of the "modèle intérieur." [44] This lies at the heart of Diderot's doctrine. One aspect of his greatness as a critic and theorist, as well as a creative writer, is his constant preoccupation with the relation of art to reality. This was a problem to which his predecessors had found a ready-made answer in the doctrine of imitation, either of the ancients or of "la belle nature," which they had accepted without reservation, and frequently made the center of their poetic doctrines. With Diderot, that perpetual question-raiser, the whole problem is reopened.

From the beginning Diderot, with all his enthusiasm for the ancients, was opposed to a slavish imitation of their works. The only way to rival them was to do what they had done, to imitate nature. But for Diderot nature was not the traditional "belle nature" which in the *Lettre sur les sourds et muets* he had criticized Batteux for not defining. What he would have the poet imitate is nature untrammeled by civilization or by conventional standards. "Why," he asks, "is an old split, crooked, broken tree, which I would have cut down if it were at my door, just the tree that the painter would plant there if he were painting my cottage?"[45] The traditional "belle nature" has no real existence; "those people who keep talking about the imitation of 'la belle nature' honestly believe that there is a 'belle nature' in reality, that it exists, that one can see it at will, and that there is nothing to do but to copy it. If you told them that it is a purely ideal entity, they would open their eyes wide, or laugh in your face." [46] It is not "la belle nature" but simply nature that the poet and artist must imitate.

How then are they to imitate nature? In a few passages in his earlier works Diderot seems to be demanding a realistic and close copy: "The products of art will be commonplace, imperfect, and feeble as long as we do not aim at a more rigorous imitation of nature." [47] In the *Troisième Entretien* he answers the question "Qu'est-ce que la beauté d'imitation?" by saying simply, "La conformité de l'image avec la chose." [48] But the next year this is interpreted in such a way as to give greater liberty to the imitator. We know that in nature all is unity and harmony; but with our limited experience this harmony may escape our direct observation, and it is the poet's task to make it apparent to us, "so that he is less literally true, and more true to nature than the historian." [49] In the "Imitation" article in the *Encyclopédie* Diderot, still insisting that art must keep close to nature, reiterates the contrast between the "imitation rigoureuse" of the historian and the "imitation libre" of the poet.[50]

The concluding pages of *De la poésie dramatique* introduce the conception of the "modèle idéal," created from elements found in nature, and aiming at the greatest possible perfection. But the model can only be approximate: "If one means by a man of taste one who bears within himself the general ideal model of all perfection, he is a chimera." But once this model is achieved as far as is humanly possible, how is it to be imitated? It is to be modified according to circumstances, Diderot answers — altered, strengthened, weakened, distorted, reduced. "Thus from a single image an infinite variety of different representations will emanate." [51] The ideal model, derived from nature, restoring the unity and harmony not always apparent in nature, is modified by the artist in his imitation, as it is modified by nature.

The ideal model is treated at length in the opening pages of the *Salon de 1767*, the locus classicus of Diderot's conception. Addressing himself to "one of our most enlightened artists," he forces him to admit that his portrait of a woman is not a rigorous imitation of the model he had before him. "You have added to it, you have taken away from it; otherwise you would not have made an original image, a copy of the truth, but a portrait or a copy of a copy." In copying the model found in nature the artist would have been thrice removed from the truth or prototype; he would have put between the prototype and its "fantôme subsistant" which should be his model, the individual woman he had before him. If this is so, the artist answers, where then is the true, the original model? Diderot replies that neither the whole nor any part of any existing creature can be taken as the original model. This model is purely ideal, and is not borrowed directly from any individual in nature, present or remembered. The difference between the "portraitiste" and the man of genius is that the former reproduces nature faithfully, and thus deliberately puts himself in the third rank, whereas the latter, seeking after truth, the original model, makes a constant effort to attain the second. This is to be reached, not by picking out from a multitude of individuals the most perfect parts and making them into a whole, by combining "une infinité de petits portraits isolés," but by a close study of the changes and deformations produced by nature, by the gradual elimination and correction of these, until finally the "vrai modèle idéal de la beauté" is reached.[52]

This passage is a difficult and in some ways confusing one. At many points its language is strongly reminiscent of Plato, and indeed at the end Diderot, quoting Garrick's statement that the actor must have an ideal model, says that it contains "the *secundus a natura* and the *tertius ab idea* of Plato, the germ and the proof of all that I have said." The resemblance has led a number of critics to find in Diderot a return to neoclassicism, to the imitation of the *beau idéal*.[53] But, as Yvon Belaval has so well observed, Diderot materialized the Platonic doctrine; "the ideal model is no longer an immutable archetype in the heaven of intelligibles, but, by the medium of genius, a natural creation. . . . Diderot's ideal model is to Plato's what the normative is to the norm; one is immanent, the other transcendent." [54] In the creation of the ideal model the artist has a certain latitude; Diderot says at the end of the *Salon de 1767*: "There is an original model which does not exist in nature, and which exists only vaguely and confusedly in the mind of the artist. Between the most perfect creation of nature, and the original and vague model, there is a latitude along which artists are scattered." [55] Each artist, each poet, has his own "modèle intérieur." Diderot advises the painter: "Illuminate your objects by your own sun, which is not that of nature; be the disciple of the rainbow, but not its slave." Of such imitation he says: "Where is the model? In the spirit, in the mind, in the more or less vivid imagination, in the more or less tender heart of the author. So an inward model is not to be confused with an outward model." [56]

The other essential difference, to my mind, between the classical doctrine of the ideal model and Diderot's lies in the way in which the artist and the poet transform their model into a work of art. As Diderot makes very clear in the passage from *De la poésie dramatique* quoted above, the ideal model is not to be copied slavishly, any more than nature is. Here Diderot is brought back to the central problem of the relation of art and reality: "The great man . . . is the one who best knows how to reconcile falsehood and truth." [57] The ideal model has been derived from reality, and in order to reproduce it convincingly the artist must return to reality;

"The truth of nature is the basis of verisimilitude in art." [58] At the same time Diderot warns his reader of the danger of assuming too easily that what seems extraordinary to us does not exist in nature: "Nature is so varied . . . that there is nothing in a poet's imagination so bizarre that experience and observation cannot find a model for it in nature." [59]

In any case a compromise must be effected between the imaginative and the natural: "Les plans se forment d'après l'imagination; les discours d'après la nature." [60] The sentence comes from the essay on dramatic poetry, and obviously applies to the general structure of a play on the one hand, and to the speeches, the dialogue, the concrete elements, on the other. But it is applicable in a wider sense, not only to literature but to art. In the *Salon de 1761* Diderot says that color in a painting is the equivalent of style in a literary work.[61] He may well have had in mind what Batteux had said, that *dessein* in painting corresponded to *fable* in literature, *coloris* to *versification*. Measure and harmony constitute the color of poetry, imitation its structure.[62] On this last point Diderot is completely at odds with Batteux; for him the plan, the *dessein*, is the work of the imagination, and the imitation comes in the details, the expression. So in *Les Deux Amis de Bourbonne* Diderot advises his interlocutor to create the illusion of reality by sprinkling his story with such simple incidents and natural touches that the reader is bound to say: "How true that is. That sort of thing can't be made up." Thus "la vérité de la nature couvrira le prestige de l'art," and the author will be at the same time historian and poet. In the same way a painter, by adding a slight scar or a wart to a beautiful face, will convince the spectator that here is an authentic portrait.[63]

Diderot never found the exact ratio between fiction and reality, and, wisely, believed that it could not be established: "Dans toute production poétique, il y a toujours un peu de mensonge dont la limite n'est, et ne sera jamais déterminée." [64] And he asks: "Where is the line which poetry cannot cross without falling into monstrosities and chimeras, or rather what is this borderland beyond nature along which Le Sueur, Poussin, Raphael and the ancients occupy different positions; Le Sueur, on the edge which touches nature, from which the ancients allowed themselves the greatest divergence possible? More truth on one side, and less genius; more genius on the other side, and less truth. Which is the most valuable?" [65] But whatever the proportions may be, poetry is primarily concerned with verisimilitude rather than with truth.[66]

The idea of the ideal model is applied in the *Paradoxe* to the actor as well as to the poet and the painter. Instead of collaborating with the poet in the imitation of nature, as the *Second Entretien* had suggested ("Il y a des endroits qu'il faudrait presque abandonner à l'acteur" [67]), the actor must now follow the "modèle intérieur" of the poet. "He who leaves the least to the imagination of the great actor is the greatest of poets." All through the *Paradoxe* the importance of the ideal model is emphasized. Instead of being guided by his own feelings, imitating nature directly, the actor must have his ideal model, drawn from memory and imagination. Like the poet, instead of depending on his own limited resources, he must draw from the inexhaustible fountainhead of nature. The final pages of the *Paradoxe* remind us again that nature, even "la belle nature," must not be imitated too closely.[68]

The importance of the "modèle intérieur" in Diderot's conception of the artist, the poet, and the actor, explains, even more perhaps than his scientific interests, the changing ratio in his theory between feeling and enthusiasm on the one hand, and judgment on the other. It stresses above all the need for rising above immediate experience to imaginative vision. This leads us straight to the consideration of what was for Diderot the chief faculty of the poet, imagination. For it is imagination that produces the ideal model, and again and again Diderot allies the two conceptions: "The astonishing thing is that the artist recalls these effects when he is two hundred leagues away from nature, when his model is present only in his imagination. . . . It is his imagination, as accurate as it is fertile, that supplies him with all his truths." [69]

Diderot's interest in the imagination has been commented on by all writers on his aesthetics. Few, however, have attempted to analyze in detail the exact meaning the term had for him, and the precise part it played in his idea of artistic and literary creation. Those who have done so tend to conclude that the word had different meanings for him at different times, in different contexts.[70] Yet I believe that there is a basic unity in his conception. It would be an exaggeration to claim that his use of the word is entirely consistent; particularly in his early works, when the idea has not taken on its full importance for him, he occasionally uses the word in a rather loose way.[71] Yet there are not several different and alternating ideas of imagination, but a single central and predominant one, from which there are occasional and minor deviations. Once his conception has been fully developed, his use of the word, wherever it is significant, seems to me remarkably consistent.[72]

As we have seen, the problem of the imagination had been of particular interest to a long line of English philosophers and writers, and had begun to be seriously considered in France, particularly by Condillac and Voltaire. Diderot was familiar with all of these, as well as with other writings on the subject. But his conception of imagination is no mere compendium of borrowed notions. Many of the questions he brings up had been raised before; some of his answers had already been given. But he always approaches the problem in the light of his own experience as a human being, a writer, and a critic. If he agrees with his predecessors, it is because his experience has confirmed their conclusions; if he disagrees, the reason is again to be found in his own experience. And on certain points, particularly the role of imagination in the making of poetry, he goes far beyond his predecessors.

Diderot was interested in imagination both in itself, as one of the great human faculties, and because of its role in artistic creation. At times he emphasizes the definition of imagination — what it is, what it does, how it works — at times its function for the artist and the poet. The question is only slightly touched on in his early works, but begins to preoccupy him seriously about 1758. His interest may well have been stimulated by Voltaire's "Imagination" article for the *Encyclopédie*, which reached him about this time.[73] But in any case it was practically inevitable that his conception of the ideal model should lead him to the problem of the imagination.

Diderot's basic definition of imagination is given in *De la poésie dramatique*: "L'imagination est la faculté de se rappeler des images." All his discussions of the nature of imagination center on this definition and the precise meaning of its two terms, *se rappeler* and *image*. The chief problem presented by the latter is the distinction between imagination and memory, treated most fully in the *Entretien avec D'Alembert* and the *Rêve de D'Alembert*. In the former the role of memory, its source, and its workings are discussed, with the comparison of "les fibres de nos organes" to "des cordes vibrantes sensibles." Here memory seems to be taken in its broadest sense, the power of remembering, regardless of what is remembered. Only later on, in the *Rêve*, is imagination distinguished as a special type of memory: "L'imagination, c'est la mémoire des formes et des couleurs." But Diderot had made the distinction earlier, in *De la poésie dramatique*, where, after stating that imagination is "the quality without which one is neither a poet, nor a philosopher, nor a man of intelligence, nor a reasonable being, nor a man," he says of the philosopher that the moment when he passes from memory to imagination comes when he moves from the abstract to the concrete. Then he becomes a painter or a poet. The same distinction is also made in a number of passages in the *Eléments de physiologie*, such as "la mémoire est des signes, l'imagination des objets." It had been made, it will be remembered, by Hobbes, and after him by Condillac. This is the imagination no one can afford to be without; otherwise "speech is no more than a mechanical habit of using combinations of sounds." Without imagination there are only abstractions; it is "the faculty of borrowing from sense-objects images to serve as comparisons . . . the faculty of giving bodily form to an abstract word." [74]

So for Diderot the images recalled by the imagination are concrete images, opposed to the signs of words recalled by the memory. Then comes the question: are these images visual only, or are they furnished by all the five senses, as Voltaire maintained against Addison? This was a difficult problem for Diderot; his own imagination was above all visual, and the possibility of another kind of image was difficult for him to conceive. He says himself: "I have Raphael's pictures more clearly present to my mind than Corneille's verses, than Racine's most beautiful passages." It should be observed, however, that this visual imagination is not only "pictorial" in a static sense, but also "cinematographic." Movement is recalled, as well as form and color. Yet the possibility of an imagination other than visual seems to Diderot unavoidable, as he worries over it in the *Lettre sur les aveugles*: "If we have scarcely any idea of the way in which a man born blind registers, recalls and combines touch-sensations, it is a result of the habit we have acquired through our eyes of reproducing everything in our imagination in color." In the "Addition" to the *Lettre*, composed some thirty years later, Diderot is still worried: "What is a blind man's imagination? This phenomenon is not so easy to explain as one might think." [75] He is uncomfortably aware of the difficulty of limiting imagination to visual images only, yet his own experience leads him to think and speak constantly of imagination in these terms.

Then there is the other term of the original definition, describing the activity of the imagination: *se rappeler*. Just what does imagination do? This brings up another basis on which to distinguish between memory and imagination, by assigning to memory a purely reproductive power, and to imagination a combining power. As a note in the *Eléments de physiologie* puts it, "La mémoire est un copiste fidèle. L'imagination est un coloriste." [76] But this cuts across the previous distinction made on the basis of the respective objects of memory and of imagination. Either memory must be allowed to reproduce images as well as signs, or two categories of imagination, reproductive and combining, must be set up. The dilemma is found in Hobbes, who adds to his memory-sign and imagination-picture distinction two types of imagination, simple and compounded. Condillac also notes these two forms of imagination, and the central thesis of Voltaire's article is his distinction between passive and active imagination.

It seems to me that Diderot managed to avoid any sharp distinction by conceiving the imagination as a single faculty with a tremendous range, from the photographic recall of images, through the uncontrolled vagaries of dream and fancy, to the combining and fusing power that reaches its height in the genius. It is true that the first of these is sometimes called memory, as in the passage quoted earlier from the *Paradoxe*: "Memory joins with imagination, the one to retrace, the other to magnify the pleasure that is past." And memory has an important role. [77] In the great passage of the section "Mémoire" of the *Eléments de physiologie* Diderot says:

I am inclined to believe that everything we have seen, known, perceived, or heard — even the trees of a great forest, yes, even the arrangement of the branches, the form of the leaves, and the variety of colors, of greens and of light and shade; even the appearance of the grains of sand on the seashore, the irregularities of the surface of the waves, whether stirred by a light breeze or foaming and tossed by tempestuous winds; even the multitudes of human voices, animal cries, and the sounds of nature, even the melody and the harmony of all the tunes, all the musical compositions, all the concerts we have ever heard — that all this exists within us without our knowing it. . . . The sound of a voice, the presence of an object, a certain place . . . and there is an object, yes even a long stretch of my past recalled . . . and I am plunged into pleasure, regret, or grief.[78]

The passage may possibly have been suggested to Diderot by a few lines of a work of Francis Hutcheson he must certainly have read: "In like manner it is known, that often all the circumstances of *actions*, or *places*, or *dresses* of persons, or *voice*, or song, which have occurred at any time together, when we were strongly affected by any passion, will be so connected that any one of these will make all the rest recur." [79] But Diderot has given concrete form, as so often, to a general idea, and produced a striking illustration of the conception of involuntary memory which was to be so fruitful for later writers, above all Proust. One passage on this theme, in Ruskin's *Modern Painters*, is so strikingly close to Diderot that if it had not been published twenty years before the *Eléments de physiologie* first appeared one would be greatly tempted to think that Ruskin had been familiar with Diderot's passage. Ruskin has been speaking of the "mental chemistry by which dream summons and associates its material," and goes on:

How far I could show that it held with all great inventors I know not, but with all those whom I have carefully studied (Dante, Scott, Turner and Tintoret) it seems to me to hold absolutely; their imagination consisting, not in a voluntary production of new images, but an involuntary remembrance, exactly at the right moment, of something they had actually seen. Imagine all that any of these men had seen or heard in the whole course of their lives, laid up accurately in their memories as in vast storehouses, extending, with the poets, even to the slightest intonations of syllables heard in the beginning of their lives, and, with the painters, down to minute folds of drapery, and shapes of leaves and stones; and over all this unindexed and immeasurable mass of treasure, the imagination brooding and wandering, but dream-gifted, so as to summon at any moment exactly such groups of ideas as shall justly fit each other: this I conceive to be the real nature of the imaginative mind.[80]

Here we have a remarkable anticipation of Proust, with the

very phrase "involuntary remembrance," as well as echoes of Coleridge's "brooding spirit of imagination" and Baudelaire's "vaste magasin d'images," all in a passage that immediately brings Diderot to mind. It shows too how tenuous are the boundaries between memory and imagination. And Diderot himself, in a passage preceding and leading up to the one I have quoted, sees the imagination at work: "How does the imagination disturb the orderly progress of reason? It resuscitates in man voices, sounds, all the features of nature, images which become just so many opportunities for straying from the straight path." This imagination is more than a purely reproductive faculty, in that it leads away from the domain of reason (and thus carries an amusing echo of the unreliable faculty so suspect to earlier French writers). "The man of imagination strolls about in his head like a sightseer in a palace where at every moment he is distracted by interesting objects; he goes on, he comes back, he cannot tear himself away. Imagination is like childhood, attracted by every thing at random." [81]

For Diderot imagination, as a poetic faculty, is above all the power of combining as well as recalling images. As early as the *Lettre sur les aveugles* it is "la faculté de se rappeler et de combiner." Its workings are described in the *Rêve*, where Bordeu and D'Alembert reach the conclusion that sense impressions can be transformed by the "instrument sensible" which in recording them exaggerates, leaves out details, adds them, distorts or embellishes the data, so that the record is not historical, the actual facts, but poetic, the impressions of the recording instrument, in which related ideas set one another reverberating. The great definition comes in the *Salon de 1767*: "Imagination creates nothing, it imitates, compounds, combines, exaggerates, magnifies, reduces. It is constantly concerned with resemblances." And, after defining judgment, Diderot concludes: "Judgment is the predominant quality of the philosopher; imagination, the predominant quality of the

poet." [82] In associating imagination with the poet Diderot is
of course following a long tradition. But he does not stop
with the mere statement; he indicates the precise part that
imagination plays in the poetic process, and its relation to the
other faculties involved. In his discussion of the nature of
imagination he is often dealing with problems that were already familiar, and his contribution lies in the clarity with
which he put the essential questions, and the way in which he
tested the answers by his own experience. When he comes to
the role of imagination in artistic creation he is on less trodden
ground, and his ideas are often original, and always worthy
of close attention.

When he says that imagination is "la qualité dominante du
poète," he is, as so often, using the word *poète* in its broadest
sense. His "Prospectus" of the *Encyclopédie* follows Bacon's
great divisions: "It is from our faculties that we have derived
our knowledge; history came to us from memory; philosophy,
from reason; and poetry, from imagination." Later he explicitly includes all the arts under the heading of poetry.[83] All
the arts "imitent ou contrefont la Nature"; the difference is
only in the materials and techniques they employ. It is in the
domain common to all the arts that imagination functions. Its
great work is the creation of the "modèle intérieur." [84] Long
before Diderot arrives at this conception it is foreshadowed
in his earliest mention of imagination, in one of the notes to
his translation of Shaftesbury, *Essai sur le mérite et la vertu*:
"What do you mean by a *monster?* A being which bears some
resemblance to something, such as the siren, the hippogriff,
the faun, the sphinx, the chimera, and the winged dragons?
But don't you see that these offsprings of painters and poets
have nothing absurd in their structure; that although they
don't exist in nature, they in no way contradict the ideas of
relationship, harmony, order, and perfection?" Diderot already
sees that the composite creature so often cited as examples of
the combining imagination must be put together in accordance

with the fundamental laws of proportion and of harmony. In "Sur le beau" the connection with the ideal model is even more apparent: "Purely imaginary beings such as the sphinx, the siren, the faun, the minotaur, the ideal man, etc., are those concerning the beauty of which opinion is least divided, and this is not surprising: these imaginary beings are, in truth, formed in accordance with the relationships we see in real beings; but the model which they must resemble, dispersed among all the products of nature, is, properly speaking, everywhere and nowhere." [85] And in the *Salon de 1767*, after the conception of the ideal model has been developed, Diderot cites the very same examples of the sphinx, the centaur, and their like.

This active imagination, forming the "modèle intérieur" from the images it has stored up, is so close to later ideas of the "creative" imagination that it is worth pausing over Diderot's use of *créer* and its derivatives. Now although he says specifically that "l'imagination ne crée rien," he goes on to describe its activity in almost precisely the terms that Coleridge and Baudelaire were to use: "elle imite, elle compose, combine, exagère, agrandit, rapetisse." It would seem that Diderot, like Voltaire, Condillac, and other eighteenth-century writers, insisted on using *créer* in the strict sense of a creation *ex nihilo*, God's creation of the world. The products of the imagination, though they have no direct models in nature, are still composed of elements found in nature.[86] So, with a few exceptions, Diderot does not use the word *créer* for the work of the imagination. He does however use it on several occasions for the whole activity of the poet, and particularly of the genius.[87]

Together with his ideas on imagination and on the ideal model, one of the things which makes Diderot seem most "modern" is his emphasis on the importance of suggestion in art. He takes a long stride along the road we are following. No longer is clarity a requisite for the poet; indeed clarity is harmful to enthusiasm, and Diderot exclaims: "Poètes . . . soyez ténébreux." Also in the *Salon de 1767*, he advises poets to select a single part of a figure: "this part exaggerated by a standard which exhausts the total capacity of my imagination; a choice of expression, a rhythm, a corresponding harmony; this is the way to create infinite, immeasurable beings, who will go beyond the limits of my intelligence, and will hardly be contained within the limits of the universe." Suggestion is achieved first of all by a choice of features or parts rather than by detailed description. "Movement, action, passion itself are indicated by a few characteristic traits; and my imagination does the rest. I am inspired by the divine afflatus of the artist." [88] Hence Diderot's insistence on the importance of preserving the "esquisse" in the finished work. The imagination of the poet must arouse the imagination of the reader. Too much detail cramps the imagination: "The more vague expression is in the arts, the more imagination is at ease." [89]

Another means of suggestion is the artist's technique, whatever it may be: "the sublime, in either painting, poetry, or eloquence, does not always arise from the exact description of phenomena, but from the emotion which the genius observing them has felt, from the art with which he communicates to me the trembling of his soul, from the comparisons he uses, from his choice of expressions, from the harmony with which he strikes my ear, from the ideas and feelings he is able to arouse in me." It is true that for Diderot technique often seems secondary, and technique alone he finds intolerable: "O mon ami! la plate chose que des vers bien faits! la plate chose que de la musique bien faite! la plate chose qu'un morceau de peinture bien faite, bien peinte!" Of Saint-Lambert he says that he possesses the technique of versification, a good ear, and a sense of harmony, but then asks, "What does he lack then in order to be a poet?" The reply is: "What does he lack? a troubled soul, a vehement spirit, a strong and impetuous imagination, a lyre with more strings; his has too few." Technique is no substitute for imagination. Diderot says to Hubert Robert: "You have technique, but the ideal is missing," and of Vien: "Notice that, with the greatest understanding of art, he is without ideal, without fervor, without poetry, without incident, without interest." [90]

Yet Diderot never ceases to insist that if imagination is not seconded by technical skill the model will be inadequately represented. One of Casanove's paintings is "a beautiful poem, well conceived, well organized, and badly written." As for the poet, "Le Mierre has only one of the qualities of the poet, a vivid imagination; he is absolutely ignorant of harmony." [91] Diderot himself seems one of the most spontaneous of writers, yet in 1766 he writes to Falconet, "Ce n'est pas au courant de la plume qu'on fait une belle page," and the section "Sur ma manière de travailler" of the *Conseils et confidences d'un philosophe à une impératrice* reveals the conscious method that underlay his apparent spontaneity. And in the *Salon de 1767* he writes: "When one has fervor, unusual ideas, an original and forceful way of seeing and feeling, the great torment is to find the particular, individual, unique expression which will characterize, distinguish, move, and impress." [92]

So it is true for the poet as for the painter that "a great and powerful imagination must be seconded by firm, sure, and effortless brushwork." But both imagination and technique must be fired by enthusiasm. Diderot writes of a painting by Le Prince: "Everything is well conceived, well organized, the figures well placed, the objects well distributed, the lighting convincing; but no painting, no magic." All through his art criticism Diderot stresses this double function of enthusiasm, "l'enthousiasme d'âme et celui du métier." "Without the one, the idea is cold; without the other, the execution is feeble; the two together make the work sublime." And he says that if Loutherbourg had possessed, together with "le sublime du technique," "le sublime de l'idéal," he would be an object of worship.[93] Only by the collaboration of enthusiasm, imagination, and technique can the truly great work of art be achieved.

All that has been said so far is valid for the poet in the broadest sense, the artist whatever his medium. One of Diderot's chief preoccupations was to point out the relationships of the arts: "What is still to be done is to bring together the beauties common to poetry, painting and music; to show the analogies between them; to explain how the poet, the painter, and the musician reproduce the same image; to grasp the fleeting emblems of their expression; to inquire whether there is not some resemblance between these emblems, etc." [94] This was written in 1751, and the problem keeps recurring in Diderot's later criticism. Poetry and painting have much in common,[95] and there is a constant interchange, or rather ferment, between them: "Looking at the pictures of the great masters is as useful for an author as reading great works of literature is for a painter." [96]

However, Diderot was well aware of the differences among the arts, particularly between poetry and painting. Painting is simultaneous, poetry successive; "The painter has but a single moment; and he can no more include two moments than two actions." [97] Before Lessing he attacked the famous *ut pictura poesis* doctrine. In the *Salon de 1767* he says that his colleagues have the doctrine firmly fixed in their heads, "and have no inkling that it is still more true that *ut poesis pictura non erit.*" He cites the example he had already used in the *Lettre sur les sourds et muets* of Neptune rising from the waves, so admirable in Virgil's verse, so unsuited for a painting.[98]

Diderot then realized fully that "chaque art imite d'une manière qui lui est propre." [99] Each art has its own special technique, its own means of suggestion. Later one of the chief of these means of suggestion for the poet was to be the image, glorified into the symbol. With Diderot the word *image* often has the sense, so frequent in the eighteenth century, of simply a word picture.[100] With his strong feeling for the concrete, such pictures are essential for him, and no reader needs to be reminded how frequent they are in his own writings. But the poet's image differs from that of the painter. As La Fontaine had said in "Le Tableau":

> Et comme celle-ci [l'action] déchet dans la peinture,
> La peinture déchet dans une description.
> Les mots et les couleurs ne sont choses pareilles
> Ni les yeux ne sont les oreilles.

Only at its peril can poetry indulge in the kind of detailed description that a picture gives. Ariosto's detailed description, from top to toe, of Angelica's beauty only exasperates the reader, and leaves him unconvinced. Homer knew better, Diderot says; he describes not Helen herself, but the effect of her beauty on the old men on the walls of Troy. The example is used in the *Salon de 1767*, and also in one of Diderot's poems:

> Du front et des sourcils d'Hélène
> Homère ne m'entretient pas.
> Mais j'entends des vieillards attroupés autour d'elle,
> Stupéfaits, transportés, s'écrier: "Qu'elle est belle! . . ."
> Oubliant, à l'aspect de ses divins appas,
> Et la fureur d'Ajax, et le courroux d'Achille,
> Et le désastre de leur ville,
> Et l'approche de leur trépas.

Always the poet must avoid an overabundance of detail. Le Mierre tries to reproduce the thing itself and not his impression of it; "he forgets that he is a poet, and deserts his role for that of the painter." [101]

When it comes to imagery as a figure of speech, it is clear that a long tradition of conventional and faded allegories and so-called symbols had made Diderot wary of these categories. "Allegory, rarely sublime, is almost always cold and obscure." [102] Even a sublime allegory should only be used once. Diderot is vehement on the subject: "I shall never cease to consider allegory as the resource of a mind which is feeble, sterile, incapable of making use of reality, and calling on the hieroglyph for aid; the result is a jumble of real people and imaginary beings which shocks me, compositions worthy of Gothic times and not of ours." [103] Symbol is hardly distinguished from allegory; in "Un Petit Mot sur le genre allégorique" Diderot says that in general the symbol is frigid, and that the only way to get rid of this insipid and fatal frigidity is by the simplicity and sublimity of the idea. And he advises painters to prefer, as far as possible, real people to symbolic beings. Yet he does admit the possibility of finding in the "emblem" a unique expression, "l'image unique et forte d'une qualité individuelle." [104]

In spite of his general harshness towards allegory and symbol, Diderot has a good deal to say about other types of images. He praises Du Marsais' *Des tropes*, finding it full of excellent observations.[105] He sees the value of metaphor, defining his phrase "expressions heureuses" as those expressions "which are proper to one sense, touch for example, and which are at the same time metaphorical for another sense, such as sight; the result is a double illumination for the listener, the true and direct light of expression, and the reflected light of metaphor." [106] Even for the philosopher the use of imagery is of value: "Happy is the systematic philosopher to whom nature has given . . . a powerful imagination, great eloquence, and the art of presenting his ideas in the form of striking and sublime images!" [107] It is by metaphors that the writer keeps in touch with nature.[108] For the metaphor is the expression of the *rapports* of which Diderot speaks so constantly: "What is an exact, new, and stimulating comparison, what is a bold metaphor, what is an original expression, if it is not the expression of certain special relationships between beings known to us?" [109] So Diderot is led to the role of analogy, the analogy of images and sentiments, which guides the artist in his choice of accessories. In the *Essai sur la peinture* the idea is developed in terms which prefigure the later doctrine of *correspondances*: "Is not one color more analogous than another to certain states of mind, certain passions?" [110] The rest of the passage brings out by examples the suggestive power of such carefully chosen analogies. For Diderot the significant images are not the artificial and conventional allegories of his time, but the metaphors and comparisons which lead us back to nature and its hidden harmony, and thus are rich in suggestive power. But for the poet the supreme instrument of suggestion is language.

Language in general was one of Diderot's great preoccupations. In his article "Encyclopédie" he says that the first concern of the *encyclopédistes* is the study of language, and goes on to devote twenty pages to the subject.[111] For him the great danger is that, whereas for children words evoke images, with age the image is no longer noticed; we judge only by shape and weight, as with coins.[112] Language tends towards abstraction, and becomes more and more remote from concrete experience. And by its very nature it has difficulty in expressing experience: "Our spirit is a picture in constant motion, which we are always having to paint; we take a long time to reproduce it faithfully: but it exists as a whole, and all at once: the mind does not progress step by step as expression does." [113] In his earlier writings Diderot sees the solution for this problem in the imitation of spontaneous expression: "C'est au cri animal de la passion à dicter la ligne qui nous convient." [114] In this conception Diderot follows a line of development very similar to that of the ideal model in the domain of the imagination. At first he insists on as close an imitation as possible of natural language, difficult though this is to achieve,[115] and warns the writer against sacrificing everything to harmony of style.[116] But as his conception of "l'harmonie imitative" develops, a greater freedom is allowed: "If the exact word is never sacrificed except when the mind will not be too much diverted from it by melodious expression, the understanding will supply it . . . the spectacle becomes more complicated and more

varied, and in proportion its charm increases in my mind; the
ear is satisfied, and truth is not offended." [117]

Diderot constantly distinguishes between the language of
the philosopher, which aims above all at clarity and precision,
and the language of the poet. In the *Lettre sur les sourds et
muets* he describes the difference between eloquence and
poetry: "There passes into the discourse of the poet a spirit
that moves and quickens its every syllable. What is this spirit?
I have sometimes felt its presence; but all I know about it is
that through it things are at the same time spoken and pictured;
that at the same moment that the understanding grasps them,
the soul is moved by them, the imagination sees them, and
the ear hears them, and discourse is no longer only a linking
together of strong terms that set forth the thought nobly
and forcibly, but a fabric of closely interwoven hieroglyphs
that picture it. I might say that in this sense all poetry is emblematic." [118] This famous and familiar passage shows clearly
how the hieroglyph is the means by which the ideal model is
conveyed from the imagination of the poet to the imagination
of the reader. The poet's imagination forms the model; the
reader's imagination perceives it; the transmitting agent is
language, raised to its highest power by enthusiasm.

Diderot's use of the term *hiéroglyphe* has been much discussed.[119] There seems little doubt that the term came to him
from Warburton, probably by way of Condillac. For Diderot
the term seems to be a solution of the linguistic problem he has
been discussing, the difficulty of finding adequate expression
for the "tableau mouvant" of the spirit. The idea is suggested
before the word occurs: "Since we have but one mouth, this is
what we have done: we have attached several ideas to a single
expression. If these forceful expressions were more frequent,
instead of the tongue forever lagging after the mind, the
number of ideas expressed at the same time might be so great
that the tongue would go faster than the mind, and the mind
would have to race after it." Then the word *hiéroglyphe* is

attached to such expressions, and Diderot proceeds to give a
number of examples, including the often-quoted line from
Boileau,

Soupire, étend les bras, ferme l'œil et s'endort.

This leads to a more precise definition of the term: "The
exquisite emblem, the subtle hieroglyph which dominates a
whole description, and which depends on the distribution of
long and short syllables in languages in which quantity is
marked, and on the distribution of vowels among consonants
in the words of all languages: all this necessarily disappears in
the best of translations." [120]

The term *hiéroglyphe* used in this sense disappears from
Diderot's criticism after the *Lettre sur les sourds et muets*,[121]
but the concept behind it, that of verbal harmony, remains of
the first importance. In the conclusion of the *Lettre* he brings
together the terms *harmonie* and *hiéroglyphe*: "*I have compared* the harmony of style to the harmony of music; and *I
have been convinced*: 1° that in words the former is a result of *quantity* and of a certain interweaving of vowels and
consonants, suggested by instinct, and that in sentences it is
the result of the arrangement of the words; 2° that syllabic
and periodic harmony will engender a kind of hieroglyph
peculiar to poetry." This idea of harmony is a favorite one
with Diderot. In 1766 he writes to Falconet: "I doubt whether
the magic of chiaroscuro is any more difficult to grasp than
the subtleties of imitative harmony." [122] In the *Salon de 1767*
he addresses the would-be poet: "You write verses? You think
so, because you have learned from Richelet to arrange words
and syllables in a certain order, according to certain given
conditions; because you have acquired the facility of ending
these arrangements of words and syllables with consonances.
You are not painting; you hardly know how to trace." After
quoting a stanza of Horace, Diderot goes on: "You have felt

the beauty of the image, which is nothing; here the rhythm is everything; perhaps you will never perceive the prosodic magic in this bit of a picture. What then is rhythm? you ask me. It is a special choice of expressions; it is a certain distribution of syllables, long or short, harsh or soft, muted or shrill, light or heavy, slow or swift, plaintive or gay, or else a concatenation of little onomatopoeias analogous to the ideas with which one is preoccupied; to the sensations which one experiences and wishes to arouse; to the phenomena the features of which one is trying to reproduce; to the passions one feels, and to the animal cry they would wring from one; to the nature, the character, the movement of the action one proposes to reproduce; and this art is no more conventional than the effects of the rainbow; it cannot be acquired; it cannot be communicated; it can only be perfected." This harmony cannot be learned from books: "Nature, and Nature alone, can dictate the veritable harmony of a complete period, of a certain number of verses." Rhythm is inspired by natural taste, by the mobility of the spirit, by sensibility. On this rhythm the power of the image depends: "The quality of the sounds fortifies or weakens the image; their quantity contracts or expands it. How great then is the power of rhythm, harmony, and sound!" [123] It is this harmony above all that makes poetry suggestive: "these soft expressions, these fleeting accents, these flexible and varied numbers of Racine's and Voltaire's poetry; this harmony which goes straight to the heart, which stirs the inward parts; that art which makes us imagine, see, hear, conceive things which the poet does not say, and which move us more deeply than those he expresses." [124] The passage not only recalls the earlier one on the hieroglyph, but foreshadows much that was to be said later on the power of suggestion in poetry. When Diderot speaks of "la magie du clair-obscur" and "la magie prosodique" he seems to suggest that the painter and the poet weave a magic spell which makes the spectator or the reader see the visions they conjure up. Here we are close to Baudelaire's "magie suggestive" and "sorcellerie évocatoire." [125]

In such a conception matter and form are inseparable. Diderot stresses this particularly in connection with translation. During the long ramble he takes with the abbé and his pupils in the *Salon de 1767*, the Virgil lesson the abbé is giving sets Diderot to reflecting on the difficulty of transposing from one language to another the passages one knows best. He had earlier discussed the question at some length in his *Réflexions sur Térence*: "In the different judgments one hears expressed every day, nothing is so common as the distinction between style and matter. This distinction is too generally accepted not to be correct. I agree that where there is no matter there can be no style; but I cannot imagine how it is possible to detract from the style without detracting from the matter." Even prose, the great oratorical prose of Cicero or Demosthenes, loses in translation, and poetry even more so. "The fact is, strictly speaking, that when the style is good there is not a superfluous word; and that a word which is not superfluous stands for something, and something so essential, that by substituting for a word its closest synonym, or even for the synonym the word itself, one will sometimes give an impression contrary to what the orator and the poet intended." To translate Virgil as Abbé Desfontaines did, is to kill a poet. There is only one way to translate an author faithfully; "it is to be imbued with the impressions one has received from him, and to be satisfied with one's translation only when it arouses the same impressions in the reader." Diderot goes back to the question again in his article on some translations of Jacobi (1771): "Harmony paints; the harmony appropriate to the subject moves us, arouses a variety of sensations. The most remarkable thought, without the harmony appropriate to it, has no effect; the most commonplace thought, with its appropriate harmony, becomes a rare and precious thing." [126]

For Diderot form and content are then inseparable. If there must be a choice, content rather than form has the primacy; content will indeed suffer if the form given to it is inadequate, but form without adequate content is condemned to sterility. "Poetry and painting without ideas are two sorry things." [127] And Diderot never ceases to uphold the moral role of art: "Rendre la vertu aimable, le vice odieux, le ridicule saillant, voilà le projet de tout honnête homme qui prend la plume, le pinceau ou le ciseau." [128] But his moralizing is never a dry didacticism; it is closely allied with sensibility and enthusiasm. Art instructs by moving the emotions of the reader, and giving him a combination of moral and aesthetic pleasure, such as that which Diderot himself so often experienced, and which explains certain of his special enthusiasms, for Greuze and Richardson, for example. He does not hesitate to say: "Certainly it is more difficult to write an admirable page than to perform a noble deed; but the latter is of a different order of importance." [129] In the realm of art form is essential, not indeed as a goal in itself, but as the *sine qua non* for the communication of whatever the artist or poet is seeking to express. Diderot indeed believed — and he is by no means the only great critic to do so — that art has a moral function. But no one could emphasize more strongly the fact that art has its own laws, by which it must abide.

For all too many critics Diderot's moral preoccupations and his overemphasized sensibility have obscured his originality and his greatness. It is true that in his early writings the role of sensibility seems excessive. Yet even here it should not be forgotten that Diderot was reacting against a conception of poetry in which emotion, with rare exceptions, had hardly any role. And he himself, in his later writings, redressed the balance, and indeed in the *Paradoxe* swung for a time towards the opposite extreme. Likewise enthusiasm, while always essential, ceases to be completely unrestrained, and is curbed by reason and judgment. If Diderot's pronouncements to this effect sometimes sound to us very like those of his predecessors, it is well to remember how his idea of enthusiasm differs from theirs; they were damming what was already a sedately flowing stream; he, a roaring torrent.

At the heart of Diderot's doctrine is the *modèle intérieur*, opposed alike to a universal *beau idéal* and to a rigorous imitation of nature. This is allied with Diderot's constant preoccupation with the problem of the relation of art to reality, about which he thought and wrote more deeply and searchingly not only than his predecessors, bound by traditional doctrines of imitation, but also, I believe, than any of his successors in France up to Baudelaire. And it is no coincidence that for him, as for Baudelaire, imagination was the chief faculty of the poet. For imagination is the mediator between reality and art; ranging in the vast storehouses of nature and of memory, perceiving relationships everywhere, it chooses, modifies, combines, and thus creates the *modèle intérieur*.

Hardly less important is all that Diderot has to say of the necessity of form and technique for the adequate translation of the model into a poem or a painting, for the communication of the relationships perceived by the imagination. In the case of the poet, whose medium is language, his idea of *harmonie imitative* goes far beyond that of earlier writers. The language of poetry has much the same relationship to natural language that the ideal model has to nature. It does not imitate, but suggests; it is not a copy, but a hieroglyph, a symbol. This realization of the quality of suggestion in art not only makes of Diderot a precursor of modern symbolist theory, but also leads him to an intimate understanding of the relation between matter and form, and the untranslatable nature of great art.

Diderot himself was not a great, nor even a very good poet in the narrow sense of the word; his own verse is hardly more than mediocre. But rarely has anyone had a more sure and sensitive appreciation of poetry than that which appears in his comments on Homer and Virgil, and his other favorite poets. Of Virgil he says: "C'est une âme, une chaleur, une douceur qui vous enchante." His poets are identified with his own experience; "Tibulle sentait comme moi," he writes to Sophie Volland.[130] For this philosopher poetry meant as much as truth: "O sweet illusions of poetry! you have no less charm for me than truth. May you touch and please me to my last moments." [131] And if we take the word poet in its larger sense, as Diderot himself so often did, he was indeed a poet, and a great one. His experience of art and of literature, his practice of his own craft, his philosophical meditations on a multitude of problems converged in a body of critical theory which fully justifies Baudelaire's inclusion of him among the great critics: "Diderot, Goethe, Shakspeare, autant de producteurs, autant d'admirables critiques." [132]

SENSE AND SENSIBILITY

To turn from Diderot to the poetry and poetic theory of his contemporaries is somewhat disheartening. With the second half of the eighteenth century one might well expect a revival of poetry. The preromantic period, so much studied in the twentieth century, brought to the surface the sentiment and emotion, the confidences and confessions, the feeling for nature, that were to furnish the great themes of romantic poetry.[1] But in all too many respects the poetry written from the middle of the century up to Chénier carries on the tradition of the preceding period. The same genres continue to flourish, and the anthologies all have their quota of odes, elegies, idylls, eclogues, fables, madrigals, epigrams, and every variety of "pièces fugitives et légères." The more serious genres are indeed on the wane; in 1760 D'Alembert observed that the sonnet was disappearing, the elegy dying, the eclogue failing, and even the haughty ode beginning to lose its supremacy.[2] Poetry is more and more a pastime, the poets are less and less conscious of any high calling. As Cardinal de Bernis wrote in his ode, *Les Poètes lyriques*:

> Amoureux de la bagatelle,
> Nous quittons la lyre immortelle
> Pour le tambourin d'Erato.
> Homère est moins lu que Chapelle;
> Et si nous admirons Apelle,
> Nous aimons Teniers et Watteau.

The writers of odes are followers of Anacreon rather than of Pindar. Ponce-Denis Le Brun (nicknamed Le Brun-Pindare) endeavored indeed to carry on the tradition of Jean-Baptiste Rousseau, as in his seven-page ode *Sur l'enthousiasme*:

Aigle qui ravis les Pindares
Jusqu'au trône enflammé des Dieux,
Enthousiasme! tu m'égares
A travers l'abîme des cieux.
Ce vil Globe à mes yeux s'abaisse,
Mes yeux s'épurent, et je laisse
Cette fange, empire des Rois.
Déjà, sous mon regard immense,
Les astres roulent en silence:
L'Olympe tressaille à ma voix.

But Le Brun's enthusiasm is pompous, his style forced, and his poetry comes from the head rather than from the heart. Rivarol pictured him "sitting up in bed in the morning, surrounded by Homer, Pindar, Anacreon, Virgil, Horace, Racine, Boileau, etc., and fishing up a word now from one, now from another, with which to make up his poetic mosaics." [3] His reputation among his contemporaries was considerable, but the modern reader can agree wholeheartedly only with the last phrase of Sainte-Beuve's judgment of him: "Le Brun's lyric talent is great, sometimes immense, almost always incomplete." [4] Some other writers attempted to carry on the tradition of the ode, and Marmontel's account of his poetic début is sadly characteristic. He had, he writes, been impressed by hearing about the Jeux Floraux prizes: "I took it into my head to be a poet. I had never studied the rules of versification. I quickly went and bought a little book on these rules; and, on the advice of the bookseller, I acquired at the same time a copy of Rousseau's *Odes*." [5] It is consoling to know that Marmontel's ode, on the invention of gunpowder, beginning

Toi, qu'une infernale Euménide
Pétrit de ses sanglantes mains,

was not awarded a prize.

The majority of Le Brun's contemporaries, however, had less lofty aims, and the subjects they treat are rarely serious or philosophical. In Parny's *Dialogue entre un poète et sa muse* the poet replies to the muse's protest against too exact rhyme:

Il est vrai, mais le monde a changé de nos jours;
On pense rarement, et l'on rime toujours.

The poets were "des gens d'esprit qui se piquent de rimer," [6] their verse is facile, their themes light, gallant, often sensual, embellished with mythology and periphrase. The adjectives their critics repeat, *aimable*, *agréable*, *ingénieux*, apply alike to Dorat, to Gentil-Bernard, to Parny and his innumerable imitators. These poets have no thirst for immortality. Bertin says:

Et si l'Europe aux immortels écrits
Ne mêle point mes chansons périssables,
On daignera peut-être dans Paris
Me mettre aux rangs des poètes aimables.[7]

The laws of verse are treated as cavalierly as is subject matter, and the poets chafe under classical restraint:

La houssine à la main, Boileau, grave et sévère,
Châtia de mon vol l'aisance irrégulière.
Je ne pus avec lui faire un pas sans trembler.
Je l'estimais beaucoup, mais je ne l'aimais guère.[8]

None of these poets achieved the perfection of Voltaire's light verse, and although their poems, particularly Parny's, have an occasional grace and charm, their banality and superficiality tend to become wearisome. One of their historians has said: "As one reads the verses of Parny's disciples, one has the impression that literature as well as politics had its émigrés. They had forgotten nothing and learned nothing." [9]

Two genres, the elegy and the descriptive poem, deserve somewhat more special consideration, for it is in them that a new hope for poetry, however timid, appears. In the elegy, more than in any other genre, sentiment begins to find fuller expression. The genre had declined in popularity in the earlier part of the century, and the amorous elegies of Parny and his school did little to rehabilitate it. Towards the end of the century it became more serious, a change observed with regret by Clément, who noted in 1797 that the *Almanach des Muses*, that thermometer of the taste of the moment, which had formerly been characterized by a pleasant and delicate badinage, had now become "triste comme le *Bonnet de nuit* de Mercier." [10] It is true that the melancholy of the elegists often seems as artificial as their gayety, but here and there a true note is struck, as when Bertin anticipates *Le Lac*:

> Je vous revois, délicieux séjour!
> Mais ces moments de bonheur et d'ivresse,
> Ces doux moments sont perdus sans retour.[11]

or the dying Gilbert gives us a foretaste of *L'Automne*:

> Salut, champs que j'aimais, et vous, douce verdure,
>   Et vous, riant exil du bois!
> Ciel, pavillon de l'homme, admirable nature,
>   Salut pour la dernière fois! [12]

In the elegy sentiment begins to leak into poetry; in descriptive poetry the feeling for nature, for the picturesque, takes its first timid steps. Poetry must no longer reason, but paint, according to Gilbert:

> Maudit soit à jamais le pointilleux sophiste
> Qui le premier nous dit en prose d'algébriste:
> Vains rimeurs, écoutez mes ordres absolus;
> Pour plaire à ma raison, pensez, ne peignez plus!
> Dès lors la poésie a vu sa décadence;
> Infidèle à la rime, au sens, à la cadence,
> Le compas à la main, elle va dissertant;
> Apollon sans pinceaux n'est plus qu'un lourd pédant.[13]

There is an increasing use of description, particularly in didactic poetry, which culminates in the descriptive genre: Saint-Lambert's *Les Saisons* (1769), Roucher's *Les Mois* (1779), Delille's *Les Jardins* (1782). The poets declare themselves inspired by nature:

> A la voix du tonnerre, au fracas des autans,
> Au bruit lointain de flots se croisants, se heurtants,
> De l'inspiration le délire extatique
> Versera dans mon sang la flamme poétique.[14]

But with the eruption of nature into poetry it is nature, not poetry, that is changed. True to the *ut pictura poesis* doctrine, the poets launch into interminable descriptions, too often of scenes they have never looked upon with their own eyes, and embellish them with well-worn metaphors and periphrases, yet slip all too often into an abstract and prosaic language reminiscent of the didactic poem. We have already seen what Diderot found lacking in Saint-Lambert as a poet. His long article on *Les Saisons* points out the lack of poetic vision, the conventional vocabulary and poetic ornaments: "M. de Saint-Lambert a étouffé quelques beaux vers dans une foule de vers communs." [15]

The best known of the descriptive poets is Delille, pilloried by Victor Hugo in the *Préface de Cromwell* as "l'homme de la description et de la périphrase." [16] It has been suggested nevertheless that Delille is as authentic an ancestor of the romantic poets as Chénier.[17] One can indeed find in his poems lines which do suggest romantic poetry and, in spite of their rhetorical structure have something of a simple, sensuous, and passionate quality:

> Dirai-je ces forêts d'arbustes, d'arbrisseaux,
> Entrelaçant en voûte, en alcôve, en berceaux,
> Leurs bras voluptueux et leurs tiges fleuries?
>
> . . . .
>
> Les arbres frémissaient, et la rose inclinée
> Versait tous ses parfums sur le lit d'hyménée.[18]

But when these passages are winnowed out, an intolerable deal of chaff remains. Rivarol's witty criticism of Delille, concluding "sa gloire passera, les navets resteront," [19] is at one with Sainte-Beuve's judgment that Delille, with his "faux goût," retarded the progress of poetry rather than advanced it.[20]

It would be unjust to condemn the poetry of the second half of the eighteenth century in quite the same wholesale manner as that of the first half. Artificial and rhetorical as much of it is, conventional as the images and vocabulary are, there are still passages in Gilbert, in Fontanes, in Delille, where simplicity and spontaneity of feeling infuse new life into old forms. In the later romantic poetry we shall often find traces of the old rhetoric; here the proportions are reversed, and occasional foreshadowings of the new are mingled with the old. Yet on the whole poetry, which would seem to be the natural channel for the new currents, proved to be too much shackled by convention. The wealth of poetic material which the preromantic period discovered became the portion of the prose writers, such as Rousseau and Bernardin de Saint-Pierre, and had to wait until the next century for its poets. The statement so often repeated is fundamentally true: French preromanticism rediscovered poetry, but produced no poets.

Still the need for poetry is reborn, and is less and less satisfied with the poetry that is being written. It is in the great prose of the period that the craving for poetry finds its satisfaction, for the readers of poetry were born before the writers. In prose the great themes of poetry come to life, and originality and spontaneity of feeling are given free rein. From a dissatisfaction with poetry as it was, from a realization of what it might and should be, a new conception of poetry gradually emerged. Unfortunately the circumstances which produced it led to a separation of content and form, a tendency to conceive poetry in large vague terms, to let it speak the language of prose as readily as that of verse, which resulted in an entanglement of poetry with eloquence and rhetoric which was to have far-reaching effects in the nineteenth century.

As in the poetry of this period, so in the poetic theory we find a very slow development. Grimm writes in 1763 that there are few good *arts poétiques*, most of them narrowing the limits of art rather than extending them. He praises Du Bos and Diderot, and says that the *Essai sur la poésie dramatique* and the *Entretiens* are themselves poems.[21] But no writer attained the stature of Diderot, whose influence throughout the period was slight, except on Grimm and to some extent on Marmontel. It is true that many of his most significant writings on art and literature were not published until many years after his death. Furthermore, many discussions of poetry are inextricably entangled with the quarrels between the *philosophes* and their opponents, which often degenerate into personalities, so that Diderot's aesthetic doctrines are thrown into the discard along with his philosophical and moral ones.[22] The majority of writings on poetry echo ideas that we have met earlier in the century; at most there is a change in emphasis rather than a new orientation. The opposition to poetry on philosophical and moral grounds gradually fades away, but the classical tradition is carried on in the great majority of treatises on poetry, which often are no more than compendia of "les règles tirées des auteurs les plus célèbres de notre nation." [23]

One might expect to find significant ideas on poetry in the relevant articles in the *Encyclopédie*, but most of them prove disappointing.[24] Hardly any of the articles on literature and art were written by Diderot himself. Abbé Mallet wrote a number of articles in the early volumes (he died in 1755), which simply echo his *Principes*. The major contributor of literary articles was Jaucourt, seconded in the *Supplément* by Marmontel. Voltaire contributed a few important articles, and the *Supplément* borrows largely from the German Sulzer's *Théorie universelle des beaux-arts*, translated into French in 1772.

Of these writers Jaucourt is the least original.[25] The very large number of articles signed by him are nearly all borrowed, with or without acknowledgement, from Du Bos, Batteux, Voltaire, and others. Marmontel, who took many of his articles from his own *Poétique*, is often almost as traditional. In his *Mémoires* he tells how, during the five years he spent at Versailles, he made a methodical study of ancient and modern writers on poetics, and accumulated a mass of material.[26] Grimm, reviewing the *Poétique* in the *Correspondance littéraire*, says that Marmontel lacks sensibility, tact, and delicacy; the first volume is deadly, the second better, partly because many of the ideas in it are borrowed from Diderot.[27] But some of Marmontel's later articles and his *Eléments de littérature* (1782) are more interesting and independent, especially his "Analogie" article.

On the whole the poetic doctrine found in the *Encyclopédie* is indicative of the movement of the times: an emancipation from a narrow doctrine of imitation, as when Jaucourt says in his "Poème épique" article, "Let us admire the ancients; but let us not make of our admiration a blind superstition"; a broader conception of beauty and of taste; more room for feeling and imagination. Yet there is a wide range from the strict traditionalism of Mallet to Sulzer's ideas, from the original definition of *Poème*, "une imitation de la belle nature, exprimée par le discours mesuré," to Sulzer's assertion that the only perfect poem is one conceived in the mind of a poet who owes his talent to nature, whose enthusiasm is not feigned, but who at the same time is familiar with the rules of art and uses them with delicate and sure taste. But the *Encyclopédie* is far from being the firebrand in the field of literature that it was in other domains.

The classical tradition continued to have its strong defenders, led by Voltaire, who maintained to the last his admiration for Boileau.[28] But whereas earlier the classicists had played an important part in defending poetry against the onslaughts of reason and philosophy, their later concern was rather to preserve it from the contagion of foreign influences, the barbarian invasions from the North in the shape of countless translations of English and German authors, with their passion and gloom and violence. Yet the wave of emotion became increasingly strong, and towards the end of the century a more revolutionary doctrine begins to appear, especially in the works of such minor writers as Mercier and Cubières-

Palmézeaux. Sense and sensibility come into more and more open conflict.

In the general movement of poetic theory the ideas discussed are much the same as in the first half of the century, but with a different emphasis. The scornful attitude towards poetry, based on philosophical grounds, gradually disappears, although a few unregenerate philosophers still subordinate poetry to reason. But little by little reason yields to sentiment, and the cults of primitivism and of nature come to the support of poetry. What we do find very frequently is a kind of defeatism about poetry as practiced in France. Suard, writing in 1762, says that the French are timid in poetry, afraid of metaphors and images, putting abstract and arid terms in the place of picturesque and musical expressions.[29] In a "Discours sur l'ode" Sabatier, maintaining the superiority of the poetry of antiquity, deplores the servitude to which poetry has been reduced by philosophy and the resulting decline in taste.[30] The conviction grows — and is all too well justified by the poetry of the time — that the French language is not suited to poetry. The great master of poetic prose, Rousseau, writes in his *Lettre sur la musique*: "Although we have had notable poets and even some musicians who were not without genius, I really think that our language is little suited to poetry, and not at all to music." [31] And Rivarol felt that the French poet's imagination was hampered by the circumspect spirit of his language.[32] In all these cases this attitude stems not from a distrust of poetry itself, as is the case with similar statements earlier in the century, but from a profound dissatisfaction with the poetry that was being written in France.

Hence it was natural that poetry should be sought abroad. As early as 1762 Grimm says that German poetry and literature are becoming as fashionable in Paris as English literature had already been for some years.[33] The two influences became increasingly strong; the poetry of untamed nature, of graveyards and ruins, of violent and somber passions, cast its shadow over the lighthearted verse characteristic of the period. And such a work as Young's *Conjectures on Original Composition* gave new emphasis to the conceptions of originality and of genius.[34] But this injection of "northern" poetry met with stubborn resistance. Le Brun writes acidly:

> Nous changeons l'or du goût, l'or pur de Castalie,
> Au pinchbek des Anglais, au clinquant d'Italie;
> Sakeispir [sic] est sans doute un Sophocle nouveau.[35]

And Gentil-Bernard comes to the defense of Boileau:

> De l'étranger importants amateurs,
> Infatués des muses britanniques:
> Tout ce que Londres a pour eux enfanté
> Est aussitôt lu, cité, translaté.
> Aussi voit-on dans nos champs littéraires
> Changer l'émail de nos vives couleurs,
> Et par l'effet des teintes étrangères
> Dénaturer nos primitives fleurs.
> Ils nous diront, serviles tributaires,
> Que la nature excelle en ce tableau;
> Que ce beau sombre est la teinte du beau.
> Non, mes amis, consultons nos modèles,
> Imitons-les; pensons comme Boileau.[36]

What was to produce the greatest change in poetry was, more than literary influences, the changing spirit of the times and the emergence of the "âme sensible." A climate more favorable to poetry is created, and emotion and strong feelings, so neglected in the poetic doctrine of the earlier part of the century, come to be considered the basis of poetry. French preromanticism rediscovered the lyric vein, the intimate confidence, and opened up a new vein for future poets. One result is that emotion and enthusiasm are closely allied, sometimes confused. According to Marmontel, "enthusiasm is not then a vague and blind frenzy, it is the passion of the moment in all its truth and natural ardor." [37] Jaucourt, in his *Encyclopédie* article "Verve" (which he takes to be synonymous with *enthousiasme*), gives emotion its share: "c'est une vive représentation de l'objet dans l'esprit, et une émotion du cœur proportionnée à cet objet." [38] But in his "Ode" article he makes a distinction: "This feeling is not properly called enthusiasm when it is natural, that is to say when it is found in a man who experiences it as a result of the actual state he is in; but only when it is found in an artist, poet, or musician, and when it is the effect of an imagination artificially stimulated by the objects it pictures to itself in the process of composition." This leads us back to the old definition of enthusiasm as "une imagination échauffée."

In some quarters enthusiasm is still suspect, and carefully harnessed to reason. The *Encyclopédie* article on it, by Cahusac, says that it is "rien moins qu'une fureur," but rather "un des plus beaux privilèges de la raison." Yet the control of reason is more and more relaxed, especially for the ode. Le Brun says: "I laugh when I see La Motte (a man of definitions, if ever there was one) coming along with his little yardstick and his cramped compasses to measure the bold strides of our lyric giants." [39] A *Discours sur la poésie lyrique* requires this "divine enthusiasm" for the ode, especially the Pindaric ode, which is "an impetuous torrent which roars down from the top of a high mountain, and whose rushing floods carry away everything that stands in the way of their fury." [40] Only as an afterthought is it suggested that, though genius must never be a slave, art must rein its impetuosity.[41] The series of "Ode" articles in the *Encyclopédie* (by Jaucourt, Marmontel, and Sulzer) all stress the emotion that must be felt by the poet, and justify his flights of enthusiasm, his "beau désordre." Sabatier writes a nineteen-stanza ode entitled *L'Enthousiasme*, in which he says:

> Animé d'une noble audace,
> Je cède à mes transports brûlants;
> La route que la raison trace
> Fut toujours l'écueil des talents.
> Souveraine de l'harmonie,

Ivresse, mère de génie,
Epuise sur moi ta fureur.
Quel accès violent m'agite?
Il m'embrase, un Démon l'excite;
Tous mes sens ont frémi d'horreur.[42]

From Grimm too comes a defense of unbridled enthusiasm; the poet "abandons himself to transports he has never before experienced. . . . He is beside himself, he is above himself; he creates; in his delirium he brings forth works such as he never would have believed himself capable of producing." [43]

Voltaire is one of the few to prophesy the disappearance of the ode, on the grounds that it is the domain of exaggeration, and that the more philosophical a nation becomes the more odes based on enthusiasm, which have nothing to teach mankind, will lose their value.[44] Still "l'enthousiasme raisonnable est le partage des grands poètes." And Voltaire defines and limits the role of reason: "How can reason govern enthusiasm? First of all the poet outlines the composition of his picture: at this point reason holds the pencil. But when he is ready to give life and passion to his characters imagination is aroused, enthusiasm acts; it is a steed carried away on its course: but the course has been carefully laid out." [45]

For Seran de la Tour, the author of a work with the significant title of *L'Art de sentir et de juger en matière de goût*, reason's domain is still further limited. He says of enthusiasm: "one prepares for it, one waits for it, one is seized by it, one grasps it, one knows nothing else. Apparently it is not the man who is functioning, it is a higher intelligence that has taken possession of all his spiritual faculties." In some ways this is like a "fureur divine"; but the term "intelligence supérieure" is striking. There is no longer a conflict between reason and enthusiasm; the two merge in this higher intelligence. The whole passage, like others in the same work, is reminiscent of Diderot. There is the same emphasis on feeling, on nature, on a broader conception of beauty, giving room for a "beau singulier et inconnu," such as that of a landscape with a rocky crag instead of a broad green slope.[46]

More and more sensibility becomes a prerequisite for enthusiasm, and hence fundamental for the poet. Sulzer demands for the poet "une extrême sensibilité de l'âme." [47] In this connection it is interesting to note the emergence of the modern sense of lyric in Jaucourt's article "Poésie lyrique," which he defines as an "espèce de poésie toute consacrée au sentiment." Voltaire too gives emotion its due share: "Le vrai poète est, à ce qu'il me semble, celui qui remue l'âme et qui l'attendrit; les autres sont de beaux parleurs." And again: "La poésie est la musique de l'âme, et surtout des âmes grandes et sensibles." [48]

One question often raised is that of the relation of emotion and the moment of poetic creation. Trublet maintains that the elegy has fallen into desuetude because of its unnaturalness: "what is less natural than that a man should be bursting with jealousy or dying of grief, and thereupon set to writing a hundred lines of verse?" [49] But Diderot had found the answer in his "emotion recollected in tranquillity" passage in the *Paradoxe sur le comédien*, and Marmontel picks it up in his "Elégie" article in the *Encyclopédie*: "Just as imagination dissipates and weakens in the poet the sense of his present situation, so it deepens the traces of his past situation. Memory is the foster-mother of genius." And in his preface to his translation of Young's *Night Thoughts* Le Tourneur speaks of the importance for the poet of finding the moment to express his feelings before they become dim, "not in the first moments of disturbance, when the soul, absorbed in feeling, can produce only monosyllables, and spreads disorder throughout the system; but in the moment when the soul, divided between sensation and reflection, begins to become calm enough to be aware of its own agitation." [50]

Memory leads to the poetic faculty often put side by side with sensibility at this time, imagination. Sulzer says in his

"Poète" article that "le fond du génie poétique ne peut être placé que dans une extrême sensibilité de l'âme, associée à une vivacité extraordinaire de l'imagination." Imagination is more frequently discussed than it had been earlier. The definitions of it vary a good deal, some distrust of it still remains, and many writers are careful to restrain its flights by a controlling judgment. According to Trublet it is the source of both great beauties and great defects. Yet even he lessens the control of the judgment: "Imagination should be superior to judgment, and much superior." But there should be moments of reflection after the fire of composition, when the poet should examine what he has composed.[51] Earlier Trublet had written: "the operation of judgment should precede and follow that of imagination; precede it, so that one may know what to do, follow it, so that one may know whether one has done it."[52] Even Sulzer says, in his "Poète" article, that a good poet always listens to the voices of wisdom and reason, and does not allow imagination to stifle them.

There is more opposition to imagination on aesthetic than on moral and philosophical grounds; the conception of imitation as the essence of poetry, repeated in Jaucourt's definition of poetry as "l'imitation de la belle nature exprimée par le discours mesuré," lingers on. But the conception of imitation was changing; Seran de la Tour says that "l'esprit vulgaire copie, et ne fait rien de plus. L'esprit supérieur crée en copiant."[53] While imagination is frequently defined simply as "la faculté de peindre vivement tout ce que l'esprit conçoit,"[54] its active, combining activity is often noted, particularly after Voltaire's *Encyclopédie* article "Imagination," which, as suggested earlier, may well have stimulated Diderot's thinking on the subject. Later Voltaire in his turn follows Diderot when he says that the poet "a pour base de son ouvrage la fiction: ainsi l'imagination est l'essence de son art."[55]

Marmontel's treatment of imagination is almost entirely borrowed from Voltaire, except that he vacillates between calling it creative and refusing it the term. Both he and Voltaire still have their reservations about it. Voltaire insists that "the imagination of a great poet must be much chastened. He must never present images which are incompatible, incoherent, too much exaggerated, too little suited to the subject." [56] And at one point Marmontel has a curious diatribe, reminiscent of Pascal, on "the most corruptible of all the faculties." "It is by imagination that barbarism brings forth its monsters, superstition its phantoms, error its bizarre systems; hence come all the fantasies which darken understanding and corrupt judgment, whether in human beliefs and customs, or in the conceptions of genius and the products of art. The first cause of these deviations of the imagination is its natural liberty. To counterfeit and to create seem to it an unlimited privilege, which emancipates it from all the rules of verisimilitude and of suitability. Thus, we see that the more reason is corrupted and feeling clouded, the more imagination is bold but flighty, impetuous but disordered, and rich in inventions that in no way differ from the dreams of a sick man." [57]

In any case the conception of the active imagination gains ground steadily. The *Dictionnaire de Trévoux* in its 1771 edition adds to its previous definition (1762) a very long passage in which it is said that imagination "retains and recalls the images which have reached it through the senses; but it also arranges, compounds and separates them; it combines them in a thousand different ways, in order to discover different relationships. It is thus that it invents and seems to create. It is precisely this infinite combining of different images which makes and characterizes great poets, great orators, great painters, in a word men of genius." [58] One of the most interesting discussions of imagination is that of Rivarol. For him imagination, a "magasin d'images," is a memory which is not under our control. Unlike pure memory, it has no sense of perspective or of time, it reveals new figures, it brings forth chimeras and monsters, "its magic wand opposes the world

it creates to the world it inhabits." Rivarol makes the distinction which Diderot had suggested between memory which
recalls signs and imagination which recalls images. He also
gives a new turn to the distinction between active and passive
imagination. When things are represented without order, as
in dreams, we have "pure" (or passive) imagination; when
they are perceived in their natural order we have memory;
and when a new order is imposed on them we have genius.
"De là vient qu'on donne quelquefois à l'esprit ou au génie le
nom d'*imagination active* ou créatrice, par opposition à
l'imagination pure ou passive." [59]
Many of these discussions are psychological rather than
literary, dealing with the nature of imagination rather than
with its role in poetry. But similar definitions begin to appear
in the treatises on rhetoric. Thiébault distinguishes four different kinds of imagination, the last of which is "the kind of
imagination which forms groups, composes masses, combines
planes, and creates systems, sometimes rises to the heights of
genius and is blended with it, or else falls into delirium, and
disappears buried beneath the chimeras it has brought forth." [60]
The place of imagination in poetry becomes larger, although some of the poems supposedly inspired by it hardly
show its mark. Such is the case with Delille's long poem,
L'Imagination, which expands into two volumes the prose of
the preface. "Les sens sont frappés par les divers objets qui se
présentent à eux, ces impressions se gravent dans la mémoire;
phénomène inexplicable de cette faculté, c'est dans son vaste
dépôt que l'imagination les choisit, les colore, les modifie, les
assortit à son gré." In the poem this becomes:

> L'Imagination, féconde enchanteresse
> Qui fait mieux que garder et se souvenir,
> Retrace le passé, devance l'avenir,
> Refait tout ce qui fut, fait tout ce qui doit être,
> Dit à l'un d'exister, à l'autre de renaître;
> Et, comme à l'Eternel quand sa voix l'appela,
> L'être encore au néant lui répond: me voilà.[61]

In spite of the increasing number of references to imagination as an important poetic faculty it is often not easy to see what its exact role in poetry is considered to be. At the center, to be sure, is the idea of an image-retaining faculty, and this often seems to be all that is meant by the term. For the chief theorists, such as Voltaire, what seems to be significant is the work of the active imagination. But there is little attempt to relate this conception to poetic practice, to show just how the imagination functions in poetic creation. Much of what is said is negative, merely opposing imagination to imitation. And the frequent substitution of the term invention seems to indicate the absorption of imagination into a general creative process, in which emotion and enthusiasm share. The equation of imagination and genius, by Marmontel and by Rivarol for example, broadens the conception still further. On the other hand the word *imagination* is often used, though not always explicitly, in a more limited sense; the "imaginative poet" is simply one who uses a wealth of concrete images and pictures in his poetry. Finally imagination is occasionally envisaged as a purveyor not only of pictures but of images in the modern sense, tropes.

The question of the image is again much discussed. In many cases the word still means only a picture, as in the *Encyclopédie* definition, "a short and vivid description, which presents objects to the eyes as well as to the mind." Here is the great aim of descriptive poetry, to paint nature. But this painting follows the old doctrine of imitation; Saint-Lambert says in his "Discours préliminaire" that nature must be magnified, embellished, made interesting. The descriptive poet must not only picture, but also move and teach, "graver dans le cœur et la mémoire des hommes des vérités et des sentiments agréables." [62] Poets other than the descriptive ones also found in the image the chief mark of poetry. Dorat insists that, "whatever feeble arguments may be brought forward by reason, images are always the essence of poetry, just as rhythm is its form." [63]

The use of *image* in the sense of *trope* becomes increasingly frequent. Marmontel's "Image" article in the *Supplément* notes the original *Encyclopédie* definition, and then goes on to say that in connection with the "coloris du style" the word has a much more precise meaning. It signifies "cette espèce de métaphore, qui, pour donner de la couleur à la pensée, et rendre un objet sensible s'il ne l'est pas, ou plus sensible s'il ne l'est pas assez, le peint sous des traits qui ne sont pas les siens, mais ceux d'un objet analogue." Much of what is said about poetic images repeats Du Marsais, whose *Des tropes* went through edition after edition, and was constantly referred to and quoted. But there are still many reservations about the use of imagery. Rivarol goes so far as to find in it a resemblance between the poet and the savage (and from Rivarol this was no compliment): "The poet is no more than a very ingenious and very animated savage, to whom all ideas present themselves in the form of images. The savage and the poet both go around in a circle; both speak only in hieroglyphs, with this difference, that the poet's orbit of ideas is much more limited." [64] Even by those who recommend its use, imagery is circumscribed by a series of precepts. Marmontel's *Poétique* reminds the reader that "all is not image and feeling in poetry; there are intervals when thought shines alone in its glory; for it must never be forgotten that the image is but its ornament." [65] Voltaire too demands a rigid conformity of the image to verisimilitude. Discussing Corneille's line, "Ce dessein avec lui serait tombé par terre," he says: "Any metaphor which does not present a true and perceptible image is a bad one; this is a rule to which there are no exceptions; now, what painter could represent an idea falling to the ground?" [66]

In this connection a question occurs which was to come up frequently in the early romantic period: that of the admissibility of the "reversed" image — the abstract used to represent

the concrete. In his "Comparaison" article in the *Supplément*
of the *Encyclopédie* Marmontel allows this, and Delille, in his
preface to *L'Imagination*, points with pride to his use of such
images as:

> La rose au doux parfum, de qui l'extrait divin
> Goutte à goutte versé par une avare main,
> Parfume, en s'exhalant, tout un palais d'Asie,
> Comme un doux souvenir remplit toute la vie.[67]

Allegory, which Diderot had criticized so severely, is
generally accepted. Marmontel praises it, and Sulzer says in the
"Allégorie" article of the *Supplément*: "In general the effect
of allegory is that of any image, to present abstract ideas in a
form perceptible to our senses, and by this means to give us an
intuitive knowledge of them. But in this respect *allegory* is
superior to all other kinds of images; as it suppresses the object
itself, its brevity gives it more vividness." Here there is a hint,
rare in this period, of the poetic value of concision. Although
the word *symbole* turns up occasionally, it is still used in a
completely traditional sense: "The symbol is a sign relative
to the object one wishes to suggest; and this relationship is
sometimes real, sometimes fictitious and conventional. The
sickle is the symbol of harvest; scales are the symbol of
justice." [68] Only the suggestion that there is sometimes a "real"
relationship takes us a step beyond earlier definitions.

Occasionally, however, the later conception of the symbol
is foreshadowed, perhaps most of all in Marmontel's remarkable "Analogie" article in the *Supplément*. He discusses first
a form of analogy which recalls Diderot's hieroglyph: "When
speech expresses an object which, like speech itself, affects the
ear, it can imitate sounds by sounds, speed by speed, slowness
by slowness, by using analogous poetic numbers." And he
gives the classic example, "Soupire, étend les bras, ferme l'œil
et s'endort." Then he goes on to a form of the "analogie du
style" which "paints, not sound or movement, but the ideal
or perceptible character of its object. . . . This kind of

analogy presupposes a natural relationship and a close correspondence between the sense of sight and sense of hearing, and between both of them and the inner sense which is the organ of the passions. . . . The *analogy* of habit is that which repeated impressions have established between the signs of our ideas and our ideas themselves." By its vocabulary, especially the term *correspondances*, the passage is so suggestive of later theories that one may be dangerously tempted to read too much into it. Yet the very fact that Marmontel considers this form of analogy a step beyond the relation between sound and sense shows that he is tending towards the nineteenth-century doctrine of *correspondances*. There is no question, to be sure, of a relationship between the natural and the supernatural; the analogy is between the physical world and the mind and soul of man. Delille expresses the same idea in his preface to *L'Imagination*: "The more one observes the physical world and the moral world, the more one becomes aware of the eternal correspondence nature has established between them." [69] And in the preface to the 1801 edition of *Les Jardins* he says, obviously having in mind Rivarol's parallel between the poet and the savage: "Heavens, what relationship is there between the formless song of this savage and the talent of the man who can see the beauties of nature with the practiced eye of the observer, and reproduce them with the palette of imagination; paint them, now with the richest colors, now with the most delicate shades; who can grasp that secret but eternal correspondence that exists between physical nature and moral nature, between the sensations of man and the works of God." [70]

Except in relation to imagery, there is relatively little discussion of poetic language during this period. Some writers still maintain that there is little or no difference between the language of prose and that of poetry, others insist on a distinct difference. Unfortunately the latter usually tend to see this difference in the very factors which were fatal to the poetry of the time, inversion, periphrase, and above all a special poetic vocabulary, carefully differentiated from everyday language. Joannet says that "the expressions which are less in use in familiar language seem more suitable to poetry, which is the language of the gods," and advises the use of *azur* rather than *bleu*, *nef* rather than *vaisseau*, *L'Eternel* rather than *Dieu*, and a host of other terms that are the stock in trade of eighteenth-century poetry.[71] Clément, maintaining against Voltaire that the prose writer and the poet have two entirely different languages, says that poetry is characterized by images and periphrases.[72] This use of periphrase is criticized severely by Bernardin de Saint-Pierre, in an eloquent plea for a language that will describe nature so as to make it recognizable.[73]

On the other hand the followers of Voltaire continue to insist that there is little difference between eloquence and poetry. For Marmontel the only difference between poetic eloquence and oratorical eloquence is that "one should be the elixir of the other." [74] Much of this is a battle of words, depending on the definition of prose. If it means everyday speech, then poetry has a different language; if it means eloquence, the two languages are much the same.

Yet the musical values of poetry are frequently referred to, and their importance admitted. Even D'Alembert says in his *Encyclopédie* article "Goût": "Verse is a kind of song for which the ear is so inexorable that reason itself is sometimes constrained to make slight sacrifices to it." But almost everything that is said about the music of poetry, such as Jaucourt's *Encyclopédie* articles "Poétique (harmonie)" and "Style, poésie du," cites and copies Du Bos and Batteux, or else talks in vague and loose terms. This neglect of the question of the language of poetry seems to be the result of the new stress on emotion and spontaneity. The general opinion is that the *poète sensible*, filled with enthusiasm, will find a suitable language flowing naturally from his pen, and needs no guidance. Thus Sulzer says, in his "Poète" article, that the source of language is a kind of secret inspiration.

The question of verse and prose continued to be much discussed. The prose poem became very popular, and there were many prose translations of foreign poets such as Young, Gray, Ossian, and Gessner; indeed many original prose poems are disguised as translations. These poems are of all sorts, didactic, philosophical, descriptive, meditative. And besides the prose works that are labeled poetry, there is the great poetic prose of Rousseau and Bernardin de Saint-Pierre. In the face of this rising tide the defenders of verse diminished in number. Voltaire remained the most stalwart of them all, both attacking the prose poem and defending verse passionately: "What is a poem in prose if not a confession of weakness? Don't you know that it is easier to write ten volumes of passable prose than ten good lines of verse in your language, that language encumbered with articles, deprived of inversions, poor in poetic terms, barren of bold turns of phrase, enslaved to the eternal monotony of rhyme, and yet lacking rhymes for noble subjects?" [75] In the *Dictionnaire philosophique* article, "Epopée" Voltaire goes back to the value of rhyme as a "difficulté vaincue": "I am convinced that rhyme, which is for genius a perpetual irritation, so to speak, is as much a help as a hindrance to him; that by forcing him to cast his thought in a thousand different forms it also forces him to think more precisely and to express himself more correctly. Often the artist who abandons himself to the facility of blank verse is conscious of the lack of harmony in these verses and tries to atone for it by monstrous images which have no basis in nature. Finally, he lacks the merit of having overcome difficulties. As for prose poems, I do not know what these monsters are. I see in them only an inability to write verse." [76] Dorat too comes to the defense of verse: "Verses are indeed the language of sentiment; they give value to the smallest details. . . . They bring together, as it were, the fragments of a thought, strike sparks from its very precision, and often make of an otiose sentence, dragged out by the circuitousness of prose, a shaft that goes straight to the heart." [77] Seran de la Tour, with all his emphasis on sentiment, still asserts the value of verse: "Why is poetry constrained to a servile subjection to measure? Because this constraint heightens the expression of colors and the vividness of images, and because the result is a more faithful and more pleasing imitation. Otherwise poetry is only a discourse more embellished than prose." [78]

Usually the defense of verse is allied with the antiforeign attitude that has been noted, and is a bulwark against the invasions from the north. But the prose poem is slowly accepted, even by so traditional a writer as Jaucourt, who defines it in the *Encyclopédie* as "a kind of work in which the fictions and the style of poetry are found, and which thus, except for measure and rhyme, is a true *poem*; it is a very happy invention." Many of the Encyclopaedists were opposed to the "shackles" of verse. D'Alembert asserts that "with an ear sensitive to harmony, a happy gift for expression, which only taste can give, and above all ideas and feeling, a man will be a lyric poet; these are conditions enough, without adding to them the tyranny of arbitrary laws." [79] For Trublet poetry is common to prose and verse, for it is a matter of style, while versification is only a mechanical arrangement of words which constitutes a major obstacle to perfection of style.[80] Even Marmontel, usually faithful to Voltaire, says that rhyme is not necessary to poetry: "C'est le fond des choses, non la forme des vers, qui fait le poète et qui caractérise la poésie." [81]

Most of these writers have a negative and somewhat defensive attitude, much like that of the earlier part of the century. Verse is a hindrance to accurate expression, an unnecessary difficulty. Only a few writers are concerned with the crucial question of how to free poetry from verse, yet keep it poetry. Bitaubé, the translator of Gessner, apostrophizes his original: "Je ferai parler à la prose le langage élevé de la poésie: puissé-je, en secouant un joug pénible, réussir comme toi, et obtenir comme toi un rang entre les poètes." [82] And Jean-Jacques Rousseau asks with a note of despair: "Comment être poète en prose?" [83]

In the latter part of the century the antagonists of verse take the offensive. Rivarol has a diatribe against verse: "Nothing is said in verse that cannot be equally well said in our prose; and the contrary is not always true. The prose writer keeps a firmer hand on his thought and guides it into the most direct path, while the versifier raises his voice, arms himself with rhyme and measure, and leads a commonplace thought off the main road; but what weaknesses are concealed by the art of verse! . . . The mechanism of verse wearies us, without offering us more audacious turns of style; especially in our language, in which verses often seem to be the débris of the prose which preceded them." [84] The most persistent partisan of prose poetry is Mercier, who turns the tables on Voltaire by starting off with the very statement that the great defender of verse had so often made, that there is no essential distinction between poetry and eloquence. "Our poetry is only prose differently arranged; it is no more noble, no more harmonious, no more precise, no more cadenced than the fine passages of our prose writers." And Mercier asks: "Can there be poems in prose? Could not this question be put in different terms: is the profession of the poet inseparable from that of the versifier? Nowadays it is thought certain that one can be a versifier without being a poet: witness Abbé Delille. A work written in verse, but without episodes, without figures, without movement, without images, would not be the work of a poet. But once there is genius, force, imagination, and variety in prose, that author will be a poet without being a versifier." [85] All through his writings Mercier keeps up the attack: "To decrease the number of versifiers is to promote the glory of true poets." And he adds a long footnote: "Who could help being sorry for all those young people who are lost, engulfed in French versification, getting farther and farther from poetry! . . . Prose belongs to us; its progress is unhindered; all we have to do is to give it a more vivid character. . . . The prose writers are our true poets; let them be bold, and our language will speak with new accents. . . . Let us guarantee to our writers liberty to combine both entirely new expressions and audacious inversions; the result will be a livelier coloring and a greater harmony." [86] For Mercier liberty is a positive value. Freedom from verse is not merely escape from shackles, but a glorious and constructive freedom, which opens up new possibilities for poetry. This is the "liberté dans l'art," which was to be a battle cry of the romantics.

The period from the middle of the eighteenth century to the Revolution is marked by a good deal of incoherence and hesitation in respect to poetry. The general level of mediocrity of the verse written during the period is all too accurately reflected in the poetic theory, which often shows a not unnatural discouragement as to the future of poetry in France. But at the same time there are the beginnings of a remarkable awakening of the *spirit* of poetry. Feeling and emotion are more and more freed from reason and rules, and there is an outpouring of lyric confidences and intimate confessions. Originality and spontaneity are preferred to imitation and taste. The great themes of romantic poetry appear — but in prose rather than in verse. Early in the period the "official" definitions begin to speak of poetry as spirit as well as form. In 1771 the *Dictionnaire de Trévoux* adds to its earlier definition: "Poésie se prend quelquefois pour le feu de la poésie; voilà des vers, mais il n'y a point de poésie." The 1798 *Dictionnaire de l'Académie* also has an addition: "On dit d'un ouvrage en prose qui tient du caractère et de l'élévation poétique qu'il y a de la poésie dans ses idées, dans son style." Even such a traditionalist as Laharpe gradually liberalized his definition of poetry. In one of the earlier volumes of his *Lycée* it is "the language of the imagination, guided by reason and taste." Later on, "Poetry is an art, an art of the spirit, of the ear, of the imagination." [87]

The rebirth of the spirit of poetry is accompanied by a new respect for the poet and his role. Even such a poet as Dorat, who seems to us all that is conventional and artificial, has a vision of a very different kind of poet: "A reasoner, shut up in his study, dictates formal apothegms and thinks that he is delivering oracles: the poet, seized by enthusiasm, paints objects which are dear to all men; he makes our spirit perceive more clearly the great spectacle of the universe, which often escapes our eyes dulled by habit." [88] This is followed by a long passage on the vision of land and sea and mountains in which the poet, with the magic wand of imagination, discovers hidden treasures.

The poet is increasingly freed from the rules of pedants, and may well produce his greatest work in defiance of those rules. As early as 1763 Grimm wrote: "It seems indeed as if genius wanted to make sport of the solemn precepts of criticism, and punish the audacious presumption of an art which dares to dictate laws to nature. No sooner has the learned pedant set up his poetic system on supposedly invariable principles, no sooner has he opened up all possible sources of beauty and laid a curse on all those who would seek it elsewhere, than a man of genius appears, does the contrary of what the critic has ordered, and produces an immortal work." [89] Nature must guide the poet, not art. For Cubières-Palmézeaux poetry is a flower produced spontaneously by nature, and should be left to its own devices; squeezed into a narrow vase, or imprisoned in a hothouse, it fades and withers. The sound of the trumpets of liberty is heard when Cubières-Palmézeaux writes on the eve of the Revolution: "In general everyone detests rules. . . . The spirit of liberty is engraved in every human soul, and nothing has ever been able to destroy it." [90] Here is no longer the somewhat apologetic liberation of a prisoner laden with too heavy chains; as with Mercier, liberty has become a positive and fundamental concept.

So this is a period of discovery of the spirit and matter of lyric poetry. Unfortunately this step was accompanied by a neglect, often a scorn, of poetic form, indicated not only by the attacks on versification, but also by a more general tendency to consider poetic language as well as poetic ideas as the product of a spontaneous and unconscious genius. The neglect of poetic language was also allied with the discouragement that was felt about the state of poetry. If the language of the eighteenth-century poets was the model of "poetic" language, it is not to be wondered at that a less artificial and more spontaneous one seemed highly desirable. Again we see the disastrous effects of the break with the great lyric tradition; the "poetic language" at issue is not the language of Villon, of Ronsard, of Du Bellay, but the language of Jean-Baptiste Rousseau, of Le Brun, of Delille. Early French poetry was little more known or appreciated than it had been during the first half of the century. Ronsard is mentioned more frequently, but the same clichés on his lack of taste are repeated. [91] Occasionally a more favorable judgment is found, as when Joannet, after the usual reservations, assigns to Ronsard "a distinguished place among the lyric poets who are characterized by animation, force and imagination," or Sabatier de Castres calls him a poet "too highly considered in his own time, and too looked down on in ours." [92] Sabatier de Castres has some kind words for other sixteenth-century poets, especially Du Bellay, whom he admires for the softness and harmony of his verse. [93] The *Annales poétiques* has a long section on Ronsard, and high praise of Du Bellay. There is even a section on Scève, but *Délie* comes off badly: "Love poems, which will never be cited as models of taste. The author, who seems to have studied the Italians, had adopted all their faults: false wit, affectation and repetitions make the reading of this work tedious." [94] For most critics Jean-Baptiste Rousseau, though his prestige was somewhat undermined, remained the great French poet. Joannet exclaims, "Quelle sublimité de génie!"; André Sabatier writes a vehement "Lettre sur le grand Rousseau, ou Réponse aux observations de M. de Vauvenargues sur ce poète"; and Sabatier de Castres proclaims that "as long as the conception of beautiful poetry and a taste for true beauty exists among us Rousseau will be considered the most amazing genius our nation ever produced." [95]

It was inevitable that with this neglect of poetic form the failure to perceive the intimate relation between matter and form should continue. Delille says: "In every poetic work there are two kinds of interest, that of the subject and that of the form." For him, style is an ornament which makes up for a lack of dramatic or emotional interest in the subject; "This interest must be added by the most carefully chosen details, and by the charms of the most brilliant and pure style." [96] Images too remain poetic embellishments, although there is an occasional hint of a closer relation between image and meaning which has something secret and mysterious about it. But any obscurity in poetry is frowned upon. Marmontel claims that the first quality of poetry is clarity: "No one is so foolish as to write with the purpose of not being understood; but the intention of being understood is sacrificed to a desire to appear subtle, refined, mysterious, profound. . . . It is not enough to write *for oneself and for the Muses*." [97] Later Marmontel heaps scorn on the poet whose aim is to dream and to describe his dream; a volume of dreams could not possibly be interesting. This is far indeed from any conception of poetry as suggestion, and one realizes afresh how far Diderot was in advance of his times. Only Voltaire saw the poetic value of concision and density, first in the letter to Frederick the Great quoted in my first chapter, and later in the *Dictionnaire philosophique*: "Un mérite de la poésie dont bien des gens ne se doutent pas, c'est qu'elle dit plus que la prose, et en moins de paroles que la prose." [98] But it was to be many years before this idea took root, and in the meantime torrents of poetic eloquence were to roll by.

During this period the reaction against the narrow doctrines of imitation and of taste, against reason and rules, acquired new momentum in most European countries. The old "belle nature" is replaced by a larger conception of both external nature and human nature. Reason gives way to inspiration, genius, and sentiment. Originality, sincerity, and spontaneity are prized above technique. But in France all these ideas emerge slowly, with the millstone of tradition weighing them down and poetry itself lagging far behind. Still, at the end of the period, a new conception of poetry is apparent. The earlier period had grounded poetry in form; the later one saw it above all as spirit. But in both the relation of form and content is little considered. The antagonism between them drives poetry into prose, so that the authentic ancestors of the romantic poets are prose writers. The reconciliation of matter and form was to be the gradual achievement of the nineteenth century, but a long road still lay ahead.

Aᴛ its close the eighteenth century finally produced one poet worthy of the name, André Chénier. His poetry was not published until 1819, and most of his prose later, but by right of birth he belongs to the eighteenth century. To turn from the poetry of his predecessors to that of Chénier is to find depth and sincerity of feeling, a poetic vision that reaches out into time and space, a sense of plastic and musical form and beauty, a power of renewing old themes and finding new ones. Yet in spite of the "romantic" elements stressed by earlier critics Chénier was firmly rooted in his own century. Sainte-Beuve's judgment remains valid: "Chénier est le révélateur d'une poésie d'avenir, et il apporte au monde une lyre nouvelle; mais il y a chez lui des cordes qui manquent encore." [1] At times his style and phrasing seem unsuited to the subject, and even in some of his best poems lines of true and spontaneous emotion, pure and natural language, are allied with lines in which the emotion is stifled by traditional and conventional phraseology. One of the best examples is the first stanza of *La Jeune Captive*:

> L'épi naissant mûrit de la faux respecté;
> Sans crainte du pressoir, le pampre tout l'été
>   Boit les doux présents de l'aurore;
> Et moi, comme lui belle, et jeune comme lui,
> Quoi que l'heure présente ait de trouble et d'ennui,
>   Je ne veux point mourir encore.

In the first three lines the somewhat banal images placed in the mouth of the "Jeune Captive," the slightly pompous tone, the periphrase of the third line contrast unhappily with the moving simplicity and harmony of the last three lines.

There is often an effect of mosaic, or, more unkindly, of

patchwork, which comes from too frequent reminiscence, a lack of spontaneity, a sense of effort. What Chénier says in one of his *Epîtres* on his method of composition is reflected in his poetry:

> Tantôt chez un auteur j'adopte une pensée
> Mais qui revêt, chez moi souvent entrelacée,
> Mes images, mes tours, jeune et frais ornement;
> Tantôt je ne retiens que les mots seulement;
> J'en détourne le sens, et l'art sait les contraindre
> Vers des objets nouveaux qu'ils s'étonnent de peindre.
> La prose souvent vient subir d'autres lois,
> Et se transforme, et fuit mes poétiques doigts;
> De rimes couronnée, et légère et dansante,
> En nombres mesurés elle s'agite et chante.[2]

It is a conscious, deliberate method of composition, requiring long labor. Chénier's manuscripts are full of isolated lines and phrases stowed away for later use, sometimes under such headings as "Notes pour l'expression de sentiments variés." What he too often lacks is the force and intensity of imagination which in greater poets fuses equally disparate elements into a harmonious and perfect whole.[3] Chénier's enthusiasm, in spite of occasional bold flights, is all in all the "enthousiasme raisonnable" of his century. He reaches his greatest heights, to my mind, not when the old and the new are painstakingly joined together, but when the old is re-experienced and re-expressed, as in *La Jeune Tarentine* or *L'Aveugle*, or when the poet is carried away by the power of strong emotion, as in the beautiful "Salut, ô belle nuit" passage of *L'Amérique*, or the great *Odes* and *Iambes*.

Chénier's poetry was practically unknown until 1819, and until then the stream of poetry flows on undisturbed from the eighteenth century. The years between the political revolution and the literary one are particularly sterile. Again it is not quantity of poetry that is lacking. Even if one leaves out of account the plethora of official verse that celebrated the glories of Napoleon and later the return of the Bourbons, of so-called lyric poetry there is God's plenty.[4] Fontaines, Loyson, the numerous poetesses of whom Madame Desbordes-Valmore is the only one undeserving of oblivion, Chênedollé, Millevoye, to mention only a few, poured out their newly discovered emotions in verse that is all too reminiscent of the eighteenth century. Collenot is said to have foretold to the child Millevoye, "Oui, vous serez un jour un Delille," and the prophecy was not unfulfilled.[5] The old verse, the old style and vocabulary are perhaps stretched a little by a fuller content, but the waters of poetry still flow sedately within well-defined bounds. These poets talk of a bold and lofty poetry:

> Auteur, qui que tu sois, dans ton élan rapide,
> Brûles-tu de voler à l'immortalité,
> Fuis la froide Raison, prends l'audace pour guide;
> Trace, à pas de géant, un cercle illimité.[6]

But their own verse remains timid, with only occasional attempts at a more precise and picturesque vocabulary, as when *crocus* and *hépatique* jostle "les riantes tribus de Flore" in the same poem.[7] And they slip all too easily into prose, as at the end of this stanza of Chênedollé:

> J'ai vu de la moisson superbe
> Le soleil couronner la fin;
> Joyeuse, à la dernière gerbe
> La grange vient d'ouvrir son sein.
> Là, dans une enceinte profonde,
> Repose le riche froment
> Qui, pour deux ans, assure au monde
> Un intarissable aliment.[8]

The most personal poems are those of Millevoye, such as *La Chute des feuilles* and *Le Poète mourant*, which form a link between Gilbert and Lamartine. But Millevoye too is pale and timid.

There is no question that, as Madame de Staël was among the first to point out, the true poetry craved by the "âmes sensibles" was to be found in the prose of Rousseau, Bernardin de Saint-Pierre, and Chateaubriand.[9] It is curious to note that both Rousseau and Chateaubriand had made early attempts at verse. The former says in his *Confessions*: "From time to time I have composed some mediocre verses; it is a fairly good exercise for forming the habit of elegant inversions and learning to write better in prose; but I never found enough charm in French poetry to give myself up to it completely." [10] Chateaubriand, contrary to the usual practice, used his verse as a source for his prose; he says that the reader will find in his early poetic efforts descriptions which he later transferred to his prose.[11]

The most interesting ideas on poetry during this period are those of Chénier, Joubert, and Madame de Staël. Those of the first two were not published until many years after they were composed; Chénier's poems and the introduction to the *Essai* in 1819, a selection of Joubert's *Pensées* in 1838. Both were circulated in manuscript earlier, but only among a few privileged souls. And Madame de Staël's important discussions of poetry are to be found in *De l'Allemagne*, close to the end of the period with which we are dealing.

Chénier's ideas on poetry are developed in the fragmentary prose *Essai sur les causes et les effets de la perfection et de la décadence des lettres et des arts*, and also in *L'Invention* and other poems.[12] In reading the *Essai* one finds its climate different from that of much of the poetic doctrine of Chénier's time. It is not that Chénier is detached from the general movement of his century; all his thinking on philosophy, science, civilization, politics, is proof to the contrary. In this very essay he names as the great masters of his thought, along with Montaigne, Montesquieu and Rousseau. But it is the Rousseau of the *Discours* and the *Contrat social* rather than the Rousseau of the *Confessions* and the *Rêveries d'un promeneur solitaire*. Chénier's debt is to the general philosophy of the eighteenth century rather than to its aesthetics.

The point of departure of the *Essai* is the decadence of literature and the arts in modern times, and the causes, economic, social, and political, which help or hinder their progress. The arts can develop only in a democracy, free from the harmful influences of courts, salons, literary associations, as well as from the domination of an inferior literature. Hence the pre-eminence of the Greeks and the failure of the moderns, particularly the French. But although Chénier looks back nostalgically to the Greeks, "nés pour les beaux-arts plus que nul peuple du monde," and finds nothing to compare with them in the literatures so popular at the moment — "la plupart de ces poètes du Nord, surtout Anglais, se tourmentent toujours et en toute occasion" — he believes that a revival of poetry is possible. It must come through a revival of mankind, a rediscovery of "those great impulses of the soul which alone make the invention of sublime forms of expression possible." [13] From these premises Chénier goes on to develop his doctrines of *naïveté* and of "l'imitation inventrice," to which we shall return later.

Chénier's doctrine owes much to Le Brun in its emphasis on technique, on the imitation of nature and of the ancients, and on the independence of the poet. And his admiration for Malherbe must not be forgotten. But one is reminded even more frequently of the manifestoes of the Pléiade; there is the same intention of restoring poetry to the high place it had occupied in ancient times, of exalting the poet as prophet and interpreter of nature; the same conception of a liberal imitation of the great poets of antiquity; the same insistence that nature must be seconded by art. And as had been the case with the Pléiade, the potential danger of the doctrine lies in the opportunity it gives for overstressing imitation and subordinating originality. Yet in Chénier's doctrine there is at the same time a belief in emotion as the fountainhead of poetry, a constant plea for naturalness and spontaneity. He never succeeded, it seems to me, in fully reconciling these two conceptions, and this is the chief weakness of his theory as well as of his poetry.

In the early years of the nineteenth century the most perceptive thoughts about poetry are found in Joubert's *Carnets*. In the long period (1774–1824) during which Joubert jotted down in his beautiful handwriting, in a long series of tiny notebooks, his thoughts on all sorts of subjects, an interest in poetry appears very early, and Diderot's influence is obvious. But it is in the years around 1800 and immediately after, that the *Carnets* are especially rich in ideas about poetry and imagination. Aside from Diderot's influence it is to his own reading of the poets and his special love for La Fontaine, "l'Homère des Français," [14] that Joubert's idea of poetry owes most. For him poetry is a special language by means of which the poet etherealizes and lightens the images supplied by the imagination, and expresses them in concise and perfect form. He reached, I believe, a more valid conception of poetry than the somewhat vague and hazy one of many of the romantics who followed him. On the other hand, to see in him even a remote ancestor of the symbolists [15] seems to me to misread his meaning, to forget that he found in La Fontaine the exemplification of his ideal. Joubert is not dreaming of a poetry of obscurity and mystery; he is cherishing a poetry of clarity and harmony.

The poetic theory of both Chénier and Joubert is rooted in their reading of the great poets of the past, for Chénier the Greeks and Latins, for Joubert above all La Fontaine. The core of their doctrines is an enlightened classicism, a conception of poetry corresponding to an ideal long since attained. With Madame de Staël and *De l'Allemagne* the idea of a poetry different from that of the "great tradition" comes to the fore. In her earlier work, *De la littérature*, Madame de Staël's ideas are still those of the eighteenth century — and not always its most admirable ones. "Of all the arts poetry is the one that is most closely allied to reason." She is a very

Cassandra on the future of poetry: "The poetry of imagination will make no further progress in France: philosophical ideas or passionate sentiments will be put into verse; but in our century the human mind has reached a stage of development which no longer allows either illusions or the enthusiasm which creates pictures and fables destined to make an impression on our minds." [16] But Madame de Staël's contact with German romanticism produced in *De l'Allemagne* the conception of a poetry fraught with emotion, enthusiasm, and imagery, possessed of a mysterious, even mystical quality.

The other great forerunner of romanticism, the inspirer of so many poets, the popularizer of so many poetic themes, Chateaubriand, has curiously little to say about anything except the subject matter of poetry. What he does say is usually an old story: "*Divertir* afin *d'enseigner* est la première qualité de la poésie"; "Le *beau idéal* [est] l'art *de choisir et de cacher*." [17] But behind these clichés there is a poetic attitude towards nature the influence of which was to be enormous. Chateaubriand practiced this more than he preached it; he did however spell it out very clearly in regard to painting in his early "Lettre sur l'art du dessin dans les paysages" (1795): "The painter who depicts human nature must concern himself with the study of the passions; if one does not know man's heart, one cannot really know his face. A landscape, like a portrait, has its spiritual and intellectual side; it too must be expressed; one must experience by means of the material execution the reveries or the sentiments which different sites inspire." [18] The passage anticipates Amiel's "un paysage est un état d'âme," indicating a feeling for nature that the earlier descriptive poetry had so sadly lacked, and that was to reach poetry through the prose writers.

Between 1813 and 1820 the great debates between romanticists and classicists get under way. Most of these, however, are focused on drama, and only occasionally, with A. W. Schlegel and Sismondi and a few lesser writers, are the new principles applied specifically to poetry. During the same period we can trace the first beginnings of the impact on poetry of the illuminist tradition, which was to play so large a part in poetic theory later in the century.

The discouragement about poetry felt in the previous period is still evident. Chénier takes up the tale: "Of all the nations of Europe, the French are those who care least about poetry and know least about it." [19] Madame de Staël is almost equally pessimistic: "The difficulties of language and versification in French are almost always opposed to the free play of enthusiasm." [20] And Sismondi comments: "Of all nations the French is the only one which asks for the reason for everything in poetry; of all peoples they perhaps know best how to go straight to their objective; therefore they always want to have one, whereas other peoples consider it the essence of the fine arts not to have a precise goal, to abandon oneself to an inner spontaneous impulse, and to seek for poetry in inspiration alone." [21]

The only hope for poetry is seen in a stirring and deepening of human emotions. Chénier, starting from the statement that *Homo sum* is the principle and aim of all art, insists on the role of *naïveté*, which alone can produce lively and deep feeling. In his *Epilogue* comes the line which could be the motto of so much romantic poetry: "L'art ne fait que des vers; le cœur seul est poète." For Chénier emotion and enthusiasm are sisters:

> Aimer, sentir, c'est là cette ivresse vantée
> Qu'aux célestes foyers déroba Prométhée.[22]

Joubert too writes of the necessity of emotion and inspiration: "The intelligence has no part in true poetry, which comes from the soul alone. It comes during moments of revery, and by no efforts can it be found by reflection. It is a gift of heaven, which has blessed us with it!" But Joubert does not reject the cooperation of the intelligence completely, for he goes on: "However the intelligence prepares the way by presenting objects to the soul. Reflection, which unearths them as it were, is helpful for the same reason." [23] But for Joubert there is no poetry without enthusiasm.

In *De l'Allemagne* the glorification of sentiment reaches its height: "La première condition pour écrire, c'est une manière de sentir vive et forte." Madame de Staël introduces the idea so common with the romantics, that sentiment is in itself poetry, the poetry of the heart. "The gift of revealing in words what one feels in the depths of one's heart is rare indeed; yet there is poetry in all men capable of lively and deep affections; its expression is lacking in the case of those who have not practiced it. The poet does nothing but liberate, so to speak, the feeling imprisoned in the depths of the soul; poetic genius is an inner inclination, of the same sort as that which makes one capable of a noble sacrifice; to write a beautiful ode is to dream of heroism." Again emotion is closely allied with enthusiasm, which Madame de Staël describes as "love of beauty, elevation of soul, delight in devotion, united in a single feeling of greatness and of calm." [24]

This opening of the floodgates of emotion and its association, and often confusion, with enthusiasm are the most important features of poetic theory at this time. Enthusiasm can no longer be provoked; it can only be wistfully awaited, as when Chênedollé writes one autumn day: "The days of inspiration are arriving, this is the season of poetry and of meditation. Will they produce anything? Will this most poetic of seasons be sterile? Is the time of inspiration past for me? O poetry, beautiful as love and sweet as hope, hast thou fled from me forever?" [25] More and more, in spite of all efforts to restrain it, emotion takes over the chief role in poetry, although the expression of it often seems to us far from spontaneous. But Joubert, like Diderot, warns the poet not to compose under the immediate stress of feeling: "One should write what one feels only after a long period of tranquillity in the soul. One must not express oneself as one feels, but as one remembers." [26]

As a result of this predominance of emotion, imagination is often pushed into the background. Chénier does say that a penetrating and lively imagination (in the sense of image-making) is essential for the poet. But for him the activity of the imagination was circumscribed on two counts. First of all, his doctrine of "l'imitation inventrice" meant that the poet does not follow untrodden paths but continues in the road indicated by the great writers of the past, "tastes them, savors them, digests them, so that their sap becomes his substance." [27]

> Et sans suivre leurs pas imiter leur exemple,
> Faire, en s'éloignant d'eux, avec un soin jaloux,
> Ce qu'eux-même ils feraient s'ils vivaient parmi nous! [28]

Imagination is also limited for Chénier (and this was also the case with the early romantic poets) by his stress on fidelity to truth, naturalness, *naïveté*: "In the arts it is not enough never to deviate grossly from the truth; one must be truthful with force and precision, that is to say *naïf*." [29]

> Mais inventer n'est pas, en un brusque abandon,
> Blesser la vérité, le bon sens, la raison.

Chénier rejects all

> Délires insensés! fantômes monstrueux!
> Et d'un cerveau malsain rêves tumultueux!

On the contrary "dans les arts l'inventeur est celui / Qui peint ce que chacun put sentir comme lui." [30] Yet this sobriety is counterbalanced by the lofty flights in which Chénier glorifies the poet-creator: "He is true, sure, infallible as nature; he creates, he imitates the work of God. . . . Everything in nature inspires him and makes him dream: all nature belongs to him. . . . He sees everything, feels everything, paints everything . . . he creates a world." [31]

For Joubert the nature of the imagination was a constant

problem. In 1796 he notes that "imagination is the eye of the soul," and then, almost in the same breath: "Reason. Imagination is her tirewoman." Then he sees in imagination a kind of memory of colors and forms.[32] But also "memory is a storehouse on which imagination draws." Then there is the idea of imagination as "the faculty of giving body and form to that which has none. Imagination is a painter. It paints within our soul and outside it to the souls of other men. It clothes ideas in images." And finally "imagination is active, creative." [33] All these jottings are reminiscent of ideas which Diderot had expressed more fully.

Certain passages however might lead one to think that Joubert was at least groping toward a more mysterious conception, that of the imagination which perceives the *correspondances* between the visible and the invisible, the natural and the supernatural. "Genius is the aptitude for perceiving things invisible, for touching things intangible, for painting things which have no features." The Baudelairian tone is even more marked in a passage written in 1815: "Imagination at its best is the knowledge of things invisible, the faculty of picturing them to oneself." I believe however that one should be cautious in ascribing to Joubert all that Baudelaire meant by imagination, especially in view of a passage written in 1816: "To picture to oneself and to reproduce to others, in a form which it does not possess but which makes it perceptible, the abstract or invisible — that is imagination." [34] Does the invisible mean for Joubert the hidden mysteries of the universe, or merely what cannot be perceived by the senses because it is an abstraction? The question is a difficult one, and Joubert never makes the point entirely clear. I should say that for him imagination is above all the power of retaining images and of using these images to translate the abstract into the concrete, but that at times he had at least an inkling of its power of discovering the analogies between the natural and the supernatural.

In the early nineteenth century there are several long poems, most probably inspired by Delille's *L'Imagination*, on the subject of poetic invention and imagination. It is amusing to note that the very poets in whose work emotion was becoming less and less restrained put a leash on imagination and imaginative language. Millevoye's *L'Invention poétique* [35] has a long apostrophe to invention, followed by counsels of prudence:

> Il est nuit: je suis seul, du silence entouré,
> Et du besoin des vers je me sens dévoré.
> Viens, talent créateur, noble enfant du génie!
> Embrase de tes feux ma féconde insomnie.
> Invention! O toi, sans qui les plus beaux vers
> Meurent comme un vain son dans le vague des airs,
> C'est pour te célébrer que ma bouche t'implore!
> . . . .
> L'abus des beautés même enfante la langueur;
> C'est la sobriété qui nourrit la vigueur.
> N'allez point adopter l'effronté barbarisme,
> Ni l'absurde jargon du froid néologisme;
> N'allez point, au mépris du bon sens et de l'art,
> Accorder votre lyre aux pipeaux de Ronsard.

Chênedollé's section on imagination in *Le Génie de l'homme* is suggestive both of Rivarol, who is mentioned in a footnote, and of Chénier, whose poems Chênedollé knew in manuscript:

> L'Imagination, rapide messagère,
> Effleure les objets dans sa course légère,
> Et bientôt rassemble tous ces tableaux divers,
> Dans les plis du cerveau reproduit l'univers.
> Elle fait plus: souvent sa puissante énergie,
> Au monde extérieur opposant sa magie,
> Dans un monde inconnu cherche à se maintenir,
> Se dérobe au présent, et vit dans l'avenir.
> . . . .
> Pouvoir incorruptible, immortel Jugement,
> Viens donc et ralentir et diriger sa flamme,
> Et, sage conducteur, prends les rênes de l'âme.[36]

The first important prose work devoted to the imagination

came from Switzerland, from a member of Madame de Staël's circle, Bonstetten. What he says is often close to earlier treatments: "l'imagination crée, invente; l'intelligence dispose, ordonne." He also has a great deal to say about the imagination as expressing relationships between sensibility and the images the five senses present to it: "La vérité de l'imagination est dans le *rapport des idées avec la sensibilité matrice*; c'est une vérité intérieure et pour ainsi dire poétique." [37] Madame de Staël herself mentions imagination frequently, but usually in rather vague terms. In her early works it is a faculty necessary to human happiness, and seems to be not so much creation as an incoherent mixture drawn from the very nature from which we would escape.[38] In *De l'Allemagne* it is "this eminent faculty of thought, which soars and is lost in vagueness, penetrates and disappears into the depths, annihilates itself by its impartiality, confounds itself by analysis, and finally lacks certain defects which might circumscribe its virtues." Madame de Staël is undisturbed by the possibility of a conflict between truth and imagination: "Imagination, far from being an enemy of truth, makes it stand out as no other faculty does." [39] All this is somewhat woolly, and there is no evidence that Madame de Staël was very seriously concerned with either the nature or the function of imagination. She does however refer to it more than once as "creative."

On the whole, imagination, glorified by Diderot as the chief faculty of the poet, tends to lose its precision and importance during this period. It is often mentioned, rarely defined. Soumet suggested that this timidity in the domain of the imagination is characteristic of the French, who tend to prefer faithful imitations to idealized visions.[40] This is certainly true in many instances, but I believe that in many others the neglect of imagination is due rather to the growing belief that poetry is above all a product of emotion.

Like imagination, poetic imagery is frequently mentioned,

but much of what is said is already familiar. As late as 1817 François de Neufchâteau, in a long poem, *Les Tropes*, turned Du Marsais into verse, in order, he says in his preface, to give the work a less forbidding aspect:

> . . j'ose le premier, sur le Pinde français,
> Essayer d'être en vers l'écho de Du Marsais.

On the whole he follows Du Marsais with painful fidelity, thus producing such lines as, "O que de l'Hyperbole il faut se défier!" and "Le goût de l'Euphémisme est le vrai goût français." One does not wonder that he says at one point:

> Je sens que la carrière, à fournir difficile,
> Fait souvent régimber mon Pégase indocile.

He does make an occasional addition to Du Marsais, especially in a passage which develops Rivarol's ideas on the poet and the savage:

> Il est des orateurs jusqu'à chez les sauvages:
> Allons du Saint-Laurent visiter les rivages;
> Du grand Meschacebé suivons le vaste cours;
> Là, d'un fils du désert écoutons le discours:
> Chaque mot nous étonne; il charge sa peinture
> D'images, qu'il dérobe à toute la nature,
> Et qui vont émouvoir, au fond de leurs roseaux,
> Ces fleuves qui, pour lui, sont les pères des eaux.

François de Neufchâteau insists that images must be clear and understandable:

> Mais tout symbole pris d'une chose connue,
> Doit avoir sa valeur d'avance convenue:
> Car l'œil du spectateur est bientôt détaché
> De tout hiéroglyphe obscur ou recherché.
> La clarté! la clarté! c'est la règle première.

Still he feels that Voltaire's proscriptions are too strong:

> Les Tropes, à son gré, doivent être proscrits,
> Lorsqu'on ne peut les peindre ainsi qu'ils sont écrits
> . . . .
> Non, la plume n'est pas l'esclave du pinceau.[41]

At one point Madame de Staël puts imagery on an equal footing with sentiment: "Modern poetry is made up of images and of sentiments. In the first respect, it belongs to the imitation of nature; in the second, to the eloquence of the passions." [42] The passage is a good indication of the constant conflict between poetry as imitation and poetry as emotion, and the resulting tendency to split poetry into two parts, emotion which is spontaneous and imagery which embellishes the emotion. Millevoye recalls the advice that Parny had given him: "Poetry is becoming worn out; it must be rejuvenated by new images." [43]

On the question of allegory opinion is divided. Madame de Staël, in her *Essai sur les fictions*, has harsh words for it. Allegories "debilitate thought . . . the need for images in order to grasp ideas indicates an intellectual weakness in the reader." [44] But many writers are still favorably inclined towards allegory, which is for Chénier the language of the spirit: "Poetry gives body and countenance to all the vices, virtues, and passions." [45] And Fabre d'Olivet maintains that "the essence or the spirit of poetry . . . is none other than the allegorical genius, the immediate product of inspiration." [46]

In rare cases only is a close relation between thought and image conceived. Bonstetten says that "in poetry comparisons, metaphors, and allegories embrace two series of ideas *perceived in a unique harmony* called *unity*." [47] And François de Neufchâteau writes in *Les Tropes*:

> L'Imagination libre se promène
> Dans les deux infinis qui forment son domaine;
> Elle peut combiner, en ses pensers rêveurs,
> Les bruits, les mouvements, les parfums, les saveurs;
> La nuit même ne peut lui cacher la nature.
> Voilà ce que jamais n'atteindra la peinture!
> Ce qui n'est pas visible avec elle est perdu,
> Et le monde invisible est le plus étendu. [48]

On the moot question of the "reversed" image Joubert asserts that "the most defective comparisons are those in which outward objects are compared to man, bodies to the soul, instead of comparing souls to bodies and man to external things. For example, when a tossing sea is compared to a troubled heart, whiteness to innocence, the roar of thunder to the tempests of the soul. Man exists, possesses himself, has a perpetual self-awareness. All these comparisons teach him nothing, and confine and contract instead of expanding. . . . Our illustrious Chateaubriand sometimes makes this mistake." [49] Here Joubert is undoubtedly thinking of the famous image in *René*: "Quelquefois une haute colonne se montrait seule debout dans un désert, comme une grande pensée s'élève par intervalles dans une âme que le temps et le malheur ont dévastée." [50] On the question of imagery, soon to become of central importance, these years have little to offer.

Likewise the neglect of poetic language noted in the previous period continues, with only Chénier and Joubert much concerned with the question. As earlier, there is a general tendency to believe that language comes to the poet naturally and spontaneously, with no effort on his part. At times this is also Chénier's position. While the mere rhymer struggles with language,

> Celui qu'un vrai démon presse, enflamme, domine,
> Ignore un tel supplice: il pense, il imagine;
> Un langage imprévu, dans son âme produit,
> Naît avec sa pensée, et l'embrasse et la suit;
> Les images, les mots que le génie inspire,
> Où l'univers entier vit, se meut et respire,
> Source vaste et sublime et qu'on ne peut tarir,
> En foule en son cerveau se hâtent de courir.[51]

In the *Essai* Chénier condemns the poets who are "incapable of experiencing those great impulses of the soul which alone lead to the invention of sublime expressions, to the perception of the numerous relationships in nature which strike a sensitive imagination and inspire it with that glowing metaphorical language which gives life to everything, and by which objects

illuminate one another." [52] But Chénier also advises the poet
to borrow the language of the great poets of the past, as in the
well known lines:

> Changeons en notre miel leurs plus antiques fleurs;
> Pour peindre notre idée, empruntons leurs couleurs;
> Allumons nos flambeaux à leurs feux poétiques;
> Sur des pensers nouveaux faisons des vers antiques.[53]

This vacillation between natural language and a language
imitated from the ancients is yet another example of the un-
resolved conflict in Chénier's poetic theory.

For Joubert the special mark of poetry seems to be "trans-
parency, translucence, lack of solidity, magic; the imitation
of the divine which created all things out of so little and, so
to speak, out of nothing." Poetry is variously described in
terms of air, of color, of light, of nectar and ambrosia, of
perfume, of music, "la musique de l'âme." All this might seem
somewhat vague, foreshadowing many romantic pronouncements on poetry which echo one of Joubert's best known
sayings: "Les beaux vers sont ceux qui s'exhalent comme des
sons ou des parfums." What distinguishes Joubert from most
of the romantics, however, is his insistence that poetry is not
only an "état d'âme," but words:

> Imagine a spiritual power which softens everything that is harsh in
> words, makes everything clear that is obscure, and colors everything
> that is somber.
> With his breath the poet puts air into words, makes them light and
> gives them color: a tincture, a potion, like the nectar by which the
> bee changes the pollen of flowers into honey.
> Make words take wing.[54]

One is reminded of what Diderot had said in the *Lettre sur
les sourds et muets*: "Il passe alors dans le discours du poète
un esprit qui en meut et vivifie toutes les syllabes." The poet,
for Diderot the creator of "un tissu d'hiéroglyphes," is for
Joubert a magician who with a wave of his wand builds out
of words a fairylike and ethereal structure. It is by his handling

of words that the poet proves himself, by his ability to make the common word beautiful, the worn-out word new, to restore to the words whose images, as Diderot had said, have been effaced by usage, their pristine freshness.

When, after much groping, Joubert finds his definition of poetry, he writes to Molé on March 10, 1805: "Il me semble que je sais très bien maintenant ce que c'est que la poésie, le poète et la versification: *architecture de mots*." [55] The poet can by his labor make any material poetic. At this point Joubert is far from any theory of pure inspiration. Poetry is a conscious construction, the work of an architect, of an artist. Yet the finished work is no solid structure, but light as air, aglow with color and light. "Poésie proprement dite, c'est-à-dire celle qui est tout par elle-même. En n'opérant que sur une matière fantastique et sur ses propres créations." [56] Here Joubert seems very close to the modern doctrine of pure poetry. Yet it is above all La Fontaine who exemplifies his poetic ideal. In any case, his great originality, at a time when poetry was more and more being conceived as an overflow of emotion, was his realization that poetry is first of all language.

Joubert also stresses a quality of poetic language which is not mentioned by Diderot before him nor by the romantics after him: concision. In 1797 he writes: "Concise like a poet. Poetic concision. — The character of the poet is to be brief, that is to say perfect, *absolutus*, as the Latins said. That of the orator is to be flowing, abundant, spacious, wide-spread, varied, inexhaustible, immense." The adjectives applied to the orator seem to the modern reader to characterize admirably the French romantic poetry to come. Joubert goes back to the same distinction later, at the time when he was thinking most about poetry: "In eloquence elocution rolls its waves as rivers do. But in poetry there is more art. Fountains, cascades, lakes, arrangements of words of all kinds are disposed carefully." [57]

Though to some extent implicit in what Joubert says, the idea of the suggestive power of language is rarely mentioned.

Emotion is poured out into poetry freely and effusively, without choice or constraint. Chênedollé, although his practice of poetry seems far from his theory in this case, does have one interesting remark on the subject: "Poetry must always paint, and even, in its light-footed progress, it must perceive more than it paints. Often it must suggest more than it shows, and leave to the imagination, once it has been alerted, the task of filling in the picture." [58] Here is at least an adumbration of the poetry of suggestion.

The controversy between the partisans of verse and of prose goes on. In *De l'Allemagne* Madame de Staël praises the art of versification, "a remarkable art, the study of which is inexhaustible: words which, in the ordinary circumstances of life, serve only as signs of thoughts, reach our souls by the rhythm of harmonious sounds, and give us a double enjoyment, which arises from the union of sensation and reflection." But she maintains that in France versification is a despot. "In France our greatest lyric poets are perhaps our great prose writers, Bossuet, Pascal, Fénelon, Buffon, Jean-Jacques, etc. Often the despotism of alexandrines forces us not to put into verse what would nevertheless be true poetry; while in foreign countries, where versification is much more easy and natural, all poetic thoughts inspire verses." [59] One of the greatest of the prose poets, Chateaubriand, makes a strong defense of the primacy of verse: "I am not one of those barbarians who confuse prose and verse. Whatever people may say, the poet is above all other men, and whole volumes of descriptive prose are not worth fifty beautiful lines of Homer, Virgil, or Racine." [60]

Above all the inflexibility of rhyme is criticized. Fabre d'Olivet says: "Wherever rhyme is part of poetic form, it will make this form inflexible, and will absorb all the efforts of talent and make those of intellectual inspiration futile. Never will the people that rhymes its verses attain perfection in poetry." [61] Whether it is a question of versification or of language, the attacks on the rules become increasingly violent, particularly on the part of Mercier and Cubières-Palmézeaux.[62] And Madame de Staël says, though with more restraint: "While Boileau perfected taste and language, it cannot be denied that he gave to the French mind an orientation far from favorable to poetry." [63] All that is needed is to write from the heart. Cubières-Palmézeaux advises:

> Livrez-vous donc, amis, j'en ai l'expérience,
> A ce noble abandon qui vous fait tout oser
> Et croyez que sentir est l'art de composer.

To Boileau's "Vingt fois sur le métier remettez votre ouvrage" he opposes several illustrious, though questionable, examples: "Voltaire, *en quinze jours*, a composé Zaïre"; "J'ai connu Diderot, il ne corrigeait rien." [64] For Madame de Staël language presents no difficulty for the true poet, who "conceives, so to speak, his whole poem at a single moment in the depths of his soul." [65]

During this period one can discover the beginnings of an influence which was to be very great on later poetry, that of the illuminist and occult traditions of the eighteenth century. I shall recall only very briefly this curious recrudescence of religion, with such leaders as Martines de Pasqually, Swedenborg, and Saint-Martin, and such popularizers as Cazotte, Cagliostro, Mesmer, and Rétif de la Bretonne.[66] In the leaders of the movement what is particularly significant for the future of poetry is the belief in a contact with the invisible and celestial world, of which this world is but an allegory. The words allegory, analogy, emblem, type, image (used in a spiritual, not an aesthetic sense) recur constantly. These movements were strong in the latter part of the eighteenth century, and it is quite possible that the references to the role of analogy quoted in the preceding chapter derive, directly or indirectly, from these ideas which were so much in the air. After the

Revolution illuminism and occultism went underground, but were revived towards 1810, particularly by the émigrés who had come in contact with them in Germany. Among their most notable disciples were Madame de Staël and Joseph de Maistre.

De Maistre deserves mention as an interesting example of illuminism in the bosom of orthodox Catholicism, and above all as one of the many sources of Baudelaire's interest in illuminism.[67] He writes, for example: "The physical world is but an image, or, if you will, a repetition of the spiritual world." [68] But his literary influence was slight in his own time, and far more important is the penetration of illuminist ideas into Madame de Staël's thought in the early years of the nineteenth century. A letter of Bonstetten says: "Nothing could be more changed than Coppet . . . all these people are going to become Catholics, Boehmists, Martinists, mystics, and all this thanks to Schlegel. . . . When Madame de Staël goes out for a drive alone, she reads the works of the mystics!" [69] Later Dussault, in one of his articles on De l'Allemagne accuses Madame de Staël of concealing under her doctrine of enthusiasm all the reveries of illuminism, Martinism, and magnetism, all the visions of alchemy, all the pretensions of white magic.[70] One of the chapters of De l'Allemagne is entitled "Des philosophes religieux appelés théosophes." There is a summary of the beliefs of the mystics, who "see in man the epitome of the world, and in the world the emblem of Christian dogmas." Later comes the term correspondance: "Not only does nature repeat herself, but she seems to wish to imitate the works of men, and thus to give them a special token of her correspondence with them." All this is mere repetition of the mystics she had been reading, but she then takes an important step in connecting these doctrines with poetry: "In order to conceive the true greatness of lyric poetry, one must wander by revery in ethereal regions, forget the noise of earth in listening to celestial harmonies, and consider the entire universe as a symbol of the emotions of the soul." And a little later, foreshadowing

Baudelaire, she sees in the perception of *correspondances* the work of the imagination: "It is this secret alliance of our being with the marvels of the universe which gives to poetry its true greatness. The poet is able to reestablish the unity of the physical world and the moral world: his imagination forms a link between the two." [71]

An interesting connection between Madame de Staël and the romantics is Alexandre Soumet. In 1814, in *Les Scrupules littéraires de Madame la baronne de Staël*, after noting that Madame de Staël had been accused of wanting to revive the dreams of illuminism, he observes that she does not define poetry, but merely describes a state of enchantment.[72] Ten years later, reviewing Baour-Lormian's *Jérusalem délivrée* in the *Muse Française*, and using much of the material of the *Scrupules*, some of it almost verbatim, he adds a new paragraph just after the one referred to. In it he develops more fully than had yet been done the connection between the poet and the symbol:

The poet is essentially the interpreter of nature and of destiny, and poetry has been called the first of the arts only because it explains and completes, so to speak, the work of the Creator. It strips beings of their everyday wrappings, so as to force them to yield to our gaze all the secrets of their marvellous existence. To the eyes of the poet everything is symbolic, and, by a continual interchange of images and comparisons, he seeks to discover traces of that primitive language revealed to man by God Himself, of which our modern tongues are but a faint echo. It is he who finds innocence in the lilies of the field, he who takes the wings of the dove to flee from the injustice of men into solitude, he who divines beneath the different objects that surround him something other than those objects themselves.[73]

Here is the essence of a symbolist theory of poetry. But Soumet's own mediocre poetry was untouched by it, and for the time being it bore no fruit.

A more influential figure was Ballanche.[74] Steeped in the illuminist tradition, he repeats over and over again "tout est symbole," "tout est symbolique," and "l'ordre matériel est un emblème, un hiéroglyphe du Monde spirituel." [75] Fabre d'Olivet too makes the connection with poetry: "Once the poet has received his inspiration, once his soul has been transported into the realm of intelligibles, all the ideas which come to him are universal, and consequently allegorical." [76] But such suggestions are rare, and only slowly did the conception of the symbol, so common in the illuminist writers, make its way into poetry.

Except for Chénier, poetry itself made little progress during this period. And a good deal of poetic theory is hardly more than a passionate plea for the free flow of emotion in poetry, with a resulting neglect of imagination, imagery, and poetic form. It must not be forgotten that there was steady neoclassic resistance to this encroaching tide, but it became increasingly ineffectual.

Yet, in spite of the obvious weaknesses in most of the poetic theory, certain important ideas do emerge. The poet is restored to his high calling; he is no longer earth-bound, but soars into the empyrean:

> Le poète divin, tout esprit, tout pensée,
> Ne sent point dans un corps son âme embarrassée;
> Il va percer le ciel aux murailles d'azur,
> De la terre, des mers, le labyrinthe obscur.[77]

The creative function of the poet is expressed in almost Coleridgean terms by Charles de Villers:

Poetic talent in man is a precious reflection of the omnipotence of his Creator: it is the need we too feel to create, which our limited nature derives from his divine nature: it is the need to escape from the commonplace world which hems us in, which cramps and stifles the best in us; the need to rise up towards eternal beauty and sublimity; the need to find within ourselves and above ourselves an ideal world as pure, as noble, as radiant with light and love as is fitting for the human soul glorified by the idea of Beauty. . . . But what in the Omnipotent Being is a tremendous reality, in man is no more than an ideal imitation, a flight of his intelligence. . . . Man's poetic talent is only a simple form, yet a form made of fire, a white-hot crucible which dissolves into nebulous and ethereal figures the terrestrial objects and figures which are entrusted to it. This is the only mode of creation permitted to man.[78]

The poet is no longer of this world, but above it, dominating and transforming it. According to Madame de Staël, "Fine verses are not poetry. . . . Lyric poetry tells no story, is in no way bound by the limitations of time and space; it soars above nations and centuries; it prolongs that sublime moment during which man rises above the pains and pleasures of life. Amid the marvels of the world he feels himself at once creator and creature." [79]

In these writers we find a new conception of poetic experience. The poet is no longer the mouthpiece of his fellow men, who gives form to ideas and sentiments already familiar to them; he is a voyager in a different and mysterious world, which he recreates in his poetry. This idea recurs in other writers in the early nineteenth century, chiefly those most marked by German influences, who echo the contrast made by A. W. Schlegel: "Ancient poetry and art can be considered as rhythmic laws, so to speak, as the harmonious and regular revelation of the wise and well-ordered legislation of an ideal world. Romantic poetry, on the contrary, is the expression of a mysterious force, ever tending towards a new creation, and bringing forth from the womb of chaos a world of wonders." [80] Joubert refers to the "magic" of poetry,[81] and a little later Nodier writes: "Poetry is wholly enchantment and magic; it requires sensitive and trusting hearts, excitable and credulous minds, a naïveté of ideas and feelings which belong only to unspoilt nature and to primitive societies." [82] The element of mystery, so ponderously eliminated from poetry a century before, begins to creep back into it. Poetry begins to be considered not only as lyric effusion, but as secret and mysterious discovery.

Both these conceptions are concerned almost exclusively with the spirit and matter of poetry, and at no period have questions of poetic form been more neglected. Fabre d'Olivet makes form definitely secondary: "A form, however admirable it may be, passes away and yields to destroying time, whereas the essence of Spirit which animates it, immutable as the Divinity from which it emanates, resists all vicissitudes." [83] The ignorance and neglect of earlier French poetry continues.[84] The only French poet who found the appreciation he deserved was La Fontaine, in whom Joubert found "une plénitude de poésie qu'on ne trouve nulle part dans les autres auteurs français." [85] Those who craved for poetry continued to find their needs satisfied by foreign poetry, often read in translation, which again meant that form was secondary to content.

So the rift between matter and form continues. It is evident in Chénier's doctrine. He does indeed say that "c'est aux pensées de créer le style . . . elles ont leur expression propre que le génie rencontre toujours sans la chercher jamais." [86] But the famous line, too often quoted as if it expressed the whole of Chénier's doctrine, "Sur des pensers nouveaux faisons des vers antiques," indicates an antagonism between content and form which neither Chénier's practice nor his theory resolves. He is fully aware of the problems of both content and form, but he fails to perceive their interdependence. He brings out a wealth of new poetic material, but his unlimited admiration of the ancients leads him to seek his poetic language in them rather than in the nature of his subjects.

Even when lip service is paid to the unity of matter and form it is with the assumption that poetic inspiration will naturally and inevitably find its perfect expression. Thus Schlegel writes: "Ce qui est surtout nécessaire pour qu'un ouvrage soit poétique dans son essence, c'est qu'il soit produit d'un seul jet, que l'esprit en détermine la forme, et que la forme y soit l'expression de l'esprit." [87] The perception of the intimate relation of spirit and form is wholly admirable; the danger comes when the production of the poem "d'un seul jet" is made a necessary condition of this relation. Only Jou-

bert was fully aware of the need of dominating and controlling
the initial poetic impulse.

During the long period covered by this chapter and the
preceding ones poetry remained at a low level. It was in the
poetic theory, with all its timidity and weaknesses, that a new
conception of poetry slowly evolved. In general the innovations in theory were due less to the poets themselves than to
critics and readers and lovers of poetry who were dissatisfied
with French poetry as it was, and had a vision, sometimes
clouded indeed, of what it could and should be.

V

THE ROMANTIC REVOLUTION

W ITH the romantic period there began the great revival of poetry which was to reach its full flowering towards the middle of the century. At the same time there was continual discussion of the nature and problems of poetry. For the first time (except for Chénier) the most important pronouncements came from the poets themselves rather than from theorists and critics. Hardly any of the great poets failed to set down, sometimes at length, sometimes only in casual remarks, their ideas on the nature and function of their craft. Thus there is a far closer relation between the theory and the practice of poetry than there had been in the earlier period.

For these years it would be difficult and ill-advised to make such chronological divisions as were possible, with some simplification indeed, for the long period preceding. The work of many of the writers covers all or nearly all of the years from 1820 to the death of Baudelaire, and the main currents of ideas run parallel and overlap. Three major trends can be distinguished. First there is the strictly "romantic" conception of poetry as the spontaneous overflow of emotion, released from all bonds by a poetic revolution compared by its leaders to the great political revolution of the previous century. Then around 1830 there is a revival of interest in poetry as art, leading from *Les Orientales* and Gautier to the Parnasse. Parallel with these, but developing more slowly, is an increasing sense of poetry as a special and mysterious experience; in this the penetration into literature of the illuminist and occultist traditions plays a large part. Poetic experience is enriched and deepened to extend from the visible world to the invisible, and the poetic image is transformed from ornament into symbol. With the achievement of a poetry of magic, of suggestion, the long and deplorable tendency to separate matter and form comes to an end. The result is a poetry liberated from convention yet concerned with form, intensely aware of mystery yet translating that mystery in terms of the visible world. In this and the two following chapters I shall follow these three trends one by one, and in the last chapter consider their meeting and fusion in the poetry and doctrine of Baudelaire.

It is of course true that we rarely find any one of these doctrines proclaimed absolutely and exclusively; but for practically all the poets with whom we are dealing one or the other of them has the place of honor. For Lamartine and Musset poetry was above all an effusion of emotion, for Gautier and Banville it was form, for Gérard de Nerval it was an adventure into the unknown and invisible. Yet even in these cases the central doctrine is colored and modified by reflections from other conceptions and from the poet's own individuality. Other poets either shifted their ground from time to time or formulated a composite doctrine. Vigny, for example, allies a poetry of ideas and a poetry of form. Most of all Victor Hugo, the "écho sonore," was blown about by one wind of doctrine after another during his long poetic career. Many of the critics too, such as Rémusat and Magnin and above all Sainte-Beuve, attempt to ally and to reconcile different points of view. Hence certain writers, especially Hugo, will appear in more than one chapter. Yet the three trends I have noted are so basically distinct, so significant for the future of poetry, that, even at the cost of breaking up the doctrine of certain individual poets, a clearer picture of the movement of poetic theory is to be gained by treating the three trends separately.

It is traditional, and justifiable, to date the beginnings of romantic poetry from the publication of Lamartine's *Méditations poétiques* in 1820, followed by Hugo's and Vigny's first volumes of verse in 1822.[1] Chénier's poems had been published for the first time in 1819.

La poésie en France allait dans la fadeur,
Dans la description sans vie et sans grandeur,
Comme un ruisseau chargé dont les ondes avares
Expirent en cristaux sous des grottes bizarres,
Quand soudain se rouvrit avec limpidité
Le rocher dans sa veine. André ressucité
Parut . . . .

Lamartine ignorant, qui ne sait que son âme,
Hugo puissant et fort, Vigny soigneux et fin.[2]

The change was not such a sudden one as Sainte-Beuve's lines suggest; the great poets, and still more the minor ones, detached themselves only gradually from the eighteenth-century tradition. The walls of the classical Jericho did not fall with a crash at the sound of the romantic trumpets, and the continuers of the classical tradition made frequent sorties against the besieging army.[3] In the years in which romanticism was coming to the fore many works appeared which reiterated the sound doctrine of the past. François de Neufchâteau's verse version of Du Marsais' *Des tropes* has already been mentioned. J.-C. Laveaux states in the "Discours préliminaire" to his *Dictionnaire raisonné* of the French language that most of his material is taken from eighteenth-century writers, especially Condillac.[4] It seems indeed familiar to us; enthusiasm is an "imagination réchauffée," its dangers are pointed out, the same reservations about the use of imagery are made. On the question of language Carpentier's *Le Gradus français* is in effect a book of recipes for poetry such as mother used to make. Periphrases "are useful particularly to our poets, who may not use a large number of terms which our delicacy excludes not only from poetic language, but from any noble style." For the convenience of poets Carpentier gives a long list of "poetic" words, by which the language of poetry is to be distinguished from that of prose. Often he offers a wide variety of choice; thus for *ciel* one may substitute *Olympe, séjour des Dieux, voûte azurée, voûte éthérée, empyrée*. The only point on which Carpentier allows some licence is in versification, where he admits the use of *enjambement* in certain cases where it adds a beauty. Otherwise all his definitions and rules are well-worn, his advice timid.[5]

The future romantic poets themselves were in the beginning far from jettisoning tradition, as is apparent from *Le Conservateur Littéraire* (1819–21), of which Victor Hugo was the leading spirit, and its successor, *La Muse Française* (1823–24). These ardent defenders of tradition in religion and in politics are still far from the idea of a revolution in poetry. The idea of poetry as a school of virtue and morality is maintained. Victor Hugo blames Delille for using his pure and noble talent in a genre "qui ne demande que de l'esprit" — descriptive poetry.[6] On form the young critics are equally conservative. Poetry, says Abel Hugo, must be clear in order to be read. He criticizes the abuse of *enjambement*, as well as too great effusiveness, and advises the poet under consideration to compress his thought into fewer lines, and to pay particular attention to his rhymes.[7] Victor Hugo, it is amusing to note, is severe when he finds "in the middle of a lofty passage, a touch of affectation or a neologism, a bizarre coupling of words, one of those bombastic sentences which have been called *phrases à effet.*" Here Hugo is writing of an obscure and forgotten poet, but he is almost equally severe on Chénier: "One may indeed be contemptuous of this incorrect and barbarous style, these vague and incoherent ideas, this effervescent imagination, these tumultuous dreams of an awakening talent, this mania for mutilating sentences, and, so to speak, carving them in the Greek style, these words derived from the ancient languages used in their etymological sense, these bizarre verse patterns, this lack of knowledge of the true nature of French versification; these defects are great but they are by no means dangerous." Likewise in reviewing the *Méditations* Hugo points out certain neologisms, repetitions, and obscurities, before concluding in a decidedly patronizing manner: "Courage, young man, you are among those whom Plato wished to crown with honors and banish from his republic." [8] In *La Muse Française*, founded, according to the "Avant-propos," to rekindle the languishing flame of poetry, moral values are again upheld, Soumet praising Victor Hugo for upholding the noble and primordial aim of poetry, to kindle in men's souls the love of virtue.[9] Yet in the *Conservateur* occasionally, more often in the *Muse*, the beginnings of a new doctrine of poetry emerged, which were to be more fully developed as the romantic movement gained momentum.

This timidity of theory is echoed in the poetry published in the two periodicals. One has only to leaf through the *Conservateur* to find poems with an all too familiar ring: fables, "poésies légères," didactic poems, satires, translations from Virgil (several by Hugo), Horatian and Anacreontic odes, elegies, idylls, and a "poème ossianique," again by Hugo. Most of this poetry is rhetorical and diffuse, and the reader is tempted to agree with one of the poets that

> Ce don de ne jamais finir,
> Les Dieux l'accordent au poète.[10]

The only poems of note are some of Victor Hugo's odes on a variety of subjects, chiefly historical and political. In his *Vers à M. V.-M. Hugo* François de Neufchâteau says: "Le Louvre s'est ému, jeune homme, à votre voix." [11] It may be that the admirable royalist sentiments expressed made the Louvre more susceptible than the modern reader, who is left somewhat cold by the grandiose rhetoric of the odes, their innumerable apostrophes and exclamations. Yet if one thinks not of later, but of earlier poetry, the odes, in spite of all that is artificial in them, have a new vigor and strength, a new mastery of verse.

If one turns from the *Conservateur* to the *Muse* one still finds a plentiful supply of epistles, elegies, and odes in the best eighteenth-century manner. But in many of these the sentiment begins to seem more personal, more profound; the love poetry treats of "passions fatales," of absence, and of memory, and there are many poems on religion and on death. The external themes too are more varied — the Middle Ages and modern Greece are particularly important — and many of the poems are narrative, not infrequently with more than a touch of melodrama. The language shows signs of becoming more precise, more picturesque. And there is often a naïve faith in the ability of unaided sentiment to produce poetry:

> Ces vers que, dans ma solitude,
> Tracent sans art et sans étude
> Le sentiment et le loisir! [12]

Along with Hugo's *La Bande noire* and *A mon père*, the only notable poems are Vigny's *Fragment d'un poème de Suzanne* and *Sur la mort de Lord Byron*. Otherwise what strikes the reader most are the constant reminiscences of Chénier, and above all of Lamartine.

In the very numerous discussions of poetry of the romantic period, the great problem is that of the nature of poetry and of the qualities necessary for the poet as well as his function. In dealing with these discussions a frequent difficulty is the vague and imprecise use of terms. In the eighteenth century the theorists were careful to define their terms, and, while one may often deplore the narrowness of the definitions, one is at least reasonably sure what is meant. Whereas the romantic tendency is to use such terms as enthusiasm, imagination, nature, truth, and poetry itself with little or no indication of the significance or scope of the term.

The term poetry takes on a broader and broader meaning. In the preromantic period the essence of poetry had been found in a spirit, a state of mind, to which form and language were secondary, so that poetry could be found in prose or verse indifferently. In the romantic period this conception is carried still further, and poetry can exist without any verbal expression, can be lived as well as written. Thus poetry comes to be defined by a series of abstractions — life, virtue, delight, and beauty — and literary expression is at best secondary.

This tendency is carried to its extreme by Lamartine. Although, early in his poetic career, he wrote to his friend Virieu: "A poet should not speak in prose, nor make up poetic theories about his works," he continued through his long life to set down his ideas about poetry. Very early there is the suggestion that the poetry of nature is superior to the written word: "There is more poetry in the tiniest corner of one of [nature's] pictures than in all your human poems." [13] In nearly all he writes about poetry expression is subordinated to spirit: "What indeed is poetry? Like all that is divine in us, it cannot be defined by one word, nor by a thousand. It is the incarnation of what is most intimate in man's heart and most divine in his thought, of what is most splendid in nature's images and most melodious in its sounds! It is at once sentiment and sensation, spirit and matter." [14] In Lamartine's later years the result of this attitude towards poetry is a somewhat curious one; a tendency to look down on *written* poetry, to consider it a minor activity: "One should devote to these works which humor the imagination only the hours left free by our duties to our family, to our country, and to our age; they are the luxuries of the mind, and must not become man's daily bread. The poet is not the whole man, just as imagination and sensibility are not the whole soul." [15] In 1842 he tells Madame de Girardin that he has given up writing verse, considering it a "sublime childish game" unsuited to his years.[16] And in the 1849 preface to the *Méditations* he insists that "to sing is not to live; it is to refresh oneself or console oneself by the sound of one's own voice. . . . I have never been wholly possessed by poetry." [17]

While Lamartine goes farther than most in his subordination of written poetry to experienced poetry, something of the same extension of the bounds is found in other romantics. For the young Hugo poetry belongs to the domain of the good as much as to that of the beautiful. In 1821 he writes to his future wife: "Poetry, Adèle, is the expression of virtue; a beautiful soul and a great poetic talent are almost always inseparable. So you see that you should understand poetry; it comes only from the soul, and can be manifested by a noble action as well as by a beautiful verse." [18]

Or poetry may be considered as an abstract and ideal beauty, distinct from its outer form. This idea is developed at some length by Lamennais, whose influence on many of the romantic poets was so marked. In his *Esquisse d'une philosophie* he claims that the different arts are but fragments of a universal poetry. "In a general and strictly true sense, poetry is Art itself, or Beauty incarnate, clothed in a perceptible form. Thus the universe is a great poem, God's poem, which we endeavor to reproduce in ours." Language is the vehicle of poetry, not poetry itself, which must not be confused with its material form. There can be poetry without verse, just as there is verse without poetry.[19] Although Vigny never separates poetry from form to this extent, he often writes of it in abstract terms. It is a delight, an elixir, and above all it is beauty: "Poetry is the *supreme Beauty of things* and the ideal contemplation of this beauty." [20]

But by the romantics poetry is envisaged above all as emotion; emotion felt, emotion expressed. The ideas of enthusiasm and of inspiration are in large measure absorbed by emotion. Inspiration is no longer an occasional and hard-won gift of the gods, but is implicit in emotion. Only the young Victor Hugo writes, in practically eighteenth-century terms: "Poetic composition is the result of two intellectual phenomena: *meditation* and *inspiration*. Meditation is a faculty; inspiration is a gift. . . . The poet evokes inspiration by meditation." [21] Vigny, whose emotions are more controlled than those of the other romantic poets, is the one who most emphasizes poetic enthusiasm. In 1837 he writes: "The world is growing cold. The sacred fire of enthusiasm has taken refuge with the poets. — Let them remain masters of themselves and they will be able to nourish themselves on it and in their hearts burn incense to the divinity." There follows an admirable definition, "La Poésie, c'est *l'Enthousiasme cristallisé*." [22] It is the adjective *cristallisé* that sets Vigny's idea apart from that of poetry as pure emotion.

Most of his contemporaries gave emotion the place of honor in poetic creation. Poetry is the revelation of the soul, it is passion put into words. Soumet, reviewing Hugo's *Nouvelles Odes*, asks that the writer possess above all "le génie des émotions." [23] Earlier Hugo himself had noted in Chénier's poetry "the imprint of that profound sensibility, without which there is no genius, and which perhaps *is* genius. . . . Poetry is almost entirely sentiment." [24] And the 1822 preface to the *Odes* has the famous statement: "Poetry is not in the form of ideas, but in ideas themselves. Poetry is what lies at the heart of everything." Hugo's ideas on poetry varied a good deal later on, and he never again treated form in so cavalier a fashion. Yet, with variations and accrescences, the idea of poetry as emotion persisted; more than thirty years later he writes that "la poésie est une avidité de l'âme." [25] The same idea echoes throughout the romantic period. In 1833 Maurice de Guérin writes to his sister: "Poetry cannot be taught. The poetic doctrine of every poet is written in his inmost soul; there are no others." [26]

Such a conception of poetry as pure feeling leads to a neglect and often a scorn of form, or at best a belief that the form which comes "du premier jet" is sacred and not subject to revision and correction. Vigny, who did not share this belief, quotes from the preface of a poem he is reviewing in 1824: "I have refrained from retouching in my calmer moments what I had written in the fervor of profound inspiration." [27] Lamartine makes this point again and again. In 1818 he writes: "To create is splendid, but to correct, change, spoil is dreary and boring, it is work for masons not for artists. I believe that great works are *in posse* in the soul and that it matters very little whether they come forth or not." [28] His preface to the *Harmonies poétiques* (1830) states that what is strongly felt is quickly written, and his commentaries on the *Méditations* are full of references to poems composed on horseback or scribbled in pencil "presque d'une seule haleine." However a study of the manuscripts of his poems and of the earlier versions found in his letters shows that with him practice did not always follow theory. The manuscripts are full of variants, and it seems doubtful that Lamartine's emotions were entirely responsible for the transformation of the lines found in a letter of 1814,

> Coulez, jours fortunés, coulez plus lentement,
> Pressez moins votre course, heures délicieuses,
> Laissez-moi savourer ce bonheur d'un moment.
>   Il est si peu d'heures heureuses! [29]

into the great stanza of *Le Lac*,

> O Temps, suspends ton vol, et vous, heures propices,
>   Suspendez votre cours!
> Laissez-nous savourer les rapides délices
>   Des plus beaux de nos jours!

For Lamartine this negligence in poetic composition comes from his giving an inferior place to written poetry as compared to experienced poetry. In Musset there is a similar lack of belief in conscious artistry, but for him this comes from the sacredness of sentiment: "l'art, c'est le sentiment." [30] In 1831 he writes to his brother: "What the artist or the poet must have is emotion. When, as I am composing a verse, I feel a familiar beating of my heart, I am sure that my verse is of the best possible quality I can produce." [31] In *Namouna* he writes:

> Sachez-le, — c'est le cœur qui parle et qui soupire
> Lorsque la main écrit, — c'est le cœur qui se fond;
> C'est le cœur qui s'étend, se découvre et respire,
> Comme un gai pèlerin sur le sommet d'un mont.

His poetic creed is put into verse in *Impromptu*:

> Chasser tout souvenir et fixer la pensée,
> Sur un bel axe d'or la tenir balancée,
> Incertaine, inquiète, immobile pourtant;
> Eterniser peut-être un rêve d'un instant;
> Aimer le vrai, le beau, chercher leur harmonie;
> Ecouter dans son cœur l'écho de son génie;
> Chanter, rire, pleurer, seul, sans but, au hasard;
> D'un sourire, d'un mot, d'un soupir, d'un regard,
> Faire un travail exquis, plein de crainte et de charme,
>   Faire une perle d'une larme,
> Du poète ici-bas voilà la passion,
> Voilà son bien, sa vie, et son ambition.

This rule of emotion is hardly challenged during the first ten years of the romantic movement. Vigny is alone among the romantic poets in choosing to write not under stress of immediate emotion, but rather in emotion recollected in tranquillity. "My mind is never more free than when the work I am composing has no relation to my situation of the moment. And I have always had such a horror of the present and the real in my life that I have never presented in art a painful or delightful emotion at the time I was experiencing it, seeking to take refuge in the skies of poetry from this earth where at every step thorns wounded my feet which are perhaps too delicate and bleed too easily." [32] But the idea of emotion, immediate and spontaneous, as the chief element in poetic creation and poetic enjoyment was a persistent one. For example Henri de Latouche writes *A un amateur*:

> Vos accents imparfaits savent-ils émouvoir?
> Plaisent-ils? vous savez tout ce qu'il faut savoir.
> Que vos vers, comme vous, à la gêne indociles,
> Volent près des amours sur des routes faciles.[33]

And for Paul Ackermann "to be moved and to delight in this emotion constitutes the poetic state." [34] So as late as 1852 Sainte-Beuve could say that the influence of Musset was stronger than that of either Lamartine or Victor Hugo.

Yet even sympathetic contemporary critics noted the dangers of this extreme faith in emotion. In the first of a series of articles published in *Le Globe* in 1825 Charles de Rémusat, accepting the premise that inspiration is the source of all enduring beauty in poetry, maintains that inspiration is not the lack of all reason and restraint, but rather a state into which the poet is plunged by his sentiments and sensations, and which becomes a kind of irresistible urge to express and communicate them. But the poet must not be beside himself, else at the height of passion he will lack the freedom of mind necessary to art. This leads Rémusat to a plea for emotion recollected in tranquillity: "Thus it is rather the memory of his emotions than his present emotions that [the poet] should describe or sing. It is true that individuals differ in this respect; in most cases, sensibility is too keen during the first moments to leave room for talent; in some cases, on the contrary, it is only with time that sensibility becomes acute enough to become poetic; in other cases, finally, sensibility and imagination are simultaneous and evoke one another: these men are the improvisors in all genres. Inspiration and naturalness can hardly be distinguished." [35]

In the latter articles of the series Rémusat points out the relation between the needs of the time and lyric poetry: "Such poetry cannot but give pleasure to our age. By presenting personal feelings, it satisfies the need for naturalness and truth which is the predominant taste of our time; and by its general character, endowed with the vagabond swiftness of thought and even of revery, it corresponds remarkably to the mood of doubt and contemplation into which we are cast by the doctrines and events of our century. The universe and a single man, infinity and the individual, such is the contrast which is the basis of lyric poetry as of human thought." [36] Unfortunately Rémusat is less perceptive in his criticism of individual poets than in his general observations; he singles out for special mention three lyric poets, Lamartine, Delavigne, and Béranger, with the statement that of the three it is perhaps Delavigne who gives most promise for the future. However his criticism of Lamartine is far from unjustified: "Poetry is to the poet as sound is to the lyre: left to itself, exposed to the touch of the wind, the lyre gives forth sounds which are indeed pure, but vague and monotonous; only the touch of a skilled hand gives variety to its chords and passion to its harmony." [37]

The torrents of poetic emotion were less kindly treated by other critics, and were an inexhaustible source of parody and satire. A long satiric poem of 1825, *Le Parnasse moderne*, exclaims to the romantic poets:

> Pleurez surtout, pleurez lorsque renaît l'aurore;
> Pendant le jour pleurez, la nuit pleurez encore.[38]

And the author of another poem with the same title, published in 1830, says sarcastically:

> Mon faible est, il est vrai, la sensiblemanie,
> Et tout ce qui la flatte est pour moi du génie.[39]

The very entertaining *Physiologie du poète*, illustrated by Daumier, distinguishes among other species "le poète lyrique," "le poète échevelé," and "le poète lamartinien." The last of these, the most numerous of all, is "la troisième eau d'un thé, dont le premier défaut est d'être un peu faible." [40]

Romantic doctrine sees poetry above all as the spontaneous expression of personal emotion. The poet is first and foremost a man. In his early article on Chénier Hugo says: "What indeed is a poet? A man who feels strongly, and expresses his feelings in a more expressive language." [41] The preface to the *Feuilles d'automne* describes the poems as "elegies such as the heart of the poet pours forth unceasingly through all the rifts made by the shocks of life." Sainte-Beuve's idea is very similar: "A lyric poet is a naked soul which passes singing through the world; and according to the times, the various inspirations, and the different tones to which it is pitched, this soul can give forth many a different sound." [42] This is the core of the doctrine of all the great romantic poets in their early years, although, with the exception of Musset, they all, especially Hugo, were to modify and enlarge their poetic beliefs in their later years.

In their poetry as in their doctrine personal emotion is the key theme. Man is at the center of all things. The poet, treating the great themes of love, death, nature, religion, draws them all into his own personal sphere. In Lamartine's verse the readers of 1820 found the poetry of which the "âmes sensibles" of the eighteenth century had dreamed. All that is traditional and conventional in it, the rhetoric, the "poetic" vocabulary, the timidity of its imagery, is infused with a power and depth of emotion such as poetry had not known for many a year. [43] This is enhanced by a quality which Lamartine rarely mentions in his vague and loose statements about poetry: the extraordinary music of his verse. It is somewhat of a shock to find him writing towards the end of his life: "Poetry does not consist of this empty sonority of verses; it lies in the idea, the sentiment, the image. . . . To change speech into music is not to perfect it, but to materialize it." [44] For it is above all by its music that Lamartine's poetry has survived. My own experience must be that of many readers; when one thinks about Lamartine's poetry, one remembers exaggerated sentiments, banal philosophy, vague religiosity, all expressed with too much eloquence, too much effusion. Yet as soon as one begins to reread one is captivated by the exquisite harmony of the lines, the delicate accord of sound and sense.

While Lamartine gradually expanded the scope of his poetry, one poet, Musset, remained faithful to the end to the poetry of pure sentiment, and touched all the chords of a broken heart. The neglect of form which made his name anathema to many later poets blinded them to the desperate sincerity of his confessions, the delicate shades of his feelings, and made them neglect the wistful charm of some of his lighter poems, such as *Une Soirée perdue*, which have stood the test of time better than the tears and moans of the *Nuits* and *Souvenir*, though they too have their moments of lyric beauty.

Except for the "later" Hugo, it is Vigny who has best maintained the poetic pre-eminence which later generations have perhaps been too ready to deny to the romantic poets. Vigny, with emotions no less deep, refrained from a too facile and effusive expression, and translated his personal feelings into generalizations, expressed not directly, but by parables and images. This discretion of emotion is accompanied by a preoccupation with form, an attempt to impose order on verbal as well as emotional chaos. Unfortunately his poetry is often shortwinded; the enthusiasm which the poet invoked was for him a capricious muse. Vigny, in more than one way the legitimate successor of Chénier, shares with him a certain difficulty in maintaining a high poetic level. The most striking example is perhaps *La Maison du berger*, in which the passage on railroads intervenes between the beginning and ending stanzas to Eva, which contain some of the most lovely lines in all French poetry. For Vigny prose seems to be a more natural vehicle than verse; his journal is filled with prose "projets de poèmes" and images, and when he comes to translate them into verse the flame often does not burn strongly enough to fuse them into poetry. Too many lines lack internal stress, some are painfully prosaic, such as "L'Anglais-Américain, nomade et protestant," and there are too many weak verbs and abstract nouns. Vigny himself wrote, "Je me suis toujours trouvé le génie épique," [45] and one wonders whether, with his great gift of narration (at its best in *Servitude et grandeur militaires*) his true gift was not for a genre that demands less intensity than the lyric poem.

Victor Hugo is by far the most varied, the most complex of all the romantic poets.[46] He will reappear in the two following chapters, and here I would only say a word on his more purely romantic poetry. He was perhaps the slowest of the romantics to find himself, and it is a blessed thing that he was not numbered among the poets who die young. For much of his early work is shot through with false rhetoric, questions, exclamations, repetitions, and his vocabulary reeks of harps, lyres, lilies, muses, angels, and azure. The rhetoric was never fully tamed, but the banal vocabulary was gradually replaced by one of the richest and most picturesque lexicons any poet ever created for himself. But even the early rhetoric, though it overlays, cannot entirely disguise a strong and powerful vein of emotion. And this persists throughout Hugo's poetry. Its expression sometimes continues to be rhetorical and magniloquent, as in *A Villequier*, but there are many poems in which it is set forth with moving simplicity.

> Demain, dès l'aube, à l'heure où blanchit la campagne,
> Je partirai. Vois-tu, je sais que tu m'attends.
> J'irai par la forêt, j'irai par la montagne,
> Je ne puis demeurer loin de toi plus longtemps.

It would be easy to draw up a long list of poets who shared with the great romantics this poetry of personal emotion. There is a whole gamut of tones, from the pageant of Musset's bleeding heart to the more discreet and homely "intimiste" poetry which Sainte-Beuve derived from the Lake poets, and which Lamartine also practiced. Sainte-Beuve writes: "I have endeavored, after my predecessors, to be original in my humble and bourgeois fashion, observing nature and man closely, but without a microscope, calling everyday things by their names, but preferring the cottage to the boudoir, and in every case seeking to ennoble these prosaic details by depicting human feelings and natural objects." [47] And Lamartine says to a correspondent that he has been writing verses in a new style, less pompous and less solemn; "not romanticism à la Hugo, but something more intimate, more true to life, more free from affectation in costume and style." [48]

After 1830 there is, side by side with this personal poetry, much poetry which expresses strong feeling allied with philosophical, religious, political and social convictions. Hugo very early, Lamartine somewhat later, became aware of the social responsibility and function of the poet. It is not enough that he should sing to ease his own aching heart; he has a responsibility towards his fellow men, to console their sorrows and be their guide.

> . .   le poète sur la terre
> Console, exilé volontaire,
> Les tristes humains dans leurs fers;
> Parmi les peuples en délire,
> Il s'élance, armé de sa lyre,
> Comme Orphée au sein des enfers.[49]

Even Musset, the most self-centered of poets, puts this obligation, expressed by the famous image of the pelican, in the mouth of the Muse of the *Nuit de mai*. The poet must also be a guide to right thinking. Poetry is bound up with moral and social beliefs. However much Hugo's ideas changed, his poetry never ceased to proclaim them, from the moment he wrote in the 1822 preface to the *Odes*: "The history of mankind offers poetry only when judged from the heights of monarchical ideas and religious beliefs." The poet leads the people onwards:

> Un jour vient dans sa vie, où la Muse elle-même,
> D'un sacerdoce auguste armant son luth suprême,
>   L'envoie au monde ivre de sang,
> Afin que, nous sauvant de notre propre audace,
> Il apporte d'en haut à l'homme qui menace
>   La prière du Tout-Puissant.[50]

In the December, 1822, preface to the *Odes* Hugo maintains that the chief object of the poet is to be useful, and in the 1824 preface that he should "march before the people like a light, and show them the road." After the brief deviation marked by the preface to *Les Orientales* he remains faithful to his belief in the mission of the poet: "The art of the present must no longer seek only the Beautiful, but also the Good." He is not however a partisan of "the *direct utility* of art, a puerile theory," and continues: "After all, art must be its own goal, and teach, moralize, civilize, and edify on the side; with-

out turning aside, just going straight ahead." [51] In the preface
to *Les Voix intérieures* "le poète a une fonction sérieuse."
Poetry is the weapon of the leader:

> Secouant mon vers sombre et plein de flamme
> J'entrerai là, Seigneur, la justice dans l'âme
> Et le fouet à la main.[52]

And art is never sufficient in itself: "Art for art's sake may be
fine, but art for the sake of progress is finer still. To dream
dreams is good, to dream utopias is better." [53]

Towards 1830 Lamartine enlarged his early conception of
poetry: "Poetry will be reason set to music; that will be its
destiny for a long time; it will be philosophical, religious,
political, social, like the eras the human race will pass through;
above all it will be intimate, personal, meditative and serious." [54] Vigny too very early notes this role of poetry: "In
the ages of simplicity poetry was entirely devoted to the
beauties of the physical forms of nature and of man; each step
that it has since taken with society towards our ages of civilization and sorrow has seemed to unite it with our arts as well
as with the sufferings of our souls; now at last, serious like
our religion and like destiny, it borrows from them its greatest
beauties; never discouraged, it has followed man in his great
voyage, a beautiful and tender companion." [55] So beside the
lyric, elegiac, and disheveled poets, the *Physiologie du poète*
puts the humanitarian and proletarian poets, as well as the
Olympic poet, who "does not write for the public; he writes
for the people, because he has received from God the mission
of speaking to the masses; he does not write to write, but to
teach." [56]

In the years following 1830 many poets developed a social
conscience, and a different kind of emotion is introduced into
poetry.[57] The common humanity of the poet is stressed. In
1830 Sainte-Beuve writes that art is now on a common footing,
down in the arena with the crowd, side by side with unwearied

humanity, remembering the past, but looking forward towards the future.[58] There is an alliance between socialism and romanticism noted by Hugo many years later: "Romanticism and socialism, as has been said with hostility, but with justice, are one and the same thing." [59] Hugo is indeed oversimplifying here — many of the romantics followed a very different path — but it is certainly true that the conception of "l'art social" was of great importance. It was defined indeed in various ways. For some it meant pure propaganda, the popularization of ideas; for others, such as Saint-Simon and Fourier, the artist together with the *savant* presided over and guided the activities of society; and for others the role of the artist was a Messianic one. The poet speaks, not for himself, but for his fellow men:

> Mais la voix du poète est la voix, à toute heure,
> De la société; comme elle, il chante ou pleure.[60]

This tendency was by no means limited to poetry; it embraced all art, all literature. As far as poetic theory is concerned its scope is limited, in that it considered the function of poetry, the mission of the poet, only in relation to society. Yet, as has been well pointed out, there is no real break between the early individualist romantics and the later socialist ones.[61] Those poets who turned away from their individual sentiments and sorrows to broader themes still believed that poetry was above all the expression of feeling; their philosophical and political attitudes might change, their focus might shift from past to future, but the change in poetic belief is at most one of emphasis. The matter and function of poetry are stressed, rather than its nature or form.

Second only to the great key word *sentiment* in romantic theory are *vérité* and *nature*. The frequent failure to define terms leads to a good deal of difficulty when one encounters these two words. It is often far from easy to distinguish between them; truth frequently seems to mean a faithful representation of nature. Both terms recur constantly. For Hugo, romantic literature draws poetry from the wellsprings of truth.[62] Guirard, in his important article, "Nos Doctrines," after quoting Boileau's line,

> Rien n'est beau que le vrai; le vrai seul est aimable,

makes a distinction between absolute truth, that of epic and drama, and relative truth, that of works in which the author is present, and communicates his own feelings and the mysteries of his own nature. In this relative truth no direct imitation is possible; poetry is the expression, not the imitation of nature.[63] Much later Sainte-Beuve uses truth as a stick with which to beat Gautier: "Truth is what the poet of our times must seek for above all, since forms, colors, rhythm are easy enough to borrow." [64]

Most often *vérité* and *nature* are coupled, as in the 1826 preface to the *Odes et ballades*: "The poet must have only one model, nature; only one guide, truth. He must not write with what has been written, but with his soul and with his heart." Here truth is opposed to the imitation of literary models. Rességuier likewise writes in the *Muse Française* that when people reproach poets for not imitating the ancients they forget that by not imitating they are doing what the ancients did.[65] Rémusat has severe criticism for young writers who seek their inspiration in books, and advises them to be men before being poets.[66] *Vérité* is the imitation, not of models, but of nature; not an idealized "belle nature," but living nature in all its details and all its variety. This leads Hugo in the *Préface de Cromwell* to his doctrine of the grotesque, with its necessary complement of the sublime: "True poetry, complete poetry, is found in the harmony of contraries." Again truth and nature are allied: "The poet must take counsel only of nature, of truth, and of inspiration which is also a nature and a truth." Later in the *Préface* Hugo does face the problem of the relation of art to reality: "Nature then! Nature and truth! . . . let us try to indicate what is the impassable barrier which, to our way of thinking, separates the reality of art from the reality of nature. . . . The truth of art, as has been said, cannot be absolute reality." [67] But for the majority of the romantics truth is fidelity to nature in all its manifestations, all its variety. In this opposition to the imitation of a *beau idéal*, this contrast of absolute and relative, we often find a parallel between *vérité* and *variété*. Rarely is there any restriction on the wholesale imitation of nature. Only Vigny, in a concise phrase, makes a reservation: "l'art, c'est la vérité choisie." [68] So it was inevitable that this opening up of all nature to poetry should meet with the opposition of the classicists and attract the barbs of the satirists. The *Parnasse moderne* of 1830 describes a monster cast ashore by the tides, who becomes "le Toutou de la société":

> L'animal est décrit d'espèce domestique,
> Et d'accord unanime appelé romantique.[69]

Sentiment, vérité, nature; and along with them the all-embracing battle cry, *liberté*. Hugo's aesthetics outstrip his politics when he proclaims in the 1828 preface to the *Odes et ballades:* "La liberté dans l'ordre, la liberté dans l'art." And in the preface to *Les Orientales* the following year he proclaims that the poet is free to go where he will, to do what he pleases. In his preface, "But de cette publication," to *Littérature et philosophie mêlées* (1834) he writes of "the spirit of liberty, which the author's instinct will apply first to art, then, by an irresistible logic to society." [70] This liberty manifested itself alike in the opening of the floodgates of emotion and in the liberation of poetry from classical doctrines of imitation. Above all it loosened the chains of poetic language and versification. Hugo proclaims in the *Préface de Cromwell:* "A language cannot be fixed. The spirit of man is always on the march, or, if you prefer, in motion, and languages along with it. . . . In vain do our literary Joshuas call on language to stand still; neither languages nor the sun stand still. The day that languages become fixed, they die." [71] In his maniloquent lines in the *Réponse à un acte d'accusation* Hugo claimed to have carried out a revolution in poetic language equivalent to the great political revolution of the previous century:

> Je fis souffler un vent révolutionnaire.
> Je mis un bonnet rouge au vieux dictionnaire.

The *Parnasse moderne* of 1830 had its word to say on the subject:

> Parsemez vos discours de ces tropes hardis,
> Qui, moins ils ont de sens, plus ils sont applaudis.
> Tels qu'un *fleuve de flamme* et des *pleurs intrépides*,
> Une *molle clarté*, des *nuages limpides*.
>
> . . . .
>
> J'aime à voir s'accoupler deux pensers ennemis,
> Qui de se fuir toujours semblaient s'être promis.[72]

For many of the romantic poets, most of all for Hugo, the romantic movement appeared a complete break with tradition, a complete revolution in the spirit and the form of poetry. In 1829 Émile Deschamps asserted that a great literary century is never the continuation of another century. Hugo with the ode, Lamartine with the elegy, Vigny with the "poème," had created great poetry, because they applied their talents to genres of which the French language offered either no examples or inadequate ones.[73] Looking back in 1863 Hugo wrote: "The writers and poets of this century have the amazing advantage of not proceeding from any ancient school, of working first-hand, without models. . . . The poets of the nineteenth century, the writers of the nineteenth century, are the sons of the French Revolution." [74] The parallel had been made much earlier — and deplored — by Maurice de Guérin, who saw in the word *liberté* the guiding principle of the romantic movement. "Instead of detaching themselves from the past, they broke violently with it. . . . Thus, having quarreled with its venerable ancestors, and thinking itself capable of doing without their help, our new literature was at the mercy of its stormy imagination, with little aid from those serious and difficult studies which act as ballast to the mind, and make its progress both safe and majestic." [75]

For a good many years literary historians echoed these claims and opinions with docility, and they are still to be found in many histories of literature.[76] But in our time there has been an increasing awareness of the links between French romanticism and the literature of the eighteenth century.[77] In 1904 Emmanuel Barat observed that Delille, Le Brun, and Parny were the masters from whom the French romantic poets had learned their versification and style, their manner of speaking, writing, and even feeling poetically.[78] Some ten years later Gustave Lanson remarked that romanticism was a great deal more classical than it had believed itself to be. By the time that Pierre Moreau came to write *Le Classicisme des romantiques*, in 1932, he was able to cite a number of recent uses of his title phrase. And in 1935 Paul Hazard pointed out, not without a certain pride, that French romanticism, far from being a deviation from tradition, had, while assimilating foreign influences, kept its native tang, its traditional classical qualities.[79]

At first such views were chiefly historical in character, simply demonstrating the persistence of tradition in romanticism. Then they came to be associated with a judgment of values. Henri Peyre, in some admirable pages, brought out the differences between French and English romantic poetry, the eloquence and the oratorical tone of the former, the concentration and intensity of the latter. He emphasized again the continuity between the poets of the late eighteenth century and the romantics, the differences being only in the degree of individual talent.[80] The extreme of belittlement of the romantics was reached by Thierry Maulnier, who asserted that their place in the history of French poetry is negligible, that they brought nothing new except a few technical changes, and those timid ones.[81]

When one turns back to romantic poetry it is difficult to deny that along with much that is new — the intensity of emotion, the extent and variety of subject matter, the new vocabulary and imagery, the freedom of versification — many bonds attach it to the eighteenth century — its rhetoric, its eloquence, its frequent diffuseness. A good deal of evil has been spoken of eloquence in poetry. Recently it has found a defender, and an eloquent one, in Henri Peyre. "Eloquence is after all one of the ways in which literature, and poetry in particular, can escape the perpetual nightmare of art: immobility which is death, and capture that prerogative of life: motion." [82] He rightly points out that the English and German romantic poets are by no means free from rhetoric, and that such generally admired poems as *Le Lac* and *Ischia* contain some of the most eloquent passages in French poetry. So far I agree entirely, and I would say that eloquence has its roots in that overflow of strong feeling which is at the heart of lyric poetry. The danger lies in the fact that eloquence, codified into the laws of rhetoric, offers a tempting opportunity to substitute the language of feeling for feeling itself, or at best to exaggerate personal feeling to an oratorical level which gives it a certain unreality, a sense that the friend or the beloved is being addressed from the pulpit or the rostrum. In other words, I would say that there is a good poetic eloquence, in which heightened feeling finds expression in a speech similarly elevated, but that there is also a bad eloquence, in which the language overreaches and is at variance with the tone of the poem. And I should say that both these types of eloquence are to be found in the two poems which Henri Peyre cites. *Le Lac* starts off with a grandiloquent image and a great rhetorical question:

> Ainsi toujours poussés vers de nouveaux rivages,
> Dans la nuit éternelle emportés sans retour,

> Ne pourrons-nous jamais, sur l'océan des âges,
>   Jeter l'ancre un seul jour?

Then it moves on to some of the most poignant lines in French poetry, those put in the mouth of the absent beloved, "O temps, suspends ton vol! . . ." The theme is the same as that of the first stanza, but in the interval Lamartine has moved from the general to the particular, and the lines speak with the sound of the human voice. But once the quotation is ended the poet relapses into a more ponderous rhetoric, in which the lengthy enumerations of the appeal to nature are too heavy a weight on the sentiment.

The same is true of *Ischia*, where the lines in quotation marks have an intensity and simplicity that is lacking in what precedes and follows. Sometimes too the poet's own words have this tone of personal speech, as when Vigny ends *La Maison du berger*:

> Nous marcherons ainsi, ne laissant que notre ombre
> Sur cette terre ingrate où les morts ont passé;
> Nous nous parlerons d'eux à l'heure où tout est sombre,
> Où tu te plais à suivre un chemin effacé,
> A rêver, appuyée aux branches incertaines,
> Pleurant, comme Diane au bord de ses fontaines,
> Ton amour taciturne et toujours menacé.

One might note too that French romantic poetry is rich in great passages rather than in great poems. Rarely does a poem of any length maintain a high level throughout, and this is most often, I believe, because of an intrusion of false rhetoric. Some of the romantics themselves noted these connections with the eighteenth century. Guiraud — a timid romantic to be sure — says: "Our literary century began before the end of the last century; Gilbert's verses . . . Delille's poems, Ducis' tragedies, some of Lebrun's odes, marked in a striking way the transition from one period to another, and prove without question that even before the Revolution there were distinguished writers who felt the need of returning to the models of the 'grand siècle', and seeking within their own souls the poetic inspiration which the eighteenth century had sought in vain." [83] And in 1827 Sainte-Beuve remarked that the *Muse Française* school of poets "soon had its commonplaces, its mythological insipidities, its artificial ardor, and most of the defects which it criticized in the older poetry. What it lacked above all was style." [84]

What is relevant here is the relation of the weakness of the poetry to the poetic theory. Often it seems that the practice is simply at variance with the theory. Two examples will suffice, one from the least, one from the most revolutionary of the romantic poets. While Lamartine made no pretence of a complete breach with the past, he still claimed to have made definite innovations: "I was the first to bring poetry down from Parnassus, and to give to what we call the muse, instead of the conventional lyre with seven strings, the very fibres of the human heart, touched and moved by the innumerable thrills of the soul and of nature." [85] Yet when Lamartine sets out to turn his emotions into poetry they all too easily stiffen into a conventional mold. In 1814 he writes to his friend Virieu:

Hier je découvris, assez loin de la ville, un petit sentier ombragé par deux buissons bien parfumés; il me conduisit au milieu des vignes qui sont parsemées de cerisiers. Je me couchai sous leur ombre fraîche et épaisse, j'ôtai mon épée et mes bottes, l'une me servant de pupitre et l'autre d'oreiller. Je sentais dans mes cheveux un vent doux et frais; je n'entendais rien que les bruits qui me plaisent, quelques sons mourants de la cloche des vêpres, le sourd bourdonnement des insectes pendant la chaleur et les rapaux d'une caille cachée dans un blé voisin. . . . Voilà ce que j'y griffonnais au crayon:

> Ah! rendons grâce au ciel qui nous créa sensibles:
> Aurait-il pu nous faire un plus heureux présent!
> L'imagination, d'un pinceau complaisant,
> Crée, embellit pour nous des mondes invisibles
> Où nous nous égarons loin du monde présent.
> Pour nous tout est plaisir et tout est jouissance:
> La chute d'une feuille, une fleur que balance
>   L'haleine invisible du vent,
> Ce ruisseau paresseux qui murmure en fuyant,

L'obscurité, le jour, le bruit ou le silence,
Tout dans un cœur sensible éveille un sentiment.
Soit que le jour finisse ou que le jour commence,
Il nous trouve plongés dans un songe charmant.[86]

There is little to be said for this as poetry except what can always be counted on in Lamartine, the music of many of its lines. Any personal note is absent; the whole first part of the poem is a series of general statements, prosaic in form, conventional in tone, vague to a degree. The poet says that imagination creates new worlds for us, but his imagination does no such creating. In the lines which follow the concrete details of the prose disappear, and are replaced by such general terms as noise and silence, leaf and flower. The original experience, instead of being enriched and intensified, has evaporated into a series of banal reflections expressed in conventional language.

Hugo, the later flamboyant revolutionary, says in the December 1822 preface to the *Odes* that the monotony of the ode is due to the abuse of apostrophe, exclamation, prosopopoeia and other such figures used in too great abundance. But his own odes too often are examples of this very fault. Take a few lines from *Le Rétablissement de la statue de Henri IV* (first published in the *Conservateur Littéraire* in 1820):

Où courez-vous? — Quel bruit naît, s'élève et s'avance?
Qui porte ces drapeaux, signe heureux de nos rois?
Dieu! Quelle masse au loin semble, en sa marche immense,
    Broyer la terre sous son poids?
Répondez . . . Ciel! c'est lui! je vois sa noble tête . . .

These may be extreme examples, but the fact remains that in this "revolutionary" poetry there are but rare poems that do not strike some note all too familiar to those who know their eighteenth-century poetry.

The reasons for this conflict between theory and practice need be mentioned only briefly here. Sainte-Beuve, in his 1855 article on Ronsard, inclines to blame the schooling of the French romantics for some of their poetic weaknesses.[87] He puts first the teaching of rhetoric, which played so large a part in the curriculum. In theory, of course, the romantics were far from accepting their rhetoric lessons in docile fashion.

> Guerre à la rhétorique et paix à la syntaxe!

says Hugo in the *Réponse à un acte d'accusation*. Yet as early as the middle of the nineteenth century Sainte-Beuve, who rarely missed an opportunity of attacking the friends of his romantic youth, wrote: "What used to be called *rhetoric* is now called *poetry*. Just because the rhetoricians and sophists are disguised as poets, we think they have disappeared. The author who flatters himself that he is a poet is all too often only a magnificent rhetorician." [88] Later writers have shown that in poem after poem of these revolutionary romantics there is hardly a line in which one or more of the despised figures of rhetoric cannot be detected.

The romantics' failure to free themselves from the practice of rhetoric is due in part to their formal education. But it might well be suggested that formal training should not be overstressed, that the budding poet may well react against what he is made to read and write in school, and be far more influenced by what he reads of his own free will. Vigny for example writes in his journal in 1847: "My true literary education was that which I gave myself, when, delivered out of the hands of my teachers, I was free to follow at will the swift flight of my insatiable imagination." [89] But what the French romantics lacked, in or out of school, was contact with the fountainheads of their own lyric poetry. We have seen how neglected and misjudged Villon and the sixteenth-century poets had been, and there is no evidence that any of the romantic poets had read them before their rehabilitation by Sainte-Beuve in 1828. They read their own great dramatic poets, but for lyric poetry in their own language they were limited to their predecessors in the eighteenth and nineteenth centuries. Much as they reacted against these poets in theory, it is easy to trace in their practice the stilted phrasing, the oratorical style of the earlier poets. And although the romantics turned to foreign poets they all too often read them in translation.

As both the romantics themselves and later critics pointed out, their real masters were the great prose writers who preceded them: Rousseau and Bernardin de Sainte-Pierre, Chateaubriand and Madame de Staël. Sainte-Beuve noted in 1825 that the prose writers had had to take over the role of the poets.[90] And in 1828 Emile Deschamps wrote: "The true poetry of the nineteenth century came into France through prose. M. de Chateaubriand and Madame de Staël were the first poets of the period. . . . And then it must be admitted that the poems of the school of Delille, and, later, those of the Empire, however well constructed they were, were above all well calculated to create discouragement about French poetry." [91] So the romantics turned to the prose writers, and with a vengeance. As Sainte-Beuve remarked with his customary acidity, "M. de Chateaubriand has been spoiled by the poets of his time; almost all of them have struggled to put his prose into verse." [92] Indeed passage after passage of these poets is borrowed from the great prose writers, as a glance at the footnotes of modern critical editions will indicate. Lamartine wrote in 1816, "I am sharpening my pen to put *Atala* into verse." [93] A long passage in Vigny's *Eloa* does precisely this; he picks out sentences and phrases from some five pages of the prologue to *Atala*, puts the resulting mosaic into alexandrines, and produces twenty-five lines of the kind of poetry of which Henri Peyre has said: "Only a difference of rhythmical form, and, as it were, of degree, separates this poetry from the finest prose." [94] One cannot, I think, overemphasize the disastrous effect on the French romantics of having been cut off from their own lyric tradition, of having had to discover poetry through prose.

This led to certain weaknesses which are to be found in their poetic theory as well as in their poetry. When they write in the rhetorical tradition, when their verse is all too reminiscent of the eighteenth century, then they are indeed unfaithful to their poetic beliefs. But when the poetry is diffuse, effusive, loose in form, lacking in concision and density, there is no basic infidelity to the conception of poetry as emotion, truth, nature, and liberty.

The aspect of romantic theory that has been treated in this chapter was above all a liberation. Emotion was set free, truth and nature were delivered from the bonds of *bienséances* and imitation, and the shackles binding versification and language were unloosed. It is probably true that such a revolution was necessary for the rebirth of poetry; we have seen all too well the failure of more timid attempts to produce a poetic revival. The weakness of the doctrine lies in the fact that it had too little that was positive to put in the place of what it had destroyed. To these romantics cut off from their own poetic tradition one may apply what Santayana says: "The misfortune of revolutionists is that they are disinherited, and their folly is that they wish to be disinherited even more than they are." [95] But this applies above all to the romantic doctrine of the 1820's and to the poets who carried it out unchanged. For the greatest of them this theory of effusion and liberty was to be modified by the renewal of interest in form and art which began shortly before 1830.

VI

To poetry conceived as emotion, sometimes even as un-written emotion, was to be opposed the conception of poetry as belonging above all to the realm of art. This alliance of poetry and art has two aspects, often found in conjunction but basically distinct. First of all poetry is envisaged as closely allied to the plastic arts, and is therefore essentially pictorial, a poetry of images, either descriptive or metaphorical. The first great manifestation of this is *Les Orientales*,[1] and it is carried on by Gautier and the Parnassian poets, and indeed colors much of the poetry of the nineteenth century. This poetry turns its back on social trends, is opposed to any idea of utility, and sets up against the poet-guide the poet-artist. But poetry is also seen as art in another sense, not as competing with the plastic arts, but as concerned above all with its own particular tools, language and versification. The poet is an artist in words.

It would of course be absurd to pretend that the early ro-mantics had no conception of pictorial poetry, no interest in it. Their scorn of the descriptive poetry of the eighteenth century did indeed make them somewhat wary of it. Soumet, echoing Madame de Staël, writes in the *Muse Française* that there are two great divisions of poetry, the poetry of images and the poetry of sentiment. "The poetry of sentiment belongs to the different moods of the human soul; the poetry of images to the wonders of creation. The first, to be sublime, must be attuned to a heart which is deeply moved; the second needs only to represent natural objects faithfully: one is an echo, the other a mirror. In the ode, according to M. Victor Hugo, these two kinds of poetry are united, and each expresses the other." ² The passage is worth pausing over. First of all it suggests a clear superiority of poetry of sentiment. Then *image* is plainly used in the sense of description or picture, and Soumet's two categories recall, in an uncomfortable way, the elegy and the descriptive poem of the previous century. Only the last sentence suggests a possible fusion of the two.

Even the least pictorial of the romantics, Lamartine, gives images a place, though it is the last place, in one of his descriptions of poetry: "Poetry, for a long time turned by a kind of intellectual profanation into a skilful distortion of language, a sterile diversion for the mind, has now remembered its origin and its goal. It has been reborn as the daughter of enthusiasm and inspiration, as the ideal and mysterious expression of what is most ethereal and inexpressible in the soul, as the harmonious sense of the sorrows and pleasures of the spirit; after having entranced the youth of the human race by its fables, it now lifts it up with stronger wings to a truth as poetic as its dreams, and seeks for newer images in which to speak to the human race the language of its strength and its virility." ³ But the poetry of Lamartine is most often considered as being that of pure sentiment, while the poetry of images is attached to Chénier. Hugo admired in Chénier a truth of detail and abundance of images characteristic of ancient poetry.[4] Much later Gautier was to affirm that modern poetry dated from Chénier. And in 1829 Sainte-Beuve defended the disciples of Chénier against those of Madame de Staël, the precise against the abstract: "The picturesque is not a paintbox, which is emptied and exhausted in a single day; it is an eternal source of light, an inexhaustible sun." ⁵

In the development of pictorial poetry the close relation between poets and painters was an important element.[6] Both in the "Cénacle de Joseph Delorme" and later in the Jeunes-France group painters and poets mingled. In his poem, *Le Cénacle*, Sainte-Beuve, looking back to this time when poetry and painting were sisters, hailed this "Fraternité des arts! union fortunée!" [7] Most of the artists in the group were minor ones; the important thing was the constant interchange of ideas, the treatment of the same subjects in poetry as in painting. The influence of painting, on Hugo especially, should not however be exaggerated. He did indeed borrow some of his subjects from painters, good and bad; *L'Enfant grec* from Delacroix's *Massacre de Scio*, *Mazeppa* from Boulanger's painting of the same subject as well as from Byron. But one of Hugo's greatest gifts was his powerful and vivid visual imagination, which is shown in his drawings as well as in his literary work, and which needed no painter to stimulate it.

Les Orientales was hailed by Sainte-Beuve as "ce trône merveilleux dressé à l'art pur." [8] In his preface Hugo asserts that in poetry there are no good or bad subjects, only good and bad poets. Somewhat on the defensive over this reversal of his earlier opinions, he goes on: "If the author is asked today what is the use of these *Orientales*? who put it into his head to spend a whole volume wandering through the Orient? what is the sense of this useless book of pure poetry, flung out amidst the serious preoccupations of the public? . . . what is its relevance? what rhyme or reason is there to the Orient? . . . He will answer that he knows nothing about it, that it is just an idea which came into his head in a rather absurd way last summer, as he was going to watch the sun set." The preface represents a certain deviation from the development of Hugo's poetic doctrine, though not so extreme as has sometimes been said, for his interest in form was never to die out. But he was not long in returning to a belief in the utility and social value of art, heeding the appeal made to him by Pierre Leroux in 1831: "Woe to the artist who is thus apart from his time! or rather woe to the artist who, seeing his hesitant epoch wavering between the past and the future, without a destiny, thus divides himself and ends by having no social religion other than the cult of art, the religion of art!" [9] The *Feuilles d'automne* and the *Chants du crépuscule* marked the road which

Hugo was to follow. Yet in them, as in his later work, the visual element continued to predominate; Nisard said severely of the *Chants du crépuscule*: "there is no surer symptom of decadence in poetic matters than a profusion of description." [10] The change is in the theory rather than in the poetry. Many years later Hugo did his best to deny the paternity of the term "l'art pour l'art," which had been attributed to him: "It is the contrary of this term which is written in my works. . . . One day, thirty-five years ago, in a discussion . . . of Voltaire's tragedies, the author of this book flung in this interruption: 'This tragedy is not a tragedy. These are not living men, these are oratorical words. Better a thousand times art for art's sake!' " [11]

Yet *Les Orientales* and its preface were an inspiration and a rallying point for many later poets, from Gautier with his "transpositions d'art" and Aloysius Bertrand with his picturesque evocations of the past to Leconte de Lisle and the Parnassian poets. A younger generation raised the standard which Hugo had pulled down. [12] Many of the Jeunes-France group learned their first lessons from Hugo. This group included a number of artists, as well as such writers as Gérard de Nerval, Pétrus Borel, Philothée O'Neddy, and Gautier. [13] The group was labeled in the *Figaro* of August 30, 1831: "The Jeunes-France was born the day painting formed an alliance with romantic literature. The poet said to the painter: You paint, but you do not know how to talk; take my jargon. . . . The painter answered the poet: You write, but you do not know how to paint; take my brush." Speaking more seriously, Gautier wrote many years later in his *Histoire du romantisme* of "those youthful bands who fought for idealism, poetry, and the liberty of art." Later on in the book he described them more fully: "The characteristic which is found in all the budding poets of that time is the overflow of lyricism and the pursuit of passion. To develop freely all the caprices of thought, however much they might shock taste, propriety and rules; to hate and repulse as much as possible what Horace called the *profanum vulgus*, and what the art-students with their moustaches and flowing hair call grocers, Philistines, or bourgeois; to sing of love with such ardor as to burn the paper, to consider it the only goal and the only means of happiness; to sanctify and deify art as a second creator; such was the program which each one endeavored to carry out to the best of his abilities, the ideal and the secret yearning of the young romantics." [14] First of all then, the Jeunes-France carried on certain essential parts of the earlier romantic program, the outbursts of lyricism, the search for passion, the glorification of love. Philothée O'Neddy wrote:

> Je prends mon moi pour thème avec emportement.
> Volontiers je traduis, en phrases cadencées,
> Le rhythme intérieur du bal de mes pensées. [15]

For O'Neddy this goes hand in hand with the cult of art: "Poetry, that twin sister of God, who bestows on the physical world light, harmony, and perfume; on the spiritual world, love, intelligence, and will. . . . Poetry possesses a city, a kingdom where she displays at will her two natures: her human nature which is *art*, her divine nature which is *passion*." [16] For the Jeunes-France again, one of the keywords is liberty; Pétrus Borel cries out: "J'ai besoin d'une somme énorme de liberté." For him

> L'Art ne saurait souffrir de verrou ni de chaîne;
> Il brise tout lien qui l'entrave ou le gêne.
> Il prend pour lui le ciel, le temps, l'immensité,
> Il ne met sous sa dent qu'un pain de liberté.

This cult of art leads to a rejection of the world around us:

> L'art vrai sur tous les flots toujours vogue en aval.
> Il est jaloux, tyran, et n'a point de rival.
> . . . .
> Si vous choisissez l'Art, repoussez loin le monde,
> A l'Art tous nos pensers, point de commerce immonde. [17]

The poet takes pride in his poverty and his need, scorns the bourgeois, and dreams of a revolution no longer purely literary, but social. In 1862 O'Neddy wrote that his preface to *Feu et flamme* had been the expression of a desire for social revolution: "We had among us adherents of Saint-Simonism and Fourierism." [18] But for this group revolution is above all revolt, not a desire to change the world (as with the later romantics), but a desire to escape, to take refuge in another world. Some recent critics have seen in this revolt "une tentative de conquête, une volonté de transcender la condition d'artiste et d'homme," with a distinction between "poésie moyen d'expression" and "poésie activité de l'esprit" which points forward to surrealism.[19] This seems to me somewhat exaggerated, overemphasizing the metaphysical aspect of a movement which sought escape above all in art, "the philosopher's stone of the nineteenth century." [20] For most, at least, of the Jeunes-France, the escape was through literature and imagination rather than through any transcendental experience. Gautier's caricature is perhaps overdrawn, but possibly closer to the truth, when he describes his Onuphrius: "He read nothing but marvellous legends and old romances of chivalry, mystic poetry, cabalistic treatises, German ballads, books on witchcraft and demonology; with all this he created for himself, in the midst of the real world buzzing around him, a world of ecstasy and vision which it was given to few to enter." For Onuphrius the experiment leads to failure; he could make no contact with the world of reality. "Without this fatal tendency, he could have been the greatest of poets; as it was, he was only the most extraordinary of madmen." [21]

For most of the group, which broke up in 1833, the ideal outstripped the achievement. But they put into circulation the idea of the poet as artist.[22] The term had been used by Saint-Simon as early as 1825: "I mean by artist the poet in the largest sense of the term; the word *artist* then means *man of imagination*, and embraces the works of the painter, the poet, the writer, etc.; in a word, everything which has sensation as its object." [23] Here we have the reverse of the use, earlier by Diderot, and later by Baudelaire, of *poète* as the all-embracing term. Between 1827 and 1834 the use of *artiste* becomes more and more frequent. In Gautier's "Daniel Jovard" Ferdinand explains to Daniel "ce que c'était que ficelle, chic, galbe, art, artiste, et artistique." [24] In January, 1833 the *Revue de Paris* said: "*Art*, for these gentlemen, is everything, poetry, painting, etc.; these gentlemen are in love with *art*; these gentlemen despise anyone who does not work for *art*, and they spend their lives talking *art*, discussing *art*." And in 1834 Félix Pyat writes that the name of artist belongs to all creative geniuses.[25] So the *Physiologie du poète* includes both the "poète-touriste," the pictorial poet, and the Olympian poet, who has the greatest scorn for all that is not art: "It is he who invented the well-known aphorism, *art is a priesthood*, a sublime saying that means absolutely nothing." [26]

In 1837 Nisard referred to "the theory of *art for art's sake*, a literary caprice which prevailed for a moment, but disappeared suddenly in the July tempest." [27] The conception was, on the contrary, to have a long life. The poet who remained most faithful to it was Gautier. His first volume of *Poésies* (1830), written under the influence of Hugo, has little originality of theme, but shows a marked pictorial quality and preoccupation with technique. Gautier long hesitated between becoming a painter and becoming a poet, and compromised by making words paint, making poetry a "transposition d'art." His advice was, "Fuyez toujours l'épithète musicale pour l'épithète qui peint." [28] The preface to *Albertus* (1832) echoes the *Orientales* preface: "What is the use of this? — Its use is to be beautiful. . . . In general, as soon as something becomes useful, it ceases to be beautiful. . . . Art is liberty, luxury, efflorescence, it is the flowering of the soul in idleness. — Painting, sculpture, music are of absolutely no use." [29] The preface to *Mademoiselle de Maupin* is the great manifesto of art for art's sake. It begins with a violent attack on virtuous and utilitarian critics, and goes on to proclaim the supremacy of art: "There is nothing truly beautiful except what is useless; everything that is useful is ugly; for it is the expression of some need; and the needs of man are ignoble and disgusting, like his miserable and weak nature." [30]

Yet with all his passionate belief in the primacy of art Gautier never went so far as to deny the need for an innate poetic gift. In his article on "Excellence de la poésie" (1873) he starts out by saying that to write verse, "in addition to an abundance of ideas, a knowledge of language, and a gift for imagery, one needs a certain intimate sense, a secret inclination, something which cannot be acquired and which depends on temperament and individuality." But his stress on form leads him to a return to the eighteenth-century doctrine of the "difficulté vaincue": "Even if beautiful prose had the same value as beautiful verse, which I deny, should the merit of difficulty overcome count for nothing? . . . What is art, if not the means of overcoming the obstacles which nature opposes to the crystallization of thought, and if that were easy, where would be the merit and the glory?" [31] Art is above all a *making*: "Art is beauty, constant invention of detail, choice of words, exquisite care in execution; the word poet means literally *maker*; anything which is not well *made* does not exist." More and more Gautier sees in art a struggle with a resistant material, and prefers to compare poetry with sculpture rather than with painting. "Verse is a gleaming and hard material like Carrara marble, which permits only pure and correct lines, the result of long contemplation. It has been said that painting is the sister of poetry; this would be even more true of sculpture." [32] This idea is reiterated in verse in *L'Art*, with its series of plastic parallels and its conclusion:

> Les dieux eux-mêmes meurent;
> Mais les vers souverains
>   Demeurent
> Plus forts que les airains. [33]

All through his life Gautier remained faithful to this doctrine. It is repeated in the program he set forth when he became editor of *L'Artiste* in 1856:

Enamored, from my childhood, of statuary, painting, and all the plastic arts, I have carried the love of art to the verge of delirium; — now that I have reached maturity, I in no way repent of that glorious madness. . . . The Scriptures speak somewhere of the lust of the eyes, *concupiscentia oculorum*; — that is my sin. . . . After having looked my fill, my greatest pleasure has been to transpose into my own art monuments, frescos, pictures, statues, bas-reliefs, often at the risk of straining language and making the dictionary into a palette. . . . So I bring to *L'Artiste* a passion for art. . . . I believe in the autonomy of Art; for me Art is not a means, but an end; — an artist who has any other aim than beauty is not an artist in my eyes; I have never been able to understand the separation of idea and form, any more than I could understand a body without a soul or a soul without a body, at least on our mortal sphere — a beautiful form *is* a beautiful idea, for what would a form be which expressed nothing? [34]

The last part of this passage seems indeed to bring out the all too neglected idea of an intimate relation between matter and form. Gautier returns to this point in his article, "Du beau dans l'art," also published in 1856: "The great error of the adversaries of the doctrine of art for art's sake . . . is to believe that form can be independent of idea; form cannot exist without idea, nor idea without form. . . . An artist is above all a man; he can mirror in his work, whether he shares or rejects them, the loves, the hates, the passions, the beliefs, and the prejudices of his time, on condition that art the divine always be for him the end and not the means. . . . Art for art's sake means, not form for form's sake, but form for beauty's sake." [35]

Yet it cannot be denied that for Gautier form has the place of honor; he reversed the romantic doctrine. The Goncourt brothers describe him repeating lovingly a phrase Flaubert had just used to him, "de la forme naît l'idée." [36] Gautier indeed played an important part in stemming the tide of overeffusive romanticism. But it is difficult not to agree with Gide's remark, "Gautier occupe une place considérable; c'est seulement fâcheux qu'il la remplisse si mal." Gide had said earlier: "I do not reproach Gautier for this doctrine of 'art for art's sake,' outside of which I find no meaning to life, but for having reduced art to expressing so very little." [37] Except for his earlier poems — and it was these that Baudelaire so greatly admired — Gautier tends more and more to the "transposition d'art," the translation of the plastic arts into words. Curiously enough, he saw very clearly the dangers of the opposite procedure, that of translating poetry into painting: "In spite of Horace's *ut pictura poesis*, painting and poetry have nothing in common; it is this unfortunate preoccupation with poetry in painting and in music that has made us for so long the most ridiculous dilettantes and connoisseurs in the world." [38] His own poetry is as close to purely visual as possible; he once told Sainte-Beuve that his one aim had been to look carefully at nature and to reproduce it, as far as possible, just as he saw it.[39] For him poetic form has almost a plastic sense; he is keenly aware of the shape of the poem and of the stanza, and language is a palette. But it is not difficult, as Gide pointed out, to find weaknesses, platitudes, and carelessness in his language. The renewal of poetic language in its widest sense was not the work of Gautier.

The beginnings of that renewal are to be found in the late 1820's. Looking back in 1855 to the early days of romanticism Sainte-Beuve remarked that the eighteenth-century sources had been exhausted and that "it was necessary to find new strength elsewhere, not so much for sentiments (those we had within ourselves) as for expression, color, and style. There was where a large part of the difficulty lay." [40] And in 1857 he outlines what the romantic program had been: "To restore to French poetry truth, naturalness, even familiarity, and at the same time firmness and vividness of style . . . to make it express the agitations of the soul, and the subtlest gradations of thought; to make it reflect external nature not only by colors and images, but sometimes by a simple and felicitous combination of syllables." [41] On this program Sainte-Beuve and Victor Hugo were united. Which of them inspired the other has been the subject of much discussion; from what Sainte-Beuve himself wrote in 1835 it seems to have been a meeting of two minds both already preoccupied with the subject rather than a one-sided influence. "Hugo took this opportunity to explain to me his views and his methods in the art of poetry, some of his secrets of rhythm and color. At this time I was already writing verse. . . . I quickly grasped the new ideas that I heard for the first time and that immediately cast a new light on the style and structure of verse; as I was already working on our old sixteenth-century poets, I was fully prepared to apply what I heard and to find supporting arguments. A second visit completed my conversion and initiated me into some of the reforms of the new school." [42]

The new source to which the romantic poets were to turn was the great early lyric poetry of France, so long neglected and unappreciated. In 1826 the French Academy announced as the subject for its "prix d'éloquence" French literature of the sixteenth century. The prize was divided between two staunch antiromantics, Saint-Marc Girardin and Philarète Chasles, neither of whose works was in any way calculated to revive enthusiasm for sixteenth-century poetry. An unsuccessful competitor for the prize was Gérard de Nerval. His essay proposes that instead of imitating foreign poets the moderns should follow their example and study their own early poets. He deplores the scorn heaped by the poets of the Pléiade on their predecessors, although he appreciates the progress in style and poetic color they brought about, the "style primitif et verdissant" that makes up for so many defects, and particularly the perfection of Ronsard's later style. Gérard's severest criticism is reserved for the classical period: "Art, always art, cold, calculated, no gentle revery, no true religious feeling, nothing inspired directly by nature; nothing but the correct and the beautiful; a uniform nobility of thought and expression; a Midas who changes to gold all that he touches. Classic poetry is set in motion: only La Fontaine will resist; so Boileau will forget him in his *Art poétique*." [43]

In spite of Gérard's reservations on the Pléiade and his preference for a more naïve and popular poetry, he was for a time greatly influenced by Ronsard: "En ce temps, *je ronsardisais*." He was particularly struck by Ronsard's *odelettes*; a concentrated form which seemed to him no less precious than the sonnet.[44] For Gérard the question of form was a crucial one. He says in his 1840 introduction to *Faust*: "Art always requires an absolute and precise form, without which all is trouble and confusion." [45] He was to be among the first of the poets of magic and mystery, but his concern for form never deserted him, and in *Les Chimères* he crystallized his dreams and reveries into the perfect form of the sonnet.

But it was above all to Sainte-Beuve that the romantics owed the rediscovery of the poetic tradition that had been interrupted for so long. "To enrich the palette with some tones agreeable to the eye, to add some notes to well-known accents, some numbers and couplets to the rhythms then in use, above all to justify, by discovering appropriate examples, what the poetic innovators of our time dared to do by instinct, to disclose a tradition where only débris had been seen; this was my highest ambition. I focused it on the name of Ronsard." [46] On the advice of Daunou, Sainte-Beuve had set to work to compete for the Academy prize, but he did not complete his study in time, and it was published in *Le Globe* in 1828 as the *Tableau de la poésie française au seizième siècle*, and in volume form in the same year.[47] It should be noted that Sainte-Beuve's interest in style dates back to his earliest criticism, as is shown in his successive studies of the various editions of Hugo's *Odes et ballades*. In the first volume of *Odes* he finds "a style all afire, sparkling with images, leaping with harmony; bad taste due to grandiosity and brusqueness, but never to niggardliness or calculation." On the 1826 edition he is more severe; Hugo has done violence to his sublime reveries in the process of transforming them into poetry, and overloaded them with exaggerated comparisons, frequent digressions, and over-refined analyses." But Sainte-Beuve also has high praise for the harmony and movement of Hugo's style, the richness of his rhyme.[48] In 1827 an article on Malherbe also stresses the importance of style: "The special merit, the immortal glory of our poet is that he was the first in France to have had a feeling, and developed a theory of style; to have understood that the choice of terms and of thoughts is, if not the principle, at least the condition of all true eloquence, and that the felicitous arrangement of things and of words is usually more important than the things and the words themselves." [49]

In his preface to the *Tableau* Sainte-Beuve says that when he began his study of the literature of the sixteenth century by reading its poetry he became so absorbed in it that he went no further, and above all lost no opportunity to connect his sixteenth-century studies with the literary and poetic questions of his own time.[50] It is here especially that the interest of the *Tableau* lies. A good part of Sainte-Beuve's actual criticism (particularly on Villon) [51] is somewhat timid. He is at his best on style, as when he says of Du Bellay's *chansons*: "Among other merits, one is struck by the easy grace, and as it were the flowing current of the poetic phrase, which winds and meanders effortlessly through the sinuosities of rhyme." He stresses the freedom of *césure* and *enjambement*, the rich rhymes of the sixteenth-century alexandrine, recreated by Chénier and cultivated by the romantics.[52]

The *Tableau* is centered on Ronsard. "Admiring the ancients with a certain independence of mind, instead of translating them, he imitated them; all his originality, all his audacity, lies in having created this imitation." Ronsard's great aim was nobility and splendor of language; "often his periods seem to us well turned and harmonious, and his thought is clothed in

brilliant images," only occasionally spoiled by trivial and grotesque expressions (much the same criticism that Sainte-
Beuve had made earlier of Victor Hugo). Sainte-Beuve goes
on to trace the development of French poetry from Malherbe,
who by his correctness and prudence led a number of his
followers into prosaic platitude. After Malherbe poetry and
prose came to resemble each other more and more. In the
seventeenth century imitation was still original and creative,
the mirror of a great civilization, but with the appearance of
"la pruderie" (Sainte-Beuve's word for *bienséances*) "periphrase got the upper hand, and our poetic instrument was
corrupted. All the efforts of the modern school are now
centered on bringing art back to truth." But in casting off the
yoke of the two preceding centuries the new school could not
but concern itself with what had gone before, and seek to ally
itself with a national tradition. Chénier began by liberating
the line of verse, Hugo, "harmoniste et architecte en poésie,"
renewed the stanza. The new school followed the sixteenth
century in structure and rhythm, but "aside from a certain
common movement of style and of verse-form, one cannot see
how our own literary period can be compared with the one
which we have just covered." [53]

At the beginning of his second volume, composed of selec-
tions from Ronsard with an introduction and notes, Sainte-
Beuve says: "For anyone who will take the trouble to put
together the doctrines scattered through this commentary and
my *Tableau de la poésie au seizième siècle*, a whole new
poetic doctrine will emerge, of which I am far from pretend-
ing to be the inventor." [54] It may be well to pause briefly here
to summarize the main points of this doctrine, and to compare
it with the romantic doctrine that preceded it. Sainte-Beuve
has little to say of sentiment or enthusiasm; he does insist on
vérité of language, as opposed to periphrase and prudery. His
great interest is in style, in a poetic language different from
that of prose, in a variety and freedom of versification, in a

harmony of sound. His admiration for Ronsard is based on style alone: "Since his power of invention is practically non-existent, it is only by his style that he redeems himself in our eyes, and is truly a creator, that is to say a poet." [55] One of Sainte-Beuve's great contributions is to have attached the revolution in style to the great tradition of the French lyric, to have added a revival to a revolution. It has been truly said that much of what Sainte-Beuve says in theory Hugo had already carried out in practice, but Sainte-Beuve deserves the glory of having consolidated and expressed the doctrine.

His ideas met with some opposition. Rémusat discussed them at length in three articles in *Le Globe*, saying that for him the Pléiade did not deserve Sainte-Beuve's praise, that Ronsard's school was an accident which disturbed the natural course of French poetry. His final article begins with a sentence which should endear him to the New Critics: "I do not really see what poetry has to do with the history of literature." Sainte-Beuve's belief that the new school of poets should go back to Ronsard "pour trouver *à quoi se rattacher*" aims at a reform of style; but, says Rémusat, the height of art is to write, or to appear to write, naturally. He rejects the idea of a poetic language essentially different from that of prose, maintaining that French is one of the languages in which there is the least difference between the two, and he asks, "Why should a poetry which aspires only to truth seek for a conventional language?" His advice to poets is: "Seek first and foremost for novelty of genre and subject; innovate, if possible, in inspiration; and then you will find a suitable language, or rather your own will be modified naturally, if necessary, and shape itself like a garment on the body that it is to adorn." [56] Here Rémusat echoes both the earlier conception of poetic language as an ornament and the romantic belief that language is the natural result of inspiration.

Rémusat's articles bring out very clearly the differences between the poetic doctrine that stresses sentiment and inspiration and the one that stresses form. Neither Sainte-Beuve nor Rémusat represents an extreme position. Sainte-Beuve is very far from denying the importance of content; his concern is to find a true expression of that content. Nor does Rémusat ignore form; he simply believes that if the sentiment is true and natural the form will inevitably be so. The discussion centers on the way in which the poet finds his form, by inspiration or by conscious artistry and imitation. There is not the sharp contrast between a poetry of form and one of content that the eighteenth century offers, and that is found in the nineteenth century between the pure romantic doctrine and that of the minor Parnassians. The two are moving towards a common ground, both basing their positions on a fidelity to truth and to nature.

In the *Pensées de Joseph Delorme*, published the following year, Sainte-Beuve's preoccupation with questions of language continues. Again it is the problem of a special language of poetry, of its metrical, rhythmic, and musical qualities, that interests him. He stresses the use of the "mot propre et pittoresque," but adds: "While the precise and picturesque word should ordinarily be used, the vague and general word sternly rejected, one should use occasionally and in the right place some of those undefined, unexplained, elusive words beneath the extent of which the thought must be divined." [57] Words, that is, that suggest rather than paint.

Among the musical qualities of poetry Sainte-Beuve puts rhyme first:

> Rime, l'unique harmonie
> Du vers, qui, sans tes accents
>   Frémissants,
> Serait muet au génie.[58]

He notes again the value of the *assouplissement* of the alexandrine by the disciples of Chénier, as opposed to the neglect of form by the followers of Madame de Staël. "In the midst of such a whirlpool of ideas and words, one feels that *form, style* (to use the word in its broadest sense) must often have been neglected and sometimes treated with scant courtesy." The followers of Chénier, on the contrary, "approached art as artists, and lovingly set about the work of creation." But Sainte-Beuve, with all his emphasis on form, never gives it the pre-eminent place that the disciples of art for art's sake did: "While we give certain counsels about style, reveal certain new secrets of form, we do not presume to contest the pre-eminence of sentiments and ideas." [59] He sees in the absorption in form a refuge in hours of sadness: "The artist, to escape from this sterile and painful ennui, will seek distraction in questions of pure art, separating them, as far as possible, from literary quarrels, which are always so bitter and harassing; he will find pleasure in technical details, in the subtle grasp of relationships, in analyses of *style* and *form*; he will have ready for future inspiration resources and secrets which it may use at need and which will make it, unconsciously, more powerful and more free; thus he will succeed in filling a temporary vacuum in his life; and by degrees, through brooding over the means of expressing things, he will soon find himself again able to feel the things which are expressed." Thus Sainte-Beuve's motto is *"l'art dans la rêverie, et la rêverie dans l'art."* [60] He has the clearest conception we yet met of the balance of form and matter. Later, under the influence of Wordsworth, he arrived at a belief in a simpler and more natural poetic language:

> Plus est simple le vers et côtoyant la prose,
> Plus pauvre de belle ombre et d'haleine de rose,
> Et plus la forme étroite a lieu de le garder.[61]

This results in a poetry often too close to prose, in which the poet's theories of style have not resulted in sound practice.

Unlike Sainte-Beuve, Hugo arrived slowly at a belief in the importance of poetic form. In a letter of 1821 he writes to Adèle: "Poetry lies in ideas, ideas come from the soul. Verse is but an elegant garment on a beautiful body. Poetry can be expressed in prose, it is merely more perfect when it is clothed in the grace and majesty of verse." [62] Even when his practice shows an increasing concern with form he is hesitant about allowing it a conscious role. Explaining, in the preface to *Les Orientales*, his changes and corrections, he maintains that they must come naturally, irresistibly, with something like inspiration. In his article on Ymbert Gallois (1833) form is far from sufficient in itself: "It is not everything for a verse to have a good form; in order that there may be perfume, color and savor in it, it is absolutely necessary that it should contain an idea, an image or a sentiment. The bee constructs like an artist the six sides of its waxen cell, and then fills it with honey. The cell is verse; the honey is poetry." [63] Yet many of the notes published in *Littérature et philosophie mêlées* show a strong sense of the importance of style: "The artist who has no style spends his life between a dream and a sketch." Artistic creation is compared to divine creation: "There is nature which is what God makes directly, and there is art which is what God makes through man." [64] A series of pages is devoted to the renewal of poetic language, with the repetition of the comparison of the poet and the bee, but now with more stress on the importance of language and of the return to the sixteenth century, and on the contribution of the romantic school. Hugo concludes: "It is style which makes the work enduring and the poet immortal. Beautiful expression embellishes beautiful thought and preserves it; it is at the same time ornament and armor. Style on an idea is enamel on a tooth." [65] Yet in all these passages Hugo tends to talk of style as something separate, *parure*, *armure*, *émail*. It is only rarely that he and Sainte-Beuve have a momentary vision of a fusion of matter and form.

Hugo early became dissatisfied with the poetic language of the past: "Nothing is so *common* as this conventional elegance and nobility. Nothing discovered, nothing imagined, nothing invented in this style. Just what has been seen everywhere, rhetoric, bombast, commonplaces, scholastic flowers, poetry straight out of Latin verses. Borrowed ideas clad in shoddy images." [66] In the *Réponse à un acte d'accusation* Hugo's great claim was that he had overthrown traditional vocabulary, rhetoric, and versification:

> Je mis un bonnet rouge au vieux dictionnaire.
> Plus de mot sénateur! plus de mot roturier!
> Je fis une tempête au fond de l'encrier,
> Et je mêlai, parmi les ombres débordées,
> Au peuple noir des mots l'essaim blanc des idées;
> Et je dis: Pas de mot où l'idée au vol pur
> Ne puisse se poser, toute humide d'azur!
> Discours affreux! — Syllepse, hypallage, litote,
> Frémirent; je montai sur la borne Aristote,
> Et déclarai les mots égaux, libres, majeurs.
>
> . . . .
>
> J'ai dit à la narine: Eh mais! tu n'es qu'un nez!
> J'ai dit au long fruit d'or: Mais tu n'es qu'une poire!
> J'ai dit à Vaugelas: Tu n'es qu'une mâchoire!
> J'ai dit aux mots: Soyez république! soyez
> La fourmillière immense, et travaillez! croyez,
> Aimez, vivez! — J'ai mis tout en branle, et, morose,
> J'ai jeté le vers noble aux chiens noirs de la prose.

So while for Sainte-Beuve the renewal of poetic language was above all a return to an earlier tradition, for Hugo it was a revolution.

The cult of versification was carried on by Banville. "My tool," he says, "is the versification of the sixteenth century, perfected by the great poets of the nineteenth century." [67] He acknowledges his debt to Sainte-Beuve in the dedication of the *Odelettes*: "The *Pensées de Joseph Delorme* taught me my theories, the *Notes et Sonnets* at the end of the *Pensées d'août* gave me model formulas." [68] And throughout Banville's career Hugo is his god, from the *A Victor Hugo* of *Les Cariatides* to the *Ballade de Victor Hugo père de tous les rimeurs*, dated 1869:

> Gautier parmi ces joailliers
> Est prince, et Leconte de Lisle

Forge l'or dans ses ateliers,
Mais le père est là-bas, dans l'île.[69]

And in the *Petit Traité* Banville maintains that Hugo "sums up in himself the final perfection, the creative force of all our poetry, epic, lyric, and dramatic." [70]

Banville started as, and to some extent remained, a poet of sentiment; a poet, as Baudelaire said, "purement, naturellement et volontairement lyrique." [71] The poet, he himself wrote, must always be ready to show his whole soul. His sentiments are not the characteristically romantic ones of melancholy and despair, but, as Baudelaire again said, those of life's happy hours. Banville himself said in the preface to *Les Stalactites*: "A great yearning for happiness and hope is in every soul. To recover the joy that has been lost, to remount with courageous step the azure staircase which leads to the skies, is the ceaseless aspiration of modern man." In this same preface Banville assigns a mission to the poet: "it is the eternal task of lyric poetry to precede human philosophy like a dawn." [72] Up to this point Banville would seem to differ from the romantics only in the nature of his sentiments, in his preference for sunshine rather than shadow, in his return to the Greek rather than to the mediaeval past. His early poems are essentially romantic; he said of *Les Cariatides* (1841) that the poems in it were written "at that divinely unconscious age when we are truly intoxicated by the Muse, and the poet produces odes as the rosebush produces roses." [73] But he soon came to distrust the spontaneous flow of emotion. "One almost never shows oneself a good craftsman when one writes under the impact of a true emotion, at the moment when one is experiencing it." [74] The word *ouvrier* is the key to the preoccupation which increased steadily, throughout Banville's career; he was "stubbornly determined, . . . as craftsman and artist, to restore old poetic forms and to try to create new ones." [75] His cult was the cult of art, and he himself found his roots in the "race de 1830": "I was, and I still am, one of

those for whom art is an intolerant and jealous religion." [76]
The search for new and difficult forms absorbed him more and
more. Poetry was all in all for him:

> Pourquoi je vis? pour l'amour du laurier.[77]

The precarious balance between matter and form becomes
loaded on the side of form, and Baudelaire's "parfait classique"
is more and more the acrobat perilously balanced on the
complicated structure of his verse. He comes closer to
Gautier's conception of art, as is seen in the poem,

> Sculpteur, cherche avec soin, en attendant l'extase,
> Un marbre sans défaut pour en faire un beau vase,

and in the one to which Gautier's *L'Art* is the answer:

> Maître, qui nous enseignes
> L'amour du vert laurier,
> Tu daignes
> Etre un bon ouvrier.[78]

The final manifesto of his creed is the *Petit Traité de poésie
française*, in which poetry is treated as form, and most of all
as rhyme: "the *imagination of rhyme* is the quality above all
others which makes the poet." Indeed Banville goes so far as
to say that in a line of verse one hears only the rhyme word.
But this must come naturally: "Le poète *pense en vers.*" Yet
Banville never denies the role of inspiration, and writes to the
would-be poet in terms very reminiscent of the sixteenth
century: "Know then that, however great your genius and
your learning may be, you can never succeed in writing
beautiful poems without divine and supernatural help." Unlike Gautier, Banville saw poetry as essentially lyric, and defines lyricism as "the expression of the supernatural in us, of
that which transcends our material and terrestrial appetites,
in a word of those of our emotions and thoughts which can
be truly expressed only by song." [79]

With Gautier and with Banville the cult of form was predominant, as it was to be with the Parnassian poets. The only great romantic poet besides Hugo whose writings on poetry show a constant interest in form was Vigny. Gautier saw in him one of the greatest glories of the romantic school, and admired particularly "the exquisite balance of form and idea." [80] Whether Vigny's poetry, as I have suggested earlier, entirely deserves this praise is open to question, but there is no doubt that form was an ever-present problem for him. He criticizes Lamartine severely for his formal weaknesses, and in 1839 he writes that "the defect of our time is great diffusion and perpetual improvisation." [81] As far as he himself is concerned, "the Poet's constant struggle is the one which he wages with his idea. If the idea triumphs over the Poet and moves him too deeply, he become its dupe. . . . If the Poet is stronger than the idea, he molds it, forms it, and makes it into a work of art. It becomes what he wished it to be, a monument." Form is a creation of the intelligence; poetry is "reason raised to its supreme power in matter and in form." [82]

Vigny's conception of form differs from that of the poets with whom we have just been dealing. For him versification is secondary as well as difficult: "When one makes verses with one's eye on the clock, one is ashamed of the time one wastes in trying to find a rhyme which will be so kind as not to be prejudicial to the idea." Versification is for him a mechanical process: "Judgment, memory, and imagination go their own way in our heads. But beside them there is, I believe, a fourth faculty which can keep going without them; the one which manufactures rhyme and metre. One might call it the mill or the hurdy-gurdy. It keeps going without our paying any attention to it, and produces a soothing and regular sound. It is the mechanical faculty of poetry, the one which makes the rhymester but not the poet; it is nothing but it often leads us astray." Yet for Vigny poetry is to be found only in verse: "There is no such thing as a Poet in prose. Ballanche is the writer who would come closest to being a Poet if it were possible for a Poet to exist without that divine part of his work, harmony." [83] This rejection of poetry in prose, it may be noted, was shared by Hugo, who wrote in *A un écrivain* (dated 1859):

> . . La prose poétique
> Est une ornière où geint le vieux Pégase étique.
>
> . . . .
>
> La prose en vain essaie un essor assommant,
> Le vers s'envole au ciel tout naturellement.[84]

Vigny tends to maintain the old separation of matter and form. "External form is but a suitable garment which adapts itself, drops or rises to fit the fundamental idea; and the whole construction of the edifice, with the skilful structure of its lines, serves only as an ornament to the idea, ensuring its duration and remaining its most perfect symbol." [85] Yet for him style is more than words and images: "At first, when we are at the age when form alone impresses us, we believe that it is the arrangement of words alone that constitutes style, and that it is made up of rich images and novel expressions. . . . But in truth a man's character is his style." Vigny, with his philosophical interests, is, in spite of his interest in form, far from being a partisan of art for art's sake: "L'Etude pour l'Etude est ce qu'il faut dire plutôt que: l'Art pour l'art." [86]

It has often been said, with too much simplification, that the Parnassian movement was a reaction against romanticism.[87] This might have been true if romanticism had been only sentimental and effusive. But, as we have seen throughout this chapter, the cult of form developed within the framework of romanticism many years before the Parnasse came into being. Leconte de Lisle found his earliest inspiration in *Les Orientales*: "I cannot remember without the deepest gratitude the sudden impression I experienced, at an early age, when this book was given to me on the mountains of my native island, when I had this vision of a world full of light, when I admired this wealth of new and daring images, this irresistible lyrical movement, this precise and sonorous language. It was like an immense and sudden flash of light, illuminating the sea, the mountains, all the nature of my own land." [88]

In 1861 Baudelaire, seeking to situate Leconte de Lisle in his century, noted on the one hand his gift for picturesque description and on the other his innate taste for philosophy, and thus was led to compare him to Gautier and to Renan.[89] To the cult of form was added a philosophical content. Thus many critics have seen an affinity between Leconte and Vigny. Leconte himself emphasizes the differences between them. Not only did Vigny lack the historical sense, the power to relive and re-create the past instead of using it as a vehicle for his own emotions, but also his art was inadequate, marred by an incurable elegance: "One feels that the artist is not the despotic master of his instrument." [90] Still the two have in common a conception of poetry in which content as well as form is important, and which appealed to readers weary of sentimental effusions. Sainte-Beuve wrote in 1865: "Today the world is busy and distracted; it no longer gives ear to the poet who complains in solitude . . . for some time it has had enough of these lamentations over lakes and rocks. For the world today poetry lies elsewhere . . . in history, in erudition, in criticism, in art applied to everything, in the living reconstruction of the past, in the conception of languages and of the origins of the human race, in the perspectives of science and of future civilization; its original personal source has diminished and is now only a solitary torrent, a monotonous cascade, while the surrounding country, in the distance, is watered, fertilized and invigorated by a subterranean and universal current." [91] Leconte believed that art and science, in its widest sense, should be closely united. Born, as he said, three thousand years too late, preferring the past to the present, he re-created that past in a poetry born of intelligence, of passion, of revery. He maintains that all true and lofty poetry contains a philosophy. The poet must also be a thinker: "The work of a true poet, a master of his language and of his instrument, must contain a superabundance of thought. 'At the first glance he sees farther and more deeply than anyone else, because through visible beauty he contemplates the ideal, and concentrates and enshrines it in its proper, precise and unique expression." [92]

But for Leconte de Lisle "Beauty is not the servant of Truth, for it contains within itself both human and divine truth." [93] Outside the creation of beauty there is no salvation for him, and the highest praise he can give to Baudelaire is that he has loved beauty alone. He criticizes Lamartine, both for his practice and for his lack of love and respect for Art. And we have seen his severity for Vigny. The true poet must use all the resources of his art. "The poet, the creator of ideas, that is to say of forms visible or invisible, of images real or imagined, must give form to Beauty, to the extent that his powers and his inner vision permit, by a complex, skilful, harmonious combination of line, color, and sound, no less than by all the resources of passion, meditation, science, and fancy; for any work of man's mind which is lacking in these necessary conditions of perceptible beauty cannot be a work of art." [94]

Leconte de Lisle's own art was close to the plastic: "For him, *to write verse* was the same thing as to carve marble, to cast bronze, to set crystal in gold; it was to devote himself to all that gives density, precision, strength, greatness, durability." [95] He was moved to violent protest by a preface in which Thalès Bernard had written: "Let us have done with sculptured and painted poetry, let us have done with the jeweled phrase, let us lay down the chisel and the graving-tool and take up the pen." [96] In a letter to Emile Deschamps Leconte commented: "Since in the life of Art nothing can exist save by style and formal perfection, woe to the pen which is not also a chisel and a graving-tool!" [97] Yet his own poetry rarely has the fixed and static character of Gautier's, in spite of his prayer to the Venus of Milo,

Et fais que ma pensée en rythmes d'or ruisselle,
Comme un divin métal au moule harmonieux.

His *Pan* is no marble statue, but an avid faun who "poursuit la vierge errante à l'ombre des halliers," his *Hylas* "plonge sous le flot azuré." Even in poems inspired by works of art the sculptured stone is awakened to life, as in *Le Vase*, where "un pêcheur vient en hâte . . . deux renards arrivent de côté." In the poems inspired directly from nature there is a constant sense of movement; the upward flight of the condor, the slow march of the elephants across the burning desert, the swift leap of the jaguar. It is true that at the end of many of these poems motion is arrested and fixed, but the vigor and force of the verbs saves them from a frozen and sculptural immobility.

What was most repugnant to Leconte de Lisle was the poetry which, "a confused reflection of the impetuous personality of Byron, of the artificial and sensual religiosity of Chateaubriand, of the mystic reveries that come from across the Rhine, and of the realism of the Lake poets, becomes blurred and melts away." Of his own poems Leconte says: "Personal emotions have left few traces in them; contemporary passions and events, none at all." [98] This reticence and detachment are expressed in the apostrophe to the "plèbe carnassière" of *Les Montreurs*:

Je ne livrerai pas ma vie à tes huées,
Je ne danserai pas sur ton tréteau banal
Avec tes histrions et tes prostituées.

Yet in many of Leconte's poems we find neither the much talked of *impassibilité*, nor even, to use Leconte's own words, "impersonnalité." There is no lack of feeling, but rather extreme discretion in expressing it. In the poems based on personal experience, such as *L'Illusion suprême*, the intensity of personal feeling makes itself felt in every line, despite the general terms, the restraint of expression. Sainte-Beuve was right in finding in Leconte's poetry, not the impassibility of marble, but "un flot large et continu, une poésie amante de l'idéal." [99]

Except for Leconte de Lisle the Parnassian poets fall outside the time limits of this study.[100] None equaled the master, and nearly all either tried so hard to put science and philosophy into poetry that they remind us uncomfortably of the didactic poets of the eighteenth century, or carried the cult of art to an extreme that would have shocked even Gautier. Art "must give up subject matter and devote itself exclusively to form," wrote Anatole France in 1874.[101] The impassibility which Leconte de Lisle had avoided, in practice if not entirely in theory, is erected into a central doctrine:

> Poète, garde ainsi ton âme intacte et fière;
> Que ton esprit, vêtu d'impassibilité,
> Marche à travers la vie au but qu'il a tenté.[102]

As the Parnassians had reacted against the effusiveness of romanticism, so in due course a reaction against undue emphasis on form took place. In 1862 Madame Ackermann wrote in her journal: "In the young poets of our time, form is exaggerated, while matter is reduced to nothing. A true feeling finds its right and natural expression without effort. There is no need to use force." [103] Even the great ancestors turned against the last of their progeny. Sainte-Beuve criticized Gautier's "excès dans le *rendu* des choses réelles," and wrote of Lefèvre's *La Flûte de Pan* (1862): "In my opinion the only defect of these stanzas which are so well constructed, so well designed, is that they are too close to sculpture, that they have its polish and also something of its hardness: this poetry affects the ear as marble does the touch. And why translate one art by another?" [104] Hugo, long opposed to art for art's sake, uttered a protest against the new doctrine of impassibility: "There was a moment in recent years when impassibility was recommended to poets as one of the necessary conditions of divinity. To be indifferent was to be Olympian. . . . The Olympians are all passion." [105]

So in much of the poetic theory of this period we find a constant struggle between matter and form. The extremists base their entire conception of poetry on one or the other, and even those with more moderate views seem to seek a precarious balance. But by the middle of the century a new conception of poetry, and a poetry corresponding to it, was already in existence; a poetry which found not only a balance between matter and form but a fusion of the two into one. It too had its roots in romanticism, as will be seen in the following chapter.

VII

T HE poetic theories, and to a somewhat lesser degree the
poetry that we have considered in the two previous chapters,
continue the old division between the partisans of matter and
those of form. For the early romantics poetry consisted above
all in the expression of emotion, whether purely personal or
allied to philosophical, religious, political, or social beliefs,
whether the poet spoke for himself or was alike the mouthpiece
and the guide of his fellow men. Opposed to this is the cult
of poetry as form, either as closely allied to painting and
sculpture, and therefore concerned with reproducing plastic
form and creating "transpositions d'art," or as linguistic form,
concerned with the language of poetry and with versification.
Only with Hugo and Sainte-Beuve, and to a lesser degree with
Vigny and Banville, is there some attempt to bridge the gap
and to relate form and matter. Otherwise the two currents
pursue their separate ways and the rift continues.

These two currents, in many respects antithetical, have at
least one thing in common: a certain lack of depth. This is
obvious for the artists, less so for the other group. Yet even
the most romantic effusions express universal feelings; understandable to the average reader, they are expressed with order
and eloquence, often with a dramatic quality, and they keep
to the surface, avoiding the undertow of the subconscious.
The poets are not courageous explorers of the universe; with
all their "sentiment de la nature" they seek above all in the
mirror of nature the reflection of their own emotions, and are
none too pleased if the image is not a faithful one. Thus in
Tristesse d'Olympio Hugo reproaches nature:

Est-ce que vous serez à ce point insensible
De nous savoir couchés, morts avec nos amours,
Et de continuer votre fête paisible
Et de toujours sourire et de chanter toujours?

Themes

Man remains in the center of the universe and does not submit
to nature, but either dominates her, like Lamartine in *Le Lac*,
or resents her, like Vigny in *La Maison du berger*. Much the
same is true of religion; there is little or no deep religious
experience, but rather a vague religiosity. Much of the religious poetry is a dialogue on equal terms between man and
his Creator — sometimes indeed a monologue addressed to a
Creator who has little or no chance to answer. Again in the
love poetry the most passionate emotions are brought to the
surface, scrutinized in the clear light of day, and ordered and
arranged.

Towards the middle of the century a change began to be
apparent, which has been pointed out again and again by
modern critics.[1] Sainte-Beuve noted it in 1866, in a passage to
which I have referred earlier, and which deserves to be quoted
in full here:

Indeed our ideas about poets have changed almost entirely in recent
years. It is no longer the question of classicism and romanticism, if
you will; it is a question of something very different from a cockade,
from verse divisions and the unities, — from forms and colors; it is a
question of the very basis and substance of our judgments, of the
habitual attitudes and principles according to which we feel and are
moved. Can I succeed in characterizing this new state, this mental
attitude which has become almost universal? Formerly, during the so-
called classical period, the best poet was considered to be the one who
had composed the most perfect work, the poem that was the most
beautiful, the most clear, the most pleasant to read, the most finished
in every way, the *Aeneid*, the *Jerusalem Delivered*, a great tragedy.
Today we want something different. For us the greatest poet is the one
who in his works has given the reader the most to imagine and to
dream about, who has most moved him to be himself a poet. The
greatest poet is not the one whose work is the most accomplished: he
is the one who suggests the most, with whom at first one does not
grasp entirely all that he has meant to say and express, and who leaves
one much to ask, to explain, to study, much for one to finish. There

is nothing like these incomplete and inexhaustible poets to arouse and foster our admiration; for henceforth we want poetry to be in the reader almost as much as in the author. Since criticism was born and has grown up, since it has invaded everything, has outdone everything, it cares little for poetic works bathed in a clear and perfect light; it will have nothing to do with them. The vague, the obscure, the difficult, if they are combined with some greatness, are what it prefers. It must have material which it may itself construct and work on. For its own part it is far from displeased at having its skein to untangle, and at being given from time to time, if I may say so, a tricky job to do. It is not displeased at feeling that it has its share in a creative work.[2]

Here are the words which were to recur so often in symbolist theory: "imagine," "dream," "vague," "obscure," "difficult," and above all "suggest." For it seems to me that the great poetic change which took place about the middle of the century can be summed up as a passage from a poetry of statement to a poetry of suggestion. The change is not so clear-cut, to be sure, as Sainte-Beuve's passage implies. Surely all great poetry, even all good poetry, is to some extent suggestive, in the sense that it implies more than the literal and prosaic meaning of the words.[3] Musset, though he hardly practiced what he preached, pointed this out: "In every noteworthy line of a true poet, there is three or four times as much as is said; it is for the reader to supply the rest, according to his ideas, his powers, his tastes." [4] Nevertheless there is no doubt that at this time the idea of suggestion as a major factor in poetry comes to the fore in France in poetic theory as well as in poetry itself.

It might well be expected that suggestion would be allied, as it had been by Diderot and the English romantics, and was to be by Baudelaire, with imagination. As a matter of fact, for none of the French romantic poets, with the possible exception of Vigny, did imagination have the star part in poetic creation. The question is a somewhat vexing one, because of the frequent failure, noted earlier, of romantic writers to define their terms, and also because, even when the meaning of the term is expressed or implicit, we find that imagination has not one, not even a few, but a large variety of meanings.[5]

With certain neoclassical critics the traditional distrust of imagination is to be found undiluted. Thus Nisard writes in 1836: "With us imagination, even in works which are properly considered works of imagination, is an ornamental quality which embellishes literary compositions rather than inspires them. Reason . . . is the mistress of all literary works in France." Nisard's great criticism of Hugo is that in his works imagination is "a queen who rules without restraint." A later passage in the same article suggests what the role of imagination was for Nisard: "Description, born of memory and imagination; of memory, which arranges objects in order, and of imagination, which colors them." [6] In the following year Nisard lashes out with a diatribe against imagination reminiscent of Pascal: "This restless faculty, ever surfeited and ever insatiable, as easily amused as quickly bored, which carries everything to extremes and takes no pleasure in reflection, which is excited rather than satisfied by its own pleasures." [7] A certain distrust of imagination is to be found in Sainte-Beuve's criticism of the *Nouvelles Odes*, in which he blames Hugo's imagination for his overindulgence in description. For a number of critics imagination was, as Hugo says in the *Réponse à un acte d'accusation*, a

> . . . . . tapageuse aux cent voix,
> Qui casse des carreaux dans l'esprit des bourgeois.

The definitions of imagination tend to recall the distinction so often made between the poetry of sentiment and the poetry of images, and to attach imagination, however defined, to the latter. The critic Artaud says in his discussion of imagination: "What makes the poet is the gift of feeling and the art of painting: his domain is the heart of man and nature. This explains the opinion of those who have distinguished two schools of poetry, one of which delights in external nature, the other of which is the echo of a strong emotion that clamors for expression." Imagination seems to be a receptivity to nature, a sensitivity to the outer world, the ability to see and thus to describe. It is "that faculty which reflects like a mirror the impression of the tangible world." [8] Certain of Hugo's earlier definitions hardly go beyond this. In a note of about 1832–1834 he says that "l'imagination est la sensibilité de l'esprit," [9] and in the preface to *Les Rayons et les ombres* (1840): "One of the poet's two eyes is fixed on humanity, the other on nature. The first of these two eyes is called observation, the other imagination." And in a group of notes dated 1841–1860 we find: "Imagination is none other than the reflection of nature in the soul of man." [10]

Also, as in the eighteenth century, imagination is often allied with memory. Lamartine writes in the 1849 preface to the *Méditations*: "I was born impressionable and sensitive. These two qualities are the first elements of all poetry. Outward things, at first glance, made a vivid and profound impression on me; and when they had disappeared from my sight they reverberated and endured in what is called imagination, that is to say memory, which sees and paints afresh in our minds." [11] Hugo, on the other hand, had protested earlier against this assimilation of imagination to memory: "Memory has been put in the place of imagination. The law has been laid down, there are aphorisms to express it: 'To imagine,' La Harpe says with his naïve assurance, 'is at bottom only to remember.' " [12] And for Vigny memory is but one element in imagination: "Imagination contains in itself judgment and memory, without which it could not exist." [13]

Beside the conception of imagination as equivalent or allied to memory we have, again as in the eighteenth century, that of a combining and modifying power. Thus Cousin states that memory is indeed the basis of imagination, but imagination is more than memory: "The mind, applying itself to the images furnished by memory, decomposes them, chooses among their different traits, forms new combinations and images from them. Without this new power, imagination would be a captive in the circle of memory, whereas it should dispose at will of the past and the future, the real and the possible." Imagination is the most important faculty of the poet, although it must be supported by both sense and sensibility.[14] For Jouffroy a fertile imagination is one in which "all the ideas associated with the principal one are promptly and quickly aroused." He contrasts with the descriptive poetry of Delille, in which nothing is omitted, a poetry inspired by imagination, in which only what is most significant is chosen.[15]

It is curious that even in these romantic discussions a certain distrust of imagination prevails. To the poets for whom emotion was all in all, imagination might indeed be conceived as interfering with the spontaneous overflow of feeling. But more particularly it came into conflict with the conception of nature and of truth. Although the romantics had jettisoned the classical doctrines of imitation which had made imagination suspect in the eighteenth century, they had substituted for them their own doctrine of *vérité*. And imagination in any other sense than that of a true picture of nature was in danger of conflicting with truth. Thus Guirard says the domain of imagination is open to poetry, "but truth is one of its first conditions, even in the strangest of fictions." [16] Imagination, "that madwoman who multiplies, who amplifies, who exaggerates," [17] was a dangerous bedfellow for truth. Even in its soberer aspect as a modifying and combining power it is treated with a certain timidity. Sainte-Beuve, in a passage in which, although he does not use the word, he is obviously describing the workings of the imagination, writes: "Often, in the evening, looking at some bit of sky, some distant roofs, with here and there an occasional tree, I have said to myself that a picture which would reproduce faithfully the simple scene would be divine; then I have seen that it was impossible to achieve this complete fidelity directly; that my emotion

came both from the scene itself and from my state of mind that
reflected it; that from the direct observation of the object, and
also from the modified reflection of this object in the inward
mirror, art should draw a third *created* image which would be
neither exactly a copy of nature, nor a visual translation of
the elusive impression, but which would have so much the
more value and truth in that it would participate of both." [18]
In other words, art should effect a compromise between truth
and imagination. Later Sainte-Beuve writes in much the same
terms, but using the word imagination explicitly: "The imagination of great poets and painters is like a lake in which natural
objects are reflected, but in which they are reflected under
new conditions that do exist in reality. . . . [Imagination]
brings together, separates, and grasps objects as it reflects
them; it groups them; in a word it composes the landscape at
the same time that it reproduces its colors faithfully. That is
what we should say to ourselves whenever we consider nature's
pictures reflected in an artist's imagination or sensibility; it is
not a perfectly plain or smooth mirror, it is always a more or
less enchanted mirror." [19]

The romantic poet in whose doctrine imagination played
the most important part was Vigny, for whom art was "la
vérité choisie," who insisted that art was not life, but the magic
mirror of life.[20] For him imagination was the first and rarest
of faculties. In it the poet finds the colors that irradiate and
illuminate his subject. Vigny says of the poet: "He is possessed
above all by imagination. His mind, powerfully built, retains
and judges everything with an all-embracing memory and a
direct and penetrating understanding; but imagination elevates
his faculties heavenwards as irresistibly as the balloon lifts its
car; at the slightest impulse it is off; with the faintest breeze
it soars aloft and roams ceaselessly in the space which has no
human paths." [21] Here imagination seems very close to enthusiasm. But Vigny also saw in it the source of poetic images:
"Imagination gives corporal form to ideas and creates for

them living types and symbols that are as it were the tangible form and proof of an abstract theory." And he says of himself: "In order to conceive and retain positive ideas, my mind is forced to cast them into the domain of the imagination." [22]

This idea of the imagination as the faculty that discovers poetic images occurs fairly often. Artaud, after seeing in it a faculty which reflects the world of the senses faithfully, goes on to say that in that world it "sees the symbols of the affections of our hearts . . . finds, to represent our feelings and our thoughts, the most vivid expressions and the most transparent images . . . it colors and animates all that it perceives; it gives tangible form to the most abstract conceptions and the most intimate feelings." [23] A note of Sainte-Beuve's sees in true imagination the power of grasping instantaneously and intuitively the relationship between idea and image: "The Image is suited only to the idea, and is immediately applied to the idea, which thus issues forth full-armed from the mind of the writer." [24] Lamennais too defines imagination in similar terms: "Art . . . corresponds to the faculty which has been called imagination, or the power man possesses of clothing the idea in a tangible form that reveals it outwardly, of incarnating eternal types in nature." Earlier Lamennais had expressed some reservations: "Imagination is in some ways the opposite faculty to judgment; for judgment, of which the immediate object is truth, demands that the idea should be disengaged from any adulteration of sensation, whereas the characteristic of imagination, on the contrary, is to bring about the union of sensation and idea, or to join to the idea an image which corresponds to it, to incarnate it, so to speak. Hence both its advantages and its drawbacks." [25]

So in the romantic period we encounter all the conceptions of the imagination we had met in the eighteenth century; it is seen as a picture-making faculty, as identical or closely allied with memory, as a combining and arranging faculty, and as a purveyor of poetic images. It is not surprising that there should also be frequent echoes of the eighteenth-century discussion as to whether imagination "creates." Nodier, who had referred to the imagination "which had created the world of fantasy," [26] explains more fully what he means when he says: "Man does not create anything out of nothing; but he rises almost to the level of the creative power when from a variety of scattered elements he forms a new individuality and calls it into being." [27] Considerably later Gautier takes up the attack in eighteenth-century terms: "The fantasy of the human mind, which might be thought immense, is in reality very limited, for it is impossible to imagine any form outside created things. The most monstrous chimeras are real; their apparent strangeness is only the result of the combination of parts which separately are true to reality." [28] One may note too that "create" and "creative" are applied more frequently to art and to poetry, to the genius and to the poet, than to imagination. Cousin says that genius is creative, that it "breaks down and rebuilds nature in order to make it more consonant with the ideal." [29] For Lamennais poetry is a creation: "As God in creating incarnated his thought in the universe, so the poet incarnates his thought in his work." And later, "Art is for man what the creative power is in God." Lamennais has just said, however, that art corresponds to imagination.[30] Charles Magnin, too, stating that poetry is creative in the sense that it discovers new relationships between images and ideas, and from those relationships draws new ideas or images, adds that this phenomenon takes place in the imagination. And earlier he makes one of the rare pleas for the primacy of imagination, "that creative power": "The present-day school of poets all accept as their first dogma that imagination is the source of all poetry. . . . In all that pertains to art, the *Folle du logis* has again become queen and mistress." [31]

It is evident from this survey that for the great majority of the French romantics imagination was far from having the significance and the importance it had for their contemporaries across the Channel. The English romantics saw in imagination the essential poetic faculty. For Wordsworth it is not only "an endowing or modifying power," it also "shapes and creates." For Coleridge it is "that synthetic and magical power," the "true inward creatrix." And for Keats it is "the Rudder of poetry." The relatively little importance given to the imagination in France may explain, in part at least, some of the weaknesses of French romantic poetry. I do not claim that a better understanding of the nature and function of imagination would inevitably have made better poets; theory and practice are not so closely allied as all that. Yet I do believe that a clearer idea of imagination might have led the French romantics to realize that poetry is more than either spontaneous emotion or technical skill, that its truth is more than the truth of observation or of logic, and to grasp "the innumerable compositions and decompositions which take place between the intellect and its thousand materials before it arrives at the trembling, delicate and snail-horn perception of beauty." [32]

Yet in a few cases a more far-reaching conception of imagination was suggested. For Maurice de Guérin it is "the name of the inner life, the collective term for the most admirable faculties of the soul, those which clothe ideas with the adornment of images as well as those which, turned towards the infinite, perpetually meditate on the invisible and incarnate it in images of unknown origin and ineffable form." [33] Here imagination is an explorer of the infinite as well as a maker of images. And for Victor Hugo no faculty penetrates into the depths more than imagination: "C'est la plus grande plongeuse." [34] It is, however, for Hugo but one of the faculties of the poet, as he says in a passage which adds to what he had said in the preface to Les Rayons et les ombres: "The poet has a triple gaze, observation, imagination, and intuition. Observation is applied especially to mankind, imagination to nature, intuition to the supernatural. Through observation the poet is a philosopher, and can be a legislator; through imagination he is a sage and a creator; through intuition he is a priest and can be a bringer of revelation." [35] This indicates a limited role for imagination, the study and penetration of nature; its function as an explorer of the unknown is assigned to intuition. Yet creation is the work of imagination, and Hugo is almost alone in insisting without reservation on the creative activity of art; "To create and to resuscitate is the almost divine goal of art." [36] In *William Shakespeare* he compares divine and human creation: "From divine creation there emerges Adam, the prototype. From indirect divine creation, that is to say from human creation, there emerge other Adams, types." [37]

The particular interest of the passage from Maurice de Guérin is that it connects imagination with the two great developments in the direction of a poetry of suggestion that took place during this period, a new conception of poetic experience, and a new conception of the poetic image. But in general imagination is held in check by the notion of *vérité*. Only when the conception of truth and reality is expanded, when it can be said that "the true is the false, — at least in art and in poetry," can Gérard de Nerval say: "I believe that the human imagination has invented nothing which is not true, in this world or in others." [38]

The great change in French poetry which begins to be apparent towards the middle of the century stems above all from a new conception of the poetic experience. In spite of all the poets misunderstood by society, all the ivory towers from which boiling oil was poured down on the bourgeois, for the romantics the difference between the poet and the ordinary man, as far as experience goes, was a difference of degree. The poet felt more deeply, saw more clearly, and was able to express more adequately what he felt and saw. The difficulty, quite unnecessary from the poet's point of view, was that the bourgeois failed to appreciate the superior merits of the poet or give him his proper place in society.

But there develops slowly a conception of poetic experience as essentially different from ordinary experience. The poet is the visionary, the adventurer in the hidden worlds of dreams, the explorer of the secret relationships of the visible and the invisible, the material and the spiritual. Thus the domain of poetry is broadened and deepened. The change is underlined by the constant use in discussions of poetry of terms we have rarely met up to now, such as "magic," "mystery," and the like.

Many explanations have been offered of the filtration into French poetry of this conception, well established long before in German and English romanticism. Some have seen in it largely a question of foreign influences. But recent critics are in general agreed that these have been greatly exaggerated.[39] The most important foreign influence was probably philosophical rather than literary, that of German idealism popularized by Cousin and Jouffroy. It has been pointed out too that Rousseau and Senancour had experienced nature more deeply than their immediate successors; Rousseau abandoning himself to the eternal flux, Senancour seeing new analogies in outward things, had pointed out the new road.[40] And perhaps most important of all was the persistent illuminist and occultist tradition.

But the sense of mystery penetrated only very slowly into poetry. Only at one point, and that very early, did Lamartine suggest a kind of poetry which he did not succeed in achieving: "If poetry is not merely a vain assembling of sounds, it is without doubt the most sublime form in which human thought can be clothed; it borrows from music that undefinable quality of harmony which has been called celestial, for lack of any other name; appealing to the senses by the cadence of sounds, and to the soul by the elevation and energy of meaning, it takes possession of the whole man; it charms him, entrances him, intoxicates him; it exalts the divine principle in him; it makes him feel for a moment that *something more than human* which has given it the name of language of the gods. . . . So metaphysics and poetry are sisters, or rather are one and the same." [41]

This sense of mystery develops above all in Hugo, though slowly. After discussing the various influences he underwent Viatte concludes: "Binding together in a single sheaf, along with the lessons he had learned from the socialists, those of the various schools which scan the perspectives of the material and spiritual universe, by the flame of his genius he gives them form, and from all their illogical bric-à-brac he extracts an intense poetry." [42] It has often been said that there is a sharp break between the "two Hugos." But Marcel Raymond has rightly pointed out that it is rather the case of a poet who only slowly finds himself and discovers his vocation of dreamer and visionary.[43] This is apparent above all in his gradually changing attitude towards nature. At first nature is either a delight to the eyes or a mirror of the poet's own feelings. It serves as background for the poet's revery:

> Le poète s'en va dans les champs; il admire,
> Il adore; il écoute en lui-même une lyre.

Then comes an increasing sense of intimacy with nature:

> Oui, je suis le rêveur; je suis le camarade
> Des petites fleurs d'or du mur qui se dégrade,
> Et l'interlocuteur des arbres et du vent.

But the poet himself is still the focus of attention:

> Quand je suis parmi vous, arbres de ces grands bois,
> Dans tout ce qui m'entoure et me cache à la fois,
> Dans votre solitude où je rentre en moi-même,
> Je sens quelqu'un de grand qui m'écoute et qui m'aime! [44]

In *A un riche* Hugo expresses a very personal doctrine of *correspondances*:

> Tout objet dont le bois se compose répond
> A quelque objet pareil dans la forêt de l'âme.[45]

But quite early we find an increasing sense of the mystery of nature, of the message it has for the poet who listens to its voice. This is suggested in *Les Orientales*:

> Mes yeux plongeaient plus loin que le monde réel.[46]

And in *Soleils couchants* Hugo exclaims:

> Oh! contemplez le ciel! et dès qu'a fui le jour,
> En tout temps, en tout lieu, d'un ineffable amour,
>   Regardez à travers ses voiles;
> Un mystère est au fond de leur grave beauté,
> L'hiver, quand ils sont noirs comme un linceul, l'été
>   Quand la nuit les brode d'étoiles.

The transition is very apparent in *Pan* (1831), which begins with the affirmation that art and poetry are not "un flux éternel de banale ambroisie." The poets, "sacrés, échevelés, sublimes," are advised, "Allez, et répandez vos âmes sur les cimes." This seems very close to Hugo's early attitude — but the long apostrophe to the poets leads up to:

> Cherchez dans la nature, étalée à vos yeux,
> Soit que l'hiver l'attriste ou que l'été l'égaye,
> Le mot mystérieux que chaque voix bégaye;
> Ecoutez ce que dit la foudre dans les cieux!

It is no longer himself that the poet is to seek in nature, but the hidden mystery of the universe. So Hugo urges the poets: "Mêlez toute votre âme à la création!" The change from the "répandez vos âmes" of the earlier stanza is significant; nature is now on an equal footing with the poet. And more and more the poet's personal feelings will become secondary, as he listens to the voice of nature and glimpses Baudelaire's "immense clavier des correspondances":

> Car, ô poètes saints! l'art est le son sublime,
> Simple, divers, profond, mystérieux, intime,
> Fugitif comme l'eau qu'un rien fait dévier,
> Redit par un écho dans toute créature,
> Que sous vos doigts puissants exhale la nature,
>   Cet immense clavier.

In *La Pente de la rêverie* the poet descends into the depths:

> Mon esprit plongea donc sous ce flot inconnu,
> Au profond de l'abîme il nagea seul et nu,
> Toujours de l'ineffable allant à l'invisible.[47]

He penetrates into the very heart of the invisible world:

> Je ne regarde pas le monde d'ici-bas,
> Mais le monde invisible.
>
> .   .   .   .
>
> J'erre sur les hauts lieux d'où l'on entend gémir
> Toute chose créée.[48]

In his wanderings the poet discovers that

> .   .   . visions, as poetic eyes avow,
> Hang on each leaf and cling to every bough.[49]

This comes out in *A Albert Dürer*, where fantasy is combined with a deeper sense of mystery:

> Aux bois, ainsi que toi, je n'ai jamais erré,
> Maître, sans qu'en mon cœur l'horreur ait pénétré,
> Sans voir tressaillir l'herbe, et, par le vent bercées,
> Pendre à tous les rameaux de confuses pensées.[50]

The long poem, *Fonction du poète*, sums up this conception:

> La nature est la grande lyre,
> Le poète est l'archet divin!

And Hugo goes on to ally this new attitude towards nature with the conception of the poet as leader and guide:

> Le poète en des jours impies
> Vient préparer des jours meilleurs.
> Il est l'homme des utopies,
> Les pieds ici, les yeux ailleurs.

But the leader no longer proclaims monarchical and Catholic, or socialist and humanitarian doctrines. He is the visionary and the prophet who has approached through communion with nature the mysteries of God and His universe:

> Peuples! écoutez le poète!
> Ecoutez le rêveur sacré!

Dans votre nuit, sans lui complète,
Lui seul a le front éclairé.
Des temps futurs perçant les ombres,
Lui seul distingue en leurs flancs sombres
Le germe qui n'est pas éclos.
Homme, il est doux comme une femme.
Dieu parle à voix basse à son âme
Comme aux forêts et comme aux flots.

. . . .

Il rayonne! il jette sa flamme
Sur l'éternelle vérité!
Il la fait resplendir pour l'âme
D'une merveilleuse clarté.
Il inonde de sa lumière
Ville et désert, Louvre et chaumière,
Et les plaines et les hauteurs;
A tous d'en haut il la dévoile;
Car la poésie est l'étoile
Qui mène à Dieu rois et pasteurs! [51]

This new attitude appears in Hugo's prose as well as in his poetry, especially in his travel books of the early 1840's: "I am a great observer of everything, that is all, but I believe that I am right; everything contains a thought; I try to extract the thought from the thing. It is a kind of chemistry." [52] This contemplation leads to the discovery of the hidden harmonies of nature: "For thoughtful minds, all parts of nature, even those that seem most disparate at first sight, are connected with one another by a multitude of secret harmonies, invisible threads which the contemplator perceives, which make of the great whole an inseparable web living one and the same life, nourished by one and the same sap, one in its variety, and which are, so to speak, the very roots of our being." [53] Behind the outer world the poet discovers the very presence of the Almighty:

Tout cet ensemble obscur, végétation sainte,
Compose en se croisant ce chiffre énorme; DIEU.

He is like the shepherd of *Magnitudo parvi*:

. . . dépassant la créature,
Montant toujours, toujours accru,
Il regarde tant la nature,
Que la nature a disparu!

. . . .

Il ne voit plus Saturne pâle,
Mars écarlate, Arcturus bleu,
Sirius, couronne d'opale,
Aldebaran, turban de feu;

Ni les mondes, esquifs sans voiles,
Ni, dans le grand ciel sans milieu,
Toute cette cendre d'étoiles;
Il voit l'astre unique; il voit Dieu! [54]

After the tragic death of his daughter in 1843 Hugo, rather than exploring the heights, descends into the depths. From his plunge into the abyss he brought back many of the poems in *Les Contemplations*, such as *Ce que dit la bouche d'ombre*. This is the Hugo that Baudelaire so sincerely admired, "the man most gifted, most clearly chosen to express in poetry what I shall call the *mystery of life*." [55] Hugo explores the world of dream: "This mystery which we call dream and which is none other than the approach to an invisible reality. Dream is night's aquarium." [56] The world of dream is the privileged territory of the poet, an imaginary world at once real and unreal, which every dreamer has within himself. [57] The poet has passed beyond the reveries inspired by nature, beyond nature as a road to the invisible world, into that invisible world itself. Yet Hugo did not, like many later poets, yield himself completely to this world. He warns poets that "the dreamer must be stronger than his dream; otherwise there is danger." [58]

Moreover, Hugo feels an obligation to return from his adventures in the invisible world to share his discoveries with his fellow men. The visionary is never separated from the prophet and guide: "God manifests himself to us in the first degree through the life of the universe, and in the second degree through the mind of man. The second manifestation is no less sacred than the first. The first is called Nature, the

second is called Art. Hence this reality: the poet is a priest.
. . . The sibyl has a tripod, the poet has none. The poet is
himself a tripod. He is God's tripod." [59] This conception of
the poet is set forth at length in *Les Mages*:

> Pourquoi donc faites-vous des prêtres
> Quand vous en avez parmi vous?
>
> . . . .
>
> Ces hommes, ce sont les poètes;
> Ceux dont l'aile monte et descend.

The poets have solved the mysteries of nature:

> Les vents, les flots, les cris sauvages,
> L'azur, l'horreur du bois jauni,
> Sont les formidables breuvages
> De ces altérés d'infini;
> Ils ajoutent, rêveurs austères,
> A leur âme tous les mystères,
> Toute la matière à leur sens;
> Ils s'enivrent de l'étendue;
> L'ombre est une coupe tendue
> Où boivent ces sombres passants.
>
> . . . .
>
> A leur voix, l'ombre symbolique
> Parle, le mystère s'explique.

These are the prophets, the messiahs, who lead mankind on-
ward and upward:

> La poésie est un pilote;
> Orphée accompagne Jason. [60]

In Hugo, more than in any other poet, it is possible to follow
the development of a new conception of poetic experience.
Many of his poems, as we have just seen, describe the nature
of this experience. He passes from an acute sensitivity to the
outer world and the reflections of his own emotions in that
world, to a more cosmic view of the poet as the decipherer
and interpreter of nature, who finally penetrates through
nature to the heights and depths of the invisible world beyond,

and brings back a prophetic and messianic message to his fellow men.

Few of Hugo's contemporaries followed his lead, absorbed as they were in their own emotions, in social and political problems, or in the cult of art. It is in such a minor figure as Hippolyte de la Morvonnais that his ideas find their most faithful echo: "Poetry is a priesthood." La Morvonnais makes a plea for "la poésie sympathique": "It is the feeling for nature, the understanding of that mysterious language spoken to us by all that surrounds us. . . . Sympathetic poetry is that poetry which understands the language of nature's harmonies, which translates it to men." [61] An otherwise insignificant book published in 1841 contains a somewhat remarkable passage on dreams: "In my opinion, there is a means as simple as it is powerful of perceiving oneself in the pure spontaneity of the imagination. This is the state of dream. Dream is based on the activity of the memory; it is like an unconscious and seething tidal wave of the images we have received, which unconsciously makes new combinations of them." [62]

The greatest adventurer of all into the world of dream was Gérard de Nerval. For him dream was a second life, a life more real than that of the everyday world in which he lived. The story of his voyage of discovery is told in *Aurélia*, beginning with "l'épanchement du songe dans la vie réelle," [63] and leading through past and present and future, through dream and suffering and struggle, to final redemption and triumph. For him past and present and future fuse into one: "It would indeed be a consolation to think that nothing of all that has impressed the mind dies, that eternity preserves in its bosom a kind of universal history, visible to the eyes of the soul, a divine synchronism." [64] Gérard attributes to the poet, though in more modest terms than Hugo, a certain prophetic function: "Are not poets to some degree augurs?" [65] The poet's task is to discover the "harmony of the magical universe," to decipher the mysterious hieroglyphs obscured by time and ignorance.

For this Gérard invokes the aid of the cabalist and occultist tradition: "My role seemed to me to be the reestablishment of universal harmony by cabalistic art and the search for a solution by the evocation of the occult forces of different religions." [66] Like Hugo, Gérard discovered the mysteries hidden beneath the surface of nature:

> Souvent dans l'être obscur habite un Dieu caché;
> Et comme un œil naissant couvert par ses paupières,
> Un pur esprit s'accroît sous l'écorce des pierres! [67]

In *Aurélia* he writes: "Everything in nature took on a new aspect, secret voices emerged from plants, trees, animals, from the humblest insects, to advise and encourage me . . . in colors, odors and sounds I discovered hitherto unknown harmonies." What follows has often been cited as an example of the doctrine of correspondences; but for Gérard the correspondences express, not a relationship between two worlds, but the fundamental unity of a single world: "Everything lives, everything acts, between all things there is correspondence; the magnetic rays emanating from me or from others pass without obstruction through the infinite chain of created things; it is a transparent network which covers the world, whose delicate filaments are in close communication with the planets and the stars." [68]

It is more difficult for Gérard than for any other of the poets with whom we are dealing to separate his strictly poetical beliefs from his metaphysical and ethical ones. For him poetry and life are inextricably involved with one another. He has been claimed as an ancestor by many of the later poets who saw in poetry above all a "moyen de connaissance." Yet for Gérard written poetry was distinct from the poetic experience. That experience indeed clamored for expression: "There is in my head a storm of thoughts by which I am constantly dazzled and wearied; there are years of dreams, of projects, of sorrows, which want to cram themselves into a sentence, a word." [69]

Poetry is to be sure an instrument to force open magic doors, leading to "that beautiful and magical universe which poetry had created for us! . . . There everything was harmonious and everything was beautiful, everything was greater, richer and perhaps truer than the works of nature and of art." [70] It is also the explanation which the poet gives to himself of his own destiny: "the mission of a writer is to analyze sincerely what he experiences in the solemn circumstances of life." [71] Poetic experience and poetry are not to be confounded, for they are not identical; knowledge comes through the transformation of experience into poetry.[72] Dream is a road to discovery, but that discovery is made, not by accepting experience passively, but by analyzing and controlling it: "Je résolus de fixer le rêve et d'en connaître le secret. . . . Pourquoi . . . ne point dominer mes sensations au lieu de les subir?" [73]

So with Hugo and above all with Nerval there is a deepening of poetic experience, a new vision of nature, a discovery of correspondences, a venture into the world of dreams. This might well have affected only the matter of poetry, and had little effect on poetic expression. Later writers were to subordinate form to a fidelity to this revelatory experience, from Rimbaud with his "si c'est informe, il donne de l'informe," to the surrealists with their automatic writing. But the doctrine of correspondences developed from a mystical to an aesthetic doctrine, and to it is due in large measure the passage from the conception of the image as embellishment to that of the image as symbol. The relationship comes out clearly in a passage from La Morvonnais: "The power of the poet will be then, to my mind, an intimate power of spiritual communion with the invisible powers of nature, and his knowledge of the art of language, the knowledge of *symbolism*, the art of clothing his feelings in images, of speaking, as God speaks in the visible universe, by means of sound, light, and form." [74]

The symbol was to be introduced into French poetry by Hugo, Gérard de Nerval, and Baudelaire. But a sound doctrine of the poetic symbol developed somewhat earlier. In formal treatises *symbole* still has its eighteenth-century meaning; Laveaux's *Dictionnaire raisonné* defines it as a "form of trope by which there is substituted for the name of a thing the name of a sign chosen by usage to designate the thing. These kinds of tropes are not images." But we have already seen how Madame de Staël and Soumet attached the idea of symbolism to poetry, how Ballanche maintained that poetry is itself a symbol. All these lead us back to the illuminist tradition.

The interest in symbolism was reinforced by the influence of German idealist philosophy, with its return to the idea of absolute beauty, as brought into France by Victor Cousin and Jouffroy. In his *Cours de philosophie*, based on the course he had given in 1818, Cousin starts with the premise, "Tout est symbolique dans la nature," and goes on to connect symbolism with poetry. "Two or three words are sufficient to arouse the most profound emotions in the soul. . . . Thus the word is the most clear and the most vast of symbols." [75] Jouffroy, in his *Cours d'esthétique*, based on a course he had given in 1826, again proceeds from the general statement, "Tout est symbolique," to the conclusion, "Poetry is but a series of symbols presented to the mind to make it conceive the invisible." Jouffroy sees perfect equality between the natural and the spiritual, and approves the "reversed" image, citing Chateaubriand's column in the desert: "First the invisible is represented by material symbols; then later material nature is expressed by images drawn from spiritual nature; this is the characteristic, one of the characteristics, of the poetry of our time." In the appendix to the *Cours* Jouffroy uses the term *hiéroglyphe*: "Matter is a hieroglyph whose only value lies in what it expresses, and which is expressive only for those who understand its language, with this difference that we all understand naturally the language spoken by matter. The universe is made up of symbols which we understand without having learned to understand them." [76]

Among those who attended Jouffroy's course in 1826 were Sainte-Beuve and Pierre Leroux, who was to contribute some of the most important discussions of symbolism of the romantic period. In his article, "Du style symbolique," published in 1829, Leroux sees the essence of the romantic movement in the substitution of emblem, allegory, and symbol for comparison.[77] "It must be granted that all poetry lives by metaphor, and that the poet is an artist who grasps relationships of all sorts with all the powers of his soul, and substitutes for them identical relationships in the form of images." Here is both the perception of relationships and the expression of those relationships by metaphor (in which Leroux includes emblem and allegory). He goes on: "Suppose that all at once there is introduced into a language a figure which allows the continual substitution of images for abstract terms, and of vague and indefinite expression for precise expression; see what the effect would be. Abstraction will disappear from the poetry of this people, and mystery will be born in it."

All this seems close to later conceptions of symbolism. What gives a modern reader pause, however, is Leroux's choice of examples, largely from Hugo. He says of the line in *Les Deux Iles*,

Il a bâti si haut son aire impériale,

"The poet does not develop the idea of Napoleon's greatness, but moves immediately to the image; there is not even a comparison, the word eagle is not so much as pronounced; and yet nothing is clearer than the thought expressed by the image. This is the symbol." This kind of image is not new, indeed, but it had hardly been used in French poetry for two centuries. This indicates quite clearly that Leroux is thinking here rather of the "poetry of images" in general than of a particular form of image. When he attempts to define the symbol more specifically he says: "The characteristic of this form of language is that it does not develop the idea . . . but the image. It is thus an intermediary form between comparison and allegory properly speaking, swifter than comparison and less obscure than allegory. It is truly an emblem . . . the metaphor of an idea." Here Leroux (whether one agrees with him or not) is making the first attempt to situate the symbol in a rhetorical category and to see its relation to the traditional tropes.

It is again somewhat disconcerting to have Leroux find in Hugo's *Mazeppa* the perfect symbol: "Mazeppa is the genius. . . . The fusion of the intellectual idea and the material image: the assimilation is perfect." The modern reader may well be tempted to reply that in *Mazeppa* the image seems to be developed for itself, with a good deal of detail irrelevant to its inner meaning, and that at the end the meaning is set forth explicitly. The image is not self-sufficient; its meaning is not implicit. Yet if one compares *Mazeppa* not with later, but with earlier poetry one must recognize a significant change. The image has moved from a peripheral to a central position. And, irrelevant as some of the details of the image seem, in the second or explanatory part of the poem Hugo relates many of them to the genius he is depicting. Granted that image and meaning are not completely fused, that the meaning is too explicitly and fully set forth, I would maintain in Leroux's defense that while the image falls short of being a symbol in our full sense of the word, it takes a long step in that direction.

It should be noted too that Leroux, like many other writers (including Baudelaire), does not really make a sharp distinction between the symbol and other forms of poetic imagery. He defines allegory as "a discourse, or in general a sign expressing something other than what it states directly. . . . In this sense, *metaphor, symbol, myth*, are but different degrees of allegory." [78] Yet in a series of articles published in 1831 Leroux, after insisting that the symbol is the central prin-

ciple of art, develops a theory which is essentially that of correspondences:

Poetry is that mysterious wing which soars at will in the world of the
spirit, in that infinite sphere of which one part is color, another sound,
another movement, another judgment, etc., yet all of which vibrate
together according to definite laws, so that a vibration in one region
is communicated to another region, so that the privilege of art is to
perceive and to express these relationships, hidden deep in the very
unity of life. For from these harmonic vibrations of the different
regions of the soul a *chord* results, and this chord is life; and when
this chord is expressed, it is art; now the expression of this chord is the
symbol; and the form the expression takes is rhythm, which par-
ticipates in the symbol; that is why art is the expression of life, the
reverberation of life, and life itself.[79]

Leroux's doctrine was drawn from a variety of sources, but
it was not basically esoteric; Hugo said that he "manquait de
folie." After the early 1830's he turned more and more from
art to society, declaring that "l'art c'est la vie qui s'adresse à
la vie."

Leroux was in close touch with several of the romantic
writers, especially with Sainte-Beuve, from their meeting in
1824 until their break in 1833. There is more than one trace of
this contact in Sainte-Beuve's work, such as the poem *A mon
ami Leroux*, in which he writes of poets:

> Ces mortels ont des nuits brillantes et sans voiles;
> Ils comprennent les flots, entendent les étoiles,
> Savent les noms des fleurs et pour eux l'univers
> N'est qu'une seule idée en symboles divers.[80]

In his article on the *Revue Encyclopédique* (1832) Sainte-
Beuve says that its doctrine is "en art, le symbolisme le plus
vaste." [81] The *Pensées de Joseph Delorme* has a long passage
on symbolism: "The sense of art implies a vivid and intimate
sense of things . . . the artist, as if he were endowed with an
extra sense, is peacefully occupied in perceiving beneath the
outer world that inner world of which most men are ignorant,
the existence of which philosophers merely state; he observes

the invisible interplay of natural forces, and sympathizes with them as if they had souls; at his birth he was given the key to symbols and the understanding of images; what seems to others incoherent and contradictory is for him only a harmonious contrast, a distant chord on the invisible lyre. He himself soon takes part in this great concert and, like the bronze vases of ancient theatres, he joins the echo of his voice to the music of the world." [82] This tone is found in Sainte-Beuve's writings only around 1830, and seems a clear echo of Leroux's ideas.

This conception of symbolism met with some unfavorable criticism. A reviewer of *Joseph Delorme* noted with regret that Sainte-Beuve, like Hugo, made too much use of figures, allegories, symbols.[83] In 1832 Buchez protested against undue stress on the symbolic form: "Form is symbol; it is the outward figure, the garment of a thought; just as a word is the sign of an idea. . . . It is only because of the sentiment it expresses that form has any value. . . . Art produces a living and moving form only when it is urged on by a strong feeling and above all that of a willing devotion." [84] On the other hand Magnin, reviewing *Les Rayons et les ombres*, maintains that through the effulgence of its symbols and the flashes of its metaphors poetry brings out a throng of truths which will later be demonstrated by science.[85] But again in 1844 a long article by Paulin Limayrac protests against the symbolist tendency: "Today . . . in spite of glorious attempts, of great and fine successes, poetry is losing itself in developments, drowning ideas in descriptions, and worshipping a recently discovered little divinity which is called the Vague." Myths and symbols belong to the infancy of society; the modern poet is not a priest of Isis, but a citizen armed with a lyre. Limayrac offers a warning: "Nature, for our symbolic poets, is an extension of humanity. Everything has a spiritual intelligence. . . . Everything lives, everything speaks; everything has an individual existence and a special eloquence. The trees in the forest and the flowers in the garden converse with each other and with the poet. Take care: all this becomes cold if you carry it too far, and verges on the ridiculous if you make it into a system." Limayrac notes the curious alliance (due perhaps to Pierre Leroux) between symbolism and socialism, which are "le vrai royaume du vague." He is severe on Laprade's *Psyché*, with its revival of allegory: "In his unconsidered enthusiasm, he arrives at a kind of illuminism." Amusingly, he cites with high approval a poem which to us seems far from symbolist: "In the midst of these obscure prolixities, I have been haunted by the memory of that striking picture by M. Victor Hugo, which has no more than forty lines, entitled *La Vache*. There is something beautiful and precise, which gives food for thought. . . . If that is symbolic poetry, well and good, it is intelligible poetry." Limayrac's conclusion is: "Symbolic poetry has no future in France, and socialism, by taking possession of it, has dealt it a hard blow." [86]

A great deal of this discussion refers, explicitly or implicitly, to Victor Hugo. The idea of the poetic symbol is implied in much that Hugo says about the poet and poetic creation, but the term is not a particularly frequent one with him, though it occurs occasionally:

> Ecoute la nature aux vagues entretiens,
> Entends sous chaque objet sourdre la parabole,
> Sous l'être universel vois l'éternel symbole.[87]

Here, as elsewhere, Hugo is referring to the symbol found in nature, not to a poetic image, and he nowhere proposes a theory of poetic symbolism in so many words. Yet such a doctrine is implicit in his conception of poetic experience and creation, and in much of his poetry.

A number of critics have seen in Vigny an ancestor of the symbolists, the one of all the romantics who is closest to later poetry. Thus Marc Eigeldinger says: "He was the first to have the idea of translating the abstractions of thought by having recourse to the prestige of the symbol." Yet Eigeldinger goes on to say that in Vigny "the symbol does not coincide entirely with the thought, there is a certain hiatus between the idea and the image, the fusion is not complete, the interpenetration does not take place naturally." [88] More recent critics have often refused to use the term symbol in connection with Vigny. The basis for this can be found in a passage which Eigeldinger himself quotes from a letter of Vigny's: "I always start from the Idea. Around this centre I evolve a fable which is the demonstration of the thought." [89] An earlier passage from his journal expatiates on his method: "To conceive and ponder over a philosophical thought; to find in human actions the one which is the most obvious *demonstration* of it; to reduce this to a simple action which can be impressed on the memory and present, as it were, a statue and a grandiose monument to men's imagination, that is the aim of this poetry which is alike epic and dramatic." Always the point of departure is the idea, which is then transformed into image. A study of Vigny's notes for future poems is revealing; we find many headings, "Comparaison poétique," or such a note as:

> Poème:
> Le lion marche dans le désert.
> Les animaux lâches vont en troupes.
> Qu'ainsi marche toujours le poète.
> (Peindre le Lion et les Loups)

It is true that Vigny himself uses the word symbol, speaking in *La Maison du berger* of the "graves symboles" of poetry, and in his journal: "DES PENATES ET DES SYMBOLES. — The image sustains the mind in adoration as figures sustain it in computation. DE LA COMPARAISON. — The greatest geniuses are almost exclusively those who have found the most exact comparisons to express their ideas." [90] Yet for Vigny, as has been seen earlier, outward form and imagery are but the vesture of ideas. So his notion of the symbol stands apart from the one we have been following.

That conception, derived from the doctrine of correspondences, expresses an inevitable relationship between the natural, concrete, and visible world and the supernatural, abstract, and invisible one. By the contemplation of nature the poet discovers these relationships and sees in the outer world symbols of the inner world. As Coleridge put it in *The Destiny of Nations*:

> For all that meets the bodily sense I deem
> Symbolical, one mighty alphabet for infant minds.

The next step is to transfer the symbol from the domain of poetic experience to that of poetic creation, to allot to it a place among the traditional rhetorical images. But there is no such rigid distinction between symbol and metaphor, symbol and allegory, as had already been made in England and in Germany. The philosophic notion of the symbol simply gives new scope and importance to the familiar categories. Not until much later was the rhetorical symbol precisely defined in France and assigned to the lofty and unique place it now occupies among poetic images.[91]

The image as practiced in poetry moved, somewhat more slowly at first, but outstripping the theory in time, from ornament to symbol. Earlier French poetry had used imagery soberly, eliciting Hazlitt's severe criticism: "The French have no poetry; that is, no combination of internal feeling with external imagery. Their dramatic dialogue is frothy verbiage or a mucilage of sentiment without natural bones or substance; ours constantly clings to the concrete, and has a *purchase* upon matter. Outward objects interfere with and extinguish the flame of their imagination: with us they are the fuel that kindles it into a brighter and stronger blaze." [92] Most images seem to have been composed according to the formula Sainte-Beuve found for Boileau: "It is evident that the metaphor almost never springs forth complete, entire, indivisible, and full armed; he composes it, and finishes it little by little, he manufactures it laboriously, and the line of the seams is apparent." [93]

With the early romantics there is no real break in this tradition. Lamartine uses images to give more precision to his vague sentiments, and almost always keeps the terms of comparison, as when he writes, "Et moi, je suis semblable à la feuille flétrie," or, in *L'Occident*, borrows Chateaubriand's famous "reversed" image, but restores its conventional form:

> Et puis il s'élevait une seule pensée,
> Comme une pyramide au milieu du désert.

And in the majority of Lamartine's poems the image is not an important element.[94]

With many of the other romantics the image is often developed for its own sake, with a wealth of detail more or less relevant to its meaning, and then that meaning is explained. This is the structure of many of Vigny's best known poems. In *La Mort du loup* there is first the story of the hunt, an admirable piece of narrative verse, and then the "moral" of the story, "Seul le silence est grand." The technique is essentially that of the fable.

In Vigny's poems the meaning is usually fairly general and abstract, and the abundance of detail belonging to the story rather than to the meaning has no disturbing effect on the reader. When, with certain other romantics, the meaning is more concrete, abundance of detail has its dangers, as in Musset's all too famous image, with its twenty-nine lines on the habits of the pelican followed by "Poète, c'est ainsi que font les grands poètes." A still less felicitous example is Hugo's *La Vache*, in which the detailed genre picture of the farmyard scene, with the children drinking from the cow's teats, leads up to the conclusion:

> Ainsi, Nature! abri de toute créature!
> O mère universelle! indulgente Nature!
> Ainsi, tous à la fois, mystiques et charnels,
> Cherchant l'ombre et le lait sous tes flancs éternels,
> Nous sommes là, savants, poètes, pêle-mêle,
> Pendant de toutes parts à ta forte mamelle.

Even more startling is Gautier's *L'Hippopotame*, with its three stanzas of excellent animal painting topped by "Je suis comme l'hippopotame." These are indeed extreme examples, and many poems could be cited in which the image has no such unfortunate effect. In the vast wealth of Hugo's poetry the "suitable" images are in the great majority. But the point I want to make is that in all these poems the image, whether it is appropriate or ludicrous, is developed for itself, with details, often very numerous, which have no bearing on what the image stands for. The reader may be interested and moved by the image itself, but its significance is rarely borne in upon him until the poet makes it explicit. According to the particular case, the reader may accept the significance willingly, as with Vigny, and at times with Hugo and Gautier, or he may have the details about the pelican, the cow, or the hippopotamus which the poet has so generously supplied so present to his mind that the application seems incongruous, even comic. This use of the image is typical of romantic poetry, and persisted with the Parnassians. It is the formula of a number of Baudelaire's early poems, before the poet arrived at a felicitous fusion of image and meaning.

But with the later Hugo, and above all with Gérard de Nerval, the image ceases to be ornamental and peripheral, and becomes the center and focus of the poem. As Hugo moves from the visual to the visionary, from perception to imagination, he adds to the purely pictorial images the metaphorical, to the metaphorical the symbolical (though all three coexist in his later poetry). The early poetry is particularly rich in similes; the forty-eight lines of the first two sections of *Les Têtes du serail* contain eleven terms of comparison. In the poetry of 1830–1840 metaphor becomes more frequent, as in the enchanting *Ecrit sur la vitre d'une fenêtre flamande* of *Les Rayons et les ombres*:

> J'aime le carillon dans tes cités antiques,
> O vieux pays gardien de tes mœurs domestiques,

> Noble Flandre où le nord se réchauffe engourdi
> Au soleil de Castille et s'accouple au midi!
> Le carillon, c'est l'heure inattendue et folle
> Que l'œil croit voir, vêtue en danseuse espagnole,
> Apparaître soudain par le trou vif et clair
> Que ferait en s'ouvrant une porte de l'air.

Hugo's metaphors gradually become more closely related to their context, as in the great line of *Pasteurs et troupeaux*, "Le pâtre promontoire au chapeau de nuées." And he begins to find in the outer world an inner meaning, to see in a simple incident a moral or philosophical sense, as in *Le Mendiant*, where the beggar's mantle "semblait un ciel noir étoilé," and the poet concludes:

> Je songeais que cet homme était plein de prières,
> Et je regardais, sourd à ce que nous disions,
> Sa bure où je voyais des constellations.

The same approach is found in "Je payai le pêcheur," with its "moral" that "l'homme rend le bien au monstre pour le mal." [95] Such poems as these are closer to allegory than to symbol; the story contains details irrelevant to the meaning, which is often made explicit at the end, so that the formula is not unlike Vigny's.

Hugo comes closest to a true symbolism in the poems where the contemplation of nature leads him to a vision of the unity of the universe; what he finds is not so much correspondence as coexistence. Image and idea are one.[96] So metaphor is gradually enlarged into symbol. Yet, as has been well observed, for Hugo the concrete, visual side of the image remains dominant.[97] His intense vision leads him, not to apperception of the relationship between two worlds, but to the discovery of one world, palpitating with life, speaking words that only the poet can hear: "L'herbe s'éveille et parle aux sépulcres dormants." In the poem, *Crépuscule*, from which this line is taken, the twilight scene, the growing darkness, the heavy step of the reaper, the rising star are not, strictly speaking, *symbols* of

love and death; they *are* love and death. In the same way, in
Eclaircie, the dawn does not symbolize God's gaze upon the
earth; it is that gaze. We have, rather than a system of correspondences, a pantheistic vision.[98] In Hugo there is no such
personal symbolism as in Baudelaire and other later poets. He
finds in nature not the image of his own — or others' — nature
and experience, but a cosmic vision; a vision indeed peculiar
to Hugo, of a world constructed by his personal philosophy.
And this philosophy is made explicit, and not left for the
reader to discover.

The most authentic practitioner of symbolism of this period
was Gérard de Nerval.[99] In translating his experience into
poetry he followed the advice that Adoniram, one of his many
counterparts, gives to Benoni: "You are copying nature coldly.
. . . My child, that is not art: art is creation." He urges the
young Benoni to seek for "unknown forms, nameless beings,
incarnations before which men recoil." [100] In Gérard's poetry
there is no split between image and meaning, no explanatory
matter; the image carries the whole weight. Gérard's poetic
world is a world of symbols, a world in which sign and object
are interchangeable. The symbols are drawn from the whole
realm of Gérard's experience and knowledge: his personal life,
his dreams, his wide reading in religious and cabalistic texts.
Concrete objects, particularly precious stones, metals, flowers,
and animals, all have transcendental values. As he says in *Vers
dorés*:

> Respecte dans la bête un esprit agissant:
> Chaque fleur est une âme à la Nature éclose;
> Un mystère d'amour dans le métal repose;
> "Tout est sensible!" Et tout sur ton être est puissant.

Personal experience and traditional relationships are fused. On
the one hand the events of Gérard's own life take on a symbolic significance for him; on the other hand he finds the
symbols of his own experience in the world around him, in
history, in legend and in myth. His own experience takes on a

mythical value, and the myths of the past are fused with this personal myth.

So in the best known of *Les Chimères*, *El Desdichado*, Gérard equates his own life with the past and discovers in himself a series of reincarnations. One cannot say that one is the symbol of the other; the descents into Hades are no more a symbol of Gérard's "crises de folie" than the latter are the repetition, in the eternal cycle, of the former. The "prince d'Aquitaine," Amour, Phébus, Lusignan, Biron are not, strictly speaking, symbols of Gérard himself; rather his own life reiterates and subsumes these figures.

> Je suis le ténébreux, — le veuf, — l'inconsolé,
> Le prince d'Aquitaine à la tour abolie:
> Ma seule étoile est morte, — et mon luth constellé
> Porte le *soleil* noir de la *Mélancolie*.
>
> Dans la nuit du tombeau, toi qui m'as consolé,
> Rends-moi le Pausilippe et la mer d'Italie,
> La *fleur* qui plaisait tant à mon cœur désolé,
> Et la treille où le pampre à la rose s'allie.
>
> Suis-je Amour ou Phébus? . . . Lusignan ou Biron?
> Mon front est rouge encor du baiser de la reine;
> J'ai rêvé dans la grotte où nage la sirène . . .
> Et j'ai deux fois vainqueur traversé l'Achéron:
> Modulant tour à tour sur la lyre d'Orphée
> Les soupirs de la sainte et les cris de la fée.

Gérard's symbolism is not based on the traditional system of correspondences, in which the outer world reflects and symbolizes the inner world, but is rather a two-way system, in which symbol and meaning are at once interchangeable and inseparable.

The new conception of poetic experience and the idea of the symbol were the chief factors in the creation of a poetry of suggestion. As external nature revealed its hidden meaning to the poet, so the poet translated that meaning by symbols. The meaning is no longer set forth directly and merely amplified and beautified by the image; it is suggested by it. As Magnin writes: "What poetry has the power to express, is not the immediate sensation we receive from objects, but the inner feeling aroused in us by these objects; its function is to express relationships." [101] But for the poet there is one further step; his symbols must be translated into words. Language too must become an instrument of suggestion.[102] In 1856 poetry is defined by an obscure critic in these terms: "It is the sensation, or better still the emotion which we receive from reality seen through the prism of the ideal and the mirages of the imagination. I will add, it is an intimate and intense penetration into facts and ideas which reveals to us their unknown, brilliant, or sombre aspects, crowned with deep darkness or with dazzling light. To translate into human language these sensations and emotions and make them pass into it with all their retinue of marvels, mirages, shadows, lights, is to produce written poetry." [103]

So there develops, especially in Hugo, along with the sense of the mysterious relationship of nature and man, of meaning and symbol, a sense of the relationship of symbol and language. In his early play, *Cromwell*, Hugo puts into Milton's mouth the words:

> Oui, je veux à mon tour créer par la parole,
> Du créateur suprême émule audacieux,
> Un monde entre l'enfer et la terre et les cieux.

Whereas in the *Réponse à un acte d'accusation* Hugo is the revolutionary who liberates language and restores the rights of common speech, in the *Suite* to the *Réponse* he develops an almost mystical conception of language:

> Car le mot, qu'on le sache, est un être vivant.
> La main du songeur vibre et tremble en l'écrivant;
> La plume, qui d'une aile allongeait l'envergure,
> Frémit sur le papier quand sort cette figure,
> Le mot, le terme, type on ne sait d'où venu,
> Face de l'invisible, aspect de l'inconnu.
> . . . .
> Les mots sont les passants mystérieux de l'âme.

The poet discovers in nature not only a meaning but the form it is to take, as Hugo says in "O strophe du poète." Verse itself is brought by the "Idée implacable" from the depths of the unknown:

> Tu m'apportes un vers, étrange et fauve oiseau
> Que tu viens de saisir dans les pâles nuées.[104]

So language is joined with symbol as an instrument of suggestion.

This led to a most important step, the bringing together of matter and form, so long separated in poetic theory. We have seen in the preceding chapters a few moves in the direction of convergence. Some of the writers cited there had moments of insight in which they envisaged a complete fusion. Emile Deschamps saw a close union of matter and form: "As if idea could be separated from expression in a writer; as if the method of conceiving were not closely united to the method of expressing." [105] And Sainte-Beuve says admirably: "Indeed verse, according to my conception, is not manufactured out of separate pieces more or less closely adapted to each other, but is conceived in the womb of genius by an intimate and obscure process of creation. Inseparable from the thought, it is born and grows up with it; thought is like the vital spirit which forms verse from within and organizes it." [106]

Hugo, who often had seen matter and form as separate, came to grasp and express their unity. "It is a mistake to believe . . . that a single thought can be expressed in several ways, that a single idea can have several forms. An idea never has but one form, which is peculiar to it; which is its pre-eminent form, its complete form, its rigorous form, its essential form, its preferred form, which always springs forth as one with it from the mind of the genius. Thus with great poets nothing is more inseparable, nothing more intimate, nothing more consubstantial than the idea and the expression of the idea. Kill the form, and you will almost always kill the idea. Take away Homer's form, and what is left is Bitaubé." To the images of form as the enamel on the tooth, the cells of the beehive, Hugo adds the image of fusion: "All great poetry should have undergone fusion, and been lava before being bronze." [107] In a number of passages, ranging in date from about 1830 to 1864, collected in *Postscriptum de ma vie*, he reiterates this need of fusing form and matter: "Expression comes forth like the idea, in its own right, no less essential than the idea, which it meets mysteriously in the depths; the idea is incarnated, the expression is idealized, and they emerge so intermingled with one another that their coupling becomes union. Idea is style, style is idea." [108]

The unity of form and matter is emphasized by a poet usually thought of as a passionate partisan of form for form's sake, Banville. And he allies it with the idea of a poetry of suggestion. "The aim of poetry is to communicate impressions to the soul of the reader and to evoke images in his mind — but not by describing these impressions and these images. . . . The old question of Thought and Form has always been not only misunderstood, but *turned inside out*. The Form that is presented to your mind is always the Form of a Thought; but a man who thinks in abstract words will never succeed in translating his thought by a form." [109] Likewise Gérard de Nerval, in his article on Heine, allies the idea of suggestion with the fusion of form and matter: "With him idea and form are completely identified. Words with him do not designate objects, they evoke them." [110]

So during this period certain writers became aware of that "perfect appropriateness of the form to the matter" which was for Coleridge the essence of poetry. In general this did not lead them, as it had led certain of the English romantics, to stress concision and density as poetic virtues, to load every rift with ore. As Keats put it in verse:

> Misers of sound and syllable, no less
> Than Midas of his coinage, let us be
> Jealous of dead leaves in the bay-wreath crown.

The only one of the French romantics, oddly enough, to mention concision was Hugo: 'One can never be too concise. Concision is the marrow." [111] But in Hugo's own poetry, and in that of nearly all his contemporaries except Gérard de Nerval, there are often all too many dead leaves in the bay-wreath crown.

Thus there developed, along with the poetry of emotion and the poetry of art, a new conception of poetry as sugges-tion, as a magic, an alchemy.[112] These are the terms used by Banville in the definition that Gide considered the most perfect one ever given of poetry: "That magic, which consists in arousing sensations by a combination of sounds and which makes a form visible and tangible as if it were carved in marble or represented in real colors, this sorcery by means of which ideas are infallibly communicated to us in a certain way by words which do not express them." [113] But before Banville wrote these words one poet had conceived poetry as above all a "magie suggestive": Baudelaire.

VIII

IMAGINATION ENTHRONED: BAUDELAIRE

WITH Baudelaire, more than any poet-critic we have encountered, the theory and the practice of poetry are inextricably interwoven.[1] In the case of such poets as Chénier, Vigny, and Hugo, the theory at times seems unrelated to the poetry; sometimes better, sometimes worse, and occasionally contradictory. But with Baudelaire the two go hand in hand. Poetry indeed comes first; as Baudelaire wrote in "Richard Wagner et Tannhäuser à Paris": "It would be an entirely new occurrence in the history of the arts for a critic to become a poet, a reversal of all psychological laws, a monstrosity; on the contrary, all great poets naturally, inevitably, become critics. I am sorry for the poets who are guided by instinct alone; I believe them to be incomplete. In the inner life of the former there comes an inevitable crisis when they wish to intellectualize their art, find out the obscure laws in obedience to which they have produced, and deduce from this study a series of precepts of which the divine aim is infallibility in poetic creation. It would be a miracle for a critic to become a poet, and it is impossible that a poet should not contain a critic. The reader will not then be surprised that I consider the poet the best of all critics." [2] The poetic experience, the production of poetry, the enjoyment of poetry are not in themselves sufficient; the true poet feels the urge to "transformer [sa] volupté en connaissance," to understand as well as to feel the joy of poetic experience and poetic creation.[3]

This does not mean that Baudelaire turned out a neatly organized *art poétique*. His ideas on poetry, like Diderot's, are scattered through his work, in his criticism of art and music as well as of literature, and indeed in his poetry itself. With all

his originality, many of these ideas have a familiar ring, just
as his poetry awakens many an echo. He himself was the last
to deny his debt to his predecessors. He admired much in the
earlier romanticism, "a grace, celestial or infernal, which has
marked us forever with its stigmata." [4] But Baudelaire is no
partisan of the poetry of pure emotion. He was indeed far
from despising sensibility: "Every man's sensibility is his
genius." [5] But he makes a distinction between the sensibility
of the imagination and the sensibility of the heart. It is the
latter that he distrusts: "I know nothing more stupid than *pure
sentiment*." And he recalls with approval a dictum of Leconte
de Lisle: "*Tous les élégiaques sont des canailles!*" [6] His article
on Gautier puts it more moderately: "The sensibility of the
heart is not entirely favorable to the poetic process: an
extreme emotional sensibility can even be harmful." [7] It is
not the existence of emotion, but its expression uncontrolled
by imagination, that Baudelaire bans. No reader of his poetry
needs to be reminded that its raw material is his own personal
experience, the emotions expressed directly in his letters and
in the *Journaux intimes*. All through his work run the tensions,
the conflicting urges that made of him a *homo duplex*, from his
earliest childhood conscious of both the horror of life and
the ecstasy of life,[8] hearing the two voices calling, one saying
"La Terre est un gâteau plein de douceur," the other,

> . . . Viens; oh! viens voyager dans les rêves,
> Au delà du possible, au delà du connu! [9]

There is the often repeated cycle of aspiration towards the
ideal, followed by discouragement and spleen,[10] then the efforts
at escape, followed by remorse and a fresh start — all summed
up in the statement: "In every man, at every moment, there are
two simultaneous attractions, one towards God, the other
towards Satan. The invocation of God, or spirituality, is a desire for ascent; that of Satan, or animality, is a joy in descent."
This is the source of what were for Baudelaire "two funda-

mental literary qualities, supernaturalism and irony. The individual vision, the aspect which things take on for the writer, then the Satanic turn of mind. The supernatural includes general color and accent, that is to say intensity, sonority, limpidity, vibration, depth and reverberation in space and in time." [11]

The basis of Baudelaire's poetry is his own human experience. For this we have his own word: "Must I tell you, you who have no more perceived it than anyone else, that into this *atrocious* book I have put all *my heart*, all *my tenderness*, all *my religion* (disguised), all *my hatred*? It is true that I shall say the contrary, that I shall swear by all my gods that it is a work of *pure art*, of *apery*, of *jugglery*; and I shall be lying like a trooper." [12] This indeed gives the lie to what he says in the "Projets de préface" for *Les Fleurs du Mal*: "This book, essentially useless and absolutely harmless, was written with no other aim than to amuse myself and to exercise my passion for obstacles." [13] Baudelaire's poetry gives us a sense of contact with a poignant human experience, reaching from the heights of heaven to the depths of hell. What first of all distinguishes him from the romantic poets who had all too often draped their emotions in eloquence and rhetoric is the intimate tone of his poetry. Not since Villon had protested to his "frères humains,"

> Si vous clamons freres, pas n'en devez
> Avoir desdaing . . . .

has a poet come so close to his readers. At our peril do we dissociate ourselves from this dubious character; Baudelaire turns on us with

> Hypocrite lecteur, — mon semblable, — mon frère!

The supreme appeal to the reader comes in the *Epigraphe pour un livre condamné*:

> . . . si, sans se laisser charmer,
> Ton œil sait plonger dans les gouffres,

Lis-moi, pour apprendre à m'aimer;

Ame curieuse qui souffres
Et vas cherchant ton paradis,
Plains-moi! . . . sinon, je te maudis!

At times Baudelaire thus addresses himself directly to his reader, or calls him into the poem, as in the last lines of *Le Masque*:

C'est que demain, hélas! il faudra vivre encore!
Demain, après-demain et toujours! — comme nous!

More often the poems have the tone of a conversation overheard; the reader almost feels guilty of an indiscretion as he catches the despairing cry,

O toi que j'eusse aimée, ô toi qui le savais!

or the softly murmured

Entends, ma chère, entends la douce nuit qui marche.

The great majority of Baudelaire's poems have this tone of conversation or of interior monologue; it is worth noting that in all but eighteen of the hundred and fifty-eight poems of *Les Fleurs du Mal* first or second person pronouns (most often both) are used. It is of course true that these pronouns are frequent in romantic poetry — but there the poet often seems to be speaking from the pulpit or the rostrum, in tones deafening to the single listener. To be sure, Baudelaire too has his moments of rhetoric — and some very great ones — but he is most himself when he speaks as man to man. His emotion is muted and controlled, but it is at the heart of his poetry.

But the poet must not imprison himself in his own experience, his own emotion. "The characteristic of true poets . . . is to be able to go outside themselves, and understand a completely different nature." [14] This is repeated in the prose poem, *Les Foules*: "The poet enjoys the incomparable privilege of being at will himself and others. Like those wandering souls who seek for a body, he enters, when he wishes, into the character of anyone." [15] One is reminded of Keats' words: "A Poet is the most unpoetical of anything in existence; because he has no Identity — he is continually filling some other Body — The Sun, the Moon, the Sea and Men and Women who are creatures of impulse are poetical and have about them an unchangeable attribute — the poet has none; no identity — he is certainly the most unpoetic of God's Creatures." [16]

So, although Baudelaire's is an intensely personal poetry, the role of the "sensibility of the heart" is a limited one in his conception of poetic creation. As for enthusiasm, he repeats after Poe that it is "a quickening of the spirit — an enthusiasm entirely independent of passion, which is the intoxication of the heart, and of truth, which is the food of reason." [17] But its role too is limited. In his article on Madame Desbordes-Valmore Baudelaire implies that spontaneous sentiment and inspiration do not suffice to make a great poet. And there is more than one warning against the danger of overconfidence in genius and inspiration.

It might well seem that, in theory at least, Baudelaire was closer to the doctrine of art for art's sake than to that of sentimental romanticism. Flaubert, thanking Baudelaire for *Les Fleurs du Mal*, wrote: "What pleases me most of all in your book is that Art is predominant in it." [18] By his emphasis on art Baudelaire dissociates himself from those romantics who relied on inspiration alone, such as Musset, condemned by Baudelaire for his "total inability to understand the labor by which a revery becomes a work of art." For Baudelaire himself "nothing less than perfection is admissible." [19] Yet he refuses to follow Poe's complete submission of inspiration to method, and questions the account Poe gives of the composition of *The Raven* in "The Philosophy of Composition." "Poetics, so they used to tell us, are made and modeled after poems. Here is a poet who declares that his poem was composed according to his poetics. . . . Did he, with an odd and amusing vanity, pretend to be much less inspired than he really was? Did he underestimate the gratuitous faculty in order to give the lion's share to the will? I am rather inclined to think so." [20]

Baudelaire is also far from following Gautier's too facile assimilation of poetry and the plastic arts. He does indeed, like Diderot, have a sense of the unity of the arts, of the great underlying principles which bind them together, in spite of the differences imposed by form and technique. "One of the symptoms of the spiritual state of our century is that the arts aspire, if not to supplement one another, at least to lend new strength to one another." [21] The sentence comes from the 1863 article on Delacroix, in which Baudelaire had just discussed the poetical and musical qualities of the painter's work. What he admired so much in Wagner was the synthesis of the arts, the relation between sound and color and ideas and emotions. Yet he was from the beginning aware of the dangers of a confusion of the arts. In his first *Salon* he wrote that Boulanger had been ruined by the influence of Hugo, and in the *Salon de 1846* he develops the point: "To seek deliberately for poetry in the conception of a picture is the surest way not to find it. It must come without the artist's knowing it. It is the result of the painting itself; for it lies hidden in the soul of the spectator, and the task of genius is to arouse it." [22] Baudelaire criticizes Hugo for having, by his overattention to surface detail, become a painter in poetry, whereas Delacroix, with his attention fixed on the ideal, is often unconsciously a poet in painting. Each art has its own ideal, its own form, which must not be confused with those of other arts: "Today, each art seems desirous of encroaching on its neighboring art . . . painters introduce musical scales into painting, sculptors introduce color into sculpture, writers introduce plastic procedures into literature, and other artists . . . a kind of encyclopedic philosophy into plastic art itself." [23] The plastic arts were among Baudelaire's richest sources of inspiration, but his poems on pictures and statues and engravings are not "transpositions d'art," they are interpretations, discoveries of the inner meanings that lie behind art as well as nature.

Moreover, Baudelaire parts company with both Gautier and Poe in regard to the aim and function of poetry. His attitude has been much discussed, and he has been seen as the Parnassian author of a "livre essentiellement inutile," as a Christian moralist, and as occupying various intermediate positions. His earliest position is that poetry is a necessity, that a man can live for some days without food, but never without poetry.[24] Poetry is then "useful," but not because it does or should teach a direct moral lesson. As the poetry of painting must be created by the spectator, so the philosophy of a poem must be created by the reader. Poetry must be involuntarily philosophical, hence poetry is a false genre. All this is apropos of Ménard's *Prométhée délivré*, and ends with the warning: "Never confuse the phantoms of reason with the phantoms of imagination; the former are equations, the latter beings and memories." [25]

For a brief period in 1848 and the following years Baudelaire was without question carried away by the conception of a popular and democratic art, and reacted violently against the doctrine of art for art's sake. "The puerile utopia of the school of *art for art's sake*, by excluding morality, and often even passion, was necessarily sterile. It was in flagrant contradiction with the genius of humanity." This is in the 1851 article on Pierre Dupont, and Baudelaire goes on to say that he prefers to skilful versifiers the poet who is in constant communication with the men of his time, and exchanges with them thoughts and sentiments translated into a noble and fairly correct language. Art must be inseparable from morality and from utility. But Baudelaire insists that it must always be utopian, always opposed to facts, always in revolt, always a negation of evil. Because Pierre Dupont seemed to him such a poet, Baudelaire maintains, even in his 1861 article on him, that in spite of his almost inconceivable carelessness of language and looseness of form, he is "one of our most precious poets." At about the same time as the first Pierre Dupont article Baudelaire came out with a violent attack on "L'Ecole païenne." "To dismiss passion and reason is to kill literature. To repudiate the efforts of the former Christian and philosophical society is to commit suicide, to refuse all possibilities and means of perfection. To surround oneself exclusively with the seductions of material art is to run the risk of damnation." The cult of beauty is fraught with dangers: "Immoderate love of form leads to monstrous and unknown disorders," all notions of right and justice disappear. And Baudelaire concludes: "Any literature which refuses to advance fraternally between science and philosophy is a homicidal and suicidal literature." [26]

This however was a passing phase, and in the article "Drames et romans honnêtes" Baudelaire expressed the position which was to be his for the rest of his life. "Is art useful? Yes. Why? Because it is art. Is there a pernicious art? Yes. It is the art which distorts the conditions of life. Vice is attractive, it must be painted as attractive; but it brings in its train strange maladies and moral sufferings; they too must be described. . . . The first condition of a healthy art is the belief in integral unity. I defy you to find a single work of imagination which fulfils all the conditions of beauty and which is a pernicious work." Art is useful because it is authentic, and a true work of art needs no special pleading: "The logic of the work is sufficient for all the demands of morality, and it is for the reader to draw his conclusions." [27]

Baudelaire indeed sympathized fully with Poe's violent attacks on the "great heresy of modern times," the idea of the direct utility of literature. But he always added that all the same poetry *is* useful, although this is not its immediate aim. In the "Nouvelles Notes sur Edgar Poe," after quoting the passage from "The Poetic Principle" in which Poe asserts that art has no aim other than itself, he interjects: "I do not mean that poetry does not ennoble morals — let that be understood — that its final result is not to elevate man above the level of commonplace interests; that would obviously be absurd. I say that if the poet has pursued a moral aim, he has diminished his poetic power; and it is not imprudent to wager that his work will be bad." [28] So Baudelaire praises Hugo because he is a moralist unintentionally, because of the depth and richness of his nature. "By describing what is, the poet degrades himself, and comes down to the level of the professor; by recounting what is possible, he remains faithful to his function; he is a collective soul which questions, which weeps, which hopes, and sometimes finds the answer." [29] Baudelaire's final word is in a letter to Swinburne: "I am not so much of a *moralist* as you kindly pretend to think. I simply believe (as you do, without doubt) that every *good* poem, every *good* work of art, naturally and inevitably suggests a *moral*. That is the reader's business. I even have a very decided hatred for any exclusively moral *intention* in a poem." [30]

Baudelaire then cannot be classified among the partisans of art for art's sake. There is in his doctrine a balance between matter and form, morality and art, which recalls the great classical tradition. In 1860 Flaubert wrote to him: "You have found a way of being classic, while remaining the transcendent romantic we love." [31] This meeting of romanticism and classicism in Baudelaire has been noted by many critics, by Valéry in his "Situation de Baudelaire," and more recently by Henri Peyre in the final chapter, "Baudelaire romantique et classique," of his *Connaissance de Baudelaire*. Baudelaire was a great critic as well as a great poet, and if, as Valéry has said, "that writer is a classicist who contains a critic within himself, and who associates that critic closely with his works," Baudelaire is indeed classic as well as romantic: by his lucidity, his power of analysis, his conscious and deliberate art, his passion for perfection. But, to quote Valéry again, "Baudelaire, in the midst of romanticism, makes us think of a classicist, but he does no more than make us think of one." [32] Baudelaire's classicism is less that ideal and serene equilibrium so rarely attained than a tension or a series of tensions so tightly drawn that one holds one's breath waiting for the snap. But in him there is more than a precarious compromise between classicism and romanticism. In a letter already quoted Flaubert wrote to him: "You have found the way to rejuvenate romanticism." [33] Baudelaire himself very early pointed the way to a new romanticism and thus to his own conception of art: "Romanticism lies not so much in the choice of subjects or in exact truth, but rather in a way of feeling. . . . For me, romanticism is the most recent, the most contemporary expression of beauty. . . . Romanticism means modern art, — that is, intimacy, spirituality, color, aspiration towards the infinite, expressed by every means available to the arts." [34] This is not perhaps a completely adequate definition of Baudelaire's ideal, but all its terms are essential to such a definition and are repeated again and again in what he writes of art and poetry.

Like Diderot, Baudelaire often uses the word poetry in a very general sense. He refers to the poetry of Delacroix's work, and to his paintings as great poems; David's *Marat* is a "poème inaccoutumé"; Decamps' early pictures are full of poetry and revery.[35] Poetry is a quality essential to written poetry, but not limited to it. One wishes that Baudelaire had carried out his intention, noted in the draft of a preface for *Les Fleurs du Mal*, to answer a series of questions, the first of which was, "What is poetry?" But, he says, "I was stopped by the appalling futility of explaining anything to anybody." [36] He does however suggest elsewhere what his answer would have been.

At one point he follows Poe in defining poetry as human aspiration towards a higher beauty, and states that "the generative principle of works of art is the exclusive love of the beautiful." [37] Here it is well to ask what Baudelaire meant by beauty, for his conception is far from the classical *beau idéal*. It appears first in the *Salon de 1846*: "All forms of beauty, like all possible phenomena, contain an eternal element and a transitory one — an absolute element and a particular one. Absolute and eternal beauty does not exist, or rather it is merely an abstraction skimmed off the surface of a variety of beauties." [38] Baudelaire's is the "multiform and multicolored beauty which moves in the infinite spirals of life," [39] a beauty which always contains a bizarre, irregular, surprising element.[40] The idea is developed most fully in "Le Peintre de la vie moderne."

This is a good opportunity indeed to set up a rational and historical theory of beauty, in opposition to the theory of unique and absolute beauty; to show that beauty is always, inevitably, double in its nature, although the impression which it produces is single; for the difficulty of discerning the variable elements of beauty in the unity of expression in no way invalidates the necessity of variety in its composition. Beauty is composed of an eternal, invariable element, the quantity of which is exceedingly difficult to determine, and of a relative, circumstantial element, which may be, in turn or at the same time, fashion, morality, passion. Without the second element, which is, as it were, the amusing, captivating, appetizing icing on the celestial cake, the first element would be indigestible, imperceptible, inappropriate to human nature. I defy anyone to discover any example whatever of human beauty which does not contain both these elements.

For the artist the variable element is to be found in the world around him, the "modern" world: "Modernity is the transitory, the fleeting, the contingent half of art, the other half of which is eternal and unchangeable." [41] From the beginning Baudelaire glorifies the poetry of modern life. Each artist, each poet, must combine with the eternal beauty elements drawn from the life of his times, his own experience, in order to create his own particular beauty. In *Fusées* Baudelaire notes: "I have found the definition of the Beautiful — of my Beautiful. It is something ardent and sad, something a little vague, leaving the way open to conjecture. . . . Mystery and regret are also characteristics of the Beautiful. . . . I can hardly conceive (could my mind be an enchanted mirror?) a type of Beauty without *Sorrow*." On the material side, the ideas of immensity and of movement are among the most precious elements of beauty. The sea, that "diminutive infinity," plays a large part in Baudelaire's poetry. "Twelve or fourteen leagues of liquid in motion are sufficient to give the highest idea of beauty offered to man in his mortal habitat." [42] It is this conception of beauty, not the statuesque one of Baudelaire's early sonnet, *La Beauté*, that is his definitive one. The *Hymne à la beauté* makes it clear that Beauty, that "monstre énorme, effrayant, ingénu," may be found, as so many of the *Fleurs du Mal* show, in what is evil and ugly. This is reiterated in the "Projets de préface," and in the Gautier article Baudelaire says that "it is one of the extraordinary privileges of art that the horrible, artistically expressed, becomes beauty." So the poet, in the unfinished epilogue, addressed to Paris, of *Les Fleurs du Mal*, claims triumphantly,

> . . . j'ai de chaque chose extrait la quintessence,
> Tu m'as donné ta boue et j'en ai fait de l'or.[43]

For Baudelaire the beauty to which poetry aspires, and which it creates, is not then a traditional *beau idéal*, but an amalgam of eternal beauty with the poet's own individuality, like Diderot's *modèle intérieur*. The poet's beauty is that of his own time, of his own experience; it may be a transmutation, by his mysterious alchemy, of ugliness and evil. It is neither an eternal and absolute ideal, nor is it to be attained by a zealous fidelity to nature. The concrete world of reality and the transcendental ideal must be fused into the poet's beauty.

The most typically Baudelairian definition of poetry is, rather than that borrowed from Poe, the one given in the unfinished article, "Puisque réalisme il y a. . . ." After a statement which at first sight seems surprising from him, "All good poets have always been *realists*," Baudelaire goes on to say: "Poetry is what is most real, what is completely true only in *another world.* This world, a hieroglyphic dictionary." [44] For him (and again we are reminded of Diderot) the great central problem is that of the relation of art to reality. True reality is not to be found in this world: "Common sense tells us that the things of this world exist only incompletely, and that true reality is to be found only in dreams." Yet the two worlds are not divorced: "The natural world penetrates into the spiritual world, nourishes it, and thus cooperates in bringing about that undefinable compound which we call our individuality." [45] It is in the meeting of the natural and the spiritual worlds that true reality is to be found. There is in Baudelaire no such detachment from concrete reality as was to be found in many later poets. To be sure the world of nature is but the raw material, the poet's dictionary, the storehouse on which imagination draws. But the realistic subject is not to be rejected; it is to be illuminated and transfigured. The writer, whether he be novelist or poet, must, as Baudelaire says in his article on *Madame Bovary*, "jeter un voile de gloire sur des aventures de table de nuit, toujours répugnantes et grotesques, quand la poésie ne les caresse pas de sa clarté de veilleuse opaline." [46]

So Baudelaire's poetry always has its point of departure in a known and familiar reality. No poetry brings us into more immediate contact with the world around us, the world of the senses. Baudelaire runs through the gamut of the five senses, the delight and the horror that each can give. For the sense of touch there is the range from the softness of "le dos satiné des molles avalanches," to the harshness of

> . . . tous les becs et toutes les mâchoires
> Des corbeaux lancinants et des panthères noires
> Qui jadis aimaient tant à triturer ma chair.

For taste we pass from the heady intoxication of

> . . . . un vin de Bohème
> Amer et vainqueur,
> Du ciel liquide qui parsème
> D'étoiles mon cœur!

to the nauseating bitterness of

> Comme un vomissement, remonter vers mes dents
> Le long fleuve de fiel des douleurs anciennes.

The extraordinary use Baudelaire made of odors and perfumes is too well known to need examples; again and again, as he says,

> Comme d'autres esprits voguent sur la musique,
> Le mien, ô mon amour! nage sur ton parfum.

With all this use of the "inferior" senses, the major ones of sight and sound are equally present. Baudelaire's poetry abounds in visual evocation, drawn from both nature and art, with a wealth of precise detail, of color and especially light and shade, "brillants soleils," "jours blancs, tièdes et voilés," "ciel bizarre et livide," "jour noir plus triste que les nuits." With sounds there is a like variety, from the strident

> Comme un sanglot coupé par un sang écumeux
> Le chant du coq au loin déchirait l'air brumeux,

to the lulling melody of *L'Invitation au voyage* or *La Musique*. All these sense images reinforce one another, and certain poems, such as *Le Balcon* or *Harmonie du soir*, are veritable symphonies of the senses.

But the poet must not be content with a purely sensuous poetry; he must penetrate beyond outer reality. How then does he arrive at the discovery of inner reality? How does he disentangle it from outward appearances? This is the question of the poetic experience as distinguished from the human experience which is the raw material of poetry. The poet has a special way of looking at things, a vision which leads him from outward appearances to inner meaning.

It seems to me unquestionable that Baudelaire's interest in the effects of hashish and opium was due in no small degree to the parallels he found between the experience of the drug-addict and that of the poet. The descriptions of the effect of

→ combines drugs with poetic
experiment – Kayon

hashish on a certain type of individual recall again and again
what Baudelaire says of the poetic experience. There is the
intensification of color and light, the distortion of time and
space, the deformation and exaggeration of sentiment as well
as of sensation: "Then come the ambiguities, misappre-
hensions and transpositions of ideas. Sounds are clothed in
colors, and colors have their music. That, you may say, is only
natural, and every poetic spirit, in its healthy and normal state,
easily conceives these analogies." [47] The difference lies only
in the extreme intensification of these phenomena produced
by the use of drugs. Later Baudelaire speaks of the seething of
the imagination, the fruition of dream, the poetic travail that
result from hashish. But even with drugs the point of departure lies in everyday reality. The imagination produces
hallucinations, but it must have a pretext. Sound will speak,
utter words distinctly; but there is a sound to start with. And
strange forms are derived from simple and known ones.

It would seem then that the use of drugs might be an easy
road to the creation of poetry. But Baudelaire warns his reader
of the dangers of this primrose path. Paradise must not be
bought at the price of eternal salvation. At the end of the
Poème du haschisch he is severe on those who have sought in
this black magic an easy way of attaining the supernatural
world, while "we, poets and philosophers, have saved our souls
by steady labor and contemplation; by an assiduous exercise
of the will and a lasting nobility of intention, we have created
for our use a garden of true beauty." [48]

The passage above contains the word *contemplation*, and
Baudelaire suggests frequently that through contemplation the
poet discovers the inner meaning of the outer world. The verb
contempler occurs often in *Les Fleurs du Mal*: "Contemple-
les, mon âme; ils sont vraiment affreux" (*Les Aveugles*): "Con-
templons ce trésor de grâces florentines" (*Le Masque*). This
contemplation is the result of a conscious effort. The chief
mark of Delacroix's style, according to Baudelaire, is "con-

cision and a kind of unobtrusive intensity, the customary result of the concentration of all the spiritual powers on a given
point." This concentration leads to revery and dream: "The
faculty of revery is a divine and mysterious faculty; for it is
by dream that man communicates with the shadowy world
by which he is surrounded. But this faculty needs solitude in
order to develop freely; the more a man concentrates, the more
apt he is to dream amply and deeply." [49] Even more than
contempler, *rêver* is a key word in Baudelaire's poetry (it and
its derivatives occur about fifty times in *Les Fleurs du Mal*).
To dream is essential for the poet, but his dream is no idle
revery, nor is it fantastic and meaningless. Dreams are a hieroglyphic language, "a dictionary which must be studied, a
language of which wise men may find the key." [50]

Contemplation and dream are then one road to inner reality.
Another is memory. "Memory is the chief criterion of art;
art is a kind of mnemotechny of the beautiful: now exact
imitation spoils a memory." Memory rejects detail, keeps only
the essential. Baudelaire, citing Poe, says that "he alone is a
poet who is the master of his memory, the sovereign of his
words, the log-book of his own emotions always ready to be
leafed through." Memory restores the vision of childhood and
youth, the time when objects are most profoundly impressed
upon the mind, when colors are visionary, when sounds speak
a mysterious language. "Some little grief, some little pleasure
of childhood, immeasurably increased by an exquisite sensibility, later become in the adult, even without his knowledge,
the basis of a work of art." [51] The idea is taken up again in "Le
Peintre de la vie moderne": "Genius is but *childhood rediscovered* at will, childhood now endowed, in order to express
itself, with virile organs and an analytical mind which permits
it to set in order the mass of materials collected involuntarily."
Baudelaire goes on to say of Guys: "All the materials with
which memory has been cluttered are ordered, arranged,
harmonized, and undergo that forced idealization which is the

result of a *childlike* perception, that is to say a perception which is keen and magical by its very ingenuousness." [52] So memory discloses its immense and complicated palimpsest, "with all its superimposed layers of defunct sentiments, mysteriously embalmed in what we call oblivion." [53] Again and again in Baudelaire's poetry a memory is the point of departure, as in *Le Cygne*. Memory is the recovery of vision, as well as a storehouse of images. In the *Salon de 1846* Baudelaire quotes Hoffmann: "True memory, considered from a philosophical point of view, consists, I think, only in a very lively and easily aroused imagination, ready to evoke in support of each of its sensations scenes from the past, and to endow them, as if by magic, with the life and character proper to each of them." [54]

Here at last we have the word *imagination*, the faculty which was to be for Baudelaire "la reine des facultés," as it had been for Diderot "la faculté dominante du poète." Diderot's interest, as we have seen earlier, was primarily in the nature, physiological and psychological, of the imagination; Baudelaire is concerned above all with its activity and role. It becomes important, by name at least, only slowly in his work.[55] At first, as in the passage from Hoffmann, there is little distinction between memory and imagination. But the idea is implicit in his constant preoccupation with the relation of art to reality. Imagination is the opposite of the imitation he so constantly criticizes. In the beginning he is particularly opposed to the imitation of models, the academic tradition, and praises those artists in whom he finds naïveté and originality. Likewise one of his severest criticisms of the writer is "Pastiche, pastiche!" Technique indeed may be learned from the masters; "It is doubtless an excellent thing to study the ancient masters in order to learn to paint, but this can be but a superfluous exercise if your aim is to understand the nature of present-day beauty." [56]

Before long however Baudelaire, following Delacroix, attacks first and foremost the direct imitation of nature. Even in 1846 he had criticized the romantics for being misled by the doctrine of truth in art. The important thing is the artist's temperament: "A beautiful picture [is] nature reflected by an artist"; "A portrait is a model plus an artist." And even more strongly: "The primary business of an artist is to substitute man for nature and to protest against nature." "The ideal is not that vague thing, that dreary and impalpable dream that floats on academy ceilings; an ideal is an individual rectified by an individual." [57] Baudelaire had learned from Delacroix that nature is a dictionary, and in 1859 he allies the idea to imagination: "No one has ever thought of the dictionary as a composition, in the poetic sense of the word. Painters who obey imagination look up in their dictionary the elements which fit into their conception; and at that, by arranging them with a certain art, they give them a totally new physiognomy. Those who have no imagination copy the dictionary." This is particularly a danger for landscape painters (and, one might add, for descriptive poets): "Most of them fall into the error I pointed out at the beginning of this study: they take the dictionary of art for art itself; they copy a word from the dictionary, thinking they are copying a poem. Now a poem is never copied; it must be composed." And in the prose *Invitation au voyage* Baudelaire writes of an art superior to nature, which is "reconstructed by dream, corrected, embellished, remolded." [58]

This aesthetic opposition to the imitation of nature was reinforced by Baudelaire's theological views. In answer to a request for some verses on nature he wrote: "You know that I am incapable of gushing over vegetables, and that my whole soul rebels against this extraordinary new religion, which, it seems to me, will for any *spiritual* being always have something *shocking* about it." The cult of Nature is a denial of the doctrine of original sin; nature is not innately good, and must be reformed. "Who would dare to assign to art the sterile function of imitating Nature?" [59]

Yet it is through nature that imagination arrives at true reality, for nature, however imperfect, is "a *logos*, an allegory, a mold." [60] One of the functions of the imagination is the discovery of *correspondances*. "Imagination is, as it were, a divine faculty, which perceives directly, without the use of philosophical methods, the secret and intimate relationship of things, correspondences and analogies." For Baudelaire correspondences and analogies are inevitable: "What would indeed be surprising would be that sound *should not be able* to suggest color, that colors *should not be able* to give the idea of a melody, and that color and sound should not be suitable translations of ideas; things have always expressed themselves by a reciprocal analogy, since the day when God brought forth the universe as a complex and indivisible whole." [61]

It has become almost a tradition among critics to classify the Baudelairian correspondences as horizontal, or synesthetic, and vertical, or transcendental. There are the correspondences between the senses, the analogies between colors, sounds, and perfumes, of which Hoffmann had written. For Baudelaire too,

Les parfums, les couleurs et les sons se répondent.

More important for Baudelaire are the correspondences between the outer and the inner worlds, the material and the spiritual, the natural and the supernatural:

La Nature est un temple où de vivants piliers
Laissent parfois sortir de confuses paroles;
L'homme y passe à travers des forêts de symboles
Qui l'observent avec des regards familiers.

These correspondences are allied to the pursuit of beauty in a passage borrowed in large part from Poe: "It is this admirable, this immortal instinct for the beautiful which makes us consider the earth and its spectacles as an insight, a correspondence to Heaven." An "innate knowledge of *correspondence* and symbolism" is one of the essential gifts of the poet; "every thing is hieroglyphic, and we know that symbols are only relatively obscure, according to the degree of purity, good will or native insight that men possess. Now what is a poet (I am using the word in its broadest sense), if not a translator, a decipherer?" [62]

Thus imagination is a way of vision, a way of knowledge: "The poet is *sovereignly* intelligent . . . he is *intelligence* par excellence, — and . . . *imagination* is the most scientific of all faculties because it alone understands *universal analogy* or what a mystical religion calls *correspondence*." Baudelaire is, I think, using *scientific* in its etymological sense, seeing in imagination intuitive knowledge of the spiritual world.[63] But imagination is also an active and creative faculty; it can "choose, judge, compare, avoid this, seek out that, swiftly and spontaneously." Baudelaire gives as his formulary of aesthetics: "All the visible universe is but a storehouse of images and signs to which imagination gives their relative place and value; it is a kind of food which imagination must digest and transform. All human faculties must be subordinated to imagination, which requisitions them all at once." Thus beauty is achieved: "The inner eye transforms everything and gives to each thing the complement of beauty which it lacks in order to be truly pleasing." [64]

The two functions of imagination, vision and creation, are allied in the definition which Baudelaire gives in the *Salon de 1859*:

How mysterious a faculty is this queen of the faculties! It touches all the others, it rouses them and sends them into combat. . . . It is analysis, it is synthesis; and yet men apt at analysis and fairly quick at abstraction can be devoid of imagination. It is that, and it is not entirely that. It is sensibility, and yet there are people who are very sensitive, perhaps too sensitive, who are without it. It is imagination which has taught man the inner meaning of color, contour, sound and scent. In the beginning of the world it created analogy and metaphor. It decomposes all creation, and with the materials accumulated and arranged in accordance with rules whose origins can be found only in the inmost depths of the soul, it creates a new world, it produces the sensation of something new.[65]

Here imagination has reached its full stature. As a modern critic has said: "Imagination is not, as its etymology suggests, the faculty of forming images of reality; it is the faculty of forming images which go beyond reality, which turn reality into song. It is a superhuman faculty." [66] Imagination discovers and creates that higher reality which is for Baudelaire true poetry. "Imagination is the queen of truth, and the *possible* is one of the provinces of truth. It is positively related to the infinite." So Baudelaire can say: "Imagination alone contains poetry." [67] This imagination is no mere picture-maker, no wandering fancy; it is the great visionary and creative faculty. Its activity is marked by what Baudelaire saw as the chief characteristics of genius, "*will, desire, concentration, nervous intensity, explosion.*" Intensity of vision, concentration in creation, these lead to a poetry of extreme density, yet never of obscurity. In it, to use Baudelaire's own words, the spirit "casts its own supernatural light over the natural obscurity of things." [68]

Through the perception of correspondences imagination discovers the symbol. "There develops this mysterious and temporary state of mind, in which the depths of life, beset with its manifold problems, are revealed completely in the spectacle, however natural and trivial it may be, which one has before one's eyes, — a state in which the first chance object becomes a speaking symbol." [69] Baudelaire praises Gautier for "his tremendous innate understanding of *correspondence* and universal symbolism, that repertory of all metaphor." And in the Hugo article he says: "In excellent poets there is no metaphor, no comparison, no epithet which is not mathematically exact in the circumstances, because these comparisons, these metaphors and these epithets are drawn from the inexhaustible well of *universal analogy*, and cannot be found elsewhere." [70] This passage, like others I have quoted on correspondences, would seem to indicate that the analogies found by the poet are those of the traditional "symbolique," in which nature is the symbol of a transcendental reality. But, as Lloyd Austin has so well demonstrated, Baudelaire's symbolism is above all the discovery in nature of symbols which translate the *état d'âme* of the poet.[71] It is more human, more personal, than the traditional doctrine. A sentence of Baudelaire's in his article on Madame Desbordes-Valmore gives, I believe, a more faithful account of his own symbolism than the passages quoted earlier: "I have always taken pleasure in seeking out in the external and visible world examples and metaphors which I could use to characterize the pleasures and impressions belonging to the spiritual order." [72] The symbol is not a traditional, but a subjective relationship, discovered by the imagination.

In Baudelaire's vocabulary, both poetic and critical, the term symbol does not have the exclusive pre-eminence that it has had for so many critics since. There seems to be no hierarchy, no invidious distinctions, among *symbole*, *hiéroglyphe*, *emblème*, *allégorie*, *métaphore*, *comparaison*, *image*. Baudelaire tends to use them indifferently, often using two of them in the same poem with the same meaning, as when in *Un Voyage à Cythère* we find

> Dans ton île, ô Vénus! je n'ai trouvé debout
> Qu'un gibet symbolique où pendait mon image . . .

From poem to poem the words vary while the underlying meaning remains the same. In *Les Petites Vieilles* we have

> La Mort savante met dans ces bières pareilles
> Un symbole d'un goût bizarre et captivant.

In *Le Squelette laboureur*

> . . . . d'un destin trop dur
> Epouvantable et clair emblème!

and in *L'Irrémédiable*

> —Emblèmes nets, tableau parfait
> D'une fortune irrémédiable.

In *L'Homme et la mer*

> Tu te plais à plonger au sein de ton image.

The word *hiéroglyphe* does not appear in the poetry, nor does *métaphore*, but in the prose both are equated with symbol and analogy. *Allégorie* is frequent in both; in *Le Cygne* "Tout pour moi devient allégorie," and in *Un Voyage à Cythère*

> Hélas! et j'avais, comme en un suaire épais,
> Le cœur enseveli dans cette allégorie.

And the prose *Invitation au voyage* gives us "Fleur incomparable, tulipe retrouvée, allégorique dahlia." In his criticism Baudelaire steadily defends allegory, about which Diderot had had so many reservations. The difference is, I think, simply in the underlying conception of the word; for Diderot it meant the conventional and banal allegorical figures he found so tiresome, while for Baudelaire it carries all the overtones of *symbole*. "Allegory is one of the most beautiful forms of art," he says in the *Salon de 1845*. Again, "Allegory, that *spiritual* form, which unskilful painters have accustomed us to despise, but which is in reality one of the primitive and most natural forms of poetry." [73]

Whatever label Baudelaire uses, the conception of the symbol dominates his poetry. The world of the senses leads into the inner world of the poet. Many later poets have plunged us into their private worlds, which too often seem to us strange and hallucinatory. Baudelaire leads us from an experience anyone might have to a vision that only the poet can perceive. In *Le Cygne* the everyday experience, "Comme je traversais le nouveau Carrousel," leads to the upsurge of memories; then all become allegory, and we have the long procession of exiles led by Andromache, closing with the final dying echo,

> Ainsi dans la forêt où mon esprit s'exile
> Un vieux Souvenir sonne à plein souffle du cor!

Or, starting from the inner experience or idea, Baudelaire translates it into concrete form. Hence the wealth of personifications: "L'aurore grelottante en robe rose et verte"; "L'Ennui . . . fumant son houka"; "les défuntes Années,/ Sur les balcons du ciel, en robes surannées." Beauty is no vague abstraction, but takes on human form and attributes: "Le Destin charmé suit tes jupons comme un chien." With many poets this move from abstract to concrete tends to give to the image a somewhat detached and artificial aspect, reminiscent of conventional allegory; one too often feels that the poet has made a deliberate and conscious search for an appropriate image. The symbolist poet, on the other hand, is more likely to find his starting point in the concrete object, which suggests to him an inner meaning. But with Baudelaire both approaches seem equally natural; the concrete object becomes a speaking symbol, and the abstract clothes itself spontaneously in concrete form. The inner and outer worlds are always linked, and the reader's experience is broadened and deepened by a sense of their intimate relationship.

But imagination is necessary for the spectator, the listener, and the reader, as well as for the painter, the composer, and the poet. In looking at a painting the spectator is "the translator of an ever clear and intoxicating translation"; in music "there is always a gap to be filled in by the imagination of the listener." This is true, Baudelaire adds, "even in the written word, which is however the most positive of all the arts." The poet and the artist must then leave room for the imagination of the reader or spectator. In other words, they must suggest. Delacroix is for Baudelaire "the most *suggestive* of all painters, the one whose works . . . give most food for thought, and recall to the memory the greatest number of sentiments and poetic thoughts once known, but believed to be forever buried in the night of the past." And art is for Baudelaire "the creation of a suggestive magic." [74]

The symbol is the great mode of suggestion. But it can produce its effect only if imagination is seconded by technical skill; otherwise the creation will be imperfect, the work will fail to suggest as it should. Hence Baudelaire's constant insistence on technique. As we have seen, he is no partisan of art for art's sake, and is by no means indifferent to subject matter: "I can never consider the choice of subject a matter of indifference, and . . . in spite of the necessary devotion which must impregnate the most humble work, I believe that the subject is for the artist a part of his genius, and for me, who am after all a barbarian, it constitutes a part of my pleasure." But no subject, no conception of the imagination can be fully realized without the aid of technique. Over and over again Baudelaire cites the example of Delacroix, who "starts from this principle, that a picture must above all reproduce the intimate thought of the artist, who dominates the model, as the creator dominates his creation; and from this principle follows a second one which at first sight seems to contradict the first, — namely, that the greatest care must be taken with the material means of execution." [75] In his last article on Delacroix, Baudelaire says: "It is obvious that in his opinion imagination was the most precious of all gifts, the most important of all faculties, but that this faculty was impotent and sterile, if it did not have at its service a swift skill capable of following the great despotic faculty in all its impatient caprices." Technique, however, is but the servant of imagination: "The more imagination one has, the more necessary it is to master technique in order that it may accompany imagination on its adventures and overcome the difficulties it eagerly seeks out. And the greater one's mastery of technique, the less one should depend upon it and display it, so that imagination may shine in all its glory. That is the voice of wisdom; and wisdom adds that he who has only technical skill is stupid, and the imagination which wishes to do without it is mad." [76]

The poet's special tool is language, and a preoccupation with poetic language appears in Baudelaire's earliest critical articles. Writing in 1846 of Ménard's "philosophical poem," *Prométhée délivré*, he says that the author's form is still vague and elusive: "He is unaware of highly colored rhymes, those lanterns which light up the path of the idea; he is also unaware of the effects that can be produced by a certain number of words put together in different ways." [77] Even in the 1851 article on Pierre Dupont, where he is least preoccupied with form, Baudelaire writes of the *mot propre* and its value, of the continued activity which goes on in the minds of writers, the series of circumstances which are necessary to bring a poet into being. He had a passion for words — "j'avais été pris très-jeune de lexicomanie" — and in his article on Banville there is a passage on the words in a poet's work which are particularly characteristic of his talent. He finds Banville's greatest claim to fame in the certitude of his lyric expression, and maintains that Leconte de Lisle's mastery of his thought would be of little use if he did not know how to use his tools. The poet is forever in search of the language which will best express the conceptions of his imagination:

> Je vais m'exercer seul à ma fantasque escrime,
> Flairant dans tous les coins les hasards de la rime,
> Trébuchant sur les mots comme sur les pavés,
> Heurtant parfois des vers depuis longtemps rêvés.[78]

The gift of language is, with the perception of correspondences, the poetic gift that Baudelaire praises most highly. In his article on Gautier he says: "To speak worthily of the tool which so well serves this passion for beauty, I should need to possess similar resources, that knowledge of the language which is never at fault, that magnificent dictionary whose leaves, stirred by the breath of divinity, open at the right place so that the right word, the unique word, may spring forth, and finally that sense of order which puts each stroke and each touch in its natural place, and omits no gradation." Gautier's understanding of correspondences and symbolism, with his gift of style, permits him "to define the mysterious attitude which the objects of creation take on in men's eyes. There is in the word, in the *logos*, something *sacred* which forbids us to gamble with it. To handle a language skilfully is to practice a kind of evocative sorcery." [79]

Even grammar takes on a poetic aspect. Baudelaire writes in the *Poème du haschisch*: "Grammar, arid grammar itself becomes something like an evocative sorcery; words are resurrected clothed in flesh, the noun in its substantial majesty, the adjective, a transparent garment which clothes and colors it like a glaze, and the verb, the angel of movement which sets the sentence in motion." The "Projets de préface" state that poetry "is connected with the arts of painting, cooking and cosmetics by the potentiality it has of expressing any sensation of sweetness or bitterness, of bliss or horror, by coupling such and such a noun with such and such an adjective, analogous or contrary." In *Fusées* Baudelaire gives an example: "*Ciel tragique.* Epithet of an abstract order applied to a material entity." [80]

Rhyme and rhythm are not artificial, but, Baudelaire says in the "Projets de préface," correspond to "man's immortal needs of monotony, symmetry and surprise." He proposes to explain:

How poetry is related to music by a prosody whose roots go deeper into the human soul than any classical theory indicates;
That French poetry has a mysterious and unrecognized prosody, like Latin and English;
Why any poet who does not know exactly how many rhymes every word has is incapable of expressing any idea whatsoever;
That the poetic phrase can imitate (and in this respect it verges on the art of music and the science of mathematics) a horizontal line, a straight line ascending or descending; that it can rise straight towards heaven without losing breath, or plunge perpendicularly towards hell with the speed of gravity; that it can follow the spiral, describe a parabola, or a zigzag making a series of superimposed angles.[81]

In the Gautier article Baudelaire specifies the rhythm particularly characteristic of lyric poetry: "It is the nature of true poetry to flow regularly, like great rivers which approach the sea, their death and their infinity, and to avoid haste and abruptness. Lyric poetry springs forward, but always with a supple and undulatory movement." Thus poetry profits by the rules of prosody and rhetoric, which "are not arbitrarily invented by tyrannies, but a collection of rules required by the very organization of our spiritual being. And never have prosodies and rhetorics kept originality from making itself clearly visible. The contrary, that they have helped the flowering of originality, would be far more true." [82]

So Baudelaire believed that "because of the constraint of the form, the idea springs forth with more intensity." [83] But he also had the idea, set forth in the dedication of the *Petits Poèmes en prose*, of a freer form: "Which of us has not, in his days of ambition, dreamed the miracle of a poetic prose, musical without rhythm and without rhyme, flexible enough and abrupt enough to adapt itself to the lyrical impulses of the spirit, to waves of revery, to sudden starts of conscience?" But the essential is that idea and form must not be separated. "Idea and form are two beings in one," and the neglect of form "results in the annihilation of poetry." This is put more poetically in the prose poem *Le Thyrse*. In the staff and the flowers twined around it Baudelaire finds a symbol: "Straight line and arabesque, intention and expression, rigor of will, flexibility of language, unity of end, variety of means, all-powerful and indivisible amalgam of genius, what analyst will have the despicable courage to divide and separate you?" [84]

Thus Baudelaire both conceived and practiced a poetry in which imagination transfigures personal experience by poetic vision, transmutes everyday reality into that poetic reality which is the highest truth, and, seconded by the gift of language, in its alchemist's crucible fuses matter and form into one. Poetry, like all art, is for Baudelaire "the creation of a suggestive magic, containing at the same time the object and the subject, the world outside the artist and the artist himself." [85]

In Baudelaire's poetic doctrine the reader finds, as Hugo found in his poetry, "un frisson nouveau." Flaubert wrote to him: "You are not like anyone else (which is the first of all qualities)." [86] Yet many aspects of his theory recall his predecessors, and his debt to them is by no means negligible. Like his own Samuel Cramer, "He was at the same time all the artists he had studied and all the books he had read, and nevertheless, in spite of this gift of mimicry, he remained profoundly original." [87]

As we look back over the road we have traveled, we realize that the chief articles of Baudelaire's poetic creed had been expressed or adumbrated earlier. Most striking are the parallels with Diderot, to my mind Baudelaire's only peer in the realm of poetic theory during this long period. Diderot, like Baudelaire, was intensely aware of the great central problems of the nature and function of poetry, the relation of art to reality, of matter to form, of imagination to technique. His solutions to those problems were, I believe, essentially the same as Baudelaire's, although at times the emphasis varies. For him too imagination was the chief faculty of the poet. His conception of imagination is a more limited one than Baudelaire's, in the sense that the poetic imagination is for him primarily the active, combining, "creative" faculty, whereas for Baudelaire it is both creative and visionary, the faculty which penetrates beyond the surface of reality, both into that spiritual world whose existence Diderot denied, and into the human correspondences of the natural world, in which it finds its symbols. There is no question, I think, that Diderot had a clearer conception than Baudelaire of the physiological and psychological nature of imagination, which for Baudelaire remained veiled in mystery. And it might well be maintained that the visionary aspect of the Baudelairian imagination is to be found, to some extent at least, in Diderot's conception of enthusiasm. What interested Baudelaire was not so much what imagination *is* as what it *does*, and he brings together under its aegis the poetic activity in its entirety. But whatever the differences in conception are, Diderot and Baudelaire are alike in seeing in the imagination, suspect earlier, little understood and viewed with some misgivings by most of the romantics, the greatest of all poetic faculties.

Yet Baudelaire, as we have seen, was far from breaking with his immediate predecessors. Much as he distrusted the sentimental effusions of romantic poetry, he inherited from it the conception of a highly personal poetry. But this poetry of sentiment was controlled and dominated by a belief in the importance of form, that all-in-all for the partisans of art for art's sake. With Baudelaire the separation between the poetry of sentiment and the poetry of images comes to an end; matter and form are united and inseparable. Finally, from the illuminist tradition and its gradual penetration into literature Baudelaire, together with Hugo and Gérard de Nerval, develops the conception of a special poetic experience by which the poet is led through nature to a higher reality, to the discovery of correspondences and symbols, and thus to a poetry of suggestion.

Baudelaire's originality and greatness as a critic are to be found then, I believe, not so much in the invention of new ideas as in an extraordinary power to illuminate old ideas with the intensity of his personal experience and vision, to see them in their right relation and proportion. To his poetic doctrine as well as to his poetry may be applied his words, "j'ai de chaque chose extrait la quintessence." The magical and synthetic power of his imagination, at work in his criticism as well as in his poetry, combines and fuses the old doctrines into a new creation. Thus it seems to me right and justifiable to see in Baudelaire the culmination of the long development we have followed.

Yet it would be arbitrary and one-sided not to recall that Baudelaire is a beginning as well as an end. It has become a commonplace with modern critics to see in him a turning point in French poetry, from which there is an unbroken line to the poetry of the twentieth century. It was from Baudelaire that his greatest successors learned to envisage poetry not as statement and rhetoric but as suggestion and magic. Many later poets were to follow Baudelaire's call, "Au fond de l'Inconnu, pour trouver du nouveau!" But there are certain sharp distinctions between Baudelaire and the majority of his successors which lead to a conception of poetry which is in certain respects radically different from his. There is a disintegration and a modification of Baudelaire's all-embracing conception of the imagination.[88] For him imagination found its point of departure in the world around us, and through that world discovered the invisible and unknown. His successors tend to distrust and disparage the world of the senses, to eliminate everyday experience, in an attempt to arrive directly at a higher reality. In the words of a modern poet, Pierre Reverdy, "The more the artist can detach himself from that tangible reality which importunes him, the more efficaciously will his work attain the hidden source of reality." [89] Everyday reality is no longer an instrument, but an obstacle. Moreover the visionary aspect of imagination was increasingly emphasized at the expense of its creative activity. Poetry was conceived as primarily experience, as a "moyen de connaissance." As Tristan Tzara said, it was no longer "to be classified under the heading of expression. . . . Poetry which expresses either ideas or feelings no longer interests anyone. To it I oppose poetry as an 'activité de l'esprit.' " [90] This would certainly have been completely inacceptable to Baudelaire. For him the "activité de l'esprit" is indeed essential to poetry, but it is not in itself poetry, which belongs to the domain of art and not to that of metaphysics. Poetry is expression and creation, the translation of experience into form, the fusion of vision and language.

Nor would Baudelaire have sympathized with the tendency on the poet's part, resulting from his complete absorption in his private experience, to turn away from his reader and in upon himself, to write, as it were, poetry for the poet's sake. For Baudelaire, as for his predecessors, however much poetry was the overflow of personal feelings, however much it was the satisfaction of the creative urge, however much it was a voyage into the unknown, it was in the end intended for a reader. The idea of a reader is implicit in the conception of poetry as suggestion as much as in that of poetry as statement. If poetry is to suggest, it must suggest to some one. We have seen how often Baudelaire speaks of the collaboration between the imagination of the artist and the spectator, of the poet and the reader. If, as Baudelaire believed, poetry is as necessary to man as his daily bread, the poet must satisfy that need. And more than one critic has noted in recent French poetry a return to a more human view, a renewal of the conception of poetry not as a metaphysical or mystical activity but as literature and as art.[91]

The long progress of the idea of poetry which we have followed through this book, starting at a moment when poetry was at its lowest ebb, is marked by doubts and hesitations and timidity, but also, very early even, by flashes of insight and glimpses into poetic truth that finally lead to the restoration of poetry to its full dignity and greatness. It is a significant chapter in the history of French literature, and one which is closely tied to the great literary movements of the eighteenth and nineteenth centuries. More than that, it is, I believe, illuminating and fruitful for an understanding of the nature and problems of the poetry of all times.

There are, as I see it, three central and ever present problems on which the discussions we have followed are focused: that of the essential nature of poetry, involving its relation to truth and to morality and, on the formal side, to prose; that of the relation of poetry, as of all art, to reality; and that of the relative importance of matter and form and the relations between them. From a position which judged poetry by its conformity to truth and to morality, which denied any essential difference, other than a purely formal one, between poetry and prose, there developed a conception of poetry as an independent form of art, having its own aims, its own laws. From a narrow conception of poetry as imitation we reach that of poetry governed by imagination, in which nature, though never lost sight of, is transformed and re-created by poetic vision. And after a long series of vacillations between the notions of poetry as spirit and poetry as form, matter and form are finally seen as inextricably related, fused into one. Poetry ceases to be embellished statement, and becomes suggestive magic. I would not claim that the doctrine of poetry thus achieved, admirable as it seems to me, is the only acceptable and valid one; there are many mansions in poetic theory as in poetry itself. I would only suggest that the story of the growth of this conception brings us face to face with the major problems of poetic theory and offers a solution which has borne fruit in great poetry.

NOTES

NOTES

Unless otherwise indicated, the place of publication is Paris. I have given the names of publishers only when it seemed that the edition referred to might otherwise be difficult to identify.

The following abbreviations are used for titles of periodicals:

MLN   *Modern Language Notes*
MLR   *Modern Language Review*
RDM   *Revue des Deux Mondes*
RHL   *Revue d'Histoire Littéraire de la France*
RLC   *Revue de Littérature Comparée*
RR   *Romanic Review*
YFS   *Yale French Studies*

I. THE NADIR OF POETRY

1. Abbé Nicolas-Charles-Joseph Trublet, *Essais sur divers sujets de littérature et de morale* (1760), IV, 215.

2. For a full discussion of these *arts poétiques* see W. F. Patterson, *Three Centuries of French Poetic Theory: A Critical History of the Chief Arts of Poetry in France (1328-1630)* (Ann Arbor, 1935), and Robert J. Clements, *Critical Theory and Practice of the Pléiade* (Cambridge, Mass., 1942).

3. Joachim du Bellay, *La Deffence et illustration de la langue francoyse,* ed. Henri Chamard (Fontemoing, 1904), pp. 300-302.

4. Jacques Peletier du Mans, *L'Art poétique* (1555), ed. André Boulanger (Les Belles Lettres, 1930), p. 221.

5. Pierre de Ronsard, "L'Art poétique," *Œuvres complètes*, Bibliothèque de la Pléiade (1938), II, 1001.

6. See especially W. Folkierski, *Entre le classicisme et le romantisme: Etude sur l'esthétique et les esthéticiens du xviiie siècle* (1925); Daniel Mornet, *Histoire de la clarté française: ses origines — son évolution — sa valeur* (1929); René Bray, *La Formation de la doctrine classique en France* (1931); Paul Hazard, *La Crise de la conscience européenne* (1680-1715) (1935).

7. Ferdinand Brunot, *La Doctrine de Malherbe d'après son Commentaire sur Desportes* (1891), p. 152.

8. The most detailed study of eighteenth-century poetry is Emile Faguet, *Histoire de la poésie française de la Renaissance au romantisme* (1923-1926), Vols. VI-XI.

9. Voltaire, *Correspondence*, ed. Theodore Besterman (Geneva, 1953-), IV, 48-49.

10. Samuel Johnson, *Rasselas* (1759), Ch. x.

11. For a full and sympathetic study, see Henry A. Grubbs, *Jean-Baptiste Rousseau, his Life and Works* (Princeton, 1941).

12. See Leo Spitzer, "*Explication de texte* applied to Voltaire," *A Method of Interpreting Literature* (Northampton, Mass., 1949).

13. See Hippolyte Rigaud, *Histoire de la querelle des anciens et des modernes* (1856).

14. For a full discussion see Raymond Naves, *Le Goût de Voltaire* (1938). Naves describes an evolution which, "de la conception simplement *régulière* de la littérature, aboutit à la conception *géométrique*. Pour l'une, la Raison contrôle l'inspiration; pour l'autre, elle est l'Inspiration elle-même" (p. 15). See also a valuable article by J. Ranscelot, "Les Manifestations du déclin poétique au début du XVIIIe siècle" (*RHL*, 33: 497–520 [Oct.–Dec. 1926]).

15. Letter to Desforges-Maillard [1735], *Correspondence*, ed. Besterman, IV, 91.

16. On Fontenelle see Louis Maigron, *Fontenelle, l'homme, l'œuvre, l'influence* (1906); on La Motte, Paul Dupont, *Un Poète-philosophe au commencement du dix-huitième siècle: Houdar de la Motte (1672–1731)*, (1898). There is a curious attempt to rehabilitate La Motte in a recent article by Léon-Gabriel Gros, "Houdar de la Motte; Accusateur et défenseur de la poésie," *Cahiers du Sud*, 38e Année (1951), no. 306. On Trublet see Jean Jacquard, *L'Abbé Trublet, critique et moraliste, 1697–1770* (1926).

17. See John R. Miller, *Boileau en France au dix-huitième siècle* (Baltimore, 1942).

18. [Gabriel-Henri Gaillard], *Poétique française à l'usage des dames* (1749), I, 2–3.

19. Abbé Charles Batteux, *Les Beaux-arts réduits à un même principe* (1746), p. 48 (Pt. III, Sec. 1, Ch. vi).

20. Louis Racine, "Réflexions sur la poésie," *Œuvres* (1808), II. Voltaire wrote of Louis Racine: "Il entendait la mécanique des vers aussi bien que son père, mais il n'en avait ni l'âme ni les grâces. Il manquait d'ailleurs d'invention et d'imagination" ("Catalogue alphabétique de la plupart des écrivains qui ont paru dans le siècle de Louis XIV. . . ." [1752], *Œuvres*, ed. Moland, 1877–1885, XIV, 118).

21. See Alfred Lombard, *Fénelon et le retour à l'antique au xviiie siècle* (1954), and also Albert Chérel, *Fénelon au xviiie siècle en France (1715–1820): son prestige — son influence* (1917).

22. [Abbé Jean-Baptiste du Bos], *Réflexions critiques sur la poésie et sur la peinture* (1719), II, 38. On Du Bos see A. Lombard, *L'Abbé du Bos: Un Initiateur de la pensée moderne (1670–1742)* (1913), p. 227. This is a valuable study not only of Du Bos himself but of his relation to the critics who preceded and followed him. See also the articles by B. Munteano, "L'Abbé du Bos, ou le Quintilien de la France," *Mélanges d'histoire littéraire et de bibliographie offerts à Jean Bonnerot* (1954), and "Survivances antiques: L'Abbé du Bos esthéticien de la persuasion passionnelle," *RLC*, 30: 318–350 (July–Sept. 1956).

23. André Monglond, *Le Préromantisme française*, I (1930), 38.

24. [Toussaint Rémond de Saint–Mard], *Réflexions sur la poésie en général, sur l'églogue, sur la fable, sur l'élégie, sur la satire, sur l'ode et sur les autres petits poèmes comme sonnet, rondeau, madrigal etc., suivies de Trois Lettres sur la décadence du goût en France*, par M. R. D. S. M. (The Hague, 1734).

25. "C'est un art si charmant que la poésie, que nous ne saurions avoir trop d'obligation à Aristote et à Horace d'en avoir donné des règles: mais d'où vient que, contents de nous les donner, ces grands hommes ne se sont

toujours mis en peine de nous faire sentir sur quoi ces règles étaient fondées? Il semble que, pour rendre une poétique complète, il faudrait aller plus haut que les règles, remonter à ce qui les a fait faire, les vérifier sur les impressions mêmes; d'où il résulterait une plus grande certitude dans les règles, et ce qui, en même temps, ne serait pas d'une petite considération pour notre orgueil, l'honneur de savoir sur quoi ces règles ont été fondées; c'està-dire leur rapport avec notre manière de sentir" (*Réflexions*, pp. iii–iv).

26. Rémond de Saint-Mard's *Réflexions* are referred to fairly frequently in the eighteenth century, most often unfavorably. In the first volume of *Le Pour et le Contre* Prévost dismisses the work briefly and somewhat scathingly (I, 232), but the criticism by Desfontaines in the second volume is both longer and, in spite of some reservations, more favorable. In his *Bibliothèque française* (1744) Goujet speaks of his "ouvrages ingénieux, où il veut qu'on sente plus qu'on ne pense, lorsqu'il pense lui-même plus qu'il ne sent; où il condamne le style *maniéré*, dans le même temps qu'il est maniéré lui-même; en un mot où il détruit dans la pratique les principes qu'il veut établir" (III, 145). When Rémond's collected works were published in 1749 the *Réflexions* were discussed at some length by Fréron and Laporte, who, though they defend Boileau, praise Rémond's "idées fines, neuves, délicates" (*Lettres sur quelques écrits de ce temps*, Geneva, 1749–54, II, 116). Crévier, in his *Rhétorique française* (1765) says that Rémond "pour la finesse et la délicatesse ne cède à personne" (II, 179–180). But Sabatier de Castres classes the *Réflexions* among "ces poétiques arbitraires, qui, dérogeant aux vrais principes, ne laissent voir que les idées de l'auteur, contre lesquelles le bon goût doit se tenir sagement en garde. Cet ouvrage, d'ailleurs, est écrit d'un style affecté qui déprécie ce qu'il y a de bon" (*Les Trois Siècles de notre littérature*, Amsterdam, 1772, III, 172–173). In the nineteenth century Rémond seems to have been almost completely neglected; Michaud's *Biographie universelle* pillories him as a "littérateur médiocre . . . sans goût, sans chaleur, sans imagination" (the article is by J.-J. Weiss). Saintsbury says that he is "not destitute of original ideas worthily put" (*A History of Criticism and of Literary Taste in Europe*, New York, Edinburgh and London, 1902–1907, II, 510–511). But the only considerable treatment of him is to be found in an article which came to my attention after this chapter had been written, Arnaldo Pizzorusso, "La 'Poetica Arbitraria' di Rémond de Saint-Mard," *Rivista di Letterature Moderne*, V (1954), 5–25. The author gives a good analysis of Rémond's theories, and of some of the criticisms made of him in the eighteenth century, but hardly does justice to the freshness and originality of his position.

Rémond's other writings, such as the *Nouveaux Dialogues des dieux* and the *Lettres galantes et philosophiques* are in the *libertin* vein, with a calculated delight in upsetting traditional notions of virtue and vice and in a heaping of paradox on paradox. In the *Réflexions* his love of pleasure stands him in good stead; he has no hesitation about expressing his personal opinions, and more than one sentence anticipates the vigor of Diderot's judgments. The eclogue is "une de mes folies"; the elegy is "le genre de notre poésie française le plus insipide"; one of La Motte's odes is introduced by "Est-ce par exemple une ode que vous allez lire?" (pp. 47, 149, 226). Whatever genre he is dealing with, he recalls the highest achievement in that genre. All fables are compared with those of La Fontaine, whom Rémond praises with enthusiasm and discrimination, above all for the naturalness of his language. For Rémond naturalness is one of the chief qualities of poetry; for this reason he puts Régnier above Boileau as a satirist (p. 189). The "beau désordre" of the ode is justified as "le langage naturel d'un poète qui, maîtrisé par la passion, est forcé de s'abandonner aux différents mouvements qu'elle lui donne" (p. 223). Rémond's great criticism of his age is that it was a century "où il n'était pas du bel air d'être naturel" (p. 331), and his final hope is that "ce beau naturel reparaîtra un jour dans tout son éclat, deviendra le langage ordinaire de nos neveux" (p. 349).

Rémond de Saint-Mard is a pleasant oasis to the reader who has plowed through an arid waste of eighteenth-century treatises. His book is not a complete *art poétique* (he characteristically puts off the treatment of epic and dramatic poetry to a future date), some of the great problems of poetry are hardly touched on, but throughout there is freshness and charm and, above all, sensitivity to poetry.

27. Irving Babbitt wrote: "The process by which the word enthusiasm itself changed in the course of the eighteenth century from a bad to a good meaning, by which the enthusiast and original genius supplanted the wit and man of the world, is one of the most important in literary history and can scarcely be traced too carefully" (*Masters of Modern French Criticism*, Boston and New York, 1912, p. 7).

28. English writers often distinguished between inspiration and enthusiasm. Shaftsbury, for example, writes: "Inspiration is a real feeling of the Divine Presence, and enthusiasm a false one. But the passion they raise is much alike" (*Lettre sur l'enthousiasme* [1708], ed. A. Leroy, 1930, p. 307). Johnson's dictionary (1755) gives as its first definition of enthusiasm: "a vain confidence of divine favor or communication." But the French do not seem to have made the distinction: *enthousiasme* carries both meanings, and *inspiration* is little used until *enthousiasme* begins to take on its modern meaning, early in the nineteenth century.

29. Antoine Houdar de la Motte, "Discours sur la poésie en général et sur l'ode en particulier," *Odes* (1713), I, 36.

30. Bernard Bouvier de Fontenelle, "Réponse à l'Evêque de Luçon, 6 mars 1732," *Œuvres*, III (1742), 355–356.

31. *Réflexions critiques*, II, 15, 103.

32. *Beaux-arts*, pp. 30–31 (Pt. I, Ch. iv); p. 238 (Pt. III, Sec. 1, Ch. ix).

33. *Cours de belles-lettres distribué par exercices* (1747–1748), II¹, 11, 15.

34. Undated fragment, quoted in Grubbs, *J.-B. Rousseau*, p. 235.

35. Luc de Clapiers, marquis de Vauvenargues, "Fragments," *Œuvres*, ed. Gilbert (1857), pp. 279–280.

36. [Louis de Cahusac], *Epître sur les dangers de la poésie*, par Monsieur le comte de Cˣˣˣ (The Hague, 1739).

37. Abbé Gabriel Girard, *Synonymes français, leurs différentes significations et le choix qu'il en faut faire pour parler avec justesse* (Amsterdam, 1737), p. 116.

38. *Réflexions critiques*, II, 41.

39. *Œuvres posthumes*, ed. Gilbert (1857), pp. 34–35.

40. François de Salignac de la Mothe-Fénelon, Lettre à l'Académie (V), *Œuvres choisies* (Garnier, n. d.), pp. 130–131, 137.

41. *Réflexions critiques*, II, 1; I, 275.

42. *Beaux-arts*, pp. 240, 244 (Pt. III, Sec. 1, Ch. ix).

43. *Cours de belles-lettres*, II¹, 24.

44. "Fragments," *Œuvres*, pp. 279, 276.

45. *Réflexions*, p. 9.

46. Charles de Secondat, baron de Montesquieu, *Lettres persanes*, cxxxviii.

47. Abbé Jean-François de Pons, *Dissertation sur le poème épique, contre la doctrine de M. D.*, *Œuvres* (1738), p. 143.

48. *Lettre à l'Académie*, *Œuvres choisies*, p. 122.

49. Abbé Guillaume Massieu, *Histoire de la poésie française, avec une défense de la poésie* (1739). The publisher's preface states that the work, published after Massieu's death, had been written fifteen years earlier.

50. December 5, 1733, *Correspondence*, ed. Besterman, III, 190–191.

51. Letter to Berger, 1736, and letter to Frederick the Great [1736], *ibid.*, V, 230, 233. See also what Voltaire says in a letter to "R." in 1738: "étant parvenu à l'âge de quarante-trois ans, je renonce déjà à la poésie. La vie est trop courte, et l'esprit de l'homme trop destiné à s'instruire sérieusement, pour consumer tout son temps à chercher des sons et des rimes" (*ibid.*, VII, 215).

52. See Murray Wright Bundy, *The Theory of Imagination in Classical and Mediaeval Thought*, University of Illinois Studies, XII, 2–3 (1937); and Livingston Welch, *Imagination and Human Nature*, Psyche Monographs No. 5 (London, 1935).

53. *Œuvres complètes*, II, 1001. In 1694 the *Dictionnaire de l'Académie* defines *inventer*: "Trouver quelque chose de nouveau par la force de son esprit, de son imagination."

54. René Descartes, *Discours de la méthode*, ed. Gilson (1925), p. 37 (Pt. IV). For a full discussion of Descartes's ideas on imagination see Jean H. Roy, *L'Imagination selon Descartes* (1944).

55. "Le sens commun, où ces idées sont reçues . . . la mémoire, qui les conserve . . . la fantaisie, qui les peut diversement changer et en composer de nouvelles" (*Discours*, p. 55, Pt. V). The word *fantaisie* gradually took on its modern meaning during the eighteenth century, as Voltaire points out at the beginning of his *Encyclopédie* article (1756): "*FANTAISIE*, s. f. Gramm.; signifiait autrefois l'*imagination*, et on ne se servait guère de ce mot que pour exprimer cette faculté de l'âme qui reçoit les objets sensibles. Descartes, Gassendi, et tous les philosophes de leur temps, disent que *les espèces, les images et les choses se peignent en la fantaisie. . . . Fantaisie* veut dire aujourd'hui *un désir singulier, un goût passager*." The following article, "*FANTAISIE*, Morale," defines the term as "une passion d'un moment, qui n'a sa source que dans l'imagination. . . . Les hommes qui ont plus d'imagination que de bon sens, sont esclaves de mille *fantaisies*."

56. Nicolas de Malebranche, *Recherche de la vérité* (Flammarion, 1935), I, 152, 182.

57. Blaise Pascal, *Pensées*, *Œuvres*, Bibliothèque de la Pléiade (1941), p. 851.

58. Jean de la Bruyère, "De la société et de la conversation," *Caractères*, V.

59. *Lettre à l'Académie* (V), *Œuvres choisies*, p. 158.

60. [Abbé Edmé Mallet], *Principes pour la lecture des poètes* (1745), I, 9.

61. Abbé Prévost d'Exiles, *Le Pour et le Contre*, VI (1735), 70.

62. *Réflexions critiques*, I, 176, 355, 210.

63. *Beaux-arts*, p. 11 (Pt. I, Ch. ii); p. 24 (Pt. I, Ch. iii).

64. "Réflexions," *Œuvres*, II, 333.
65. Jean-Pierre de Crousaz, *Traité du beau* (Amsterdam, 1715); Père Yves André, *Essai sur le beau* (1741).
66. *Poétique*, p. 2.
67. *Cours de belles-lettres*, I¹, 67.
68. Guillaume Amfrye de Chaulieu, "L'Imagination, avec l'Adieu aux muses," *Poésies* (1825), p. 179.
69. *Connaissance de l'esprit humain*, *Œuvres*, p. 6.
70. Florence D. White, *Voltaire's "Essay on Epic Poetry": A Study and an Edition* (1915), p. 83.
71. Thomas Hobbes, *Leviathan* (1651), Everyman Edition (1914), pp. 3, 5–6.
72. John Locke, *Essay on Human Understanding*, *Works* (London, 1823), I, 145. In his essay "On Taste" (1759) Burke, discussing imagination, says: "To this belongs whatever is called wit, fancy, invention, and the like," and quotes with praise Locke's distinction between wit and judgment (*Works*, London, 1913, I, 58).
73. "I have indeed a faculty of imaging, or representing to myself the ideas of those particular things I have perceived, and of variously compounding and dividing them" (George Berkeley, *A Treatise concerning the Principles of Human Knowledge* [1710], ed. T. E. Jessop, London, 1942, p. 10); "The liberty of the imagination to transpose and change its ideas" (David Hume, *Treatise of Human Nature* [1738], *Philosophical Works*, Boston, 1854, I, 24).
74. Francis Bacon, *The Advancement of Learning* (1605), ed. W. A. Wright (Oxford, 1900), p. 85 (II, i, 1).
75. Joseph Addison, *Spectator*, no. 411, June 21, 1712.
76. *Spectator*, no. 417, June 28, 1712.
77. *Spectator*, no. 421, July 3, 1712.
78. John Dryden, Preface to *Annus Mirabilis* (1666).
79. Condillac and Diderot were in such close touch at about the time that Condillac was writing the *Essai* that the question of influence is a difficult one, and Condillac may have no more than a priority of publication.
80. Abbé Etienne Bonnot de Condillac, *Essai sur l'origine des connaissances humaines* (Amsterdam, 1746), I, 113–114 (Pt. I, Sec. 2, Ch. ix).
81. *Ibid.*, I, 131–134 (Pt. I, Sec. 2, Ch. x).
82. *Spectator*, no. 421, July 3, 1712.
83. January 24, 1740, *Correspondence*, ed. Besterman, X, 24.
84. *Beaux-arts*, p. 10 (Pt. I, Ch. ii).
85. *Essai*, I, 45 (Pt. I, Sec. 2, Ch. xi).
86. Letter to West, 1742, *Correspondence*, ed. Toynbee and Whibley (Oxford, 1935), I, 192.
87. "Réflexions," *Œuvres*, II, 217.
88. *Dialogues sur l'éloquence* (1718), p. 97.
89. *Principes*, I, 83.
90. Balthasar Gibert, *La Rhétorique, ou Les Règles de l'éloquence* (1730), p. 534.
91. "Sur la poésie en général," *Œuvres*, VIII, 304.
92. "Discours," *Odes*, I, 19.
93. "De la poésie et des poètes," *Essais*, IV, 245. Trublet continues:

"Quand on ne fera plus de vers, il y a bien des sottises qu'on ne dira plus, parce qu'on n'oserait les dire en prose."

94. Letter to Berger, Aug. 4, 1735, *Correspondence*, ed. Besterman, IV, 99.

95. *Connaissance des beautés et des défauts de la poésie et de l'éloquence*, Voltaire, *Œuvres*, XXIII, 405. In a recent article, "Note on the Authorship of the *Connaissance des beautés*" (*Studies on Voltaire and the Eighteenth Century*, ed. Theodore Besterman, IV [1957], 291–294), Theodore Besterman has shown that the *Connaissance des beautés* is not by Voltaire, but by David Durand, a Protestant minister settled in London.

96. Crousaz, *Traité du beau*, pp. 161–162.

97. Letter to Cideville, Nov. 6, 1733, *Correspondence*, ed. Besterman, III, 173.

98. *Histoire de la poésie française*, p. 5.

99. César Chesnau du Marsais, *Des tropes, ou des différents sens dans lesquels on peut prendre un même mot dans une même langue* (1730), pp. 26–29, 138–140, 230–238.

100. *Cours de belles-lettres*, II[1], 25. Batteux had written earlier: "les pensées, les mots, les tours ont dans la poésie une hardiesse, une liberté, une richesse qui paraîtrait excessive dans le langage ordinaire. Ce sont des comparaisons soutenues, des métaphores éclatantes, des répétitions vives, des apostrophes singulières" (Beaux-arts, p. 167, Pt. III, Sec. 1, Ch. iii).

101. *Beaux-arts*, p. 136 (Pt. III, Sec. 1, Ch. iii).

102. *Réflexions critiques*, I, 199–200. *Symbole* is of course used here in its traditional and limited sense. The 1694 *Dictionnaire de l'Académie* defines it only in terms of the fine arts: "Figure peinte ou empreinte, qui est le signe de quelque chose, principalement de quelque vertu ou de quelque vice, de quelque bonne ou mauvaise qualité." In the 1718 edition the term is extended to language: "Figure ou image qui sert à désigner quelque chose, soit par le moyen de la peinture ou de la sculpture, soit par le discours." J.-B. Rousseau writes in one of his odes (IV, 5):

> Ces Déités d'adoption,
> Synonymes de la pensée,
> Symboles d'abstractions.

103. *Réflexions critiques*, I, 190, 264, 271.

104. *Réflexions*, pp. 6, 9.

105. William Warburton, *The Divine Legation of Moses* (London, 1741), II, 95, 148.

106. *Essai*, II, 193 (Pt. II, Sec. 1, Ch. xiv).

107. *Ibid.*, II, 195.

108. [1737], *Correspondence*, ed. Besterman, VI, 277.

109. Père Jean-Antoine du Cerceau, *Réflexions sur la poésie française* (1742), pp. 13, 24.

110. *Cours de belles-lettres*, II[2], 112.

111. *Discours sur Homère* (1714), p. cviii.

112. Letter to Du Ligne, March 25, 1715. Quoted in Grubbs, *Jean-Baptiste Rousseau*, p. 215.

113. *Lettres philosophiques*, *Œuvres*, XXII, 169.

114. *Réflexions critiques*, I, 284.

115. Abbé Pierre-Joseph Thoullier d'Olivet, *Traité de la prosodie* (1736), pp. 106–109.

116. "L'Ode de M. de la Faye," *Œuvres de théâtre* (1730), I, 389.

117. *Ibid.*, I, 238. Du Bos also opposes rhyme, on the ground that poetry came before rules (*Réflexions*, I, 302, 325).

118. [Jean Soubeiran de Scopon], "Réflexions sur la préface du *Brutus* de Voltaire," *Observations critiques à l'occasion des Remarques de grammaire sur Racine, de Monsieur l'abbé d'Olivet*, par M. S. de S. (1738), p. 69.

119. "Sur la poésie en général," *Œuvres*, VIII, 281, 290. Vauvenargues writes: "Je suis fâché qu'un esprit supérieur comme M. de Fontenelle veuille bien appuyer de son autorité les préjugés du peuple contre un art aimable, et dont le génie est donné à peu d'hommes" (Fragment 12, *Œuvres*, p. 282).

120. *Dialogues sur l'éloquence* (1718), pp. 98–99.

121. [Jean-Pierre de Longue], *Raisonnements hasardés sur la poésie française* (1737), p. 103.

122. *Le Pour et le Contre*, VI, 75 (no. lxxix).

123. "C'est à cette gêne même que nous devons une partie de ces traits neufs et lumineux, qui nous saisissent d'admiration . . . nous tentons d'autres routes, qui nous font souvent découvrir des expressions et plus fortes et plus frappantes" ([President Jean Bouhier], *Poème de Pétrone sur la guerre civile*, Amsterdam, 1737, p. x).

124. *Le Pour et le Contre*, X, 285 (the discussion of Bouhier is in nos. cxlvi–cxlvii).

125. For a full discussion of this question see Vista Clayton, *The Prose Poem in French Literature* (New York, 1936); Albert Chérel, *La Prose poétique française* (1941); and especially Alexis François, *Les Origines lyriques de la phrase moderne* (1929). Personally I should question the statement made in the first of these that the way for the nineteenth-century prose poem was prepared "by more than a century of continuous development" (p. 1). The eighteenth century aimed above all at freeing poetry from the shackles of verse, material from form; the nineteenth century was seeking a form closer to the material. As Baudelaire said: "Quel est celui de nous qui n'a pas, dans ses jours d'ambition, rêvé le miracle d'une prose poétique, musicale sans rythme et sans rime, assez souple et assez heurtée pour s'adapter aux mouvements lyriques de l'âme, aux ondulations de la rêverie, aux soubresauts de la conscience?" (*Petits Poèmes en prose*, ed. Jacques Crépet, Conard, 1926, p. vi).

126. Letter to Brossette, April 29, 1719. Quoted in Grubbs, *Jean-Baptiste Rousseau*, p. 217.

127. La Motte, *Œuvres de théâtre*, I, 382.

128. *Essay on Epic Poetry*, ed. F. D. White, p. 148.

129. Preface to *Œdipe*, *Œuvres*, II, 57.

130. *Tel Quel* (1943), II, 62.

131. *La Pucelle* (Chant xvi), *Œuvres*, IX, 256.

132. "Extrait de la nouvelle bibliothèque," *Œuvres*, XXIII, 162.

133. *Dictionnaire philosophique*, article, "Comédie," *Œuvres*, XVII, 417. Compare the letter to Cideville [1731] in which Voltaire says that Fénelon "condamnait notre poésie parce qu'il ne pouvait écrire qu'en prose" (*Correspondence*, ed. Besterman, II, 225).

134. Voltaire, *Œuvres*, VIII, 19–20.

135. Letter to Louis Racine [1736], *Correspondence*, ed. Besterman, V, 153. And in 1761 Voltaire writes to Deodati de Tovazzi: "Vous dansez en liberté, et nous dansons avec nos chaînes" (*Œuvres*, XLI, 171).

136. Letter to La Noue, April 3, 1739, *Correspondence*, ed. Besterman, IX, 72.

137. Fragment 12, *Œuvres*, p. 281.

138. *Beaux-arts*, pp. 172–173 (Pt. III, Sec. 1, Ch. iii).

139. *Cours de belles-lettres*, II², 121–122.

140. Letter to Frederick the Great [1737], *Correspondence*, ed. Besterman, VI, 224. Voltaire repeats the same idea in a note to his "Remarques sur deux épîtres d'Helvétius": "Il ne faut prendre que la fleur d'une idée, il faut fuir le style de déclamation. Les vers qui ne disent pas plus, et mieux, et plus vite que ce que dirait la prose, sont de mauvais vers" (*Œuvres*, XXIII, 23). Vauvenargues likewise says: "Un autre défaut de la mauvaise poésie est d'allonger la prose, comme le caractère de la bonne est de l'abréger" ("Réflexions et maximes," *Œuvres*, p. 483).

141. *Principes*, I, xlv.

142. *Réflexions critiques*, II, 399–401. And Gaillard says: "Je ne dirai rien des idylles gothiques du fameux Ronsard; elles n'ont pu être bonnes que dans un temps où l'on n'avait point encore d'idée du bon ni du beau" (*Poétique*, II, 255).

143. *Histoire de la poésie française*, p. 248. See Richard Switzer, "French Renaissance Poetry before Sainte-Beuve," *French Review*, 26: 278–284 (February, 1953).

144. *Beaux-arts*, pp. iv–v.

145. *Principes*, I, xi–xii.

II. A NEW VISION OF POETRY: DIDEROT

1. Part of the material of this chapter has already appeared in somewhat different form in my articles, "The Poet according to Diderot," *RR*, 36:37–54 (February, 1946), and "Imagination and Creation in Diderot," *Diderot Studies II*, ed. Otis Fellows and Norman L. Torrey (Syracuse, N. Y., 1953), pp. 200–220.

2. The list of works on eloquence and poetry recommended in the *Plan d'une université* (1775–76) suggests some of the authors to whom Diderot was more or less indebted. He singles out Batteux's *Beaux-arts réduits à un même principe*, "livre acéphale mais utile"; Longinus' *On the Sublime;* Du Bos's *Réflexions;* "mais surtout *Du choix et de la place des mots*, par Denys d'Halicarnasse, ouvrage profond" (Denis Diderot, *Œuvres complètes*, ed. Assézat and Tourneux, 1875–77, III, 486. Unless otherwise indicated, all references to Diderot's works are to this edition).

3. Saintsbury was among the first to see this clearly: "Diderot is the first considerable critic — it would hardly be too much to say the first critic — known to history who submits himself to any, to every work of art which attracts his attention, as if he were a 'sensitised' plate, animated, conscious, possessing powers of development and variation, but absolutely faithful to the impression produced. To say that he has no theories may seem to those who know him a little, but only a little, the very reverse of the truth: for from some points of view he is certainly a *machine à théories* as much as Piron was a *machine à saillies*. But then the theory is never a theory prece*dent;* it never (or so seldom as to require no correction of these general statements) governs, still less originates, his impression; it follows the im-

pression itself and is based thereon" (*A History of Criticism and Literary Taste*, III, 91).

4. *Salon de 1765*, X, 233.

5. *De la poésie dramatique* (1758), VII, 339.

6. *Salon de 1767*, XI, 241. On Diderot and the ancients see Jean Seznec, *Essais sur Diderot et l'antiquité* (Oxford, 1957), especially Ch. vi, "Le Génie du paganisme."

7. "Sur la sculpture et sur Bouchardon" (1763), XIII, 43.

8. *Plan d'une université*, III, 481. See also XVIII, 109.

9. For a fuller discussion of Diderot's reading see Hubert Gillot, *Denis Diderot: l'homme, ses idées philosophiques, esthétiques, littéraires* (1937), pp. 232–286.

10. Article "Encyclopédie" (1755), XIV, 425. See also XIV, 475.

11. See Norman L. Torrey's Introduction to *Diderot Studies II*, especially pp. 11–12.

12. See for example Lester G. Crocker, *Two Diderot Studies: Ethics and Esthetics* (Baltimore, 1952). Note also Ferdinand Brunot's very shortsighted remark: Diderot "analyse, critique, juge, loue ou blâme, sans jamais rapporter ses opinions à une doctrine qui dominerait et commanderait l'art. A peine si quelques-unes des *Pensées sur la peinture* seraient à citer" (*Histoire de la langue française*, VI¹² (1930), 801.

13. *Lettre sur les sourds et muets*, I, 369–370; *Entretien avec D'Alembert*, II, 121.

14. See for example Pierre Trahard, *Les Maîtres de la sensibilité française au xviiie siècle (1713–1789)* (1931–33), II, 49–286.

15. *Paradoxe sur le comédien* (1773–78), VIII, 408.

16. I have throughout translated by "sensibility" the term *sensibilité*, used so constantly in poetic theories of the eighteenth and nineteenth centuries. The reader should bear in mind the various meanings the term may have. The *Encyclopédie* starts with "*SENSIBILITE, SENTIMENT, Méd.*" and from the basic definition, "la faculté de sentir," develops in a very long article the physiological and neurological aspects. Then the article "*SENSI-BILITE, Morale,*" by Jaucourt, gives us "disposition tendre et délicate de l'âme, qui la rend facile à être émue, à être touchée. . . . La sensibilité est la mère de l'humanité." Finally a supplementary article, "SENSIBILITE, *Gramm.*," contrasts *sensibilité* unfavorably with *tendresse*. This slightly derogatory implication is usually transferred to *sensiblerie*, first used by Mercier in his *Néologie* (1801), and defined in the 1835 edition of the *Dictionnaire de l'Académie* as "Sensibilité fausse et outrée, affectation de sensibilité." This gamut of meanings is echoed by the definitions given by the *Oxford English Dictionary*. On the history of the word in France see Arthur M. Wilson, "Sensibility in France in the Eighteenth Century: A Study in Word History," *French Quarterly*, 13:35–46(1931).

17. *Second Entretien sur le Fils naturel* (1757), VII, 108; *Essai sur la peinture* (1765), X, 520.

18. See Yvon Belaval, *L'Esthétique sans paradoxe de Diderot* (1950), pp. 90–92. Belaval distinguishes five modes of *sensibilité*.

19. II, 170–171.

20. VIII, 368, 370, 393.

21. See what Delacroix, a great admirer of Diderot, says along the same lines about the difference between the actor and the painter, in his long

discussion of the *Paradoxe* (Eugène Delacroix, *Journal*, ed. André Joubin, 1932, I, 170–174. January 27, 1847).

22. VIII, 408.

23. VIII, 386. Compare "Ce n'est pas au premier instant de la douleur qu'on parle bien; l'on sent trop fortement, et l'on ne pense pas assez" (*Essai sur Claude et Néron*, III, 355).

24. *Réfutation de l'ouvrage d'Helvétius intitulé L'Homme* (1773–74), II, 318.

25. *Essai sur Claude et Néron*, III, 383. Marmontel's remarks, defending Diderot against the attacks made on the first edition of the *Essai*, were incorporated by Diderot in the second edition, with further comments of his own.

26. [1759], *Lettres à Sophie Volland*, ed. André Babelon (1938), 2 vols., I, 45.

27. II, 318, 337; VIII, 415; II, 323.

28. I, 374.

29. [Oct. 10, 1759], *Lettres à Sophie Volland*, I, 63.

30. VII, 102–103.

31. *De la poésie dramatique* (1758), VII, 370–371.

32. XIV, 322–323. Compare "Quel est l'effet de l'enthousiasme dans l'homme qui en est transporté, si ce n'est de lui faire apercevoir entre des êtres éloignés des rapports que personne n'y a jamais vus ni supposés?" (XIV, 313).

33. *Encyclopédie*, article "Fureur" (1757), XV, 31.

34. "Sur *L'Art de peindre* de Watelet" (1760), XIII, 17.

35. *Réfutation*, II, 342.

36. *Salon de 1767*, XI, 208.

37. *Encyclopédie*, article "Théosophes," XVII, 245.

38. "Observations sur les *Saisons* de Saint-Lambert" (1769), V, 246–247.

39. XIV, 323. Compare "Il n'y a qu'un moment heureux; c'est celui où il y a assez de verve et de liberté pour être chaud, assez de jugement et de goût pour être sage" (*Salon de 1767*, XI, 132).

40. "Réflexions sur l'ode" (1770), VI, 412.

41. VIII, 367. It is interesting to note that in this passage "les beautés d'inspiration" are opposed to "la fureur du premier jet."

42. For a full discussion of this question see Herbert Dieckmann, "Diderot's Conception of Genius," *Journal of the History of Ideas*, 2:151–182 (April 1941).

43. Undated fragment "Sur le génie," IV, 26–27.

44. See Jean Thomas, *L'Humanisme de Diderot*, revised ed. (1938), Ch. iv; Eleanor M. Walker, "Towards an Understanding of Diderot's Esthetic Theory," *RR*, 35:277–287 (December 1944); Belaval, *L'Esthétique sans paradoxe de Diderot*, pp. 93–161, and "Nouvelles Recherches sur Diderot" (IV), *Critique*, no. 109 (1956), pp. 404–412.

45. I, 385. Compare VII, 407, where the same example is used.

46. *Salon de 1767*, XI, 8–9. Compare "Les beaux-arts ne sont tous que des imitations de la belle nature. Mais qu'est-ce que la belle nature? C'est celle qui convient à la circonstance" (*Plan d'une université*, III, 485).

47. *De l'interprétation de la nature* (1754), II, 35.

48. VII, 156.

49. *De la poésie dramatique*, VII, 329.

50. XV, 168–169.

51. VII, 392–394.

52. XI, 9–17. Contrast with this the earlier statement in the *Lettre sur les sourds et muets*: "C'est la chose même que le peintre montre" (I, 388).

53. Folkierski says: "Il ne peut ainsi y avoir de doute que Diderot ne soit revenu sur ses idées fondamentales concernant la création artistique. Peut-être en faut-il chercher la cause dans l'affaiblissement de son propre enthousiasme" (*Entre le classicisme et le romantisme*, p. 514). And Crocker: "Let it at once be made clear that Diderot's concept is pure eighteenth century orthodoxy" (*Two Diderot Studies*, p. 71). René Wellek takes much the same position: "Surprisingly some of his finest criticism comes when he turns back on the past and seizes firmly on certain truths of the neo-classical creed, the impersonality of the artist, the inner ideal, the 'interior model,' the deliberate shaping of the artist's work" (*A History of Modern Criticism: 1750–1950*, New Haven, I [1955], 61).

54. *Critique*, no. 108 (1956), pp. 405, 410.

55. XI, 370.

56. *Pensées détachées sur la peinture* (1775–76), XII, 87, 128–129. For the date and sources of this work, see J. Kosciusko, "Diderot et Hagedorn," *RLC*, 16:635–669 (Oct.–Dec. 1936). A recent article with the same title, by P. Vernières (*RLC*, 30:239–254 (April–June 1956), covers much the same ground (without reference to the previous article).

57. *Salon de 1767*, XI, 254.

58. *Pensées détachées*, XII, 107. As Belaval says: "De la nature commune, telle que nous l'avons sous les yeux, nous avons dégagé le modèle idéal; de l'idéal, nous revenons à la nature; mais ce n'est pas pour l'affadir, c'est pour la rendre plus typique" (*L'Esthétique sans paradoxe*, p. 110).

59. *Jacques le fataliste*, VI, 68.

60. *De la poésie dramatique*, VII, 320.

61. X, 127.

62. Batteux, *Beaux-arts*, pp. 247, 138, 140.

63. V, 276–277.

64. *Salon de 1767*, XI, 185.

65. "Sur Bouchardon," XIII, 46.

66. "La poésie, plus soucieuse de la vraisemblance que de la vérité, l'agrandit en l'exagérant" (*Plan d'une université*, III, 486).

67. VII, 105.

68. *Paradoxe*, VIII, 405, 365–366, 419–420.

69. *Salon de 1767*, XI, 140.

70. See for example Eric M. Steel, *Diderot's Imagery: A Study of a Literary Personality* (New York, 1941), pp. 17–25. Belaval's *L'Esthétique sans paradoxe de Diderot*, which contains many illuminating remarks on the question of imagination, shows something of the same tendency (see especially p. 63, n. 1, and pp. 156–159).

71. There is an amusing example of the use of the term in the traditional French sense of "une maîtresse d'erreur et de fausseté" in the dedicatory epistle of *Le Père de famille* (1758), addressed to the Princess of Nassau-Saarbruck. Diderot is giving the princess good advice as to how to bring up her children: "C'est en les éclairant sur la valeur réelle des objets, que je mettrai un frein à leur imagination. Si je réussis à dissiper les prestiges de cette magicienne, qui embellit la laideur, qui enlaidit la beauté, qui pare le

mensonge, qui obscurcit la vérité, et qui nous joue par des spectres qu'elle fait changer de formes et de couleurs, et qu'elle nous montre quand il lui plaît et comme il lui plaît, ils n'auront ni craintes outrées, ni désirs déréglés" (VII, 181).

72. One of the chief obstacles in the way of finding a unified conception of the imagination in Diderot has been the difficulty encountered by critics in reconciling the various passages on imagination in the *Eléments de physiologie* either with one another or with passages in Diderot's other works. Yet the *Eléments* are obviously composed in large part of notes that Diderot had taken at various times, and do not always necessarily represent his own opinions. Here and there he makes this explicit: "Lorsque nous avons les yeux ouverts et l'esprit distrait, nos sens n'en sont pas moins frappés par les objets ainsi qu'à l'ordinaire, mais l'âme occupée n'en reçoit pas moins l'image et ne s'en souvient jamais: c'est pour elle comme si rien n'avait frappé la vue. (Je ne crois pas cela.)" (IX, 349–350) It seems to me that one need not, and indeed should not take the ideas set down in the *Eléments* as Diderot's own, except when they correspond with those found elsewhere in his works, or are stamped by his use of *je*.

73. On November 29, 1756, Voltaire, sending to D'Alembert a series of articles for the *Encyclopédie*, says at the end of his letter: "Vous ou M. Diderot, vous ferez sans doute *Idée* et *Imagination*; si vous n'y travaillez pas, et que la place soit vacante, je suis à vos ordres." D'Alembert answers, on December 13: "Quelqu'un s'est chargé du mot *Idée*. Nous vous demandons l'article *Imagination*; qui peut mieux s'en acquitter que vous?" On January 16, 1757, Voltaire writes: "Je vous envoie, mon cher maître, l'article *Imagination*," and D'Alembert answers on January 23, "J'ai reçu *Imagination*." On June 26, 1758, Voltaire writes to Diderot: "J'ai dit si insolemment la vérité dans les articles *Histoire, Imagination et Idolâtrie*" (Voltaire, *Œuvres*, XXXIX, 136, 139, 159, 163, 462). The "Imagination" article appeared in Volume VIII of the *Encyclopédie*, in 1765.

74. VII, 333; II, 178; VII, 333; IX, 346; VII, 334; IX, 364.

75. X, 141; I, 291, 339.

76. IX, 369.

77. Georges Poulet has said that the great discovery of the eighteenth century was that of the phenomenon of memory (*Études sur le temps humain*, 1950, p. xxix).

78. IX, 366–367, 369–370.

79. Francis Hutcheson, *An Inquiry into the Original of our Ideas of Beauty and Virtue*, 4th ed. (London, 1738), p. 81 (Section 6, xi).

80. John Ruskin, *Modern Painters*, Part V (1856), Ch. ii. *Works*, Library Edition, London, VI (1904), 41–42.

81. IX, 365. Compare "Rien ne convient tant à un poète que les écarts. . . . L'image d'un homme qui erre en se promenant au gré des lieux et des objets qu'il rencontre, s'arrêtant ici, là précipitant sa marche, m'intéresse tout autrement que celle d'un voyageur courbé sous le poids de son bagage" (XIII, 83). There is a parallel between the last sentence of the passage quoted in the text and Baudelaire's comparison of childhood and genius: "L'enfant voit tout en *nouveauté*; il est toujours *ivre*. . . . Le génie n'est que l'*enfance retrouvée* à volonté" ("Le Peintre de la vie moderne," *L'Art romantique*, ed. Jacques Crépet, Conard, 1925, pp. 59–60).

82. I, 293; II, 178–179; XI, 131.

83. XIII, 134; "Il n'est pas moins vrai de dire du peintre qu'il est un poète, que du poète qu'il est un peintre; et du sculpteur ou graveur, qu'il est un peintre en relief ou en creux, que du musicien qu'il est un peintre par les sons" (XIII, 156).

84. "Un poète est un homme d'une imagination forte, qui s'attendrit, qui s'effraye lui-même des fantômes qu'il se fait" (*Essai sur la peinture*, X, 490).

85. I, 35; X, 41.

86. In the *Rêve* D'Alembert says: "Ce qui ne m'empêchera pas de demander au docteur s'il est bien persuadé qu'une forme qui ne ressemblerait à rien, ne s'engendrerait jamais dans l'imagination, et ne se produirait point dans le récit." Bordeu replies: "Je le crois. Tout le délire de cette faculté se réduit au talent de ces charlatans qui, de plusieurs animaux dépécés, en composent un bizarre qu'on n'a jamais vu en nature" (II, 179).

87. For further details, see my article in *Diderot Studies II*, pp. 217–218. On the question of creation, see James Doolittle, "Criticism as Creation in the Work of Diderot," *YFS*, II[1] (Spring–Summer 1949), 14–23.

88. *Salon de 1767*, XI, 147, 333, 254. Compare "Le vrai goût s'attache à un ou deux caractères, et abandonne le reste à notre imagination" (XI, 328).

89. XI, 270; X, 351–352.

90. *Réfutation*, II, 330; XI, 84; *Observations*, V, 250; *Salon de 1767*, XI, 229, 33.

91. X, 328; XIII, 85.

92. XVIII, 171; Maurice Tourneux, *Diderot et Catherine II* (1899), pp. 448–451; XI, 187.

93. XII, 88; XI, 201; XII, 88; XI, 281.

94. I, 385.

95. "Il en est de la poésie ainsi que de la peinture. . . . Le poète a sa palette, comme le peintre ses nuances, ses passages, ses tons" (XI, 267).

96. *Pensées détachées*, XII, 75.

97. *Essai sur la peinture*, X, 497.

98. XI, 72–73. For discussions of the *ut pictura poesis* doctrine see: Rensselaer W. Lee, "*Ut pictura poesis*: The Humanistic Theory of Painting," *Art Bulletin*, XXII (1940), 197–269; Irving Babbitt, *The New Laokoön: An Essay on the Confusion of the Arts* (Boston and New York, 1910); W. Folkierski, *Entre le classicisme et le romantisme*, pp. 425–441; B. Munteano, "Le Problème de la peinture en poésie dans la critique française du xviiie siècle," *Atti del quinto Congresso internazionale di Lingue e Letterature Moderne* (Florence, 1955), pp. 325–338.

99. *Troisième Entretien*, VII, 162.

100. See Steel, *Diderot's Imagery*, Ch. i.

101. XI, 328–329; IX, 37; XIII, 86.

102. XII, 84.

103. XI, 363. Compare "l'allégorie, la ressource ordinaire des esprits stériles" (*Jacques le fataliste*, VI, 30); "Le mélange des êtres allégoriques et réels donne à l'histoire l'air d'un conte: et, pour trancher le mot, ce défaut défigure pour moi la plupart des compositions de Rubens" (*Essai*, X, 500).

104. XI, 51; XII, 84; XI, 19.

105. *Plan d'une université*, III, 466.

106. *Lettre sur les aveugles*, I, 301.

107. *De l'interprétation de la nature*, II, 20.

108. "Ses idées particulières, ses comparaisons, ses métaphores, ses expressions, ses images, ramenant sans cesse à la nature qu'on ne se lasse pas d'admirer, seront autant de vérités partielles par lesquelles il se soutiendra" (Article "Encyclopédie," XIV, 432–433).

109. *Réfutation*, II, 329–330.

110. X, 494.

111. XIV, 429–449. See J.-J. Mayoux, "Diderot and the Technique of Modern Literature," *MLR*, 31:518–531 (October 1936); H. J. Hunt, "Logic and Linguistics: Diderot as 'Grammarien-philosophe,'" *MLR*, 51:288–305 (July–Sept. 1951); Marlou Switten, "Diderot's Theory of Language as the Medium of Literature," *RR*, 44:185–196 (October 1953).

112. "A la longue nous en avons usé avec les mots, comme avec les pièces de monnaie: nous ne regardons plus à l'empreinte, à la légende, au cordon, pour en connaître la valeur; nous les donnons et les recevons à la forme et au poids: ainsi des mots, vous dis-je. Nous avons laissé là de côté l'idée ou l'image pour nous en tenir au son et à la sensation" (*Salon de 1767*, XI, 133–134).

113. *Lettre sur les sourds et muets*, I, 369.

114. *Le Neveu de Rameau*, V, 466.

115. "Comment se fait-il que, dans les arts d'imitation, ce cri de nature qui nous est propre soit si difficile à trouver?" (*Satire I*, VI, 304). See also *Second Entretien*, VII, 107.

116. *Lettre sur les sourds et muets*, I, 372.

117. Article "Encyclopédie," XIV, 448. See also III, 486.

118. I, 374. Diderot's point of departure may well have been Batteux's third kind of harmony: "un certain art, qui, outre le choix des expressions et des sons par rapport à leurs sens, les assortit entr'eux de manière que toutes les syllabes d'un vers, prises ensemble, produisent par leur son, leur nombre, leur quantité, une autre sorte d'expression qui ajoute encore à la signification naturelle des mots" (*Beaux-arts*, p. 178).

119. See especially James Doolittle, "Hieroglyph and Emblem in Diderot's *Lettre sur les sourds et muets*," *Diderot Studies II*, pp. 148–167.

120. I, 367, 376.

121. It is tempting to speculate on the reasons which led Diderot to discard the term. In his later works it is used only in a derogatory sense, as in the passage on allegory quoted earlier in this chapter. My guess would be that he found it too suggestive of an exclusively pictorial representation, whereas "tout art d'imitation [a] ses hiéroglyphes particuliers" (I, 385). Also at this time he saw painting as a more direct art of imitation than poetry: "C'est la chose même que le peintre montre; les expressions du musicien et du poète n'en sont que des hiéroglyphes" (I, 388). Later, when he gave to the painter as well as to the poet an ideal model, a more general term became necessary. I suspect too that Diderot may not have been entirely convinced by his own defense of the term in the "Lettre à Mlle.xxx," added to the *Lettre sur les sourds et muets*: "'Il y a, ajoutez-vous enfin, des morceaux de musique auxquels on n'attache point d'images, qui ne forment, ni pour vous ni pour personne, aucune peinture hiéroglyphique, et qui font cependant un grand plaisir à tout le monde.' Je conviens de ce phénomène; mais je vous prie de considérer que ces morceaux de musique qui vous affectent si agréablement sans réveiller en vous ni peinture ni perception distincte de rapports, ne flattent votre oreille que comme l'arc-en-ciel plaît

à vos yeux, d'un plaisir de sensation pure et simple" (I, 407). On this point see Crocker, *Two Diderot Studies*, pp. 111–112, n. 72.

122. I, 390–391; XVIII, 206.

123. XI, 267–269, 331.

124. "Sur *La Peinture*, poème . . . de Le Mierre" (1769), XIII, 90.

125. See Anne-Marie de Commaille, "Diderot et le symbole littéraire," *Diderot Studies*, ed. Otis Fellows and Norman L. Torrey (Syracuse, N. Y., 1949), pp. 94–120.

126. XI, 107–108; V, 235–236; VI, 425.

127. Letter to Falconet, 1766, XVIII, 206.

128. *Essai sur la peinture*, X, 502. Compare "La peinture a cela de commun avec la poésie, et il semble qu'on ne s'en soit pas encore avisé, que toutes deux elles doivent être *bene moratae;* il faut qu'elles aient des mœurs" (X, 501); "le vrai, le bon et le beau se tiennent de bien près" (X, 517).

129. *Plan d'une université*, III, 468–469.

130. *Lettres à Sophie Volland*, II, 271; I, 169.

131. *Encyclopédie* article "Grecs," XV, 53.

132. "Richard Wagner et Tannhäuser à Paris," *L'Art romantique*, ed. Jacques Crépet (Conard, 1925), p. 220.

III. SENSE AND SENSIBILITY

1. See especially Daniel Mornet, *Le Sentiment de la nature en France de J.-J. Rousseau à Bernardin de Saint-Pierre* (1907); *Le Romantisme en France au XVIIIe siècle* (1912); *Histoire de la clarté française* (1929); Paul Van Tieghem, *Etudes d'histoire littéraire européenne*, I (1924), II (1930); André Monglond, *Le Préromantisme français* (Grenoble, 1930).

2. Jean Le Rond d'Alembert, "Réflexions sur la poésie," *Mélanges de littérature, d'histoire et de philosophie* (Amsterdam, 1759–67), V, 434.

3. [Charles-Julien de Chênedollé], *Esprit de Rivarol* (1808), p. 162.

4. Charles-Augustin Sainte-Beuve, "Le Brun," *Portraits littéraires* (Garnier, 1864–78), I, 149. See also "Le Brun-Pindare," *Causeries du lundi*, 3d ed. (Garnier, 1851–62), V, 162.

5. Jean-François Marmontel, *Mémoires*, ed. Maurice Tourneux (1891), I, 108.

6. Henri Potez, *L'Elégie en France avant le romantisme* (1898), p. 16.

7. Antoine de Bertin, *Œuvres*, new ed. (1791), p. 47.

8. Claude-Joseph Dorat, *Dialogue de Pégase et de Clément, Poésies* (1824), p. 309.

9. Potez, *L'Elégie en France*, p. 314.

10. Jean-Marie-Bernard Clément, *Journal Littéraire* (1796–97), II, 177.

11. *Œuvres*, p. 61.

12. Nicholas-Joseph-Laurent Gilbert, *Ode IX, imitée de plusieurs psaumes, Œuvres* (1823), p. 133.

13. *Satire I: Le Dix-huitième Siècle, Œuvres*, pp. 32–33.

14. Jean-Antoine Roucher, *Les Mois, poème en douze chants* (1779), I, 2.

15. *Œuvres*, V, 245.

16. *Préface de Cromwell*, ed. Maurice Souriau (n. d.), p. 268.

17. Robert de Souza, "Un Préparateur de la poésie romantique: Delille (1738–1813)," *Mercure de France*, 285: 298–327 (July, 1938). Souza says:

"Il n'est pas pour son époque de répondant plus 'neuf,'" and "Delille fut le moins didactique de ses confrères." After this somewhat measured praise he continues, "Autant qu'à la 'nouveauté' il vise à la simplicité libre et naturelle" (pp. 299–300), and quotes a number of passages in support of his contention. See also P. Guégen, "Florilège de l'abbé Delille," *Mercure de France*, 325: 446–475 (November 1955).

18. Jacques Delille, *Les Jardins, ou l'Art d'embellir les paysages* (1782), p. 31.

19. [Antoine de Rivarol], *Lettre critique sur le poème des "Jardins,"* suivie du "Chou et du navet," par M. le comte de Barriel (Amsterdam, 1782).

20. *Pensées de Joseph Delorme* (1829), *Poésies* (1910), p. 149.

21. Grimm-Diderot, *Correspondance littéraire*, ed. Maurice Tourneux (1877–82), V, 375.

22. See for example the virulent attack on Diderot in Martial Sabatier de Castres, *Les Trois Siècles de notre littérature* (Amsterdam, 1772), I, 385, in the course of which the author says: "Nous ne dirons rien de la *Lettre sur les aveugles* ni de celle sur les *Sourds* qui semblent faites pour n'être lues ni entendues." Compare Gilbert's lines in *Le Dix-huitième Siècle*, "Ce lourd Diderot, docteur en style dur,/ Qui passe pour sublime à force d'être obscur."

23. [Abbé Joseph de la Porte], *Ecole de littérature, tirée de nos meilleurs écrivains* (1764), I, x.

24. See Jacques Rocafort, *Les Doctrines littéraires de l'Encyclopédie: ou le Romantisme des encyclopédistes* (1908).

25. See James Doolittle, "Jaucourt's Use of Source Material in the *Encyclopédie*," *MLN*, 65: 387–392 (June, 1950).

26. *Mémoires*, II, 6–7. See S. Lenel, *Un Homme de lettres au 18e siècle: Marmontel* (1902).

27. *Correspondance littéraire*, V, 377–378.

28. *Questions sur l'Encyclopédie* (1771), *Œuvres*, XVII, 429. Jaucourt says in his "Poétique" article: "Despréaux fait connaître en peu de mots tous les genres séparément, et donne les règles générales qui leur sont communes. Non seulement les jeunes gens doivent le lire, mais l'apprendre par cœur comme la règle et le modèle du bon goût."

29. *Journal Etranger*, September 1762, pp. 171–172.

30. André Hyacinthe Sabatier, *Odes nouvelles et autres poésies, précédées d'un discours sur l'ode et suivies de quelques morceaux de prose* (1766), pp. iii, ix–x.

31. Jean-Jacques Rousseau, *Lettre sur la musique* (1753), *Œuvres*, ed. Auguis (1825), XV, 164.

32. *De l'universalité de la langue française* (1783), in *De l'homme* (1800), p. 33.

33. *Correspondance littéraire*, V, 11.

34. See, in addition to the works referred to in n. 1 of this chapter, Fernand Baldensperger, *Le Mouvement des idées dans l'émigration française* (1789–1815) (1924).

35. *Œuvres*, II, 204.

36. Pierre-Joseph-Justin Bernard, known as Gentil-Bernard, *Epître à mes vers, adressés à la marquise de Pompadour en 1760*, *Œuvres* (1803), ii, 149.

37. *Poétique* (1763), I, 73.

38. This definition is borrowed by many writers, for example Sabatier de Castres, *Dictionnaire de littérature* (1770), I, 641–642.

39. *Œuvres*, IV, 294.

40. [Abbé J.-B. Gossart], *Discours sur la poésie lyrique, avec les modèles du genre* (1761), pp. ii, x.

41. *Ibid.*, p. 19. Compare what Sabatier says: "Je sais que la raison doit guider l'enthousiasme, mais sans l'asservir. Elle doit lui montrer les précipices et l'abandonner à lui-même, s'il a la force de les franchir. Cette raison qui ne saurait être trop sévère, lorsqu'il s'agit d'observer, de discuter ou d'analyser, ne doit point porter sa froide rigidité dans les ouvrages d'imagination" (*Odes nouvelles*, p. 37).

42. *Odes nouvelles*, p. 37.

43. *Correspondance littéraire*, V, 374.

44. *Dictionnaire philosophique* (1771), article "Exagération," *Œuvres*, XIX, 45.

45. *Ibid.*, article "Enthousiasme," XVIII, 554.

46. Abbé Seran de la Tour, *L'Art de sentir et de juger en matière de goût* (1762), I, 174; II, 32, 42–44.

47. Johan Georg Sulzer, article "Poète" in the *Supplément* to the *Encyclopédie*.

48. *Dictionnaire philosophique*, article "Epopée," *Œuvres*, XVIII, 572; article "Poètes," XX, 232.

49. "De la poésie," *Essais*, IV, 208.

50. *Les Nuits de Young*, traduites de l'anglais par M. Le Tourneur (1769), I, lviii–lx.

51. "De la poésie," *Essais*, IV, 209, 229–230.

52. "Du génie," *Essais*, III, 138.

53. *L'Art de sentir*, p. 150.

54. Abbé Jean-Baptiste-Claude Joannet, *Eléments de poésie française* (1752), I, 192.

55. *Dictionnaire philosophique*, article "Imagination," *Œuvres*, XIX, 433.

56. *Questions sur l'Encyclopédie*, *Œuvres*, XIX, 437.

57. "Essai sur le goût," *Eléments de littérature* (1771), (ed. 1856), I, 15–16. Compare a very similar passage in Etienne de Senancour, *Rêveries*, ed. J. Merlant (1910), I, 145. The imagination and all its works are satirized by Jean-Marie Chassaignon in his *Cataractes de l'imagination, déluge de la scribomanie, hémorrhagie encyclopédique, monstre des monstres*, par Epiménide l'Inspiré, Dans l'antre de Trophonius, au pays de Visions (1779).

58. The *Dictionnaire de l'Académie* does not admit the "creative" function of the imagination until the nineteenth century. The 1798 edition merely adds to earlier definitions "la faculté de se représenter et de rendre vivement les objets."

59. *De l'homme* (1797), pp. 71–73. Compare "Le génie étant le sentiment au plus haut degré qu'on puisse le concevoir, peut être défini faculté créatrice . . . ces beaux ouvrages du génie qu'on appelle *créations*, ne sont au fond que des arrangements, des compositions, des choses trouvées mises en ordre" (p. 79).

60. Dieudonné Thiébault, *Traité du style* (1774), new ed. (1801), I, 264–265.

61. *L'Imagination* (1806), I, xvi, 8. The preface states that the poem was composed between 1785 and 1794.

62. Jean-François, marquis de Saint-Lambert, *Les Saisons*, new ed. (1785), pp. x–xii.

63. Claude-Joseph Dorat, *Lettres d'une chanoinesse de Lisbonne à Melcour, officier français*, précédées de quelques réflexions (The Hague, 1770), p. 15.

64. *Esprit de Rivarol*, p. 116.

65. *Poétique*, I, 60. Compare "En observant ces deux règles, savoir, de ne jamais revêtir l'idée que pour l'embellir, de ne jamais embellir que ce qui en mérite le soin, on évitera la profusion d'images, on ne les employera qu'à propos" (*ibid.*, I, 195). Similar precepts are found in nearly all the treatises on rhetoric.

66. *Commentaire sur Corneille, Œuvres*, XXXII, 7.

67. *L'Imagination*, I, xxxi.

68. Marmontel, *Eléments de littérature*, II, 58.

69. *L'Imagination*, I, xxix–xxx.

70. *Les Jardins*, new ed. (1801), p. xiii.

71. *Eléments*, II, 26–27.

72. J.-M.-B. Clément, *Lettres à Monsieur de Voltaire* (The Hague, 1773–1776), I, 3e Lettre, p. 47.

73. "L'art de rendre la nature est si nouveau que les termes même n'en sont pas inventés. Essayez de faire la description d'une montagne de manière à la faire reconnaître; quand vous aurez parlé de la base, des flancs et du sommet, vous aurez tout dit; mais que de variété dans ces formes bombées, arrondies, allongées, aplaties, carrées, etc.! Vous ne trouvez que des périphrases; c'est la même difficulté pour les plaines et les vallons" (*Voyage à l'Ile de France*. Quoted by Sainte-Beuve, *Portraits littéraires*, II, 121).

74. *Poétique*, II, 70–71.

75. "Discours aux Welches, par Antoine Vadé," *Œuvres*, XXV, 241.

76. *Œuvres*, XVIII, 580. See also the articles "Rime" and "Vers et prose" (XX, 373, 562).

77. *Lettres d'une chanoinesse de Lisbonne*, pp. 11–12.

78. *L'Art de sentir*, pp. 143–144.

79. "Suite des réflexions sur la poésie et sur l'ode en particulier," *Œuvres* (1821–22), IV, 301. D'Alembert had written earlier in his "Eloge de Montesquieu" in the *Encyclopédie*: "Le style poétique, si on entend comme on le doit, par ce mot, un style plein de chaleur et d'images, n'a pas besoin, pour être agréable, de la marche uniforme et cadencée de la versification: mais si on ne fait consister ce style que dans une diction chargée d'épithètes oisives, dans les peintures froides et triviales des ailes et des carquois de l'Amour, et de semblables objets, la versification n'ajoutera presque aucun mérite à ces ornements usés: on y cherchera toujours en vain l'âme et la vie."

80. "Réflexions sur la prose et le vers français," *Essais*, IV, 392–393.

81. *Poétique*, I, 53.

82. Paul-Jérémie Bitaubé, *Joseph* (1773), p. 3. In his preface Bitaubé says: "Surtout dans les sujets simples, tels que ceux qui tiennent à la poésie champêtre, la prose a peut-être plus de naturel; l'esprit n'étant gêné par aucun joug, peut mieux s'abandonner au sentiment. . . . Mais . . . ceux qui refuseront à mon ouvrage le titre de poème ne trouveront point en moi de contradicteur" (p. xviii). On Bitaubé see André Monglond, "Le Rôle littéraire

d'un refugié: Jérémie Bitaubé et la "'Prose poétique,'" *RLC*, 3:264–275 (April–June 1923).

83. *Mémoires de Condorcet*, ed. Frédéric-G. de la Rochefoucauld-Liancourt (1824), I, 113.

84. *De l'universalité de la langue française*, in *De l'homme* (1800), pp. 35–36.

85. Louis-Sébastien Mercier, *Mon Bonnet de nuit* (Neufchâtel, 1784), II, 215–216, 256.

86. *Néologie, ou Vocabulaire de mots nouveaux, à renouveler, ou pris dans des acceptions nouvelles* (1801), I, xliv–xlvii.

87. Jean-François de Laharpe, *Lycée, ou Cours de littérature ancienne et moderne* (1823), V, 163–164; XIV, 330.

88. *Lettres d'une chanoinesse*, p. 14.

89. *Correspondance littéraire*, V, 373.

90. [Michel Cubières-Palmézeaux], *Lettre à M. le marquis de Ximenès sur l'influence de Boileau en littérature* (Amsterdam, 1787), pp. 10–11.

91. See Joannet, *Eléments*, I, ix; Sabatier de Castres, *Dictionnaire de littérature*, I, 649; Louis-Mayeul Chaudon, *Bibliothèque d'un homme de goût*, I, 188; Marmontel, *Eléments de littérature*, I, 146; *Annales poétiques ou Almanach des Muses* (1778–88), I–V; also M. Alliot and J. Baillou, *Ronsard et son quatrième centenaire* (1926).

92. Joannet, *Eléments*, III, 126; Sabatier de Castres, *Trois Siècles de littérature*, I, 202.

93. *Trois siècles de littérature*, I, 99–100.

94. *Annales poétiques*, IV, 42, 7.

95. Joannet, *Eléments*, III, 128; Sabatier, *Odes*, p. 201; Sabatier de Castres, *Trois siècles de littérature*, III, 206.

96. Preface to *Les Jardins* (1780), *Œuvres* (1834), pp. 2–3.

97. *Poétique*, I, 99–100.

98. Article "Poètes," *Œuvres*, XX, 232.

IV. THE ROAD TO ROMANTICISM

1. "M. Régnier et A. Chénier" (1829), *Portraits Littéraires*, I, 174.

2. André Chénier, *Œuvres*, ed. G. Walter, Bibliothèque de la Pléiade (1950), p. 159.

3. According to his chief biographer, Chénier's best poems "restent capables d'intéresser, de toucher, il faut en convenir; mais ils n'intéressent, ils ne touchent, que modérément; ils ne saisissent ni transportent" (Paul Dimoff, *La Vie et l'œuvre d'André Chénier jusqu'à la Révolution française*, 1936, II, 442).

4. See Potez, *L'Elégie en France*, and Gustave Merlet, *Tableau de la littérature française 1800–1815* (1878). Merlet says in his preface: "La poésie surtout, qui avait émigré dans la prose, ne nous offre que des talents distingués, mais secondaires, ou de pâles ombres dont le souffle s'épuisait à ranimer les cendres de foyers éteints" (p. ix).

5. Quoted by Potez, p. 428.

6. Charles-Julien de Chênedollé, *L'Invention, Etudes poétiques* (1820), p. 116.

7. Chênedollé, *La Gelée d'avril*, ibid., p. 131.

8. *Le Dernier Jour de la moisson*, ibid., p. 16.

9. Joubert wrote of Chateaubriand: "Ecrivain en prose, M. de Chateaubriand ne ressemble point aux autres prosateurs; par la puissance de sa pensée et de ses mots, sa prose est de la musique et des vers" (letter of March 6, 1801, in G. Pailhès, *Du nouveau sur J. Joubert*, 1900, p. 248).

10. Jean-Jacques Rousseau, *Confessions* (Flammarion, 1928), I, 245 (Livre IV).

11. François-René de Chauteaubriand, "Tableaux de la nature 1784–1790," *Romans et poésies diverses* (Furne, Jouvet et Cie, 1876), p. 553.

12. The first complete publication of the *Essai* was in Chénier, *Œuvres inédites*, ed. Abel Lefranc (1914). On Chénier's poetic doctrine see Dimoff, *La Vie et l'œuvre d'André Chénier*; M. Jouglard, "L' 'imitation inventrice' ou les contradictions d'André Chénier," *RLC*, 8: 640–653 (Oct.–Dec. 1928); Jean Fabre, *Chénier, l'homme et l'œuvre* (1950).

13. *Essai, Œuvres*, pp. 646–647, 676.

14. Joseph Joubert, *Les Carnets*, ed. André Beaunier (1938), II, 859 (Jan. 15, 1817). For a fuller discussion of Joubert's ideas see my article, "Joubert on Imagination and Poetry," *RR*, 40: 250–260 (Dec. 1949).

15. "Ainsi Joubert a eu claire conscience de cet art poétique, non formulé en France — formulé par les Wordsworth et les Coleridge — qui va présider au lyrisme romantique. On trouverait même chez lui comme le pressentiment doctrinaire du symbolisme" (Monglond, *Le Préromantisme*, II, 473).

16. Germaine Necker de Staël, *De la littérature, Œuvres complètes* (1820), IV, 49 ("Discours préliminaire"); IV, 481 (Pt. II, Ch. v).

17. *Le Génie du Christianisme* (Furne, Jouvet et Cie, 1881), pp. 155 (II, i, 2), 203 (II, ii, 11). Compare the preface to *Atala*: "Peignons la nature, mais la belle nature; l'art ne doit pas s'occuper de l'imitation des monstres" (*Romans et poésies diverses*, p. 6).

18. *Correspondance générale*, ed. Louis Thomas (1912–1924), II, 321.

19. *Essai, Œuvres*, p. 672.

20. *De l'Allemagne, Œuvres*, X, 255 (Pt. II, Ch. x).

21. J. C. S. de Sismondi, *De la littérature du midi de l'Europe* (1819), I, 301–302. In Edmond Eggli and Pierre Martino, *Le Débat romantique en France, 1813–1830*, I (1933), 56.

22. *Œuvres*, pp. 614, 143.

23. *Carnets*, I, 419 (Dec. 14, 1803); II, 528 (Dec. 22, 1805).

24. *Œuvres*, X, 190 (Pt. II, Ch. i); X, 253 (Pt. II, Ch. x); XI, 509 (Pt. IV, Ch. x).

25. Sainte-Beuve, *Chateaubriand et son groupe littéraire sous l'Empire*, nouvelle éd. (Calmann-Lévy, 1889), II, 31.

26. *Carnets*, I, 45 (1779–1783).

27. *Essai, Œuvres*, pp. 686, 690, 689.

28. *L'Invention, Œuvres*, p. 130.

29. *Essai, Œuvres*, p. 681.

30. *L'Invention, Œuvres*, pp. 123–124.

31. *Essai, Œuvres*, pp. 684–685.

32. *Carnets*, I, 124 (May 18, 1796); I, 205 (May 4, 1799); I, 260 (July 2, 1800).

33. *Carnets*, I, 282 (November 12, 1800); II, 563 (July 10, 1806).

34. *Carnets*, II, 503 (April 23, 1805); II, 834 (May 4, 1815); II, 848 (March 7, 1816).

35. Charles-Hubert Millevoye, *L'Invention poétique*, poème couronné par la Société Littéraire d'Agen (1806).

36. *Le Génie de l'homme*, poème (1807), pp. 77–78.

37. Charles de Bonstetten, *Recherches sur la nature et les lois de l'imagination* (Geneva, 1807), I, 22, 316.

38. *Essai sur les fictions* (1795), *Œuvres*, II, 161, 172.

39. *Œuvres*, X, 34 (Pt. I, Ch. ii); XI, 132 (Pt. II, Ch. xxi).

40. "On ne saurait trop répéter aux Français qu'ils marchent avec trop de crainte dans les champs de l'imagination; ils ne font point entrer assez d'idéal dans leur manière de considérer les beaux-arts; ils veulent en ramener toutes les productions à des imitations positives; et cependant le talent poétique, ce luxe de notre âme, a quelquefois besoin de dédaigner la beauté des objets réels, pour arriver à cette sorte de sublime dont il ne trouve de modèle que dans sa propre inspiration" (Alexandre Soumet, *Les Scrupules littéraires de Madame la baronne de Staël*, 1814, in Eggli and Martino, p. 219).

41. L. C. Neufchâteau (sic), *Les Tropes, ou les Figures de mots, poème en quatre chants*, avec des notes, un extrait de Denys d'Halicarnasse sur les tropes d'Homère, et des recherches sur les sources et l'influence du langage métaphorique, dédié à la jeunesse studieuse (1817), pp. 2, 51, 65, 39, 4, 22, 8.

42. *De la littérature*, *Œuvres*, IV, 65 (Pt. I, Ch. i).

43. "Sur l'élégie," *Œuvres* (1823), IV, 72.

44. *Œuvres*, II, 172.

45. *Essai*, *Œuvres*, p. 692.

46. Antoine Fabre d'Olivet, *Les Vers dorés de Pythagore expliqués, et traduits pour la première fois en vers eumolpiques français, précédés d'un discours sur l'essence et la forme de la poésie* (1813), p. 12. On Fabre d'Olivet, see Léon Cellier, *Fabre d'Olivet: Contribution à l'étude des aspects religieux du romantisme* (1953).

47. *Recherches sur l'imagination*, I, 146.

48. *Les Tropes*, pp. 8–9.

49. *Carnets*, II, 718 (May 15, 1812).

50. *Romans et poésies diverses*, pp. 88–89.

51. *L'Invention*, *Œuvres*, p. 131.

52. *Œuvres*, p. 676.

53. *L'Invention*, *Œuvres*, p. 127.

54. *Carnets*, I, 319 (February 23, 1802); I, 153 (August 22, 1797); II, 604 (March 29, 1807); II, 478 (January 21, 1805).

55. *Pensées*, ed. Raynal (1842), II, 340.

56. *Carnets*, II, 479 (January 24, 1805).

57. *Carnets*, I, 132 (February 13, 1797); II, 484 (February 4, 1804).

58. *Le Génie de l'homme*, p. vi.

59. *Œuvres*, X, 247, 250 (Pt. II, Ch. ix).

60. Preface to *Atala*, *Romans et poésies diverses*, p. 5.

61. *Les Vers dorés*, p. 65.

62. Mercier, *Satyres contre Racine et Boileau* (1808); Cubières-Palmézeaux, *Essai sur l'art poétique en général, et, en particulier, sur la versification française* (1812).

63. *De l'Allemagne*, *Œuvres*, X, 258 (Pt. II, Ch. x).

64. *Essai sur l'art poétique*, pp. 7–9.

65. *De l'Allemagne*, *Œuvres*, X, 259 (Pt. II, Ch. x).

66. The bibliography of the subject is a long one. See especially Robert Amadou, *L'Occultisme* (1950), for the essentials of the doctrine; Auguste Viatte, *Les Sources occultes du romantisme français* (1928), and *Victor Hugo et les illuminés de son temps* (Montreal, 1942); Jacques Roos, *Aspects littéraires du mysticisme philosophique, et l'influence de Boehme et de Swedenborg au début du romantisme* (Strassburg, 1954). The importance of these ideas for literature has been noted again and again, for example by Aristide Marie, in his introduction to Gérard de Nerval, *Les Illuminés* (1929), p. i; Henri Peyre, *Shelley en France*, pp. 190–191; Albert Béguin, *L'Ame romantique*, II, 321–322.

67. See E. Dermenghen, *Joseph de Maistre mystique* (1946).

68. Letter to Bonald, 1814, *Œuvres* (Lyons, 1884–1886), XII, 466.

69. *Briefe an F. Brun*, I, 282. Quoted in Viatte, *Les Sources occultes*, II, 103.

70. François-Joseph Dussantt, 3e article sur *De l'Allemagne, Les Débats*, July 2, 1814. Quoted in Eggli and Martino, I, 186.

71. *Œuvres*, VI, 493–494 (Pt. IV, Ch. ix); XI, 504 (Pt. IV, Ch. ix); X, 255 (Pt. II, Ch. x); X, 305 (Pt. II, Ch. xiii).

72. Alexandre Soumet, *Les Scrupules littéraires de Madame la baronne de Staël, ou Réflexions sur quelques chapitres du livre "De l'Allemagne"* (1814). Eggli and Martino, I, 235, 218.

73. *La Muse Française* (1823–24), ed. Jules Marsan (1907), I, 296–297.

74. See Sainte-Beuve, "M. Ballanche," *Portraits contemporains*, II, 1–51; Albert J. George, *Pierre-Simon Ballanche* (Syracuse, N. Y., 1945); Joseph Buche, *L'Ecole mystique de Lyon* (1935).

75. Pierre-Simon Ballanche, *Essai sur les institutions sociales* (1818), *Œuvres* (1830), II, 65; *Orphée* (1829), IV, 306; *Essais de palingénésie sociale* (1827), III, 188.

76. *Les Vers dorés*, p. 59.

77. *L'Amérique, Œuvres*, p. 437.

78. E. Eggli, *L' "Erotique comparée" de Charles de Villers, 1806* (1927), pp. 169–170. See F. Baldensperger, "Une Définition de la poésie romantique, par Charles de Villers," *Revue de Philologie Française*, 16: 115–122 (1902).

79. *De l'Allemagne, Œuvres*, X, 255 (Pt. II, Ch. x).

80. A. W. Schlegel, *Cours de littérature dramatique* (1814), II, 329.

81. *Carnets*, I, 319.

82. Charles Nodier, review of Ballanche's *Antigone, Journal de l'Empire*, April 4, 1815. Eggli and Martino, I, 295.

83. *Les Vers dorés*, p. 11.

84. Jean-François de Laharpe, *Cours de littérature*, I, 445; Fontanes, *Discours à l'Académie Française* (1816), *Œuvres* (1859), 293. See M. Alliot and J. Baillou, *Ronsard à son quatrième centenaire* (1926).

85. *Carnets*, II, 804 (December 16, 1814).

86. *Essai, Œuvres*, p. 636.

87. Schlegel, *Cours de littérature dramatique*, I, 52.

V. THE ROMANTIC REVOLUTION

1. There is no adequate work dealing exclusively with French poetry of the nineteenth century, although Brunetière's *L'Evolution de la poésie lyrique en France au dix-neuvième siècle* (1894) is not without value for

the early part of the century. There is an excellent brief survey in the introduction to *The Poetry of France from André Chénier to Pierre Emmanuel*, ed. Alan Boase (London, 1952), but for fuller treatment one must refer to histories of nineteenth-century literature in general or of separate movements.

2. Sainte-Beuve, "A M. Villemain," *Pensées d'août* (1837), *Poésies complètes* (Charpentier, 1910), pp. 377–378.

3. See Charles Bruneau, *L'Epoque romantique*, in Ferdinand Brunot, *Histoire de la langue française*, XII (1948), 6, and, for a discussion of the rhetorical treatises of the period, B. Munteano, "Des 'constants' en littérature. Principes et structures rhétoriques," *RLC*, 31: 388–420 (July–Sept. 1957).

4. J.-C. Laveaux, *Dictionnaire raisonné des difficultés grammaticales et littéraires de la langue française*, 2d ed. (Ledentu, 1822), I, ix.

5. L. J. M. Carpentier, *Le Gradus français, ou Dictionnaire de la langue poétique* (Johanneau, 1822), pp. 6–7, 62, 22. Carpentier quotes approvingly (p. 83) what Geoffroy had written earlier in the century: "Depuis Corneille, Racine et Boileau, nos prosateurs ont affecté le style poétique et nos poètes ont rimé de la prose. . . . Il n'appartient qu'au vrai génie de créer des beautés nouvelles, de reculer les bornes du territoire poétique: la médiocrité présomptueuse altère ce qu'elle croit embellir, et regarde comme neuf ce qui n'est que bizarre et gothique. Le vrai génie est si rare, qu'il est toujours utile de s'opposer aux innovations. Ce qu'il y a de plus sûr pour nos poètes, c'est de se renfermer dans le cercle tracé par Racine et Boileau. Ces deux législateurs ont irrévocablement fixé notre langue" (Jean Racine, *Œuvres*, commentaires par J. L. Geoffroy, Le Normant, 1808, I, 207).

6. V. [Victor Hugo], "*Œuvres posthumes* de Jacques Delille, *Le Conservateur Littéraire, 1819–21*, ed. Jules Marsan, Textes Français Modernes (1928–38), II¹, 20–21.

7. A. [Abel Hugo], *ibid.*, II², 17, 247.

8. V. [Victor Hugo], *ibid.*, I², 28; I¹, 19; I², 197–198.

9. Alexandre Soumet, "*Nouvelles Odes*, par Victor-M. Hugo," *La Muse Française*, ed. Jules Marsan, Textes Français Modernes (1907–1909), II, 145.

10. J.-J. Reda [J.-J. Ader], "Elégie," *Conservateur Littéraire*, I², 178.

11. *Ibid.*, I², 174.

12. Madame Verdier, "Epître," *Muse Française*, I, 179.

13. Alphonse de Lamartine, *Correspondance*, publiée par Madame Valentine de Lamartine (Hachette, 1882), I, 300 (May 11, 1818); II, 36 (May 21, 1819).

14. "Destins de la poésie" (1834), *Méditations poétiques*, ed. G. Lanson, Grands Ecrivains de la France (1913), II, 287.

15. "Avertissement" to *Jocelyn* (1836). See also the "Avertissement" to *La Chute d'un ange*.

16. *Correspondance*, IV, 142 (Nov. 23, 1842).

17. *Méditations poétiques*, ed. Lanson, II, 368–370. See also the preface to *Recueillements*.

18. *Lettres à la fiancée* (Ed. de l'Imprimerie Nationale, 1947), p. 99.

19. Félicité de Lamennais, *Esquisse d'une philosophie* (1840–46), III, 347, 350. See Jean-Albert Bédé, "Les Idées esthétiques de Lamennais: A propos du centenaire de l'*Esquisse d'une philosophie*," *RR*, 33: 359–378 (Dec. 1941).

20. Alfred de Vigny, *Journal, Œuvres complètes*, Bibliothèque de la Pléiade (1946), II, 1139–40 (1840), 1191–92 (1843), 1288 (1851).

21. "*Eloa*; par le comte Alfred de Vigny," *Muse Française*, II, 248–249. Compare *Littérature et philosophie mêlées*, pp. 136–137.

22. *Journal, Œuvres*, II, 1078.

23. *Muse Française*, II, 145.

24. *Conservateur Littéraire*, I¹, 27–28.

25. *William Shakespeare* (1864), (Ed. de l'Imprimerie Nationale, 1937), p. 164.

26. *Œuvres* (Les Belles Lettres, 1947), II, 71.

27. *Muse Française*, II, 156.

28. *Correspondance*, I, 347–348.

29. *Correspondance*, I, 234.

30. Alfred de Musset, "Un Mot sur l'art moderne," *Mélanges de littérature et de critique, Œuvres complètes* (Charpentier, 1866), IX, 129.

31. *Œuvres posthumes, ibid.,* X, 277.

32. *Œuvres*, II, 903.

33. Henri de Latouche, *Adieux: Poésies* (1844), p. 174.

34. Paul Ackermann, *Du principe de la poésie et de l'éducation du poète* (1841), p. 2.

35. R. [Charles de Rémusat], "De l'état de la poésie française," 1st article, *Le Globe*, January 22, 1825.

36. *Ibid.,* 2d article, "M. Casimir Delavigne," February 12, 1825.

37. *Ibid.,* 3d article, "M. de Lamartine," March 12, 1825.

38. *Le Parnasse moderne, ou Les Classiques et les romantiques* (1825), p. 7.

39. *Le Parnasse moderne, ou l'art poétique du XIXe siècle: Poème en quatre chants*, par un homme du monde (1830), p. 36.

40. Sylvius [attributed to E. Texier], *Physiologie du poète*, illustrations de Daumier (J. Laisné, 1841), pp. 30, 35.

41. *Conservateur Littéraire*, I¹, 28.

42. "J.-B. Rousseau" (1829), *Portraits littéraires* (Garnier, 1864–1878), I, 130–131.

43. See Gustave Lanson, "Le Romantisme de Lamartine," in *Le Romantisme et les lettres* (1929).

44. *Les Confidences* et *Les Nouvelles Confidences, Œuvres* (Hachette), VI (1866), 293.

45. *Œuvres*, II, 958 (1832).

46. It should not be forgotten that, as Léopold Mabilleau wrote many years ago: "Depuis 1825 jusqu'au dernier jour, son génie n'a fait que se développer de la façon la plus logique et la plus rigoureuse" (*Victor Hugo*, 1893, pp. 95–96). Two excellent general studies of Hugo's poetic scope and development are Marcel Raymond's introduction to Victor Hugo, *Poèmes choisis* (Geneva, 1945), and Henri Peyre, *Victor Hugo le poète* (New York: Cultural Division of the French Embassy, 1952). For a full discussion of Hugo's ideas on the function of the poet, see Amédée Guiard, *La Fonction du poète: Etude sur Victor Hugo* (1910).

47. *Pensées de Joseph Delorme, Poésies*, p. 157.

48. Letter to Virieu, Aug. 1, 1829, *Correspondance*, III, 151.

49. *Le Poète dans les révolutions* (dated March, 1821), *Odes*, I, i.

50. *Le Poète, Odes*, IV, i.

51. *Littérature et philosophie mêlées* (Ed. de l'Imprimerie Nationale, 1934), pp. 15–17.

52. *Les Châtiments*, II, vii.

53. *William Shakespeare*, p. 173.

54. "Destinées de la poésie," *Méditations*, ed. Lanson, II, 413.

55. *Poèmes antiques et modernes*, ed. E. Estève, Textes Français Modernes (1914), p. 4 (note to 1822 edition).

56. *Physiologie du poète*, p. 26.

57. For a full and excellent account of this movement, see H. J. Hunt, *Le Socialisme et le romantisme en France: étude de la presse socialiste de 1830 à 1848* (Oxford, 1935).

58. "Espoir et vœu du mouvement littéraire et poétique après la révolution de 1830" (October 11, 1830), Premiers Lundis, 2d ed. (Calmann-Lévy, 1875), I, 405–406.

59. *William Shakespeare*, p. 208.

60. Adolphe Dumas, *La Cité des hommes* (1835), p. 87.

61. "*L'épanchement du moi* resta à l'ordre du jour, avec cette différence, qu'en 1830 l'écrivain initiait ses lecteurs à ses douleurs et à ses désespoirs tandis que plus tard il exprimait ses ambitions et ses espérances, engendrées par un idéalisme impuissant; au lieu de chanter le passé il chanta un avenir irréalisable" (Hunt, p. 341).

62. "Sur Georges Gordon, Lord Byron," *Muse Française*, II, 302.

63. Alexandre Guiraud, "Nos Doctrines," *ibid.*, II, 3–4.

64. "De la poésie et des poètes en 1852," *Lundis*, V, 387.

65. Jules de Résseguier, "*Poèmes et chants élégiaques*, par M. Alex. Guiraud," *Muse Française*, II, 92.

66. *Le Globe*, Jan. 22, 1825.

67. *Préface de Cromwell*, ed. Souriau, pp. 223, 253, 260–261.

68. *Journal* (1829), *Œuvres*, II, 901.

69. *Parnasse moderne* (1830), p. 31.

70. *Littérature et philosophie mêlées*, p. 4.

71. *Préface de Cromwell*, pp. 288–289. On poetic language see Emmanuel Barat, *Le Style poétique et la révolution romantique* (1904); F. Brunot, "Les Romantiques et la langue poétique," in *Le Romantisme et les lettres* (1929); and Charles Bruneau's volume cited in n. 3.

72. *Parnasse moderne* (1830), p. 37.

73. *Un Manifeste du romantisme: La Préface des Etudes françaises et étrangères* (1829), ed. Henri Girard, Bibliothèque Romantique (1923), pp. 7, 14.

74. *Postscriptum de ma vie*, in *William Shakespeare* (Ed. de l'Imprimerie Nationale, 1937), p. 473.

75. Maurice de Guérin, "Correspondance littéraire: 2e Lettre à La Morvonnais," *France Catholique*, I, no. 22 (March, 1834), pp. 268–271.

76. For example Paul Van Tieghem says: "Le mouvement romantique a offert en France plus que dans tout autre pays les caractères d'une véritable révolution littéraire" (*Le Romantisme dans la littérature européenne*, 1948, p. 175).

77. I have treated some of the material which follows in my article, "Revival and Revolution in English and French Romantic Poetry," *YFS*, Sixth Issue (1950), pp. 14–26.

78. *Le Style poétique et la révolution romantique*, p. 3.

79. Paul Hazard, "Les Caractères nationaux du lyrisme romantique français," *Quatre Etudes* (New York, 1940), pp. 22–85.

80. Henri Peyre, *Shelley en France* (Cairo, 1935), pp. 149–150, 168, 293.

81. Thierry Maulnier, *Introduction à la poésie française* (1939), p. 97.

82. Henri Peyre, "Romantic Poetry and Rhetoric," *YFS*, Thirteenth Issue (1954), pp. 30–41.

83. "Nos Doctrines," *Muse Française*, II, 18–19.

84. "Victor Hugo, 'Odes et ballades'" (January 2, 1827), *Premiers Lundis*, I, 167.

85. 1849 preface to *Méditations*, ed. Lanson, II, 357.

86. *Correspondance*, I, 232–233. August 3, 1814. In my article cited above I have compared this letter with Keats's letter to Reynolds on the composition of the *Ode to Autumn*.

87. *Lundis*, XII, 59–60. On the question of education see G. Weill, *Histoire de l'enseignement secondaire en France* (1802–1921), and F. Brunot, *La Révolution et l'Empire: le français langue nationale, Histoire de la langue française*, IX¹ (1927).

88. *Chateaubriand et son groupe littéraire*, I, 299, n. 1.

89. *Journal, Œuvres*, II, 1262.

90. Review of *Voyage littéraire et historique en Angleterre et en Ecosse*, par A. Pichaut, *Le Globe*, December 17, 1825.

91. Preface to *Etudes françaises*, p. 22.

92. *Chateaubriand et son groupe littéraire*, II, 95, n. 2.

93. *Correspondance*, I, 259.

94. *Shelley en France*, p. 167.

95. *Winds of Doctrine* (New York, 1913), p. 156.

VI. POETRY AS ART

1. For the picturesque aspect of Hugo, see André Joussain, *L'Esthétique de Victor Hugo: Le Pittoresque dans le lyrisme et dans l'épopée: Contribution à l'étude de la poétique romantique* (1920). In spite of the last part of the title, the book is a study of Hugo's practice rather than his theory.

2. A. Soumet, "*Nouvelles Odes*, par Victor-M. Hugo," *Muse Française*, II, 150. See also what Guiraud says about the Revolution having opened the domain of the imagination as well as of the heart: "Ces deux conditions d'originalité dans les conceptions et de vérité dans les mœurs . . . constituent principalement la poésie" (*ibid.*, II, 22).

3. *Discours prononcés dans la séance publique tenue par l'Académie Française pour la réception de M. de Lamartine* (Firmin Didot, 1830), p. 16.

4. "*Œuvres complètes* d'André Chénier," *Conservateur Littéraire*, I¹, 22.

5. *Pensées de Joseph Delorme, Poésies*, p. 154.

6. See Louis Hautecœur, *Littérature et peinture en France du XVIIe au XXe siècle* (1942); Prosper Dorbec, *Les Lettres françaises dans leurs contacts avec l'atelier de l'artiste* (1929); Henri Girard, *Emile Deschamps: Relations d'un poète romantique avec les peintres, les sculpteurs et les musiciens de son temps* (1921); Pierre Moreau, "Le Romantisme littéraire dans ses rapports avec les arts plastiques," *Atti del quinto congresso internazionale di lingue e letterature moderne: Lingue e letterature moderne nei loro rapporti con le belle arti* (Florence, 1955), pp. 341–351; Pierre Martino, "Rapports de la littérature et des arts plastiques: Parnasse et symbolisme," *ibid.*, pp. 399–410.

7. *Poésies*, p. 64. On the Cénacle, see Léon Séché, *Le Cénacle de Joseph Delorme (1827–1830)*, (1912).

8. "Victor Hugo en 1831," *Portraits contemporains*, new ed. (Michel Lévy, 1870–71), I, 414.

9. "De la poésie de notre époque," *Revue Encyclopédique*, 52: 643 (1831). See also Leroux's "Aux philosophes," *ibid.*, 51: 513–516 (1831).

10. Désiré Nisard, "M. Victor Hugo en 1836," *Portraits et études* (1875), p. 61.

11. *William Shakespeare*, p. 178.

12. See Albert Cassagne, *La Théorie de l'art pour l'art en France* (1906), and Irving Singer, "The Aesthetics of 'Art for Art's Sake,'" *Journal of Aesthetics*, 12: 343–359 (March 1954).

13. See Gautier, *Les Jeunes-France* (Charpentier, 1875); *Les Petits Romantiques français*, ed. Francis Dumont (Cahiers du Sud, 1949); Enid Starkie, *Pétrus Borel the Lycanthrope: His Life and Times* (London and New York, 1954).

14. *Histoire du romantisme* (1874), pp. 1, 18, 64.

15. *Poésies posthumes* (Charpentier, 1877), p. 145.

16. "Avant-propos" to *Feu et flamme*, ed. Marcel Hervieu, Bibliothèque Romantique (1926), p. 2.

17. *Rhapsodies* (1830), *Œuvres complètes*, II (1922), 13, 227–228. On Borel see Baudelaire's article, *L'Art romantique*, ed. Jacques Crépet (Conard, 1925), pp. 336–340.

18. Quoted in Hunt, *Le Socialisme et le romantisme*, p. 195.

19. F. Dumont, *Les Petits Romantiques*, pp. 8–9. See also the other essays in this volume, particularly those by A. Hoog and T. Tzara.

20. Alphonse Bertrand, *Gaspard de la nuit* (1842), (Mercure de France, 1902), p. 9.

21. "Onuphrius," *Les Jeunes-France*, pp. 32, 69.

22. See Georges Matoré, "Les Notions d'art et d'artiste à l'époque romantique," *Revue des Sciences Humaines*, Nouvelle Série, Fasc. 62–63, pp. 120–136 (April–Sept. 1951).

23. Saint-Simon, *Opinions littéraires, philosophiques et industrielles* (1825), quoted in Hunt, *Le Socialisme et le romantisme*, p. 11, n. 2.

24. *Les Jeunes-France*, p. 87.

25. *Nouveau Tableau de Paris* (1834), IV, 7.

26. *Physiologie du poète*, pp. 10–11.

27. "M. de Lamartine en 1837," *Portraits et études*, p. 139.

28. Arsène Houssaye, *Les Confessions: Souvenirs d'un demi-siècle* (1891), V, 86. On Gautier's development, see René Jasinski, *Les Années romantiques de Théophile Gautier* (1929); Louise B. Dillingham, *The Creative Imagination of Théophile Gautier: A Study in Literary Psychology* (Princeton, n. d. [1927]); and, for a more debatable approach, H. Van de Tuin, *L'Evolution psychologique, esthétique et littéraire de Théophile Gautier: Etude de caractérologie "littéraire"* (Amsterdam, 1933).

29. *Poésies complètes*, ed. R. Jasinski (1932), I, 81–82.

30. *La Préface de Mademoiselle de Maupin*, ed. G. Matoré, Textes Littéraires Français (Geneva, 1946), pp. 31–32.

31. "Excellence de la poésie," *La Charte de 1830*, January 16, 1837. *Fusains et eaux-fortes* (1880), pp. 47–48, 54.

32. "*La Divine Epopée*, par M. Alexandre Soumet," *RDM*, XXVI, 4th series (April 1841), 121, 126.

33. *L'Art* (1857), *Poésies*, III, 128. The poem as originally published had an additional stanza:

Dans la matière dure
Scelle ton rêve, afin
Qu'il dure
Tant que le monde ait fin.

34. *L'Artiste*, December 14, 1856. See also in the *Poésies*: *Consolation* (II, 290); *Le Poète et la foule* (II, 292); the preface to *Emaux et camées* (III, 3).

35. "Du beau dans l'art," *L'Art Moderne* (1856), pp. 151–152.

36. Edmond et Jules de Goncourt, *Journal* (Flammarion, 1935), I, 126–127.

37. André Gide, *Incidences* (N. R. F., 1924), pp. 162, 94.

38. "Salon de 1839," *La Presse*, March 21, 1839.

39. Sainte-Beuve, "*Poésies complètes* de Théodore de Banville" (1857), *Lundis*, XIV, 73.

40. "*Œuvres inédites* de Pierre de Ronsard" (1855), *Lundis*, XII, 60.

41. "*Poésies complètes* de Théodore de Banville" (1857), *Lundis*, XIV, 77–78.

42. Postscript to 1835 article, *Portraits contemporains*, I, 469.

43. Introduction to *Choix des poésies de la Pléiade* (1830), *Poésie et théâtre* (Le Divan, 1928), p. 122. The text presented to the Academy has not been found, so that it is impossible to tell how much it was modified in the "Introduction."

44. *Petits Châteaux de Bohème*, *Œuvres*, Bibliothèque de la Pléiade, I (1952), 93.

45. *Les Deux Faust de Goethe*, ed. F. Baldensperger (Champion, 1932), p. 227.

46. *Lundis*, XII, 61. On Sainte-Beuve see W. M. Frohock, "The Critic and the Cult of Art: Sainte-Beuve and the Esthetic Movement," *RR*, 32: 379–388 (December 1941); the comment on this article by Edna Fredrick, "The Critic and the Cult of Art: Further Observations," *RR*, 33: 385–387 (December 1942); and Carl A. Viggiani, "Sainte-Beuve (1824–1830): Critic and Creator," *RR*, 44: 263–272 (December 1953).

47. For details see G. Michaut, *Sainte-Beuve avant les Lundis* (Fontemoing, 1903), and *Etudes sur Sainte-Beuve* (Fontemoing, 1905), pp. 141–287.

48. *Premiers Lundis*, I, 170, 178–179, 180, 185.

49. "*Lettres inédites* de Malherbe," *Le Globe*, April 14, 1827.

50. *Tableau historique et critique de la poésie française et du théâtre français au seizième siècle* (1828), I, Preface.

51. See Nathan Edelman, "La Vogue de François Villon en France de 1828 à 1873," *RHL*, 43:211–223, 321–339 (April–June, July–Sept, 1936).

52. *Tableau*, I, 76, 77–78.

53. *Tableau*, I, 87–88, 140; II, 236; I, 366–370.

54. *Tableau*, II, vi.

55. *Tableau*, II, xxv. It is disappointing to note that Sainte-Beuve, nearly always perceptive and reliable in his generalizations, is much less so when it comes to individuals and comparisons. Thus he says of "Quand vous serez bien vieille," "Ce tendre et mélancholique sonnet rappelle la chanson

de notre célèbre Béranger, *Vous vieillirez, ô ma belle maîtresse*, etc., etc."
(*Tableau*, II, 71–72).

56. C. R. [Rémusat], *Le Globe*, September 27, 1828, p. 718; November 5,
1828, p. 806. For a much more severe, and in many ways unjust, criticism of
the *Tableau* see A. Michiels, *Histoire des idées littéraires en France* (1842).
Michiels says that Sainte-Beuve "a l'air de croire que la forme subsiste par
elle-même," and makes a violent attack on this "matérialisme exclusif" (II,
214, 221). The *Parnasse moderne* of 1830 also had its word to say on the
subject:

> Reproduisez Ronsard, en votre style obscur,
> Mêlé d'anglo-saxon ou d'allemand tout pur (p. 74).

57. *Poésies*, p. 153.

58. *Poésies*, p. 29. This emphasis on rhyme leads Charles Magnin to say
that *Joseph Delorme* is not "tout à fait exempt du péché originel de l'école
actuelle, nous voulons parler de l'amour futile qu'elle a pour la difficulté
vaincue" (*Causeries et méditations historiques et littéraires*, 1843, I, 223).

59. *Poésies*, pp. 133–135. A little later Sainte-Beuve says of the "moderns":
"On a commencé par les accuser de mépriser la forme; maintenant on leur
reproche d'en être esclaves. Le fait est qu'ils tiennent à la fois au fond et à
la forme" (p. 140).

60. *Poésies*, pp. 157–158.

61. "A M. Villemain," *Poésies*, p. 375.

62. *Lettres à la fiancée*, p. 90.

63. *Littérature et philosophie mêlées*, p. 170.

64. "Reliquat," *ibid.*, pp. 264–265. Hugo had said earlier: "Réfléchissez.
La nature conseille l'art. Poètes, faites comme fait Dieu. Taillez largement
et ciselez finement. Ne croyez pas que la ténuité de détail nuise à l'im-
mensité de l'ensemble. Bien au contraire. Voyez la nature, vous dis-je. Plus
l'arbre est grand, plus la feuille est petite. Le chou, qui végète honteusement
le ventre contre terre, se compose de vingt grosses feuilles, le chêne qui
touche aux nuages a un million de feuilles microscopiques" (pp. 254–255).

65. *Ibid.*, pp. 12–14. See also p. 243.

66. *Préface de Cromwell*, p. 275.

67. Théodore de Banville, *Petit Traité de poésie française* (1872), (Lemerre, 1891), p. 4.

68. *Les Stalactites, Odelettes* (Lemerre, 1889), p. 100.

69. *Le Sang de la coupe, Trente-six Ballades joyeuses* (Lemerre, n. d.),
p. 256.

70. *Petit Traité*, p. 274.

71. "Théodore de Banville" (1861), *L'Art romantique*, ed. Crépet, p. 358.

72. *Les Stalactites*, pp. 5–6.

73. Preface (1877), *Les Cariatides, Roses de Noël* (Lemerre, 1889), p. 10.

74. Preface to *Roses de Noël, ibid.*, p. 299.

75. Preface (1874), *Le Sang de la coupe*, p. 6. In the *Petit Traité* Banville says: "De notre temps, dans l'artiste et le poète, on n'a voulu voir que
le penseur, le prophète, le *vates*, qui certes existe en lui; mais il doit contenir
aussi un ouvrier, qui, comme tous les ouvriers, doit avoir appris son métier
par imitation et en connaître la tradition complète" (p. 171).

76. "Commentaire," *Odes funambulesques* (Lemerre, 1892), p. 294. In
Mes Souvenirs (Charpentier, n. d.) Banville says: "Notre doctrine était celle
de l'Art pour l'Art; nous pensions qu'en dehors de son devoir absolu qui

est d'être beau, un poème n'est nullement tenu à être d'une utilité immédiate, et je suis resté fidèle à cette théorie, même après que les plus éminents esprits l'ont désertée" (p. 143).

77. *Ballade de sa fidélité à la poésie, Trente-six Ballades joyeuses*, p. 208.

78. *Les Stalactites*, pp. 95, 162.

79. *Petit Traité*, pp. 52–53, 58, 266, 128.

80. *Histoire du romantisme*, pp. 162–163.

81. Letter to the Prince Royal of Bavaria (1839), *Œuvres*, I, 589.

82. *Journal, ibid.*, II, 1071 (1837); II, 1190 (1843).

83. *Ibid.*, II, 941 (1832); II, 1034 (1835); II, 998 (1834). See also II, 1185, 1192.

84. *Les Quatre Vents de l'esprit* (Ed. de l'Imprimerie Nationale, 1908), p. 39.

85. "De Mademoiselle Sedaine, ou de la propriété littéraire" (1841), *Œuvres*, I, 916.

86. *Journal, Œuvres*, II, 1316–17 (1854); II, 1289 (1852).

87. See for example F. Calmettes, *Leconte de Lisle et ses amis* [1902], p. 163, and Maurice Souriau, *Histoire du Parnasse* (1929), p. xxi.

88. Charles Leconte de Lisle, "Discours sur Victor Hugo" (1887), *Derniers Poèmes* (n. d.), pp. 285–286.

89. "Leconte de Lisle," *L'Art romantique*, ed. Crépet, pp. 373–374.

90. "Alfred de Vigny" (1864), *Derniers Poèmes*, p. 262.

91. "De la poésie en 1865," *Nouveaux Lundis*, X, 156–157.

92. "Avant-propos" to *Les Poètes contemporains* (1864), *Derniers Poèmes*, pp. 236–237.

93. *Ibid.*, p. 235.

94. *Ibid.*, p. 236.

95. Calmettes, p. 286.

96. Thalès Bernard, Preface to Achille Millier, *Chants agrestes* (1862), p. xii.

97. Henri Girard, *Un Bourgeois dilettante à l'époque romantique: Emile Deschamps*, p. 510.

98. Preface to *Poèmes antiques, Derniers Poèmes*, pp. 217, 213.

99. "De la poésie et des poètes" (1852), *Lundis*, V, 397.

100. See Aaron Schaffer, *The Genres of Parnassian Poetry: A Study of the Parnassian Minors* (Baltimore, 1944).

101. Quoted by Calmettes, p. 214.

102. L.-X. de Ricard, quoted in Schaffer, p. 121.

103. Madame Ackermann, "Journal," Feb. 17, 1862, *MF*, 195: 566 (May 1927).

104. "*Poésies* de Banville," *Lundis*, XIV, 73; "*Le Poème des champs*," *Nouveaux Lundis*, II, 263.

105. *William Shakespeare*, p. 184.

VII. FROM STATEMENT TO SUGGESTION

1. To cite only one example, Jean Stewart speaks of French poetry through the nineteenth century as "shedding, first, sentiment and rhetoric, then realism and precision, emerging finally as the communication of an intimate spiritual experience through suggestive sound and symbolism" (*Poetry in France and England*, London, 1931, p. 155).

2. "Les Cinq Derniers Mois de la vie de Racine" (*Le Constitutionnel*, April, 1866), *Nouveaux Lundis*, 3d ed. (Michel Lévy, 1870), X, 390–391. The article is also reprinted in the appendix to *Port-Royal*.

3. Sainte-Beuve's distinction is very close to that made by E. M. W. Tillyard between "direct" and "oblique" poetry, on which he makes the wise reservation: "All poetry is more or less oblique; there is no direct poetry" (*Poetry: Direct and Oblique*, London, 1934, p. 5).

4. "Le Poète et le prosateur" (1839), *Œuvres complètes* (Charpentier, 1867), X, 149–150.

5. A typical example is what Rémusat says: "L'imagination est la muse de l'homme; riante ou terrible, elle enchante tout ce qu'elle touche. Je ne sais ce qu'elle ajoute à nos impressions, à nos sentiments, à nos pensées; mais c'est par elle que tout en nous, sensations, affections, idées, peut devenir poétique" (*Le Globe*, August 25, 1827).

6. "Victor Hugo en 1836," *Portraits et études littéraires* (1875), pp. 68–69, 70, 90.

7. "M. de Lamartine en 1837," *ibid.*, p. 144.

8. Nicolas-Louis Artaud, "Essai littéraire sur le génie poétique au XIXe siècle, *Revue Encyclopédique*, 25: 604 (1825). Later in the article Artaud makes an interesting attempt to unite the two types by a plea for the "reversed" image: "Les images naturelles, elles-mêmes, se renouvellent par un singulier artifice. Il est tout simple d'emprunter nos comparaisons à ce qui nous est le plus familier. Or, nous autres modernes, ce que nous connaissons le mieux, c'est nous-mêmes, c'est-à-dire nos sentiments, nos passions, nos idées: nous allons de nous à la nature. De là, les poètes modernes, pour rajeunir des similitudes usées, en renversent les termes, et comparent les phénomènes du monde physique aux sentiments de l'âme" (p. 607).

9. "Reliquat," *Littérature et philosophie mêlées*, p. 238.

10. "Tas de pierres," *Océan* (Ed. de l'Imprimerie Nationale, 1942), p. 287.

11. *Méditations poétiques*, ed. Lanson, II, 348–349. Compare what Lamartine wrote later: "Un poète véritable, selon moi, est un homme qui, né avec une puissante sensibilité pour sentir, une puissante imagination pour concevoir, et une puissante raison pour régler sa sensibilité et son imagination, se séquestre complètement lui-même de toutes les autres occupations de la vie courante, s'enferme dans la solitude de son cœur, de la nature et de ses livres, comme le prêtre dans son sanctuaire, et compose, pour son temps et pour l'avenir, un de ces poèmes vastes, parfaits, immortels, qui sont à la fois l'œuvre et le tombeau de son nom. Je ne fus point cet homme et je ne fis pas cette œuvre" (*Souvenirs et portraits*, I, 58).

12. *Préface de Cromwell*, ed. Souriau, p. 259.

13. Stello, *Œuvres*, I, 792.

14. Victor Cousin, *Du vrai, du beau et du bien* (1853), pp. 158, 161.

15. Théodore Jouffroy, *Cours d'esthétique* (1843), p. 129.

16. "Nos Doctrines," *Muse Française*, II, 22.

17. Pétrus Borel, *Madame Putiphar*, *Les Petits Romantiques*, p. 87.

18. "Heine, *De la France*" (1833), *Premiers Lundis*, *II*, 257–258.

19. *Chateaubriand et son groupe littéraire*, I, 208.

20. *Journal* (1850), *Œuvres*, II, 1274.

21. "Dernière Nuit de travail" (1834), *Œuvres*, I, 814–815.

22. *Journal* (1824), *Œuvres*, II, 880, 882.

23. *Revue Encyclopédique*, XXV (1825), 603.

24. *Notes inédites*, ed. C. Guyot (Neuchâtel, 1931), p. 84.

25. *Esquisse d'une philosophie*, III, 135; II, 265.

26. Charles Nodier, "Du fantastique en littérature" (1830), *Contes fantastiques* (Charpentier, 1900), p. 6.

27. "Des types en littérature" (1830), *Romans* (Charpentier, 1900), p. 5. Compare what Nodier says in "Inès de las Sierras" (1837): "c'est que l'homme est incapable de rien inventer, ou, pour m'exprimer autrement, c'est que l'invention n'est en lui qu'une perception innée des faits réels" (*Nouvelles*, Charpentier, 1898, p. 240).

28. "Du beau dans l'art," *L'Art moderne* (1856), p. 155.

29. *Cours de philosophie* (1836), p. 266.

30. *Esquisse d'une philosophie*, II, 267; III, 135.

31. Charles Magnin, "*Ahasvérus, mystère*, par M. Edgar Quinet, et de la nature du génie poétique" (1833), *Causeries et méditations historiques et littéraires* (1843), I, 157, 96–97.

32. John Keats, *Letters*, ed. Maurice Buxton Forman (Oxford, 1935), p. 71.

33. *Journal* (December 10, 1834), Biblioteca Romanica (Strassburg, n. d.), pp. 96–97.

34. *William Shakespeare*, p. 110.

35. *Postscriptum de ma vie, ibid.*, p. 611. Mabilleau says of Hugo's own imagination: "Entendez par là une impressionnabilité toujours éveillée aux spectacles changeants du monde, une perception rapide et intense des formes expressives, une collaboration de l'esprit à la vision, qui fait jaillir une 'image' là où il n'y avait qu'une apparence matérielle, qui, d'une rencontre de couleurs et de lignes, tire de la pensée et de l'émotion, qui enfin interprète toute sensation et symbolise toute figure" (*Victor Hugo*, p. 31).

36. "Reliquat," *Littérature et philosophie mêlées*, p. 261.

37. *William Shakespeare*, p. 180.

38. *Les Nuits d'octobre, Œuvres*, I, 129; *Aurélia, Œuvres*, I, 381.

39. An extreme case of the exaggeration of foreign influences is William Reymond, *Shakespeare et Goethe: Etude sur l'influence anglo-germanique en France au XIXe siècle* (1864). A more balanced presentation is to be found in Louis Reynaud, *Le Romantisme: ses origines anglo-germaniques* (1926). One of the most eminent authorities on the subject, Albert Béguin, writes: "Un des lieux communs de l'histoire littéraire traditionnelle, curieuse d'influences et de filiations, affirme que, par l'intermédiaire de Mme de Staël, le romantisme français est directement tributaire de la littérature allemande. . . . Par bonheur, des travaux de littérature comparée, des études sur le 'préromantisme français' et sur les 'sources occultes' connues aux deux pays, permettent aujourd'hui d'échapper à ces étroites condamnations. Il n'est plus possible d'ignorer que les cénacles de 1830 n'ont presque pas connu le romantisme allemand . . . le romantisme français eut avant tout des origines françaises" (*L'Ame romantique et le rêve*, 1937, II, 319–320).

40. See Marcel Raymond, *De Baudelaire au surréalisme*, new ed. (1947), p. 13; A. Béguin, *L'Ame romantique et le rêve*, II, 331–332.

41. "Avertissement" to *La Mort de Socrate* (1823).

42. *Victor Hugo et les Illuminés*, p. 151.

43. Victor Hugo, *Poèmes choisis*, préface de Marcel Raymond (Geneva, 1945), I, 11.

44. *Les Contemplations*, I, ii; I, xxvii; III, xxiv. As the manuscript shows,

Hugo predated a number of poems in the printed text of *Les Contempla-tions* (see the critical edition by Joseph Vianey, Grands Ecrivains de la France, 1922, I, lix–liv, xci–xciv). Since I am not attempting to prove any clear-cut line of development, but rather to show how new ideas develop in Hugo parallel with the older ones, I have not felt it necessary to discuss the dating of the poems in detail. It is safe to say, however, that poems or lines suggestive of a sense of the mystery of the cosmos are in the minority before 1843, whereas after that date they are increasingly frequent.

45. *Les Voix intérieures*, xix.

46. *Extase, Les Orientales*, xxxvii.

47. *Les Feuilles d'automne*, xxxv, xxxviii, xxix.

48. *A Olympio, Les Voix intérieures*, xxx.

49. Thomas Gray, letter to Horace Walpole, September, 1737, *Letters*, ed. D. C. Tovey (London, 1904–12), I, 78. The couplet is quoted by Hazlitt in his essay "On Poetry in General" (1818).

50. *Les Voix intérieures*, x. For a study of the development from fantasy to mystery in Hugo, see Jean-Bertrand Barrère, *La Fantaisie de Victor Hugo*, I (1949), especially pp. xiii, xxvi–xxxii.

51. *Les Rayons et les ombres*, i.

52. *Le Rhin* (1842), (Ed. de l'Imprimerie Nationale, 1906), p. 381.

53. "Lettre de Pasages (Pyrénées)" (1843), *En Voyage* (Ed. de l'Im-primerie Nationale, 1910), II, 352.

54. *Les Contemplations*, III, viii, xxx.

55. "Victor Hugo" (1861), *L'Art romantique*, ed. Crépet, p. 303. On this phase of Hugo, see Maurice Levaillant, *La Crise mystique de Victor Hugo (1843–1856)* (1954).

56. *Les Travailleurs de la mer* [1866] (Ed. de l'Imprimerie Nationale, 1911), p. 80. It is curious to note how Hugo draws into his magic circle even the most limpid of poets: "La Fontaine vit de la vie contemplative et visionnaire jusqu'à s'oublier lui-même et se perdre dans le grand tout. . . . Il travaille comme la création même, du travail direct de Dieu. Il fait sa fleur et son fruit, fable et moralité, poésie et philosophie; poésie étrange composée de tous les sons que la nature présente au rêveur, étrange philoso-phie qui sort des choses pour aller aux hommes. La Fontaine, c'est un arbre de plus dans le bois, c'est le fablier" (*Postscriptum de ma vie, William Shakespeare*, pp. 521–522).

57. "Promontorium somnium," *William Shakespeare*, p. 302. Hugo's in-terest in dreams may well have been stimulated by Nodier, who wrote in his preface to *Smarra*: "Ce qui m'étonne, c'est que le poète éveillé ait si rarement profité dans ses œuvres des fantaisies du poète endormi, ou du moins qu'il ait si rarement avoué son emprunt; car la réalité de cet emprunt dans les conceptions les plus audacieuses du génie est une chose qu'on ne peut contester. La descente d'Ulysse aux enfers est un rêve" (*Contes fan-tastiques*, Charpentier, 1904, pp. 295–296).

58. "Promontorium somnium," *William Shakespeare*, p. 310.

59. *William Shakespeare*, pp. 19, 21.

60. *Les Contemplations*, VI, xxiii.

61. Hippolyte de la Morvonnais, Preface to *Pharamond, Œuvres choisies*, ed. E. Fleury (1911), pp. 79, 81. La Morvonnais' preface to *Un Vieux Paysan* (1840) insists on the limited place of art in poetry. An anonymous critic [V. P. . . x] says of this preface that for La Morvonnais "la poésie est

chose sérieuse et profonde; ce n'est pas un art plastique s'arrêtant aux contours des objets extérieurs et dont la dernière limite est atteinte par l'agencement des lignes et l'entente des couleurs; c'est une ardente aspiration vers la substance même des choses, c'est l'irradiation de l'âme sur le monde visible er sur le monde moral et la réaction de ceux-ci sur l'âme; c'est le verbe humain dans son acception transcendante et mystique; le verbe, c'est-à-dire lumière, puissance, amour!" (E. Fleury, *Hippolyte de la Morvonnais: sa vie, ses œuvres, ses idées*, 1911, p. 267.)

62. Paul Ackermann, *Du principe de la poésie*, p. 20.

63. *Aurélia, Œuvres*, I, 363.

64. Introduction to *Faust*, p. 228.

65. "Notes de voyage," *Œuvres*, II, 851–852.

66. *Aurélia, Œuvres*, I, 385, 387, 402. See Jean Richer, *Gérard de Nerval et les doctrines ésotériques* (1947).

67. *Vers dorés* (1845), *Œuvres*, I, 35.

68. *Aurélia, Œuvres*, I, 403. See what M.-J. Durry says: "La plus profonde poétique de Nerval est fondée sur le besoin de retrouver l'âme qu'il a rencontrée dans des êtres qui ne sont plus que souvenirs. Voilà pourquoi les correspondances qu'il poursuit sont des esprits aux esprits, et liées à un recommencement éternel" (*Gérard de Nerval et les mythes*, p. 65).

69. "Lettres à Jenny Colon," *Œuvres*, I, 716.

70. *Lorely, Œuvres*, II, 744.

71. *Aurélia, Œuvres*, I, 304.

72. See Albert Béguin, *Gérard de Nerval* (1945), pp. 72, 102.

73. *Aurélia, Œuvres*, I, 304.

74. Fragment of unpublished work on Wordsworth (*Revue Européenne*), in Fleury, *Hippolyte de la Morvonnais*, p. 225.

75. *Cours de philosophie* (1836), pp. 260, 280–281.

76. *Cours d'esthétique*, pp. 132, 136, 136–137, 353.

77. L——x, "Du style symbolique," *Le Globe*, April 8, 1829. See also Leroux's review of the *Pensées de Jean-Paul*, *Le Globe*, March 29, 1829. For an excellent study of Leroux's literary doctrines and their sources see David Owen Evans, *Le Socialisme romantique: Pierre Leroux et ses contemporains* (1949).

78. Article "Allégorie," *Encyclopédie nouvelle* (1834).

79. "Aux philosophes," *Revue Encyclopédique*, 51: 499–516; 52: 399–415, 627–648 (1831).

80. *Consolations* (1830), *Poésies*, p. 244.

81. *Premiers Lundis*, II, 99.

82. *Poésies*, pp. 157–158.

83. C. M., *Le Globe*, April 11, 1829.

84. Philippe-J.-B. Buchez, "Des artistes d'aujourd'hui," *L'Européen*, January 28, February 4, 1832.

85. "*Les Rayons et les ombres*, par M. Victor Hugo" (1840), *Causeries*, I, 313.

86. Paulin Limayrac: "La Poésie symboliste et socialiste: *Odes et poèmes*, par M. Victor de Laprade," *RDM*, N. S. 5: 669–682 (1844).

87. *Que la musique date du seizième siècle, Les Rayons et les ombres*, xxv.

88. Marc Eigeldinger, *Le Dynamisme de l'image dans la poésie française* (Neuchâtel, 1943), pp. 62, 65. See also Fernand Baldensperger, "Le Sym-

bolisme de Vigny," *Alfred de Vigny: Contribution à sa biographie intellectuelle* (1912), pp. 137–157.

89. Letter to E. Biré, 1847, *Œuvres*, I, 583.

90. *Journal* (1829), *Œuvres*, II, 891; (1844), II, 1214; (1838), II, 1105. A burlesque of *Angelo*, played in 1835, has these lines:

> Chatterton qui se tue au lieu de travailler!
> Et quelle est la morale enfin? — Un escalier!
> Piquante allégorie, admirable symbole
> Qui semble nous montrer comment l'art dégringole.
>
> (Vigny, *Œuvres*, I, 578)

91. To cite only one example: "De l'allégorie au symbole il y a la différence du mécanique au vivant, et de la symétrie à la souplesse. Une allégorie est l'expression d'idées par des images. Un symbole donne au moyen d'images l'impression d'idées. . . . En d'autres termes, l'allégorie se présente à nous sous la forme d'une intention nette, précise, détaillée, le symbole sous la forme d'une création libre où l'idée et l'image sont indiscernablement fondues" (Albert Thibaudet, *Réflexions sur le roman*, 1938, p. 30).

92. William Hazlitt, "The Englishman," *Selected Essays*, ed. Geoffrey Keynes (1930), p. 802, n. 1.

93. "Boileau," *Portraits littéraires*, I, 21.

94. See Ernest Zyromski, *Lamartine poète lyrique* (1897), pp. 308–320.

95. *Les Contemplations*, V, xxiii; V, ix; V, xxii. Another example is *Le Pont*. (VI, i).

96. "Plus qu'une sympathie secrète, plus que la perception obscure de fragiles rapports ébauchés entre l'esprit humain et la spiritualité des choses, la puissance qui va chez Hugo engendrer l'univers — le poème — c'est la force contemplatrice du regard. . . . Le seul fait de contempler les bas abîmes du cosmos suscite en lui le mythe. Il a le regard créateur. . . . L'œil est hallucinatoire; il crée la vision qu'il contemple. . . . Il n'en reste pas moins vrai que Hugo, autant qu'un imaginatif, est un grand cérébral. . . . Hugo a su rendre leur fraîcheur à *idée*, à *abstraction*: une *idée abstraite*, c'est une certaine *image* que l'esprit *tire du réel*. Il insiste: *image* et *idée* sont le même mot. . . . Il faudrait dire que vision et pensée ne se distinguent pas chez lui, et pourtant l'une et l'autre conserve son sens plein" (Paul Zumthor, *Victor Hugo, poète de Satan*, 1946, pp. 119–120).

97. "Les images de Hugo se caractérisent par une certaine fidélité à la sensation, elles sont reliées au monde concret par des attaches profondes et nous dirons même qu'elles gardent un caractère d'extériorité qui les empêche d'être de parfaits symboles" (Eigeldinger, *Le Dynamisme de l'image*, p. 112).

98. *Les Contemplations*, II, xxvi; VI, x.

99. See *Les Chimères*, ed. Jeanine Mounin, Textes Littéraires Français (Geneva, 1949), and the notes to the "Poésies" section in *Œuvres*, I, for bibliographies of studies of *Les Chimères*. See also M.-J. Durry, *Gérard de Nerval et le mythe*, and Jean Richer, *Gérard de Nerval*, Poètes d'aujourd'hui (1950), pp. 96–111.

100. "Histoire de la reine du matin et de Soliman prince des génies," *Voyage en Orient*, *Œuvres*, II, 513.

101. "Ahasvérus," *Causeries*, I, 155–156.

102. It was with the emphasis on suggestion that poetry was to turn from painting to music as her chief sister art. As early as 1839 Musset had stressed the musical quality of poetry: "La poésie est si essentiellement musicale,

qu'il n'y a pas de si belle pensée devant laquelle un poète ne recule si la mélodie ne s'y trouve pas, et à force de s'exercer ainsi, il en vient à n'avoir non-seulement que des paroles, mais que des pensées mélodieuses" ("Le Poète et le prosateur," *Œuvres complètes*, 1867, X, 150). Only with the later symbolists was the music of poetry to become of the first importance — we are still far from "De la musique avant toute chose" — but it was the conception of poetry as suggestion that was to lead to its alliance with the most suggestive of all the arts.

103. Auguste de Vaucelle, "Du rôle actuel de la poésie," *L'Artiste*, October 12, 1856.

104. *Les Contemplations*, I, viii; V, xxv; III, xx.

105. *Préface des Etudes françaises et étrangères*, p. 58.

106. *Tableau*, I, 195. See also Sainte-Beuve's article on Fontanes: "L'expression en poésie doit être incessamment produite par l'idée actuelle, soumise à l'harmonie de l'ensemble, par le sentiment ému, s'animant, au besoin, de l'image, du son, du mouvement, s'aidant de l'abstrait même, de tout ce qui lui va, se créant, en un mot, à tout instant, sa forme propre et vive" (Fontanes, *Œuvres*, 1859, I, lxii–lxiii).

107. *Littérature et philosophie mêlées*, pp. 8, 266.

108. *William Shakespeare*, p. 484.

109. *Petit Traité*, pp. 262–263.

110. "Henri Heine" (1848), *Poésie et théâtre*, p. 128. Béguin says of Gérard's own poetry: "Jamais pareil équilibre de la forme n'a triomphé d'une aussi furieuse masse de lave" (*Gérard de Nerval*, p. 8).

111. "Tas de pierres, III (1863–65)," *William Shakespeare*, p. 513.

112. See René Lalou, *Vers une alchimie lyrique* (1927). Lalou says of the poets of 1830 to 1860: "Malgré des différences que nous marquerons, ils poursuivent un but commun: libérer la poésie du joug de l'éloquence, de l'éloquence passionnée aussi bien que de l'éloquence didactique, la transformer en une alchimie. Cet effort n'atteindra toute son amplitude qu'avec la 'sorcellerie évocatoire' de Baudelaire, mais les éléments s'en trouvent déjà chez Sainte-Beuve et Bertrand et Nerval" (p. 10).

113. *Petit Traité*, p. 291.

VIII. IMAGINATION ENTHRONED: BAUDELAIRE

1. See Henri Peyre, *Connaissance de Baudelaire* (1951) for an excellent critical bibliography of works on Baudelaire published up to that date. To these should be added, as particularly relevant to the aspects of Baudelaire treated here, Jean Prévost, *Baudelaire: Essai sur l'inspiration et la création poétique* (1953), and Lloyd J. Austin, *L'Univers poétique de Baudelaire: Symbolisme et symbolique* (1956).

2. *AR*, p. 219. Unless otherwise indicated, all references to Baudelaire's works are to the *Œuvres complètes*, ed. Jacques Crépet (Conard, 1922–1953). I have used the following abbreviations for the volumes most frequently cited: *AR*, *L'Art romantique* (1925); *CE*, *Curiosités esthétiques* (1923); *CG*, *Correspondance générale* (1947–53); *JOP I*, *Juvenilia*, *œuvres posthumes*, *reliquiæ*, I (1939); *NHE*, Edgar Allan Poe, *Nouvelles Histoires extraordinaires*, traduction de Charles Baudelaire (1933); *PA*, *Les Paradis artificiels* (1928); *PPP*, *Petits Poèmes en prose* (1926).

3. *AR*, p. 209.

4. *Salon de 1859, CE*, p. 311.

5. *Journaux intimes*, ed. Jacques Crépet and Georges Blin (1947), p. 27.

6. Letter to Madame Aupick, March 17, 1862, *CG*, IV, 70; letter to Ancelle, February 18, 1866, *CG*, V, 280.

7. *AR*, p. 162.

8. "Tout enfant, j'ai senti dans mon cœur deux sentiments contradictoires, l'horreur de la vie et l'extase de la vie" (*Journaux intimes*, p. 96). The phrase, often quoted as if it were original with Baudelaire, is borrowed from De Quincey's *Suspiria*, quoted directly in *Les Paradis artificiels*: "L'horreur de la vie se mêlait déjà, dans ma première jeunesse, avec la douceur céleste de la vie" (*PA*, p. 194).

9. *La Voix*. Compare "Sentiment de *solitude* dès mon enfance. . . . Cependant, goût très vif de la vie et du plaisir" (*Journaux intimes*, p. 58). The same idea underlies the contrast later borrowed from Emerson, "De la vaporisation et de la centralisation du *Moi*. Tout est là" (*ibid.*, p. 51).

10. "Ce que je sens, c'est un immense découragement, une sensation d'isolement insupportable, une peur perpétuelle d'un malheur vague, une défiance complète de mes forces, une absence totale de désirs, une impossibilité de trouver un amusement quelconque. . . . C'est là le véritable esprit de spleen" (*CG*, II, 108). This is the state reflected and translated in the series of *Spleen* poems. There is hardly a better example of the way emotion is expressed in prose and in poetry than the comparison of the above passage with the single line, "Le Printemps adorable a perdu son odeur!"

11. *Journaux intimes*, pp. 62, 23.

12. Letter to Ancelle, February 18, 1866, *CG*, V, 279.

13. *Les Fleurs du Mal*, ed. Jacques Crépet and Georges Blin (Corti, 1942), p. 211.

14. Letter to Madame Aupick, Janaury 9, 1856, *CG*, I, 365.

15. *PPP*, pp. 33–34.

16. Keats, *Letters*, p. 228.

17. *NHE*, p. xxi.

18. Gustave Flaubert, *Correspondance*, new ed. (Conard, 1926–1933), IV, 206.

19. Letters to Armand Fraisse, February 18, 1860, *CG*, III, 38; letter to Poulet-Malassis, April 4, 1857, *CG*, II, 38.

20. "La Genèse d'un poème," Poe, *Eureka*, traduction de Baudelaire, ed. Jacques Crépet (1936), p. 153.

21. "L'Œuvre et la vie de Delacroix" (1863), *AR*, p. 5.

22. *CE*, p. 169.

23. "L'Art philosophique," *AR*, p. 120.

24. *AR*, p. 276; *CE*, p. 82.

25. *JOP*, I, 238, 240–241.

26. *AR*, pp. 184, 369, 294–297.

27. *AR*, p. 284; "*Madame Bovary*," *AR*, p. 401.

28. *NHE*, p. xx. See also the article on Barbier, *AR*, p. 318.

29. *AR*, pp. 311, 314.

30. October 10, 1863, *CG*, IV, 198.

31. Flaubert, *Correspondance*, IV, 408.

32. Paul Valéry, *Variété II* (1930), pp. 155, 157.

33. Flaubert, *Correspondance*, IV, 205.

34. *Salon de 1846, CE*, pp. 90–91.

35. *CE*, pp. 208, 134.
36. *Les Fleurs du Mal*, ed. Crépet-Blin, p. 212.
37. "Théophile Gautier" (1859), *AR*, p. 155.
38. *CE*, p. 197.
39. "Exposition universelle de 1855," *CE*, p. 223.
40. *Journaux intimes*, p. 18.
41. *AR*, pp. 52, 66.
42. *Journaux intimes*, pp. 21–22, 85.
43. *AR*, p. 172; *Les Fleurs du Mal*, ed. Crépet-Blin, p. 216.
44. *JOP*, I, 298–299. The article was probably written in 1855.
45. Dedication of *Les Paradis artificiels*, *PA*, pp. v–vi.
46. *AR*, p. 406.
47. *PA*, p. 32.
48. *PA*, p. 69.
49. *AR*, p. 18; *PA*, p. 161 (the passage is a free adaptation of De Quincey).
50. *PA*, p. 17.
51. *CE*, p. 142; *NHE*, p. xviii; *PA*, p. 162.
52. *AR*, pp. 60, 65.
53. *PA*, p. 179. See also what Baudelaire says of "ces impressions fugitives et frappantes, d'autant plus frappantes dans leurs retours qu'elles sont plus fugitives, qui suivent quelquefois un symptôme extérieur, une espèce d'avertissement comme un son de cloche, une note musicale, ou un parfum oublié" (Poe, *Histoires extraordinaires*, traduction de Baudelaire, 1932, p. xxvii).
54. *CE*, p. 163.
55. For a fuller discussion of this development and of some of the sources of Baudelaire's conception of the imagination, see my *Baudelaire the Critic* (New York, 1943), pp. 118–133.
56. "Le Peintre de la vie moderne," *AR*, p. 67.
57. *CE*, pp. 87, 143, 168, 143.
58. *CE*, pp. 280, 333–334; *PPP*, p. 55.
59. Letter to F. Desnoyers [1855], *CG*, I, 332; *AR*, p. 100.
60. Letter to A. Toussenel, January 21, 1856, *CG*, I, 370.
61. *NHE*, p. xv; *AR*, p. 206. For a full study of the sources of Baudelaire's doctrine, see Jean Pommier, *La Mystique de Baudelaire* (1932). The most penetrating study of the nature and role of correspondences in Baudelaire's theory and poetry is to be found in Lloyd Austin, *L'Univers poétique de Baudelaire*. This chapter had been nearly completed before Mr. Austin's book appeared, but I am deeply grateful to him for confirming and developing so convincingly a point of view at which I had arrived independently.
62. *NHE*, p. xx; *AR*, pp. 164, 305.
63. Letter to Toussenel, January 21, 1856, *CG*, I, 368. This aspect of the *correspondances* is predominant in Baudelaire's theory, but as we shall see when dealing with his symbols, it is the human correspondences that play the largest role in his poetry. Jean Prévost notes that for Baudelaire "les correspondances poétiques *ont toujours l'homme pour centre*" (*Baudelaire*, p. 75). The point is developed fully by Lloyd Austin: "L'originalité essentielle de Baudelaire en cette matière est d'avoir sécularisé ce qui fut depuis des temps immémoriaux une attitude et une doctrine théologiques ou métaphysiques" (p. 54); "Baudelaire finira par le reconnaître: le 'sur-

naturel' vers lequel mènent les correspondances n'est que l'intensification, l'approfondissement des données 'naturelles,' l'augmentation du 'sentiment de l'existence' " (p. 55).

64. *AR*, p. 162; *CE*, pp. 283–284; *PA*, p. 53.

65. *CE*, p. 274.

66. Gaston Bachelard, *L'Eau et les rêves: Essai sur l'imagination de la matière* (1942), p. 23.

67. *CE*, p. 275; *AR*, pp. 160–161.

68. *AR*, p. 239; *CE*, p. 310. See Lloyd J. Austin, "Baudelaire et l'énergie spirituelle," *Revue des Sciences Humaines*, Nouvelle Série, Fasc. 85 (January–March 1957), pp. 35–42.

69. *PA*, p. 51. Compare the note in *Fusées*: "Dans certains états de l'âme presque surnaturels, la profondeur de la vie se révèle tout entière dans le spectacle, si ordinaire qu'il soit, qu'on a sous les yeux. Il en devient le symbole" (*Journaux intimes*, p. 24).

70. *AR*, pp. 164, 305. See also the passage in the *Salon de 1859* in which Baudelaire says that nature must have "un contemplateur pour en extraire la comparaison, la métaphore et l'allégorie" (*CE*, p. 333).

71. "Il s'agit simplement de réserver le terme de 'symbolique' à toute poétique fondée sur la croyance que la nature est le symbole d'une réalité divine ou transcendante, définition entièrement orthodoxe et traditionnelle; et de consacrer le mot de 'symbolisme' à toute poétique qui, sans poser la question d'une transcendance mystique, cherche dans la nature des symboles qui traduisent l'état d'âme du poète" (*L'Univers poétique de Baudelaire*, pp. 19–20).

72. *AR*, p. 329.

73. *CE*, p. 29; *PA*, p. 51.

74. *AR*, pp. 6, 71, 203

75. *CE*, pp. 344–345, 108.

76. *AR*, p. 9; *CE*, p. 262.

77. *JOP*, I, 241.

78. *Le Soleil*. Compare the description of the ragpicker in *Du vin et du haschisch*: "Il arrive hochant la tête et butant sur les pavés, comme les jeunes poètes qui passent toutes leurs journées à errer et à chercher des rimes" (*PA*, p. 206), and the lines of *Le Vin des chiffonniers*:

On voit un chiffonnier qui vient, hochant la tête,
Butant, et se cognant aux murs comme un poète.

79. *AR*, pp. 164–165. Compare *Fusées*: "De la langue et de l'écriture, prises comme des opérations magiques, sorcellerie évocatoire" (*Journaux intimes*, p. 24).

80. *PA*, p. 52; *Les Fleurs du Mal*, ed. Crépet-Blin, p. 212; *Journaux intimes*, p. 14.

81. *Les Fleurs du Mal*, p. 212. Compare what Baudelaire says of Leconte de Lisle's rhymes, *AR*, p. 376.

82. *AR*, p. 177; *CE*, p. 283.

83. Letter to Armand Fraisse, February 18, 1860, *CG*, III, 39.

84. *PPP*, p. vi; *AR*, p. 320; *PPP*, p. 120.

85. "L'Art philosophique," *AR*, p. 119.

86. Flaubert, *Correspondance*, IV, 205.

87. "La Fanfarlo," *PA*, p. 240.

88. I have discussed this question more fully in my article, "From Imagi-

nation to Immediacy in French Poetry," *RR*, 39: 30–49 (February 1948).

89. Pierre Reverdy, *Le Gant de crin* (1926), p. 29.

90. Tristan Tzara, *Essai sur la situation de la poésie* (1934). Quoted in Maurice Nadeau, *Histoire du surréalisme* (1945), p. 58.

91. See the "Avant-propos" by Jacques Charpier to the anthology, *L'Art poétique*, ed. Jacques Charpier and Pierre Seghers (1956). "Enfin la poésie cesse d'être considérée comme une mystique. Elle ne s'abreuve plus aux sources d'un absolu quelconque. Elle abandonne le royaume de la subjectivité, s'ouvre à l'histoire, à la nature, à la culture, devient un fait humain. Le poète ne respecte plus aussi religieusement cette voix qui lui dicte son poème. Il cherche à en dominer l'allure et la forme. Il oriente cette force qui l'habite, l'éjouit ou le déchire. La poésie redevient art, retrouve son sens étymologique, elle est à nouveau un *faire*, une création qui se détermine elle-même autant que cela se peut, une transformation de l'énergie créatrice en œuvre stable, une intention esthétique plus ou moins bien aboutie."

INDEX